직독직해로 읽는

소공녀

A Little Princess

직독직해로 읽는

소공녀

A Little Princess

개정판 2쇄 발행 2020년 3월 20일
초판 1쇄 발행   2011년 4월 15일

원작	프랜시즈 호즈슨 버넷
역주	더 콜링(김정희, 박윤수, 조문경)
디자인	IndigoBlue
일러스트	정은수
발행인	조경아
발행처	랭귀지북스
주소	서울시 마포구 포은로2나길 31 벨라비스타 208호
전화	02.406.0047 **팩스** 02.406.0042
이메일	languagebooks@hanmail.net
홈페이지	www.languagebooks.co.kr
등록번호	101-90-85278 **등록일자** 2008년 7월 10일
ISBN	979-11-5635-032-3 (13740)
가격	13,000원

「이 도서의 국립중앙도서관 출판예정도서목록(CIP)은 서지정보유통지원시스템 홈페이지(http://seoji.nl.go.kr)와
국가자료공동목록시스템(http://www.nl.go.kr/kolisnet)에서 이용하실 수 있습니다.(CIP제어번호: CIP2015029023)」

직독직해로 읽는

소공녀

A Little Princess

프랜시스 호즈슨 버넷 원작
더 콜링 역주

Language Books

머리말

"어렸을 때 누구나 갖고 있던 세계명작 한 질.
그리고 TV에서 하던 세계명작 만화에 대한 추억이 있습니다."

"친숙한 이야기를 영어 원문으로 읽어 봐야겠다고 마음먹고 샀던 원서들은
이제 애물단지가 되어 버렸습니다."

"재미있는 세계명작 하나 읽어 보려고 따져 보는 어려운 영문법.
모르는 단어 찾느라 이리저리 뒤져 봐야 하는 사전.
몇 장 넘겨 보기도 전에 지칩니다."

영어 독해력을 기르려면 술술 읽어가며 내용을 파악하는 것이
중요합니다. 현재 수능 시험에도 대세인 '직독직해' 스타일을 접목시
킨 〈**직독직해로 읽는 세계명작 시리즈**〉는 세계명작을 영어 원작으
로 쉽게 읽어갈 수 있도록 안내해 드릴 것입니다.

'직독직해' 스타일로 읽다 보면, 영문법을 들먹이며 따질 필요
가 없으니 쉽고, 끊어 읽다 보니 독해 속도도 빨라집니다. 이 습관
이 들여지면 어떤 글을 만나도 두렵지 않을 것입니다.

명작의 재미를 즐기며 영어 독해력을 키우는 두 마리의 토끼
를 잡으세요!

〈직독직해로 읽는 세계명작 시리즈〉의 나의 소중한 파트너 오랜 친구 윤수와 든든한 번역자 문경 씨와 일러스트레이터 은수 씨, 좋은 동역자 디자인 DX, 그리고 이 책이 출판될 수 있도록 늘 든든하게 지원해 주시는 랭귀지북스에 감사의 마음을 전합니다.

마지막으로 내 삶의 이유가 되시는 하나님께 영광을 올려 드립니다.

더 콜링 김정희

목차

Chapter **1**   Sara
track 02
8

mini test 1
34

Chapter **2**   Ermengarde
track 03
36

Chapter **3**   Lottie
track 04
54

mini test 2
76

Chapter **4**   Becky
track 05
78

mini test 3
104

Chapter **5**   In the Attic
track 06
106

mini test 4
130

CONTENTS

Chapter **6**   Melchisedec   132
track 07

mini test 5 ?   160

Chapter **7**   The Indian Gentleman   162
track 08

mini test 6 ?   192

Chapter **8**   The Magic   194
track 09

mini test 7 ?   250

Chapter **9**   "It Is the Child!"   252
track 10

mini test 8 ?   268

A Little Princess를 다시 읽어 보세요   270

1

Sara
새라

Once on a dark winter's day, / when the yellow fog hung
어느 어두운 겨울날,　　　　　　황색 뿌연 안개가 드리워져

/ so thick and heavy / in the streets of London / that the
매우 두껍고 짙게　　　　런던 거리에

lamps were lighted / and the shop windows blazed / with
램프가 커지고　　　　상점의 창문들도 눈부시게 빛나고 있을 때　　가스등으로

gas / as they do at night, / an odd-looking little girl sat
밤에 그러하듯,　　　　특이하게 생긴 한 소녀가 마차에 앉아

in a cab / with her father / and was driven rather slowly /
아빠와 함께　　　　　매우 천천히 지나갔다

through the big thoroughfares.
넓은 도로 사이를.

She sat / with her feet tucked under her, / and leaned
소녀는 앉아있었다　다리를 감싸안고,　　　　　　아빠에게 기댄 채

against her father, / who held her in his arm, / as she
　　　　　자신을 팔에 안고 있는,　　　　응시하면서

stared / out of the window / at the passing people / with a
창 밖으로　　　　　지나가는 사람들을

queer old-fashioned thoughtfulness / in her big eyes.
독특하고 고풍스러운 생각에 잠긴 채　　　　큰 눈에.

She was such a little girl / that one did not expect / to see
그토록 어린 소녀이기에　　　어느 누가 기대할 수 있을까

such a look / on her small face. It would have been an old
그런 표정을　　　그녀의 작은 얼굴에서.　　그것은 조숙한 얼굴이었다

look / for a child of twelve, / and Sara Crewe was only
열두 살 아이에게도,　　　그런데 새라 크루는 겨우 일곱 살이었다.

seven.

blaze 눈부시게 빛나다 | odd-looking 이상하게 보이는 | cab 택시, (옛날의) 승객용 마차 | thoroughfare (특히
도시의) 주요 도로 | tuck 밀어 넣다 | queer 기묘한, 독특한 | old-fashioned 구식의 | thoughtfulness 생각에
잠김, 사려 깊음 | grown-up 어른의 | voyage 여행, 항해 | captain (미국 육군·공군·해병대의) 대위, (해군의) 대령
| Lascar (외국선을 타고 근무하는) 동인도인 선원 | to and fro 이리저리 움직이는 | deck (배의) 갑판 | principally
주로 | puzzling 당혹스럽게 하는, 난해한

The fact was, / however, / that she was always dreaming
사실은 이렇다, 그러나, 새라는 항상 꿈꾸고 생각하고 있었다

and thinking / odd things / and could not herself remember
이상한 것들을 자기 자신도 기억할 수 없을 정도로

/ any time / when she had not been thinking things / about
어느 순간도 그런 것들을 생각하지 않고 있던 때는

grown-up people / and the world they belonged to. She felt
다 큰 어른들과 어른들이 속한 세상에 대해. 그녀는 느꼈다

/ as if she had lived / a long, long time.
마치 살아온 것처럼 아주 오랜 시간을.

At this moment / she was remembering the voyage / she
이 순간 새라는 여행을 회상하고 있었다

had just made from Bombay / with her father, Captain
막 봄베이로부터 떠나왔던 아버지인, 크루 대위과 함께.

Crewe. She was thinking / of the big ship, / of the Lascars
그녀는 생각하고 있었다 큰 배와, 동인도 선원들과

/ passing silently to and fro on it, / of the children / playing
배 위를 조용하게 오가던, 아이들과

about on the hot deck, / and of some young officers' wives
뜨거운 갑판 위에서 뛰놀며, 그리고 젊은 장교들의 부인들을

/ who used to try to make her talk to them / and laugh at
자신에게 말을 시키려고 시도하고는

the things she said.
자신이 한 말들을 듣고 웃곤 했던.

Principally, / she was thinking / of what a queer thing / it
주로, 새라는 생각하고 있었다 참으로 이상한 일에 대해

was that / at one time / one was in India / in the blazing
그것은 바로 동시에 한번은 인도에 있다가 불타는 태양 아래,

sun, / and then in the middle of the ocean, / and then
그리고는 바다 한가운데에 있더니,

driving in a strange vehicle / through strange streets /
다음으로 낯선 탈것에 있다는 것이었다 낯선 거리를 통과하며

where the day was as dark as the night. She found this so
낮인데도 밤처럼 어두운 곳을. 이 사실이 매우 혼란스러워

puzzling / that she moved closer to her father.
아빠에게 더 가까이 갔다.

"Papa," / she said / in a low, mysterious little voice /
"아빠," 새라는 말했다 낮고, 신비스러운 작은 목소리로

which was almost a whisper, / "papa."
거의 속삭이면서, "아빠."

"What is it, darling?" / Captain Crewe answered, /
"무슨 일이니, 애야?" 크루 대위는 대답했다.

holding her closer / and looking down into her face.
그녀를 더 꼭 껴안고 얼굴을 내려다 보며.

"What is Sara thinking of?"
"새라는 무슨 생각을 하고 있지?"

"Is this the place?" / Sara whispered, / cuddling still
"여기가 그곳이에요?" 새라가 속삭였다. 아빠를 더 꼭 껴안으며.

closer to him. "Is it, papa?"
"그래요, 아빠?"

"Yes, little Sara, it is. We have reached it / at last." And /
"그래, 새라야, 그렇단다. 그곳에 도착했구나 마침내." 그러자

though she was only seven years old, / she knew / that he
일곱 살밖에 되지 않았지만, 그녀는 알았다 아빠가 슬퍼

felt sad / when he said it.
한다는 것을 그렇게 말했을 때.

Key Expression

분사구문 해석하기

분사구문은 분사를 사용하여 절을 구로 간결하게 줄인 구문입니다. 그래서 분사구문을 해석할 때에는 생략된 접속사를 파악하여 해석합니다.
분사구문은 '~하면서(while)'라는 의미로 해석되는 경우가 가장 많으며, 이 외에도 ~때(as/when), ~하면서(while), ~한 후에(after), ~때문에(as/because), ~하면(if) 등으로 해석되기도 합니다.

ex) Captain Crewe answered, holding her closer and looking down into her face.
크루 대위는 그녀를 더 꼭 껴안고 얼굴을 내려다 보며 대답했다.

* 여자 주인을 부르는 프랑스어
** 과거 인도에서 신분이 높은 유럽 남자에게 쓰던 호칭
*** 인도인 가정부를 일컫는 말

cuddle 껴안다 | pet 애정어린, 다정한 | be fond of ~을 좋아하다 | bungalow (일부 아시아 국가의) 대저택,
단층집 | made salaams to 이마에 손을 대고 절하다 | give way 항복하다, 양보하다 | worship 숭배하다,
맹목적으로 사랑하다

It seemed to her many years / since he had begun to
새라에게는 수년이 흐른 것 같았다   아빠가 새라에게 마음의 준비를 시킨 후

prepare her mind / for "the place," / as she always called
"그곳"에 대해,   항상 그렇게 불렀던.

it. Her mother had died / when she was born, / so she had
엄마는 돌아가셨다   그녀가 태어났을 때,   그래서 엄마를

never known / or missed her. Her young, handsome, rich,
알지도 못하고   그리워하지도 않았다. 젊고, 잘생기고, 부유하며, 다정한 아빠는

petting father / seemed to be the only relation / she had /
                유일한 혈육인 듯했다   그녀에게

in the world. They had always played together / and been
세상에서.   그들은 항상 함께 놀았고

fond of each other. She only knew / he was rich / because
서로를 좋아했다.   새라는 알고는 있었다   아빠가 부자라는 것을   왜냐하면 사람

she had heard people say so / when they thought / she
들이 그렇게 말하는 것을 들었기 때문에   사람들이 생각할 때

was not listening, / and she had also heard them say / that
그녀가 듣고 있지 않다고,   그리고 또한 그들이 말하는 것을 들었다

when she grew up / she would be rich, / too. She did not
그녀가 다 자라면   부자가 될 것이라는 것을,   역시.   새라는 알지 못했다

know / all that being rich meant. She had always lived /
        부자가 의미하는 모든 것을.   새라는 항상 살았고

in a beautiful bungalow, / and had been used to seeing
아름다운 대저택에,   보아왔다

/ many servants / who made salaams to her / and called
    많은 하인들을   자신에게 인사하며

her "*Missee **Sahib," / and gave her her own way / in
"아가씨"라고 부르는,   그리고 그녀가 하자는 대로 양보해 준

everything. She had had toys and pets / and an ***ayah
모든 일에서.   새라에게는 인형과 애완동물과   자신을 떠받쳐 주는 가정부가

who worshipped her, / and she had gradually learned / that
있었고,   그래서 점차 알게 되었다

people who were rich / had these things. That, / however, /
부자라는 사람들은   이런 것들을 가진 사람이라고. 그것이,   그러나,

was all / she knew about it.
전부였다   새라가 부자에 대해 알고 있는.

During her short life / only one thing had troubled her,
짧은 삶 동안 　　　　　　　오직 한 가지가 새라를 힘들게 했는데,

/ and that thing was "the place" / she was to be taken
그것은 바로 "그곳"이었다 　　　　그녀가 가야 할,

to / some day. The climate of India was / very bad for
언젠가　인도의 기후는　　　　　아이들에게 매우 나빠서,

children, / and as soon as possible / they were sent away
가능한 한 빨리　　　　사람들은 그곳에서 멀리 떠났다

from it / — generally to England / and to school. She
— 보통 영국과　　　　학교로.

had seen / other children go away, / and had heard / their
새라는 보아왔고　다른 아이들이 떠나는 것을,　　들었다

fathers and mothers talk / about the letters / they received
그들의 부모들이 말하는 것을　　편지에 대해　　아이들로부터 받은.

from them. She had known / that she would be obliged to
새라는 알고 있었고　　자신 역시 갈 수밖에 없다는 것을,

go also, / and though sometimes / her father's stories of
비록 이따금　　아빠의 항해 이야기와

the voyage / and the new country / had attracted her, / she
새로운 나라가　　홍미를 끌어도,

had been troubled / by the thought / that he could not stay
괴로워했다　　생각으로　　아빠와 함께 지낼 수 없다는.

with her.

"Couldn't you go to that place with me, / papa?" / she had
"그곳에 함께 갈 수 없나요,　　아빠?"　　새라가 물었다

asked / when she was five years old. "Couldn't you go to
다섯 살이었을 때.　　"아빠도 학교에 갈 수 없나요,

school, / too? I would help you / with your lessons."
역시?　제가 도와줄게요　　아빠가 공부하는 것을."

be obliged to 하는 수 없이 ~하다 | keep the house 머물러 있다 | attain (보통 많은 노력 끝에) 이루다,
획득하다 | console oneself (with sth) 위로하다, 위안을 주다

12　　A Little Princess

"But you will not have to stay / for a very long time, /
"하지만 있을 필요는 없을 거야   그리 오랜 시간 동안,

little Sara," / he had always said. "You will go to a nice
새라야,"   아빠는 늘 말했다.   "넌 멋진 집에 갈 거야

house / where there will be a lot of little girls, / and you
소녀들이 많이 있는 곳인데,

will play together, / and I will send you plenty of books,
함께 놀 게 될 거야,   그리고 내가 많은 책을 보내 줄게,

/ and you will grow so fast / that it will seem scarcely a
그리고 넌 아주 빨리 자라서   1년도 채 지나지 않아

year / before you are big enough and clever enough / to
충분히 자라고 똑똑해질 거야

come back and take care of papa."
돌아와서 아빠를 보살펴 줄만큼."

She had liked to think of that. To keep the house for her
새라는 그것을 생각하기를 좋아했다.   아빠를 위해 집을 지키고;

father; / to ride with him, / and sit at the head of his table
함께 말을 타고,   식탁 머리에 앉는 것을

/ when he had dinner parties; / to talk to him / and read
아빠가 만찬 파티를 열 때;   아빠와 이야기 하고   책을 읽는 것을

his books / — that would be what she would like most / in
— 그것은 새라가 가장 좋아하는 일이었다

the world, / and if one must go away / to "the place" / in
세상에서,   그래서 만약 떠나야 한다면   "그곳"으로

England / to attain it, / she must make up her mind to go.
영국에 있는   그것을 이루기 위해,   갈 결심을 해야 했다.

She did not care very much / for other little girls, / but if
새라는 별로 좋아하지 않았지만   다른 소녀들을,

she had plenty of books / she could console herself. She
많은 책을 가지게 된다면   위로를 받을 수 있을 것 같았다.

liked books / more than anything else, / and was, / in fact,
새라는 책을 좋아했고 다른 무엇보다 ,   그리고,   사실,

/ always inventing stories / of beautiful things / and telling
항상 이야기를 지어내서   멋진 것들에 대한

them to herself. Sometimes / she had told them / to her
자신에게 들려줬다.   때때로   이야기를 해 주었다   아빠에게,

father, / and he had liked them / as much as she did.
그러면 아빠는 그것을 좋아했다   그녀만큼.   13

MISS MINCHIN, SELECT SEMINARY FOR YOUNG LADIES

"Well, papa," / she said softly, / "if we are here / I
"그런데, 아빠," 새라가 부드럽게 말했다. "우리가 여기 있다면

suppose / we must be resigned."
내 생각에 받아들여야겠네요."

He laughed at her old-fashioned speech / and kissed her.
그는 새라의 고풍스러운 말투에 웃으며 아이에게 입맞췄다.

He was really not at all / resigned himself, / though he
그는 실제로 전혀 체념한 것이 아니었다, 알고는 있지만

knew / he must keep that a secret. His quaint little Sara
그것을 비밀로 해야 한다는 것을. 별난 꼬마인 새라는

/ had been a great companion to him, / and he felt / he
그에게 훌륭한 친구였고, 그는 느꼈다

should be a lonely fellow / when, / on his return to India,
외로운 사람이 될 거라고 그때, 인도에 돌아가서,

/ he went into his bungalow / knowing / he need not
대저택에 들어갔을 때 깨닫게 되면 볼 수 없음을

expect to see / the small figure / in its white frock / come
이 작은 꼬마가 하얀 드레스를 입고

forward to meet him. So he held her very closely / in his
자신을 맞이하러 오는 것을. 그래서 그는 아이를 꼭 안았다 그의 팔로

arms / as the cab rolled into / the big, dull square / in
마차가 들어가는 동안 크고, 칙칙한 광장으로

which stood the house / which was their destination.
그곳에는 집이 있었다 그들의 종착지인.

It was a big, dull, brick house, / exactly like all the others
그것은 크고, 칙칙한, 벽돌집이었다, 다른 모든 집들과 똑같은

/ in its row, / but that on the front door / there shone a
일렬로 늘어선, 다만 정문에는 황동 판이 빛나고 있었고

brass plate / on which was engraved / in black letters: /
그 위에는 새겨져 있었다 검은 글씨로:

MISS MINCHIN, / Select Seminary / for Young Ladies.
민친 교장, 고급 신학교 어린 숙녀들을 위한.

---

resigned (괴롭거나 힘든 일을) 받아들이는, 체념한 | quaint (매력 있게) 진기한, 예스러운 | companion 동료, 친구
| frock 드레스 | dull 흐릿한, 칙칙한 | square 광장 | brass 놋쇠, 황동 | engrave (나무·돌·쇠붙이 등에) 새기다 |
Miss 선생님(여선생에 대한 호칭) | select 엄선된, 고급의 | seminary 신학교, 종교 단체에서 운영하는 교육기관

"Here we are, Sara," / said Captain Crewe, / making his
"다 왔다, 새라야." 크루 대위가 말했다, 목소리를 내어

voice sound / as cheerful as possible. Then he lifted her /
가능한 한 명랑하게. 그리고는 그녀를 안아 올려

out of the cab / and they mounted the steps / and rang the
마차에서 내렸다 그리고 그들은 계단을 올라가 초인종을 울렸다.

bell. Sara often thought / afterward / that the house was
새라는 종종 생각했다 이후에

somehow / exactly like Miss Minchin. It was respectable
그 집은 왠지 민친 교장과 똑같다고. 그 집은 훌륭했고

/ and well furnished, / but everything in it was ugly; /
시설도 잘 갖춰져 있었지만, 그 안에 있는 모든 것은 추했다;

and the very armchairs / seemed to have hard bones / in
그리고 바로 그 안락의자들도 딱딱한 뼈대가 있는 듯 했다

them. In the hall / everything was hard and polished / —
그 안에. 홀 안에 있는 모든 것이 딱딱하고 윤이 났다

even the red cheeks of the moon face / on the tall clock /
— 달 모양 얼굴의 붉은 뺨마저도 높은 시계에 그려진

in the corner / had a severe varnished look. The drawing
구석에 있는 심하게 번들거리는 모습이었다. 거실은

room / into which they were ushered / was covered by a
안내를 받아서 들어간 카페트로 덮여 있었고

carpet / with a square pattern upon it, / the chairs were
그 위에 사각형 무늬가 있는, 의자들도 사각형이었으며,

square, / and a heavy marble timepiece stood / upon the
무거운 대리석 시계가 서 있었다

heavy marble mantel.
무거운 대리석 벽난로 선반 위에.

As she sat down / in one of the stiff mahogany chairs, /
새라는 앉자 딱딱한 마호가니 의자 중 하나에,

Sara cast one of her quick looks / about her.
빠르게 둘러 보았다 주위를.

---

somehow 어떻게든, 왠지 | respectable 존경할 만한, 훌륭한 | furnished 가구가 갖춰진 | ugly 못생긴, 추한
| armchair 안락의자 | polished (잘 닦아서) 윤이 나는 | varnish 니스, 광택제를 바르다 | drawing room (큰
저택의) 거실 | usher 안내하다 | marble 대리석 | timepiece 시계 | mantel 벽난로 선반 | cast (시선·미소 등을)
던지다, 보내다

"I don't like it, papa," / she said. "But then I dare say /
"이곳이 싫어요, 아빠, " 새라가 말했다. "하지만 분명히 말씀 드리자면

soldiers / — even brave ones — / don't really like / going
군인들도 — 용감한 군인들조차 — 정말 좋아하지 않겠죠

into battle."
전쟁터에 나가는 것을."

Captain Crewe laughed outright / at this. He was young
크루 대위는 크게 웃었다 이 말을 듣고. 그는 젊고 재미있는

and full of fun, / and he never tired of hearing / Sara's
사람으로, 듣는 것에 절대 싫증을 내지 않았다

queer speeches.
새라의 이상한 이야기를.

"Oh, little Sara," / he said. "What shall I do / when I
"오, 새라야," 그는 말했다. "난 뭘 해야 하지

have no one / to say solemn things / to me? No one else
사람이 없을 때 진지한 이야기를 해 줄 내게? 아무도 없지

is / as solemn as you are."
너만큼 진지한 사람은."

"But why do solemn things / make you laugh so?" /
"그런데 왜 진지한 말을 들으면 아빠는 그렇게 웃으세요?"

inquired Sara.
새라가 물었다.

"Because you are such fun / when you say them," / he
"왜냐하면 네가 매우 재미있으니까 그런 말을 할 때,"

answered, / laughing still more. And then suddenly /
그는 대답했다, 더 크게 웃으면서. 그러다가 갑자기

he swept her into his arms / and kissed her very hard, /
그녀를 팔로 쓰다듬고 입맞춤을 퍼부었다,

stopping laughing / all at once / and looking / almost as
웃기를 멈추고 갑자기 보이면서

if tears had come / into his eyes.
마치 눈물이 나올 듯 눈에서.

outright 노골적으로, 드러내 놓고, 즉각 | solemn 엄숙한, 진지한 | sweep 쓸다, 청소하다, 털다

It was just then / that Miss Minchin entered the room. She
바로 그때   민친 교장이 방으로 들어왔다.

was very like her house, / Sara felt: / tall and dull, / and
그녀의 모습은 집과 똑같았다.   새라가 느끼기에는: 키가 크면서우중충하고,

respectable and ugly. She had / large, cold, fishy eyes, / and
훌륭해 보이지만 추한 모습이었다. 그녀는 가지고 있었다 크고, 차갑고, 수상한 눈과,

a large, cold, fishy smile. It spread itself into a very large
크고, 차갑고, 수상한 미소를.   그 미소는 함박웃음으로 변했다

smile / when she saw Sara and Captain Crewe. She had
      새라와 크루 대위를 보자.

heard a great many desirable things / of the young soldier /
교장은 바람직한 말들을 많이 들었다   이 젊은 군인에 대해

from the lady / who had recommended her school to him.
한 부인으로부터 그에게 이 학교를 추천했던.

Among other things, / she had heard / that he was a rich
다른 말들 중에,   그녀는 들었다   그가 부자 아빠라는 것을

father / who was willing to spend / a great deal of money /
      기꺼이 쓸 수 있는   굉장히 많은 돈을

on his little daughter.
자신의 딸에게.

"It will be a great privilege / to have charge / of such a
"대단한 영광입니다   맡게 되어

beautiful and promising child, / Captain Crewe," / she said,
이렇게 예쁘고 장래가 촉망되는 아이를,   크루 대위님," 교장이 말했다,

/ taking Sara's hand / and stroking it. "Lady Meredith has
새라의 손을 잡고   어루만지면서.   "메러디스 부인께서 말씀하셨어요

told me / of her unusual cleverness. A clever child is a great
      새라의 뛰어난 총명함에 대해.   총명한 아이는 대단한 보물입니다

treasure / in an establishment / like mine."
      기관에서는   저희같은."

Sara stood quietly, / with her eyes fixed / upon Miss
새라는 조용히 서 있었다.   시선을 고정한 채   민친 교장의 얼굴에.

Minchin's face. She was thinking something odd, / as
      새라는 이상한 것을 생각 중이었다.

usual.
평소처럼.

"Why does she say / I am a beautiful child?" / she was
"왜 말하는 거지   내가 예쁜 아이라고?"   새라는 생각했다.

thinking. "I am not beautiful at all. Colonel Grange's little
"난 전혀 예쁘지 않은데.   그랜지 대령님의 딸

girl, / Isobel, / is beautiful. She has dimples and rose-
이소벨이,   예쁘지.   보조개와 장밋빛 뺨에,

colored cheeks, / and long hair the color of gold. I have
긴 금발을 가졌으니까.

short black hair / and green eyes; / besides which, / I am a
나는 짧고 검은 머리에   초록색 눈이잖아;   게다가,

thin child / and not fair in the least. I am one of the ugliest
말랐고   피부도 전혀 하얗지 않아.   난 가장 못생긴 아이들 중 하나야

children / I ever saw. She is beginning by telling a story."
내가 봤던.   선생님은 거짓말을 시작하고 있어."

Key Expression ♥

with를 사용한 부대상황 : ~하면서, ~한 채로

두 가지 일이 동시에 일어나는 것을 부대상황이라고 하는데, 이런 부대상황은 with를 사용하여 다음과 같이 네 가지 형태로 표현할 수 있습니다. 해석은 '~하면서, ~한 채로'라고 하면 됩니다.

▶ with + 목적어 + 현재분사(목적어와 분사가 능동 관계)
▶ with + 목적어 + 과거분사(목적어와 분사가 수동 관계)
▶ with + 목적어 + 형용사
▶ with + 목적어 + 전치사구

ex) Sara stood quietly, with her eyes fixed upon Miss Minchin's face.
새라는 민친 교장의 얼굴에 시선을 고정한 채 조용히 서 있었다.
Sara, who lay asleep with Emily in her arms.
새라는 에밀리를 팔에 안은 채 잠들어 있었다.

---

fishy 수상한 (냄새가 나는) | desirable 바람직한, 호감이 가는 | privilege 영광 | have charge of ~을 맡고 있다 | promising 유망한, 촉망되는 | stroke 쓰다듬다, 어루만지다 | establishment 기관, 시설 | colonel (영국의 해군과 해병대, 미국의 육군·공군·해병대의) 대령 | dimple 보조개 | fair (피부·머리카락이) 옅은 색의, 금발의, 흰 피부의

She was mistaken, / however, / in thinking / she was an
새라는 틀렸다, 하지만, 생각하는 것은 못생긴 아이라고.

ugly child. She was not in the least like Isobel Grange, /
이소벨 그렌지와는 전혀 닮지 않았지만,

who had been the beauty of the regiment, / but she had an
연대의 미인으로 뽑혔던, 이상한 매력이 있었다

odd charm / of her own. She was a slim, supple creature,
자신만의. 날씬하고, 유연한 몸을 가졌으며,

/ rather tall for her age, / and had an intense, attractive
나이에 비해 다소 키가 컸고, 강렬하고, 매력적인 작은 얼굴을 지녔다.

little face. Her hair was heavy / and quite black / and only
머리 숱은 많았고 짙은 검정색으로

curled / at the tips; / her eyes were greenish gray, / it is
곱슬거렸다 끝부분만; 눈은 초록빛이 감도는 회색인데, 정말이었다,

true, / but they were big, wonderful eyes / with long, black
하지만 크고, 놀라운 눈이었다 길고, 검은 속눈썹을 지닌,

lashes, / and though she herself did not like / the color of
자신은 좋아하지 않았지만 눈 색깔을,

them, / many other people did. Still / she was very firm in
많은 다른 사람들은 좋아했다. 하지만 새라는 매우 강한 믿음을 갖고

her belief / that she was an ugly little girl, / and she was
있었다 자신이 못생긴 여자 아이라는,

not at all elated / by Miss Minchin's flattery.
그래서 전혀 신나지 않았다 민친 교장의 아첨을 듣고.

"I should be telling a story / if I said / she was beautiful," /
"난 거짓말을 하게 되겠지 만약 말한다면 선생님이 아름답다고,"

she thought; / "and I should know / I was telling a story. I
생각했다; "그리고 난 알아야 해 거짓말 한다는 것을.

believe I am as ugly as she is / — in my way. What did she
난 선생님만큼 못생겼다고 생각해 — 내 생각에는.

say that for?"
왜 저런 말을 하는 거지?"

After she had known Miss Minchin longer / she learned /
민친 교장을 더 오래 알게 되고 나서 새라는 알았다

why she had said it. She discovered / that she said the same
왜 교장이 그런 말을 했는지. 새라는 알아냈다 교장이 같은 말을 하는 것을

thing / to each papa and mamma / who brought a child / to
모든 부모에게 아이를 데려온

her school.
그녀 학교로.

Sara stood near her father / and listened / while he and Miss
새라는 아빠 곁에 서서 / 듣고 있었다 / 아빠와 민친 교장이 말하는 동안.

Minchin talked. She had been brought to the seminary /
그녀는 신학교로 보내졌다

because Lady Meredith's two little girls / had been educated
왜냐하면 메러디스 부인의 두 딸들이 / 그곳에서 교육을 받았고,

there, / and Captain Crewe had a great respect / for Lady
크루 대위는 대단히 존경했기 때문이다

Meredith's experience. Sara was to be / what was known
메러디스 부인의 경험을. / 새라는 예정이었고

as "a parlor boarder," / and she was to enjoy / even greater
소위 "특별 기숙생"으로 알려질, / 누리게 될 것이었다 / 훨씬 더 많은 특권을

privileges / than parlor boarders usually did. She was to have
특별 기숙생들이 일반적으로 누리는 것보다. / 새라는 갖게 될 것이었다

/ a pretty bedroom / and sitting room of her own; / she was
예쁜 침실과 / 자신만의 거실을; / 또 갖게 될

to have / a pony and a carriage, / and a maid / to take the
것이었다 / 조랑말과 마차와, / 하녀를 / 가정부를 대신할

place of the ayah / who had been her nurse / in India.
그녀의 유모였던 / 인도에서.

"I am not in the least anxious / about her education," /
"조금도 걱정하지 않습니다 / 새라의 교육에 대해서는,"

Captain Crewe said, / with his gay laugh, / as he held Sara's
크루 대위가 말했다, / 즐겁게 웃으며, / 새라의 손을 잡고 토닥이면서.

hand and patted it. "The difficulty will be / to keep / her
"어려운 점은 / 막는 것이겠죠

from learning too fast and too much. She is always sitting /
그 애가 너무 빨리 그리고 너무 많이 배우지 않도록. / 그 애는 항상 앉아 있어요

---

regiment (군대의) 연대 | supple (몸이) 유연한, (부드럽고) 탄력 있는 | lash 속눈썹(= eyelash) | elated 마냥
행복해 하는, 신이 난 | flattery 아첨 | parlor boarder 특별 기숙생 | sitting room 거실(=living room) | pony
조랑말 | take the place of ~에 대신하다 | nurse (과거의) 애 보는 식모 | gay 명랑한, 즐거운 | pat 쓰다듬다,
토닥거리다

21

with her little nose burrowing / into books. She doesn't
작은 코를 파묻고   책 속에.   그것을 읽는 것이

read them, / Miss Minchin; / she gobbles them up / as
아니에요,   민친 선생님;   게걸스럽게 먹어 치우는 거죠

if she were a little wolf / instead of a little girl. She is
마치 한 마리의 작은 늑대처럼   어린 소녀가 아니라.

always starving / for new books / to gobble, / and she
그 애는 항상 굶주려 있어요 새로운 책에   먹어 치울.

wants grown-up books / — great, big, fat ones — /
그리고 어른의 책들을 원하죠   — 위대하고, 크고, 두꺼운 것들을 —

French and German / as well as English / — history and
프랑스와 독일어도   영어뿐만 아니라

biography and poets, / and all sorts of things. Drag her
— 역사와 전기와 시들,   그리고 그밖에 모든 종류를.

away from her books / when she reads too much. Make
그 애를 책에서 멀리 떼어내세요   너무 많이 읽으면.

her ride her pony / in the Row / or go out / and buy a new
조랑말을 타게 하세요   로우 거리에서   아니면 나가서   새 인형을 사도록 해

doll. She ought to play more with dolls."
주세요. 그 애는 인형들과 더 놀아야 해요."

"Papa," / said Sara, / "you see, / if I went out and bought
"아빠,"   새라가 말했다.   "있잖아요,   만약 나가서 새 인형을 사 온다면

a new doll / every few days / I should have more / than
며칠에 한 번씩   더 많이 갖게 될 거예요

I could be fond of. Dolls ought to be intimate friends.
좋아할 수 있는 것보다.   인형들은 친한 친구여야 해요.

Emily is going to be my intimate friend."
에밀리는 나의 가장 친한 친구가 될 거예요."

Captain Crewe looked at Miss Minchin / and Miss
크루 대위는 민친 교장을 쳐다보았고

Minchin looked at Captain Crewe.
민친 교장도 크루 대위를 쳐다보았다.

"Who is Emily?" / she inquired.
"에밀리가 누구니?"   교장이 물었다.

"Tell her, Sara," / Captain Crewe said, / smiling.
"말씀 드려야지, 새라,"   크루 대위가 말했다.   웃으면서.

Sara's green-gray eyes / looked very solemn and quite soft /
새라의 초록빛 회색 눈은   매우 진지하고 꽤 부드럽게 보였다

as she answered.
대답할 때.

"She is a doll / I haven't got yet," / she said. "She is a doll
"에밀리는 인형이에요   아직 갖지 못한,"   새라는 말했다.   "에밀리는 인형이에요

/ papa is going to buy for me. We are going out together /
아빠가 제게 사 줄.   우리는 함께 나가서

to find her. I have called her Emily. She is going to be my
그 인형을 찾을 거예요. 저는 그 인형을 에밀리라고 불렀어요. 내 친구가 될 거예요

friend / when papa is gone. I want her to talk to / about him."
아빠가 떠나면.   난 에밀리에게 얘기하고 싶어요   아빠에 대해."

Miss Minchin's large, fishy smile / became very flattering /
민친 교장의 크고, 수상한 미소는   아첨으로 바뀌었다

indeed.
실제로.

"What an original child!" / she said. "What a darling little
"참 독특한 아이군요!"   교장이 말했다.   "엄청 사랑스러운 아이예요!"

creature!"

"Yes," / said Captain Crewe, / drawing Sara close. "She is a
"네,"   크루 대위가 말했다,   새라를 가까이 끌어당기며.

darling little creature. Take great care of her / for me, / Miss
"그 애는 사랑스런 아이예요.   잘 보살펴 주세요   제 대신,

Minchin."
민친 선생님,"

Key Expression 🎵

every+수사+시간명사 : ~마다

every few days는 '며칠마다'라는 뜻입니다. 이처럼 every에 수사와 시간명
사를 사용하여 '~마다'라는 의미를 나타낼 수 있습니다.

▶ every + 기수 + 복수명사
▶ every + 서수 + 단수명사
▶ every other day : 이틀에 한 번

ex) If I went out and bought a new doll every few days I should have more than I
could be fond of.
만약 내가 며칠마다 나가서 새 인형을 사 온다면 좋아할 수 있는 것보다 더 많
이 갖게 될 거예요.

---

burrow (~ 속으로) 파고들다, (~에) 파묻다 | gobble 게걸스럽게 먹다 | biography 전기 | intimate 친(밀)한 |
original 독창적인 | darling (대단히) 사랑하는, 굉장히 멋진, 특별한

Sara stayed with her father / at his hotel / for several days;
새라는 아빠와 함께 머물렀다   아빠의 호텔에   며칠 동안;

/ in fact, / she remained with him / until he sailed away
사실,   아빠 곁에 남은 것이었다   아빠가 다시 멀리 항해를 갈 때까지

again / to India. They went out / and visited many big shops
인도로.   그들은 밖에 나가서   함께 큰 상점들을 많이 방문했고,

together, / and bought a great many things. They bought,
엄청 많은 것들을 샀다.   그들은 샀다,

/ indeed, / a great many more things / than Sara needed; /
실제로,   더 많은 것들을   새라가 필요한 것보다;

but Captain Crewe was a rash, innocent young man / and
하지만 크루 대위는 무모하고, 순수한 젊은 사람이라서

wanted / his little girl to have / everything she admired /
원했다   어린 딸이 갖도록   좋아하는 모든 것과

and everything he admired himself, / so between them /
그 자신이 좋아하는 모든 것을,   그래서 그런 것들 중에는

they collected a wardrobe / much too grand for a child of
옷을 사기도 했다   일곱 살 아이에게는 너무 화려한.

seven. There were velvet dresses / trimmed with costly
벨벳 드레스들도 있었다   값비싼 모피로 장식된,

furs, / and lace dresses, / and embroidered ones, / and hats
그리고 레이스 드레스와,   수가 놓여진 것들,

with great, soft ostrich feathers, / and ermine coats and
크고, 부드러운 타조 깃털로 된 모자,   어민털 외투와 토시들,

muffs, / and boxes of tiny gloves and handkerchiefs and
작은 장갑과 손수건과 실크 스타킹이 담긴 상자들도 있었다

silk stockings / in such abundant supplies / that the polite
아주 많아서   예의 바른 젊은 여자들이

young women / behind the counters / whispered to each
카운터 뒤에 있는   서로 속삭였다

other / that the odd little girl / with the big, solemn eyes /
저 이상한 꼬마 여자 아이는   크고, 진지한 눈을 가진

must be at least some foreign princess / — perhaps / the
적어도 외국의 공주임이 틀림없다고   — 어쩌면

little daughter of an Indian rajah.
인도 국왕의 딸일지도 모른다고.

And at last / they found Emily, / but they went to a number
그리고 마침내　　　그들은 에밀리를 찾았다,　　　　하지만 수많은 장난감 가게를 갔고

of toy shops / and looked at a great many dolls / before they
　　　　수많은 인형들을 보았다

discovered her.
에밀리를 찾기 전까지.

"I want her to look / as if she wasn't a doll / really," / Sara
"에밀리가 보였으면 좋겠어요　마치 인형이 아닌 것처럼　　　정말로."　　새라는

said. "I want her to look / as if she listens / when I talk to
말했다. "에밀리가 보였으면 좋겠어요　마치 듣고 있는 것처럼　내가 말을 걸면.

her. The trouble with dolls, papa" / — and she put her head
　　인형들의 문제점은요, 아빠"　　　　　　— 그리고 머리를 한쪽으로 기울이고

on one side and reflected / as she said it — / "the trouble
생각에 잠겼다　　　　　　　그렇게 말하면서 —　　　"인형들이 가진 문제점은

with dolls is / that they never seem to hear." So they looked
　　　바로 전혀 듣는 것처럼 보이지 않는 거예요."　　그래서 그들은 큰 인형과

at big ones and little ones / — at dolls with black eyes / and
작은 인형들을 보았다　　　　　— 검은 눈을 가진 인형과

dolls with blue / — at dolls with brown curls / and dolls
파란 눈을 가진 인형을　— 갈색 곱슬머리 인형과

with golden braids, / dolls dressed / and dolls undressed.
땋은 금발을 한 인형을,　　　옷을 입은 인형과　　입지 않은 인형.

Key Expression

목적격 관계대명사의 생략
관계대명사가 이끄는 문장이 동사나 전치사의 목적어일 경우 생략이 가능합니다.
만약 문장이 '명사 + 주어 + 동사…'로 이어질 경우 목적격 관계대명사의 생략된
것으로 해석하세요.

ex) Captain Crewe wanted his little girl to have everything she admired and
everything he admired himself.
크루 대위는 어린 딸이 좋아하는 모든 것과 자신이 좋아하는 모든 것을 갖게 되
기를 원했다.

rash 경솔한, 무모한 | admire 감탄하며 바라보다 | wardrobe 옷 | trim (with sth) (특히 가장자리를) 장식하다(
주로 수동태로 쓰임) | embroider 수를 놓다 | ostrich 타조 | ermine 어민(북방 족제비의 흰색 겨울털. 왕들의 가운,
판사의 법복 등을 장식하는 데 쓰임) | muff 머프(방한용 토시) | rajah 인도의 국왕(왕자) | reflect 곰곰이 생각하다,
심사숙고하다 | braid 땋은 머리

"You see," / Sara said / when they were examining one
"있잖아요,"   새라가 말했다   한 인형을 살펴보다가

/ who had no clothes. "If, / when I find her, / she has no
옷을 입지 않은.   "만약,   내가 그 인형을 찾았을 때,   드레스를 입지

frocks, / we can take her to a dressmaker / and have her
않았다면,   재봉사에게 데려가   옷을 입혀줄 수 있어요

things / made to fit. They will fit better / if they are tried
몸에 맞는.   그 옷들은 더 잘 맞을 거예요   입혀보면."

on."

After a number of disappointments / they decided to walk
수많은 실망 끝에   그들은 걸어가면서 들여다 보기로

and look in / at the shop windows / and let the cab follow
결정했고   상점의 창문들을   마차를 뒤따라오도록 했다.

them. They had passed two or three places / without even
그들은 두세 곳을 지나갔다   들어가 보지도 않고,

going in, / when, as they were approaching a shop / which
어떤 상점에 다다랐을 때

was really not a very large one, / Sara suddenly started /
그리 크지 않은,   새라는 갑자기 깜짝 놀라며

and clutched her father's arm.
아빠의 손을 움켜잡았다.

"Oh, papa!" / she cried. "There is Emily!"
"오, 아빠!"   새라가 외쳤다.   "에밀리예요!"

A flush had risen to her face / and there was an expression
새라의 얼굴이 상기되어   표정이 일어났다

/ in her green-gray eyes / as if she had just recognized
초록빛 회색 눈에   마치 누군가를 막 알아본 듯

someone / she was intimate with and fond of.
                친숙하고 좋아하는.

"She is actually waiting there for us!" / she said. "Let us
"진짜 저기에서 우리를 기다리고 있어요!"   새라가 말했다.

go in to her."
"그 애한테 가요."

---

dressmaker (여성복) 재봉사 I start 깜짝 놀라다 I clutch 움켜잡다 I flush 홍조 I dear me 아 이런, 이런 어쩌나 I
intelligent 지능이 있는 I mantle 망토

"Dear me," / said Captain Crewe, / "I feel / as if we ought
"이런," 크루 대위가 말했다, "내 생각에는 필요한 것 같구나

to have / someone to introduce us."
우리를 소개해 줄 사람이."

"You must introduce me / and I will introduce you," /
"아빠가 나를 소개시키고 내가 아빠를 소개할게요."

said Sara. "But I knew her / the minute I saw her / — so
새라가 말했다. "하지만 알아봤어요 그 인형을 본 순간 — 그래서

perhaps she knew me, / too."
아마 그 애도 날 알아볼 거예요. 역시."

Perhaps she had known her. She had certainly a very
어쩌면 그 인형은 새라를 알아봤을지 모른다. 아주 똑똑한 표정을 확실히 가지고 있었다

intelligent expression / in her eyes / when Sara took her in
눈에 새라가 팔에 안았을 때.

her arms. She was a large doll, / but not too large to carry
그 인형은 컸지만, 너무 커서 쉽게 가지고 다닐 수 없을 정도

about easily; / she had naturally curling golden-brown
는 아니었다; 자연스럽게 곱슬거리는 금빛 갈색 머리를 가졌는데,

hair, / which hung like a mantle about her, / and her eyes
머리카락이 망토처럼 주위에 늘어져 있었고,

were a deep, clear, gray-blue, / with soft, thick eyelashes /
눈은 깊고, 맑은, 잿빛 푸른 눈동자에. 부드럽고, 진한 속눈썹을 가졌다,

which were real eyelashes / and not mere painted lines.
그것은 진짜 속눈썹이었다 단지 그림으로 그린 선이 아니라.

Key Expression

the minute 접속사

시간을 나타내는 명사가 뒤에 절을 동반할 경우에는 접속사 역할을 합니다.
그래서 the minute ~은 '~한 순간', every time ~은 '~할 때마다', first
time ~은 '처음 ~할 때' 등의 의미로 해석하면 됩니다

ex) But I knew her the minute I saw her — so perhaps she knew me, too.
하지만 그 애를 본 순간 난 알아봤어요 — 그래서 그 애도 역시 날 알아볼 거예요.

"Of course," / said Sara, / looking into her face / as she
"물론," 새라가 말했다. 인형의 얼굴을 들여다 보며

held her on her knee, / "of course papa, / this is Emily."
무릎에 인형을 앉히고, "물론 아빠, 얘가 에밀리예요."

So Emily was bought / and actually taken / to a children's
그래서 에밀리를 샀고 실제로 가져가서 아동용 외출복 가게로

outfitter's shop / and measured for a wardrobe / as grand
옷을 만들기 위한 수치를 쟀다

as Sara's own. She had lace frocks, / too, / and velvet and
새라의 옷만큼 화려한. 레이스 드레스도 샀다. 역시, 또 벨벳과 모슬린 드레스,

muslin ones, / and hats and coats / and beautiful lace-
모자와 코트, 예쁜 레이스로 장식된 속옷과,

trimmed underclothes, / and gloves and handkerchiefs
장갑과 손수건과 모피도 샀다.

and furs.

"I should like her always to look / as if she was a child
"에밀리가 항상 보였으면 좋겠어요 아이처럼

/ with a good mother," / said Sara. "I'm her mother, /
좋은 엄마를 둔," 새라는 말했다. "내가 엄마예요,

though I am going to make a companion of her."
친구가 될 것이긴 하지만."

Captain Crewe would really have enjoyed the shopping
크루 대위는 정말 쇼핑을 즐겼다

/ tremendously, / but that a sad thought kept tugging
엄청나게, 하지만 슬픈 생각이 계속 일어났다

/ at his heart. This all meant / that he was going to be
마음속에서. 이 모든 것은 의미했으니까 그가 헤어질 거라는 것을

separated / from his beloved, quaint little comrade.
사랑스럽고, 독특한 어린 친구와.

---

outfitter 교복 파는 상점, 야외 활동 장비점 | muslin 모슬린(속이 거의 다 비치는 고운 면직물) | underclothes (복수형) 속옷, 내의 | tremendously 엄청나게 | tug (세게, 흔히 여러 번) 잡아당기다 | comrade 동무, 동지 | mingle 섞이다, 어울어지다, 섞다, 어우르다 | lace-ruffled 레이스 주름 장식을 단 | mustache 코밑 수염 | boyish 소년같은 (매력이 있는) | heigh-ho (감탄사) 아, 어, 아이고(놀람·피로·권태·낙담 등을 나타내는 소리)

He got out of his bed / in the middle of that night / and
그는 침대에서 걸어나와　　　　그날 한밤중에

went and stood looking down at Sara, / who lay asleep /
새라를 내려다 보며 서 있었다.　　　　　　　새라는 잠들어 있었다

with Emily in her arms. Her black hair was spread out /
에밀리를 팔에 안고.　　　　　새라의 검은 머리는 흩어져 있었고

on the pillow / and Emily's golden-brown hair / mingled
베개 위에　　　　에밀리의 금빛 갈색 머리는　　　　　섞여 있었다

/ with it, / both of them had lace-ruffled nightgowns, /
　새라의 머리와,　둘 다 레이스 주름 장식을 단 잠옷을 입고 있었고,

and both had long eyelashes / which lay and curled up /
둘 다 긴 속눈썹을 가지고 있었다　　　말려 올라가 있는

on their cheeks. Emily looked so like a real child / that
뺨 위에.　　　　에밀리가 매우 진짜 아이처럼 보였기 때문에

Captain Crewe felt glad / she was there. He drew a big sigh
크루 대위은 기뻤다　　　에밀리가 그곳에 있다는 것이. 그는 깊은 한숨을 쉬고

/ and pulled his mustache / with a boyish expression.
　코밑 수염을 잡아당겼다　　　남자들이 하는 행동으로.

"Heigh-ho, little Sara!" / he said to himself / "I don't
"아아, 귀여운 새라야!"　　　그는 중얼거렸다

believe you know / how much your daddy will miss you."
"너는 모르겠지　　　아빠가 얼마나 널 그리워할지."

The next day / he took her to Miss Minchin's / and left
다음 날 　　　새라를 민친 교장네 집에 데려갔던 　　　　그곳에 두고 떠났다.

her there. He was to sail away / the next morning. He
그는 멀리 항해를 떠날 예정이었다 　다음 날 아침.

explained to Miss Minchin / that his solicitors, Messrs.
그는 민친 교장에게 설명했다 　　　사무 변호단인, 배로 앤 스킵워스 회사가

Barrow & Skipworth, / had charge of his affairs / in
　　　　　　　　자신의 일을 담당하고 있어서

England / and would give her any advice / she wanted, /
영국에서 　　교장에게 조언해 줄 것이며 　　　　그녀가 원하는,

and that they would pay the bills / she sent in for Sara's
비용을 지불할 것이라고 　　　　　　새라의 비용으로 청구한.

expenses. He would write to Sara / twice a week, / and
그는 새라에게 편지를 쓸 것이며 　일주일에 두 번,

she was to be given every pleasure / she asked for.
새라는 모든 즐거움을 누려야 한다고 　　　자신이 요청한.

"She is a sensible little thing, / and she never wants /
"새라는 현명한 아이예요, 　　　　　그러니 절대로 원하지 않을 거예요

anything it isn't safe to give her," / he said.
안전하지 않은 것을." 　　　　그가 말했다.

Then he went with Sara / into her little sitting room /
그리고 나서 그는 새라와 함께 가서 　그녀의 작은 거실로

and they bade each other good-by. Sara sat on his knee /
서로에게 작별 인사를 했다. 　　　　　새라는 아빠의 무릎에 앉아서

and held the lapels of his coat / in her small hands, / and
아빠 외투의 옷깃을 잡고 　　　　　작은 손으로,

looked long and hard / at his face.
오랫동안 열심히 바라보았다 　아빠의 얼굴을.

"Are you learning me by heart, / little Sara?" / he said, /
"아빠를 마음에 새겨 두려는 거지, 　　새라야?" 　　　그가 말했다,

stroking her hair.
딸의 머리를 쓰다듬으며.

solicitor 사무 변호사(토지·건물 매각을 위한 서류 관련 업무나 법률 자문 등을 주로 하는 변호사) | Messrs Mr의
복수형으로써 명단·회사명에 나오는 이름들 앞에 쓰임 | bade good-by ~에게 작별을 고하다 | lapel (양복 상의의
접혀 있는) 옷깃 | learn by heart ~을 외다, 암기하다 | know by heart 암기하다 | if you please (정중히 요청할
때) 괜찮다면, 죄송하지만

"No," / she answered. "I know you by heart. You are inside
"아니에요," 그녀가 대답했다.   "난 이미 아빠를 기억하고 있어요.   아빠는 내 마음속에

my heart." And they put their arms round each other / and
있으니까요."   그리고 그들은 서로를 감싸안고

kissed / as if they would never let each other go.
입맞췄다   마치 서로를 보내지 않을 것처럼.

When the cab drove away from the door, / Sara was sitting
마차가 문에서 멀어져 갈 때,   새라는 앉아 있었다

/ on the floor of her sitting room, / with her hands under
거실 바닥에,   턱 아래에 손을 괴고,

her chin / and her eyes following it / until it had turned the
눈으로 마차를 좇으며   마차가 광장의 모퉁이를 돌 때까지.

corner of the square. Emily was sitting by her, / and she
에밀리도 새라의 옆에 앉아서,   함께 그 모습을

looked after it, / too. When Miss Minchin sent / her sister,
바라보았다.   역시.   민친 교장이 보냈을 때   그녀의 여동생인,

Miss Amelia, / to see what the child was doing, / she found
아멜리아 선생을,   아이가 뭘 하는지 보도록,   she found

she could not open the door.
그녀는 문을 열 수 없었다.

"I have locked it," / said a queer, polite little voice / from
"내가 잠궜어요,"   이상하지만, 예의바른 작은 목소리가 들렸다

inside. "I want to be quite by myself, / if you please."
안에서.   "혼자 조용히 있고 싶어요,   괜찮으시다면."

Miss Amelia was fat and dumpy, / and stood very much in
아멜리아 선생은 뚱뚱하고 땅딸막했으며,   언니를 매우 두려워했다.

awe of her sister. She was really / the better-natured person
                      그녀는 실제로   천성이 더 착한 사람이었지만

/ of the two, / but she never disobeyed Miss Minchin. She
    둘 중에,   민친 교장의 말을 절대 거역하지 않았다.

went downstairs again, / looking almost alarmed.
그녀는 다시 아래층으로 내려왔다.   거의 충격 받은 모습으로.

"I never saw / such a funny, old-fashioned child, / sister,"
"본 적 없어   저렇게 웃기고, 구식인 아이는,   언니."

/ she said. "She has locked herself in, / and she is not
  그녀는 말했다. "문을 잠그고 안에 틀어박혀서,

making the least particle of noise."
전혀 소리도 내지 않고 있어."

"It is much better than / if she kicked and screamed, / as
"훨씬 낫지   발로 차고 소리지르는 것보다는,

some of them do," / Miss Minchin answered. "I expected /
몇몇 애들이 그러하듯,"   민친 교장이 답했다.   "난 기대했는데

that a child as much spoiled as she is / would set the whole
그 애처럼 버릇없는 아이는   집 전체를 소란스럽게 할 거라고.

house in an uproar. If ever a child was given her own way /
                      자기 마음대로 하는 아이라면 말이지

in everything, / she is."
모든 것을   그 애는 그렇잖아."

Key Expression 🖋

as if 가정법 : 마치 ~인 것처럼

as if는 가정법의 특수한 형태로 '마치 ~인 것처럼'이라는 의미로 쓰여요.
as if 절에는 과거동사가 오며 be 동사의 경우 인칭에 관계없이 were를 쓴다
는 점에 주의하세요.

ex) She has been provided for as if she were a little princess.
    그녀는 마치 소공녀인 것처럼 부족함 없이 받아왔으니까.
    They put their arms round each other and kissed as if they would never let
    each other go.
    그들은 마치 서로를 보내지 않으려는 것처럼 서로 껴안고 입을 맞췄다.

"I've been opening her trunks / and putting her things
"내가 그 애의 트렁크를 열고   짐을 정리했는데,"

away," / said Miss Amelia. "I never saw anything like
아멜리아 선생이 말했다.   "그런 것들을 본 적이 없어

them / — sable and ermine on her coats, / and real
— 흑담비털과 어민털로 된 외투에,   진짜 발렌시엔느

Valenciennes lace / on her underclothing. You have seen
레이스가 달려 있었어   속옷에는.   언니도 본 적 있지

/ some of her clothes. What do you think of them?"
그 애의 옷을.   어떻게 생각해?"

"I think / they are perfectly ridiculous," / replied Miss
"난 생각해   정말 터무니없다고,"   민친 교장이 답했다,

Minchin, / sharply; / "but they will look very well / at
날카롭게;   "하지만 그 옷들은 정말 좋아보일 거야

the head of the line / when we take the schoolchildren to
맨 앞줄에 있으면   학생들을 교회에 데려갈 때

church / on Sunday. She has been provided for / as if she
일요일에.   그 애는 부족함 없이 받아왔으니까

were a little princess."
마치 소공녀인 것처럼."

And upstairs / in the locked room / Sara and Emily sat
위층에   잠긴 방에서   새라와 에밀리는 바닥에 앉아서

on the floor / and stared at the corner round / which the
모퉁이를 바라보았다

cab had disappeared, / while Captain Crewe looked
마차가 사라진,   크루 대위가 뒤를 돌아보는 동안,

backward, / waving and kissing his hand / as if he could
손을 흔들고 손키스를 보내며

not bear to stop.
멈출 수 없는 사람처럼.

---

dumpy 땅딸막한 | stand[be] in awe of ~을 두려워, 경외하다 | alarmed 충격 받은, 두려워하는 | spoiled
버릇없는 | in (an) uproar 소란스럽게 | trunk 트렁크(옷·책 등을 담는 큰 가방) | put something away 치우다,
정리하다 | sable 흑담비 모피, 털(고급 외투나 화필 제조에 쓰임) | ridiculous 터무니없는 | be provided for 아무
부족함이 없다

A. 다음 문장을 해석해 보세요.

(1) The fact was, / however, / that she was always dreaming and thinking odd things / and could not herself remember any time / when she had not been thinking things / about grown-up people / and the world they belonged to.
→

(2) It seemed to her many years / since he had begun to prepare her mind / for "the place," / as she always called it.
→

(3) Sara was to be what was known / as "a parlor boarder," / and she was to enjoy even greater privileges / than parlor boarders usually did.
→

(4) If I went out and bought a new doll / every few days / I should have more / than I could be fond of.
→

B. 다음 주어진 문장이 되도록 빈칸에 써 넣으세요.

(1) 그녀는 마치 자신이 아주 오랜 시간을 살아온 것처럼 느꼈다.

She felt _____.

(2) 새라는 민친 교장의 얼굴에 시선을 고정시킨 채 조용히 서 있었다.

Sara stood quietly, _____

_____.

(3) 어려운 점은 그 애가 너무 빨리 그리고 너무 많이 배우지 못하게 막는 것이겠죠.

The difficulty will be _____

_____.

 Answer

A. (1) 그러나, 사실 그녀는 항상 이상한 것들을 꿈꾸고 생각했으며 그녀 자신도 다 큰 어른들이나 어른들이 속한 세상에 대해 생각하지 않고 있던 때를 기억할 수 없을 정도였다. (2) 그녀가 항상 "그곳"이라고 불렀던 곳에 대해 그가 그녀의 마음을 준비시키기 시작한 이후의 시간이 그녀에게는 수년처럼 느껴졌다. (3) 새라는 "특별 기숙생"으로

34   A Little Princess

(4) 슬픈 생각이 그의 마음속에서 계속 일어났다.

→

C. 다음 주어진 문구가 알맞은 문장이 되도록 순서를 맞춰 보세요.

(1) 너만큼 진지한 사람은 아무도 없어.
   (as / else / are / is / No one / solemn / you / as)
   →

(2) 난 정말로 그애가 마치 인형이 아닌 것처럼 보이길 원해요.
   (to look / a doll / she wasn't / I want / as if / her / really)
   →

(3) 저는 혼자 조용히 있고 싶어요.
   (myself / to be / I want / by / quite)
   →

(4) 그녀는 마치 소공녀인 것처럼 부족함 없이 받아왔지.
   (for / has been / were / a little princess / She / provided / she / as if)
   →

D. 다음 단어에대한맞는 설명과 연결해 보세요.

(1) cuddle   ▶   ◀ ① eat quickly and greedily

(2) solemn   ▶   ◀ ② hold and hug

(3) gobble   ▶   ◀ ③ short and fat

(4) dumpy   ▶   ◀ ④ very serious

Ermengarde
어먼가드

On that first morning, / when Sara sat at Miss Minchin's
그 첫날 아침,　　　　　　새라가 민친 교장 옆에 앉아서,

side, / aware / that the whole schoolroom was devoting
　　　인식했을 때　교실 전체가 몰두하고 있다는 것을

itself / to observing her, / she had noticed / very soon / one
자신을 관찰하는데,　　　그녀는 알아챘다　　금방

little girl, / about her own age, / who looked at her / very
한 여자 아이를,　자기 또래의,　　자신을 보고 있는　　매우 열심히

hard / with a pair of light, rather dull, blue eyes. She was
다소 경솔하고, 둔한, 파란 눈으로,　　　　　그 아이는 뚱뚱한

a fat child / who did not look / as if she were in the least
아이였다　　보이지 않는　　전혀 똑똑한 것처럼,

clever, / but she had / a goodnaturedly pouting mouth. Her
하지만 갖고 있었다　착해보이는 삐죽 내민 입을.

flaxen hair was braided / in a tight pigtail, / tied with a
금발 머리는 땋아져 있었는데　한 갈래로 촘촘하게,　리본으로 묶여서,

ribbon, / and she had pulled this pigtail / around her neck,
　　　이 머리채를 잡아당겨　　　목 주변으로,

/ and was biting the end of the ribbon, / resting her elbows
리본 끝을 씹고 있었다.　　　　　　팔꿈치를 책상 위에 올려놓은 채,

on the desk, / as she stared wonderingly / at the new pupil.
　　　놀란 표정으로 바라보면서　　　　새로 온 학생을.

Key Expression ❗

devote oneself to : 전념하다

devote oneself to는 '전념하다'라는 뜻을 가진 표현입니다. 이처럼 타동사
의 목적어가 주어 자신일 때 목적어로 재귀대명사를 사용합니다.
재귀대명사 목적어를 사용하는 자주 등장하는 표현들은 따라오는 전치사와 함께
숙어처럼 외워두는 것이 좋아요. 또한 이런 표현들은 같은 전치사를 사용한 수동태
로도 자주 사용된다는 점도 기억하세요.

ex) The whole schoolroom was devoting itself to observing her.
교실 전체가 그녀를 관찰하는 데 몰두하고 있었다.

When Monsieur Dufarge began to speak / to Sara, / she
뒤파르주 선생이 말하기 시작했을 때   새라에게,

looked a little frightened; / and when Sara stepped forward
그 아이는 약간 놀란 듯 보였다;   그리고 새라가 앞으로 나아갔을 때

/ and, / looking at him / with the innocent, appealing eyes,
그리고, 선생님을 보면서   순수하고, 호소하는 눈빛으로,

/ answered him, / without any warning, / in French, / the
대답하자,   곧바로,   프랑스어로,

fat little girl gave a startled jump, / and grew quite red /
그 뚱뚱하고 작은 소녀는 깜짝 놀라 벌떡 일어섰고,   꽤 빨갛게 상기되었다

in her awed amazement. Having wept hopeless tears / for
경외심이 담긴 놀라움으로.   감당할 수 없는 눈물을 훔치며   몇 주간

weeks / in her efforts to remember / that "la mere" meant
기억하려고 노력했기 때문에   "라 메르"는 "어머니"를 의미하고,

"the mother," / and "le pere," "the father," / — when one
"르 페르"는 "아버지"라는,

spoke sensible English — / it was almost too much / for her
— 알 만한 영어를 말할 때 —   그것은 너무 벅찬 일이었다   그녀에게

/ suddenly to find herself listening to a child / her own age
갑자기 한 아이의 말을 듣게 되는 것은   자기 또래의

/ who seemed not only quite familiar / with these words,
익숙해 보일 뿐만 아니라   이런 말들에,

/ but apparently knew / any number of others, / and could
분명히 알고 있으며   다른 수많은 단어들도,   그 단어들을 동사와

mix them up with verbs / as if they were mere trifles.
섞어 말할 수 있는 것 같아 보이는   아무 어려움이 없는 듯.

She stared so hard / and bit the ribbon / on her pigtail /
그 아이는 아주 열심히 쳐다보며 리본을 씹었기 때문에   땋은 머리의

so fast / that she attracted the attention of Miss Minchin,
매우 빨리   민친 교장의 주의를 끌었다,

/ who, / feeling extremely cross / at the moment, /
교장은   극도로 화가 나서   그 순간,

immediately pounced upon her.
그 아이를 즉시 심하게 나무랐다.

goodnaturedly 사람이 좋은, 선량한 | pouting 입을 삐죽 내민 | flaxen 금발의 | pigtail (하나 또는 두 갈래로)
땋은 머리 | pupil (특히 어린) 학생 | Monsieur ~씨, 귀하(Mr.나 Sir에 해당하는 경칭) | frightened 겁먹은, 놀란 |
awed 경외심에 휩싸인 | trifle 하찮은 것 | cross 짜증난, 약간 화가 난 | pounce 맹렬히 비난하다

"Miss St. John!" / she exclaimed severely. **"What do you**
"세인트 존 양!"　　　　교장은 심하게 소리쳤다.　　　　　　　"뭐 하는 거지

mean / by such conduct? Remove your elbows! Take your
그런 행동으로?　　　　　팔꿈치를 치워!　　　　　　리본을 빼렴

ribbon / out of your mouth! Sit up / at once!"
입 밖으로!　　　　똑바로 앉아 당장!"

Upon which / Miss St. John gave another jump, / and
이 말에　　　　세인트 존은 다시 한 번 놀라서 펄쩍 뛰었고,

when Lavinia and Jessie tittered / she became redder than
라비니아와 제시가 킥킥거리자　　　　　전보다 더 빨개졌다

ever / — so red, / indeed, / that she almost looked / as
— 매우 빨개져서, 실제로,　　　거의 보였다

if tears were coming / into her poor, dull, childish eyes;
눈물을 흘릴 것처럼　　　불쌍하고, 둔하고, 어린 애 같은 눈에서;

/ and Sara saw her / and was so sorry for her / that she
그리고 새라는 그 아이를 보자 매우 안스러워서

began rather to like her / and want to be her friend. It was
그 아이가 다소 좋아지기 시작하여　　친구가 되고 싶었다.　　　그것은 새

a way of hers / always / to want to spring into / any fray /
라의 방식이었다　　　항상　　　뛰어들고 싶어 하는 것은　　어떤 소동에

in which someone was made uncomfortable or unhappy.
누군가 불편해 하거나 불행하게 되는.

Key Expression

so~that… : 너무 ~해서 …하다

'so + 형용사/부사 + that…'은 '너무 ~해서 …하다'라는 의미로 결과를 나타
내는 구문이에요.
so와 that 사이에는 형용사나 부사가 들어가며, 명사를 넣을 경우에는 such 대
신 such (a)를 사용합니다. 또한 so대신 much 등 비슷한 의미의 단어를 사용
하는 경우도 있습니다.

ex) She became redder than ever — so red, indeed, that she almost looked as if
tears were coming.
그녀는 전보다 더 빨개졌다 — 실제로 매우 빨개져서 거의 눈물을 흘릴 것처럼
보였다.

---

titter 킥킥거리다 | childish 어린애 같은 | fray 소동, 싸움 | distress 고충, 곤경 | trouble 곤경, 문제 | take a
fancy to~ (흔히 뚜렷한 이유 없이) ~이 좋아지기 시작하다 | show 허세, 가식 | pathetic 불쌍한, 애처로운 | in
spite of oneself 저도 모르게 | giggle 피식 웃다, 낄낄거리다 | wondering 이상히 여기는, 이상한 듯한, 경탄하는
| disdain 업신여김, 무시 | savage 야만적인, 흉포한, 몹시 사나운

"If Sara had been a boy / and lived a few centuries ago,"
"만약 새라가 남자 아이이고 몇 세기 전에 살았다면,"

/ her father used to say, / "she would have gone about the
아빠는 말하곤 했다, "온 나라를 다녔을 거야

country / with her sword drawn, / rescuing and defending /
칼을 뽑아 들고, 구하고 지키며

everyone in distress. She always wants to fight / when she
곤경에 빠진 모든 사람을. 그 애는 항상 싸우려고 하니까

sees people / in trouble."
사람들을 보면 곤경에 처한."

So she took rather a fancy / to fat, slow, little Miss
그래서 새라는 약간 좋아지기 시작했고 뚱뚱하고, 느린, 세인트 존 양이,

St. John, / and kept glancing toward her / through the
그 아이를 계속 쳐다보았다 아침 내내.

morning. She saw / that lessons were no easy matter /
새라는 알았다 수업이 결코 쉬운 일이 아니라는 것을

to her, / and that there was no danger / of her ever being
그 아이에게, 그리고 위험은 없다는 것을 버릇없는 아이가 될

spoiled / by being treated as a show pupil. Her French
전시용 학생 취급을 받아서.

lesson was a pathetic thing. Her pronunciation made even
그 아이의 프랑스어 수업은 애처로운 것이었다. 발음은 뒤파르주 선생마저 웃게 만들었고

Monsieur Dufarge smile / in spite of himself, / and Lavinia
자신도 모르게, 라비니아와 제시와

and Jessie / and the more fortunate girls / either giggled
더 운 좋은 여자 아이들은 낄낄거리며

or looked at her / in wondering disdain. But Sara did not
쳐다보았다 이상히 여기는 경멸의 눈빛으로. 하지만 새라는 웃지 않았다.

laugh. She tried to look / as if she did not hear / when Miss
새라는 보이려고 애썼다 듣지 않은 것처럼

St. John called "le bon pain", "lee bong pang". She had
세인트 존이 "르 봉 팽"을, "리 봉 팡"이라고 말했을 때. 새라는 섬세하고,

a fine, hot little temper of her own, / and it made her feel
급한 성질을 갖고 있어서, 그 사실은 그녀를 화나게 했다

rather savage / when she heard the titters / and saw the
웃음 소리를 듣고

poor, stupid, distressed child's face.
불쌍하고, 멍청한, 곤경에 처한 아이의 얼굴을 보자.

"It isn't funny, really," / she said / between her teeth, / as
"이것은 우습지 않아, 정말,"   새라는 말했다   이를 악물고,

she bent over her book. "They ought not to laugh."
책에 고개를 숙이며.   "웃으면 안 되지."

When lessons were over / and the pupils gathered together
수업이 끝나자   학생들은 함께 모여

/ in groups / to talk, / Sara looked for Miss St. John, / and
끼리끼리   이야기를 나눴고,   새라는 세인트 존 양을 찾다가   그 아이

finding her / bundled rather disconsolately / in a window-
를 발견하고는   다소 절망적으로 웅크리고 있던   창가 자리에,

seat, / she walked over to her / and spoke. She only said
새라는 그 아이에게 걸어가서   말했다.   새라는 말했을 뿐이었지만

/ the kind of thing / little girls always say to each other
종류의 말을   어린 소녀들이 서로에게 말하곤 하는

/ by way of beginning an acquaintance, / but there was
안면을 트는 방법으로,   하지만 친절한 뭔가 있었고

something friendly / about Sara, / and people always felt it.
새라에게는,   사람들은 항상 그것을 느꼈다.

"What is your name?" / she said.
"네 이름이 뭐니?"   새라가 말했다.

To explain Miss St. John's amazement / one must recall
"세인트 존의 놀라움을 설명하기 위해   기억해야 할 것이다

/ that a new pupil is, / for a short time, / a somewhat
새로 온 학생은,   얼마 동안,   다소 불확실한 존재라는 것을;

uncertain thing; / and of this new pupil / the entire school
그리고 이 새로 온 학생에 대해   온 학교가 말했다는 것을

had talked / the night before / until it fell asleep quite
전날 밤에   완전히 지쳐 잠들 때까지

exhausted / by excitement and contradictory stories. A
흥분되고 모순되는 이야기로.

new pupil / with a carriage and a pony and a maid, / and
새로 온 학생은   마차와 조랑말과 하녀를 가지고 있으며,

a voyage from India / to discuss, / was not an ordinary
그리고 인도로부터 항해를 해 온   토론거리가 된,   평범하게 알고 지낼 친구는 아니었다.

acquaintance.

"My name's Ermengarde St. John," / she answered.
"내 이름은 어먼가드 세인트 존이야."   그 아이가 답했다.

"Mine is Sara Crewe," / said Sara. "Yours is very pretty. It
"내 이름은 새라 크루야,"   새라가 말했다.   "네 이름은 참 예쁘구나.

sounds like a story book."
동화책에 나오는 이름같아."

"Do you like it?" / fluttered Ermengarde. "I — I like
"넌 마음에 드니?"   어먼가드는 떨었다.   "난 — 난 네 이름이 좋은데."

yours."

Miss St. John's chief trouble / in life / was that she had a
세인트 존의 가장 큰 문제는   삶에서   똑똑한 아빠를 뒀다는 것이었다.

clever father. Sometimes / this seemed to her a dreadful
때때로   이 사실은 그녀에게 있어 끔찍한 재앙같았다.

calamity. If you have a father / who knows everything, /
만약 아빠가 있다면   모든 것을 아는,

who speaks seven or eight languages, / and has thousands
7~8가지 언어를 구사하고,   수천 권의 책을 가진

of volumes / which he has apparently learned by heart, / he
분명히 암기하고 있는,

frequently expects / you to be familiar / with the contents
그런 아빠는 종종 기대할 것이다 아이가 익숙할 것이라고   교과서의 내용이라도

of your lesson books / at least; / and it is not improbable
적어도;   그리고 있음직한 일이다

/ that he will feel / you ought to be able / to remember a
그가 생각한다는 것은   딸도 할 수 있어야 한다고

few incidents of history / and to write a French exercise.
몇 가지 역사적인 사건들을 기억하거나   프랑스어로 글을 쓰는 것 정도는.

bundle 밀어 넣다 | disconsolately 절망적으로, 적절하게 | acquaintance 면식, (약간의) 친분 | contradictory
모순되는 | story book 이야기책, 동화책 | flutter 떨다 | dreadful 끔찍한, 지독한 | calamity 재앙, 재난 |
improbable 있을 것 같지 않은

Ermengarde was a severe trial / to Mr. St. John. He could
어민가드는 엄청난 골칫거리였다   세인트 존 씨에게는.

not understand / how a child of his / could be a notably and
그는 이해할 수 없었다   어떻게 자신의 아이가   현저히 그리고 틀림없이

unmistakably / dull creature / who never shone in anything.
불멸하게   멍청한 아이일 수 있는지 그 어느 것에도 빼어나지 못한.

"Good heavens!" / he had said / more than once, / as he
"하나님 맙소사!"   그는 말했다   여러 번,

stared at her, / "there are times / when I think / she is as
딸을 쳐다보면서,   "여러 번이야   생각한 적이

stupid as her Aunt Eliza!"
저 애는 엘리자 고모만큼 멍청하다고!"

If her Aunt Eliza had been slow to learn / and quick to forget
만약 엘리자 고모가 배우는 것이 더디고   금새 전부 잊어버리는 사람이라면

a thing entirely / when she had learned it, / Ermengarde was
뭔가 배웠을 때,

strikingly like her. She was the monumental dunce / of the
어민가드는 놀랍게도 비슷했다. 어민가드는 기념비적인 지진아였다

school, / and it could not be denied.
학교의,   그리고 그 사실은 부정할 수 없었다.

"She must be made to learn," / her father said to Miss
"그 애는 공부하도록 시켜야 해요,"   어민가드의 아빠는 민친 교장에게 말했다.

Minchin.

Consequently / Ermengarde spent / the greater part of
그 결과   어민가드는 보냈다   인생의 많은 부분을

her life / in disgrace / or in tears. She learned things / and
수치스럽거나   눈물을 흘리며. 여러 가지를 배우고

forgot them; / or, / if she remembered them, / she did not
잊어버렸다;   혹은,   설사 기억했더라도,

understand them. So it was natural that, / having made
그것을 이해하지 못했다.   그래서 당연한 일이었다,

Sara's acquaintance, / she should sit and stare at her / with
새라를 알게 되자,   앉아서 새라를 쳐다볼 수밖에 없었다는 것은

profound admiration.
엄청난 존경심을 가지고.

"You can speak French, / can't you?" / she said respectfully.
"넌 프랑스어를 할 수 있지,   그렇지 않니?"   어먼가드가 존경스럽다는 듯 말했다.

Sara got on to the window-seat, / which was a big, deep
새라는 창가자리로 가서,   넓고, 깊은 자리였던,

one, / and, tucking up her feet, / sat / with her hands
          다리를 모아 올리면서,   앉았다

clasped round her knees.
깍지 낀 손으로 무릎을 감싸고.

"I can speak it / because I have heard it / all my life," / she
"난 말할 수 있는 거야   그것을 들어왔기 때문에   사는 내내,"

answered. "You could speak it / if you had always heard it."
새라가 답했다.   "너도 말할 수 있어   항상 그것을 들어왔다면."

"Oh, no, / I couldn't," / said Ermengarde. "I never could
"아, 아니야,   난 할 수 없어,"   어먼가드가 말했다.   "난 절대로 못 해!"

speak it!"

"Why?" / inquired Sara, / curiously.
"왜?"   새라가 물었다.   신기한 듯이.

Key Expression ❣

사역동사 make의 수동태

'시키다'라는 의미를 가지고 있는 사역동사 make가 들어간 문장을 수동태로 만들 때는 to가 삽입됩니다.

▶ 주어 + make + 목적어 + 동사원형(목적보어)
  → 목적어 + be made + to 동사원형

다른 사역동사는 경우가 다릅니다. 예를 들면 have의 경우에는 be asked(ordered) to, let은 be allowed to의 구문으로 바꿔서 수동태 문장을 만듭니다.

ex) She must be made to learn.
  (→ You must make her learn.)
  그 애는 공부시켜야 합니다.

---

trial 시련, 골칫거리 | notably 현저히, 뚜렷이 | unmistakably 오해의 여지가 없이, 틀림없이 | shine 뛰어나게 잘하다, 빼어나다 | Good heavens 맙소사(놀라움·짜증스러움을 나타냄) | monumental 기념비적인 | dunce 지진아 | make somebody's acquaintance ~를 알게 되다, 처음으로 만나다, 안면을 트다 | profound 엄청난, 심오한 | clasp 움켜쥐다, 껴안다 | curiously 신기한 듯이, 호기심에서

Ermengarde shook her head / so that the pigtail wobbled.
어먼가드는 머리를 세게 흔들었고   그래서 땋은 머리가 흔들렸다.

"You heard me / just now," she said. "I'm always like
"내 말 들었잖아   방금,"   그녀가 말했다. "난 항상 그래.

that. I can't say the words. They're so queer."
단어도 말하지 못하거든.   단어들이 아주 이상해."

She paused a moment, / and then added / with a touch of
어먼가드는 잠시 쉬었다가,   그리고는 덧붙였다   약간 경외심을 담은 채

awe / in her voice, / "You are clever, / aren't you?"
목소리에.   "넌 똑똑하지,   그렇지 않니?"

Sara looked out of the window / into the dingy square,
새라는 창밖을 보았다   우중충한 광장을,

/ where the sparrows were hopping / and twittering / on
거기에는 참새들이 뛰어다니며   짹짹거리고 있었다

the wet, iron railings and the sooty branches of the trees.
젖은, 철책과 거무튀튀한 나뭇가지들 위에서.

She reflected / a few moments. She had heard it said /
새라는 생각에 잠겼다   잠시.   새라는 그 말을 들어왔다

very often / that she was "clever," / and she wondered / if
매우 자주   "똑똑하다"는 말을,   그리고 궁금해 했다

she was / — and if she was, / how it had happened.
자신이 그런지   — 만약 정말 그렇다면,   어떻게 똑똑해진건지.

"I don't know," / she said. "I can't tell." Then, / seeing a
"난 모르겠어."   새라가 말했다. "모르겠어."   그리고는,

mournful look / on the round, chubby face, / she gave a
애절한 표정을 보면서   둥글고, 통통한 얼굴에 떠오른,   살짝 웃으며

little laugh / and changed the subject.
화제를 돌렸다.

"Would you like to see Emily?" / she inquired.
"에밀리를 볼래?"   새라가 물었다.

"Who is Emily?" / Ermengarde asked, / just as Miss
"에밀리가 누군데?"   어먼가드가 물었다,   민친 교장이 그랬던 것처럼.

Minchin had done.

wobble 흔들리다, 떨리다 | a touch 약간, 조금 | dingy 우중충한, 거무칙칙한 | twitter (새가) 지저귀다, 짹짹거리다
| iron railing 철책 | sooty 검댕이 묻은, 거무튀튀한 | mournful 애절한 | chubby 통통한, 토실토실한 | passage
통로 , 복도 | lose one's breath 숨차다, 헐떡이다 | gasp 숨이 턱 막히다, 헉 하고 숨을 쉬다

"Come up to my room and see," / said Sara, / holding out
"내 방으로 올라가서 보자,"　　　　　　　　　　새라가 말했다,

her hand.
어먼가드의 손을 잡고.

They jumped down from the window-seat / together, /
그들은 창가 자리에서 뛰어 내려　　　　　　　　함께,

and went upstairs.
위층으로 갔다.

"Is it true," / Ermengarde whispered, / as they went
"정말이니,"　　　어먼가드가 속삭였다,　　　　복도를 지나가면서

through the hall / — "is it true / that you have a
　　　　　　　　　— "정말이야　　놀이방을 가지고 있다는 것이

playroom / all to yourself?"
　　　　　너만을 위한?"

"Yes," / Sara answered. "Papa asked Miss Minchin / to
"맞아,"　　새라가 대답했다.　　　"아빠가 민친 교장선생님에게 부탁했어

let me have one, / because / — well, / it was because /
내가 방을 갖게 해 달라고,　왜냐하면　— 글쎄,　　그 이유는

when I play / I make up stories / and tell them to myself,
나는 놀이를 할 때　이야기를 지어내서　　　나 자신에게 말해 주는데,

/ and I don't like / people to hear me. It spoils it / if I
　좋아하지 않아　　　사람들이 내 말을 듣는 것을.　이야기를 망치거든

think people listen."
사람들이 듣고 있다고 생각하면."

They had reached the passage / leading to Sara's room /
그들은 복도를 지나　　　　　　새라의 방에 다다랐고

by this time, / and Ermengarde stopped short, / staring, /
바로 이때,　　어먼가드는 잠시 멈춰 서서,　　　　　쳐다보면서,

and quite losing her breath.
숨을 꽤 헐떡였다.

"You make up stories!" / she gasped. "Can you do that
"네가 이야기를 지어낸다고!"　　헉 하고 숨을 쉬었다.　"그것을 할 수 있니

/ — as well as speak French? Can you?"
　— 프랑스어를 말할 뿐 아니라?　　　그런 거야?"

Sara looked at her / in simple surprise.
새라는 그녀를 쳐다보았다　　단순한 놀라움으로.

"Why, anyone can make up things," / she said. "Have you
"어머, 누구나 이야기를 만들 수 있어," 　　　　　　　 새라가 말했다.

never tried?"
"넌 해 본 적 없니?"

She put her hand / warningly / on Ermengarde's.
새라는 자신의 손을 놓았다 경고적으로 어먼가드의 손 위에.

"Let us go very quietly / to the door," / she whispered, /
"아주 조용히 가자 문까지," 새라가 속삭였다,

"and then I will open it / quite suddenly; / perhaps we may
"그리고 나서 문을 열 거야 아주 갑자기; 그러면 그녀를 잡을 수

catch her."
있을지 몰라."

She was half laughing, / but there was a touch of
새라는 반쯤 웃었다, 하지만 신비스러운 희망이 있었다

mysterious hope / in her eyes / which fascinated
새라의 눈에는 그것은 어먼가드를 매혹시켰다,

Ermengarde, / though she had not the remotest idea /
비록 조금도 이해하지 못했지만

what it meant, / or whom it was she wanted to "catch," /
그게 뭘 의미하는지, 혹은 새라가 누구를 "잡기" 원하는지,

or why she wanted to catch her. Whatsoever she meant,
혹은 왜 잡고 싶어 하는지. 새라가 의미하는 것이 무엇이든,

/ Ermengarde was sure / it was something delightfully
어먼가드는 확신했다 그것은 뭔가 즐겁고 신나는 일이라고.

exciting. So, / quite thrilled with expectation, / she
그래서, 기대감으로 신이 나서,

followed her / on tiptoe / along the passage. They made
새라를 따라갔다 발 끝으로 복도를 따라. 그들은 아무 소리도

not the least noise / until they reached the door. Then Sara
내지 않았다 문에 도착할 때까지.

suddenly turned the handle, / and threw it wide open.
그리고는 새라가 갑자기 손잡이를 돌렸고, 문을 활짝 열었다.

Its opening revealed the room / quite neat and quiet, / a
그렇게 열자 방이 보였다 아주 깨끗하고 조용한,

fire gently burning / in the grate, / and a wonderful doll /
불이 부드럽게 타고 있었고 벽난로에서, 그리고 멋진 인형이

sitting in a chair by it, / apparently reading a book.
난로 옆 의자에 앉아, 책을 읽는 듯 보였다.

thrilled with 황홀해 하는, 아주 흥분한, 신이 난 | gently 부드럽게 | grate (난로 안의 연료를 받치는) 쇠살대 |
apparently 보아 하니

"Oh, she got back / to her seat / before we could see her!"
"아, 그 애가 돌아왔어   자기 자리로   우리가 보기 전에!"

/ Sara explained. "Of course / they always do. They are as
새라가 설명했다.   "물론   항상 그래.   아주 빨라

quick / as lightning."
번개처럼."

Ermengarde looked / from her to the doll / and back again.
어먼가드는 시선을 옮겼다   새라에서 인형으로   그리고 다시 새라에게.

"Can she — walk?" / she asked / breathlessly.
"저 애가 — 걸을 수 있어?"   그녀는 물었다   숨을 멈추고.

"Yes," / answered Sara. "At least / I believe / she can. At
"그럼."   새라가 답했다.   "적어도   난 믿어   할 수 있다고.

least / I pretend I believe / she can. And that makes / it
적어도   난 믿는 척 하지   할 수 있다고. 그렇게 믿으면   그렇게 보여

seem / as if it were true. Have you never pretended things?"
마치 그것이 진실인 듯.   넌 그런 척 해 본 적 없니?"

"No," / said Ermengarde. "Never. I — / tell me about it."
"아니."   어먼가드는 말했다.   "단 한번도. 난 —   그 얘기를 말해 줘."

She was so bewitched / by this odd, new companion /
어먼가드는 아주 넋이 나가서   이 이상하고, 새로운 친구한테

that she actually stared at Sara / instead of at Emily / —
사실은 새라를 쳐다보았다   에밀리를 보는 대신

notwithstanding that Emily was the most attractive doll
— 에밀리가 가장 매력적인 인형이었음에도 불구하고

person / she had ever seen.
지금까지 보아온 것 중.

"Let us sit down," / said Sara, / "and I will tell you. It's
"우리 앉자."   새라가 말했다,   "그러면 내가 말해 줄게.

so easy / that when you begin / you can't stop. You just
아주 쉬워   시작하면   멈출 수 없지.

go on and on doing it / always. And it's beautiful. Emily,
그냥 계속 하는 거야   항상.   멋진 일이지.   에밀리,

/ you must listen. This is Ermengarde St. John, / Emily.
찰 들어.   이쪽은 어먼가드 세인트 존이야,   에밀리.

Ermengarde, / this is Emily. Would you like to hold her?"
어먼가드,   이쪽은 에밀리야.   그 애를 안아볼래?"

"Oh, may I?" / said Ermengarde. "May I, / really? She is
"와, 그래도 돼?"　　　어먼가드는 말했다.　　　　　"그래도 돼,　정말?

beautiful!" And Emily was put into her arms.
예쁘다!"　　　　그리고 에밀리는 그녀의 팔에 안겼다.

Never in her dull, short life / had Miss St. John dreamed
그녀의 지루하고, 짧은 인생에서 절대로　　세인트 존 양은 꿈꿔 본 적도 없었다

of / such an hour / as the one she spent / with the queer
그러한 시간을　　　그녀가 보낸　　　이상한 새 학생과 함께

new pupil / before they heard the lunch-bell ring / and
점심 식사 종 소리가 들려서

were obliged to go downstairs.
아래층으로 내려가야 하기 전까지.

Sara sat upon the hearth-rug / and told her strange
새라는 난로 앞 양탄자에 앉아서　　이상한 일들을 말해 주었다.

things. She sat rather huddled up, / and her green eyes
새라는 몸을 웅크린 채 앉아 있었고,　　초록빛 눈은 반짝거렸으며

shone / and her cheeks flushed. She told stories of the
두 뺨은 붉어졌다.　　　　새라는 항해 이야기를 했고,

voyage, / and stories of India; / but what fascinated
인도에 관한 이야기도 했다;　　하지만 어먼가드를 가장 매혹시킨 것은

Ermengarde the most / was her fancy / about the dolls
새라의 상상력이었다　　인형에 관한

/ who walked and talked, / and who could do anything
걷고 말하며,　　　　뭐든지 할 수 있지만

/ they chose / when the human beings were out of the
자신들이 선택한　　사람이 방 밖으로 나가면,

room, / but who must keep their powers a secret / and
하지만 자신들의 힘을 비밀로 지켜야 하기에

so flew back / to their places / "like lightning" / when
빨리 돌아가 버린다는 자신들의 자리로　　"번개처럼"

people returned to the room.
사람들이 방으로 돌아오면.

breathlessly 숨이 차서, 헐떡이면서, 숨을 죽이고 | bewitched 마법에 걸린, 넋이 나간, 황홀해 하는 |
notwithstanding 그러하긴 하지만, 그래도 | hearth-rug 난로 앞에 까는 깔개 | huddle up 몸을 웅크리다

"We couldn't do it," / said Sara, / seriously. "You see, /
"우리는 그렇게 못 해," 새라가 말했다, 심각하게. "있잖아,

it's a kind of magic."
그것은 일종의 마술이야."

Once, / when she was relating the story / of the search
한번은, 새라가 이야기를 하고 있을 때 에밀리를 찾아 헤매던 일의,

for Emily, / Ermengarde saw / her face suddenly change.
어먼가드는 보았다 새라의 얼굴이 갑자기 변하는 것을.

A cloud seemed to pass over it / and put out the light /
구름이 그 위를 지나간 듯 했고 빛이 사그라들었다

in her shining eyes. She drew her breath in / so sharply
반짝이던 눈 속에서. 새라는 숨을 들이쉬었고 아주 빨리

/ that it made a funny, sad little sound, / and then she
그러자 우습고도, 슬픈 작은 소리가 났다, 그리고는 입술을 닫고

shut her lips / and held them tightly closed, / as if she
꽉 다물었다,

was determined / either to do or not to do something.
마치 결심하는 것처럼 뭔가를 해야 할까 안 해야 할까를.

Ermengarde had an idea / that if she had been like any
어먼가드는 생각했다 다른 여자 아이 같았다면,

other little girl, / she might have suddenly burst out /
갑자기 울음을 터뜨렸을지도 모른다고

sobbing and crying. But she did not.
눈물을 흘리고 울면서. 하지만 새라는 그렇게 하지 않았다.

"Have you a — a pain?" / Ermengarde ventured.
"어디 — 아프니?" 어먼가드가 조심스럽게 말했다.

"Yes," / Sara answered, / after a moment's silence. "But
"응," 새라가 말했다, 잠자코 있다가.

it is not in my body." Then she added something / in a
"하지만 몸이 아픈 건 아니야." 그리고 덧붙였다

low voice / which she tried to keep quite steady, / and it
낮은 목소리로 아주 침착하려고 애쓰면서,

was this: "Do you love your father / more than anything
이렇게 말했다: "넌 아빠를 사랑하니 다른 누구보다

else / in all the whole world?"
이 세상에서?"

Ermengarde's mouth fell open / a little. She knew / that
어먼가드의 입이 벌어졌다   약간.   그녀는 알았다

it would be far from / behaving like a respectable child /
결코 아니라는 것은   훌륭한 학생같은 행동이

at a select seminary / to say / that it had never occurred
고급 신학교에 다니는   말하는 것은 절대 일어난 적이 없었다고

to you / that you could love your father, / that you would
아빠를 사랑하는 일이,   또 필사적이었다고

do anything desperate / to avoid being left alone / in his
혼자 남겨지는 것을 피하려고   아빠와 있는

society / for ten minutes. She was, / indeed, / greatly
곳에   단 10분 동안도.   어먼가드는,   정말로,

embarrassed.
매우 당황했다.

"I — I scarcely ever see him," / she stammered. "He is
"난 — 아빠를 본 적이 거의 없어."   어먼가드는 말을 더듬었다.

always in the library / — reading things."
"항상 서재에 계시거든   — 늘 뭔가를 읽으면서."

"I love mine / more than all the world / ten times over," /
"난 아빠를 사랑해   세상 무엇보다도   열 배 이상."

Sara said. "That is what my pain is. He has gone away."
새라가 말했다.   "그것이 바로 내가 아픈 이유야.   멀리 떠나셨거든."

venture (모험하듯) 조심스럽게 말하다, 하다 | stammer 말을 더듬다

She put her head quietly down / on her little, huddled-up
새라는 조용히 머리를 숙였고   작고, 웅크린 무릎 위로,

knees, / and sat very still / for a few minutes.
가만히 앉아 있었다   몇 분 동안.

"She's going to cry out / loud," / thought Ermengarde, /
"저 애가 울 것 같아   큰 소리로,"   어먼가드는 생각했다,

fearfully.
두려워하며.

But she did not. Her short, black locks tumbled / about
하지만 새라는 그러지 않았다. 새라의 짧고, 까만 머리카락들이 떨어졌고

her ears, / and she sat still. Then she spoke / without
귀 언저리에,   새라는 가만히 앉아 있었다. 그리고는 말했다

lifting her head.
머리를 들지 않은 채.

"I promised him / I would bear it," / she said. "And I will.
난 아빠와 약속했어   견딜 거라고,"   새라가 말했다. "그리고 그럴 거야.

You have to bear things. Think / what soldiers bear! Papa
뭐든 견뎌야 해.   생각해 봐   군인들이 참아내는 것을!

is a soldier. If there was a war / he would have to bear /
아빠는 군인이야.   만약 전쟁이 난다면   아빠는 참아야 할 거야

marching and thirstiness / and, / perhaps, / deep wounds.
행군과 목마름을   그리고,   어쩌면,   깊은 상처도.

Key Expression

I wish 가정법
I wish 가정법은 가정법의 특수한 형태로 '~하면 좋을 텐데'라는 의미로 해석
합니다.
현재 사실의 반대를 가정할 때에는 가정법 과거를, 과거 사실의 반대를 가정할
때에는 가정법 과거완료를 사용합니다.

▶ I wish + 주어 + 과거동사/were : ~하면 좋을 텐데
▶ I wish + 주어 + had p.p : ~했으면 좋았을 텐데

ex) I wish we could be 'best friends'.
    우리도 '단짝 친구'가 될 수 있으면 좋겠어.

lock (머리의) 타래, 머리채, 머리털 | tumble 굴러 떨어지다 | gaze (가만히) 응시하다 | adore 아주 좋아하다 |
presently 곧, 이내 | lump 덩어리, 응어리 | huskily 늠름하게, 쉰 목소리로 | (I'll) tell you what 저 말이야, 실은
말이지, 이야기 할 것이 있는데 | gleam 언뜻 비치는 것, 어슴프레한 빛

And he would never say a word / — not one word."
그리고 아빠는 어떤 말도 하지 않을 거야   — 한 마디도."

Ermengarde could only gaze at her, / but she felt / that
어먼가드는 새라를 볼 수밖에 없었지만,   느꼈다

she was beginning to adore her. She was so wonderful /
새라를 좋아하게 되었다고.   새라는 아주 멋졌고

and different from anyone else.
다른 누구와도 달랐다.

Presently, / she lifted her face / and shook back her black
이내,   새라는 얼굴을 들었고   검은 머리를 흔들어 뒤로 넘겼다,

locks, / with a queer little smile.
            독특한 미소와 함께.

"If I go on talking and talking," / she said, / "and telling
"내가 계속 말한다면,"   새라가 말했다,   "그리고 네게 말하면

you / things about pretending, / I shall bear it better. You
척 하는 것에 대해,   더 잘 견딜 수 있을 거야.

don't forget, / but you bear it better."
잊을 수는 없겠지만,   잘 견뎌낼 수 있을 거야.

Ermengarde did not know / why a lump came into her
어먼가드는 알지 못했다   왜 새라의 목이 메어오고

throat / and her eyes felt as if tears were in them.
            마치 새라의 눈에 눈물이 날 것 것 같은지.

"Lavinia and Jessie are 'best friends,'" / she said / rather
"라비니아와 제시는 '단짝 친구'야,"   그녀는 말했다   다소 쉰

huskily. "I wish we could be 'best friends.' Would you
목소리로.   "우리도 '단짝 친구'가 될 수 있으면 좋겠어.   날 여겨줄 수 있니

have me / for yours? You're clever, / and I'm the stupidest
네 단짝으로?   넌 똑똑하고,   난 가장 멍청한 아이지

child / in the school, / but I — oh, / I do so / like you!"
학교에서,   하지만 난 — 아,   그리고 싶어   너처럼!"

"I'm glad of that," / said Sara. "It makes you thankful /
"그렇게 되면 나도 기뻐,"   새라가 말했다.   "감사한 일이니까

when you are liked. Yes. We will be friends. And I'll tell
사랑받는다는 일은.   그래.   우리 친구하자.   그리고 실은 말이지"

you what" / — a sudden gleam / lighting her face — / "I
                — 갑자기 한 줄기 빛이   그녀의 얼굴을 비췄다 —

can help you / with your French lessons."
"널 도와줄게   프랑스어 공부를."   53

3

Lottie
로티

If Sara had been a different kind of child, / the life she
새라가 다른 종류의 아이였다면,   그녀가 보냈던 삶은

led / at Miss Minchin's Select Seminary / for the next few
민친 교장의 고급 신학교에서   그 후 몇 년 동안

years / would not have been at all good / for her. She was
전혀 도움이 되지 않았을 것이다   그녀에게.   새라는 대접받

treated / more as if she were a distinguished guest / at the
았다   마치 유명한 손님 이상인 것처럼

establishment / than as if she were a mere little girl. If she
그 학교에서   그저 어린 여학생이 아니라.

had been a self-opinionated, / domineering child, / she
만약 그녀가 고집 세고,   잘난 체 하는 아이였다면,

might have become disagreeable / enough to be unbearable
무례한 아이가 되었을지 모른다   참을 수 없을 만큼

/ through being so much indulged / and flattered. If she
제멋대로 하고   아첨에 둘러싸여서.

had been an indolent child, / she would have learned
만약 그녀가 게으른 아이였다면,   아무것도 배우지 못했을 것이다.

nothing. Privately / Miss Minchin disliked her, / but she
개인적으로는   민친 교장은 새라를 싫어했지만,

was far too worldly a woman / to do or say anything /
하지만 너무 속물적인 여자라서   행동이나 말을 하지 않았다

which might make / such a desirable pupil / wish to leave
만들지도 모르는   그토록 바람직한 학생이   학교를 떠나고 싶어

her school. She knew quite well / that if Sara wrote to her
하도록.   그녀는 잘 알고 있었다   새라가 아빠에게 편지를 쓰기만 하면

papa / to tell him / she was uncomfortable or unhappy,
말하기 위해   불편하거나 불행하다고,

---

distinguished 유명한, 성공한 | self-opinionated 고집이 센 | domineering 지배하려 드는 | disagreeable
무례한, 무뚝뚝한 | unbearable 참을 수 없는 | indulge ~가 제멋대로 하게 하다 | indolent 게으른 | worldly
속물의 | amiability 상냥함, 온화 | generosity 너그러움 | sixpence 6펜스 은화(1971년까지 사용된 영국 동전) |
virtue 미덕, 덕목 | disposition (타고난) 기질, 성격 | self-satisfied 자만에 빠진

Captain Crewe would remove her / at once. Miss Minchin's
크루 대위는 새라를 데려갈 것이라고   당장.   민친 교장의 의견은 이랬다

opinion was that / if a child were continually praised /
만약 아이가 계속 칭찬을 받고

and never forbidden to do / what she liked, / she would
못하도록 금지하지 않는다면   아이가 원하는 것을.

be sure to be fond of / the place where she was so treated.
그 애는 확실히 좋아할 것이라고   자신이 그렇게 대접받는 곳을.

Accordingly, / Sara was praised / for her quickness at her
따라서,   새라는 칭찬받았다   수업에서 빨리 익히는 것이나,

lessons, / for her good manners, / for her amiability to her
수업에서,   예의가 바른 점이나,   동급생들에 상냥한 점이나,

fellow pupils, / for her generosity / if she gave sixpence / to
                너그러움에 대해   6펜스짜리 동전을 주기라도 하면

a beggar / out of her full little purse; / the simplest thing /
거지에게   가득찬 작은 지갑에서;   아주 사소한 일조차

she did / was treated / as if it were a virtue, / and if she had
그녀가 했던   대우받았다   마치 미덕인 양,   그러니 만약 그녀가 타

not had a disposition / and a clever little brain, / she might
고난 기질과   영리한 두뇌가 없었다면,

have been / a very self-satisfied young person. But the
되었을지 모른다   자만에 빠진 젊은이가.

clever little brain told her / a great many sensible and true
하지만 영리한 두뇌가 새라에게 말했고   수많은 합리적이고 진실된 것들을

things / about herself and her circumstances, / and now
        자신과 주변 환경에 대해,   그리고 이따금

and then / she talked these things over / to Ermengarde / as
새라는 이런 것들을 들려주었다   어먼가드에게

time went on.
시간이 지나면서.

"Things happen to people / by accident," / she used to
"어떤 일은 사람들에게 생겨   우연히,"   그녀는 말하곤 했다.

say. "A lot of nice accidents have happened / to me. It just
"좋은 일들이 많이 생겼어   나한테.

happened / that I always liked lessons and books, / and
그저 우연이야   내가 항상 공부와 책을 좋아하는 것은,

could remember things / when I learned them.
그리고 기억할 수 있는 것도   배운 것을.

55

It just happened / that I was born / with a father / who
그저 우연이야   내가 태어난 것은   아빠 밑에서

was beautiful and nice and clever, / and could give me
멋지고 다정하며 똑똑하고,   내게 줄 수 있는

/ everything I liked. Perhaps / I have not really a good
내가 좋아하는 것은 뭐든지.   아마도   실제로 난 착한 성격이 아닐지도 몰라

temper / at all, / but if you have everything you want / and
전혀,   하지만 원하는 모든 것을 갖게 되고

everyone is kind to you, / how can you help but be good-
누구나 친절하게 대해 준다면,   착한 성격이 될 수밖에 없잖아?

tempered? I don't know" / — looking quite serious — /
나도 모르겠어"   — 꽤 심각한 표정으로 —

"how I shall ever find out / whether I am really a nice child
"어떻게 알 수 있을까   내가 진짜 착한 아이인지

/ or a horrid one. Perhaps I'm a hideous child, / and no one
아니면 못된 아이인지.   어쩌면 난 끔찍한 아이일지도,

will ever know, / just because I never have any trials."
아무도 모르는 것일지도,   왜냐하면 시련을 겪은 적이 없으니까."

"Lavinia has no trials," / said Ermengarde, / stolidly, / "and
"라비니아도 시련을 겪지 않았어."   어먼가드가 말했다,   멍하니.

she is horrid enough."
"그래도 그 애는 아주 끔찍해."

Sara rubbed / the end of her little nose / reflectively, / as
새라는 문질렀다   작은 코 끝을   생각에 잠겨,

she thought the matter over.
그 문제를 곰곰이 생각하며.

"Well," / she said / at last, / "perhaps — perhaps / that is
"글쎄,"   그녀가 말했다   마침내,   "아마도 — 아마도

because Lavinia is growing."
그건 라비니아가 자라고 있기 때문일 거야."

This was the result / of a charitable recollection / of having
이것은 결론이었다   너그럽게 기억해 낸   아멜리아 선생이

heard Miss Amelia say / that Lavinia was growing so fast /
말하는 것을 들었던 일을   라비니아는 아주 빨리 자라고 있어서

that she believed / it affected her health and temper.
선생님 생각에   그 사실이 건강과 성격에 영향을 끼쳤다는.

Lavinia, / in fact, / was spiteful. She was inordinately /
라비니아는, 사실, 심술궂은 아이였다. 그녀는 과도하게

jealous of Sara. Until the new pupil's arrival, / she had felt
새라를 질투했다. 새 학생이 오기 전까지, 라비니아는 자신을

herself the leader / in the school. She had led / because she
대표로 여겼다 학교에서. 그녀는 이끌어왔다 할 수 있었기 때문에

was capable / of making herself extremely disagreeable /
못되게 구는 일을

if the others did not follow her. She domineered / over the
만약 다른 사람들이 자신을 따르지 않으면. 그녀는 위세를 부렸고

little children, / and assumed grand airs / with those big /
어린 아이들에게, 잘난 체 했다 큰 학생들에게

enough to be her companions. She was rather pretty, / and
자신의 또래인. 그녀는 예쁜 편이었고,

had been the best-dressed pupil / in the procession / when
옷을 가장 잘 입는 학생이었다 예배 행렬에서

the Select Seminary walked out / two by two, / until Sara's
학교 학생들이 걸어나갈 때 두 줄로,

velvet coats and sable muffs appeared, / combined with
새라의 벨벳 외투와 흑담비 모피 토시가 나타나기 전까지, 타조 깃털을 늘어뜨리며,

drooping ostrich feathers, / and were led by Miss Minchin
그리하여 민친 교장에게 이끌려

/ at the head of the line. This, / at the beginning, / had been
줄의 맨 앞에 서게 되기 전까지. 이 일은, 처음에,

bitter enough; / but as time went on / it became apparent
매우 비참했다; 하지만 시간이 지나자 명백해졌다

/ that Sara was a leader, / too, / and not because she could
새라가 대표라는 것이, 역시, 그리고 새라가 못되게 굴었기 때문이 아니라,

make herself disagreeable, / but because she never did.
절대로 그렇게 하지 않았기 때문에.

---

good-tempered 성격이 착한 | horrid 진저리나는, 지독한 | hideous 흉측한, 흉물스러운, 끔찍한 | stolidly 둔감하게, 무신경하게 | charitable 너그러운 | recollection 기억(력), 기억(하는 내용) | spiteful 심술궂은, 악의적인 | inordinately 과도하게 | domineer ~에게 위세를 부리다 | assume airs 젠체하다, 뽐내다 | procession (특히 의식의 일부로 하는) 행진, 행렬 | droop 늘어뜨린

"There's one thing / about Sara Crewe," / Jessie had
"한 가지가 있어   새라 크루에게,"

enraged her "best friend" / by saying honestly, / "she's
제시는 그녀의 "단짝"을 화나게 한 적 있다   솔직하게 말해서.   "그 애는 절대

never 'grand' / about herself / the least bit, / and you
'잘난 척' 하지 않아   자신에 대해   조금도.   그리고 너도 알다시피

know / she might be, / Lavvie. I believe I couldn't help
그 애는 그럴 만 하잖아, 라비.   나도 어쩔 수 없었을 거라고 생각해

being / — just a little — / if I had so many fine things /
— 아주 조금은 —   만약 내게 좋은 것들이 많이 있었다면

and was made such a fuss over. It's disgusting, / the way
난리법석으로 떠받들어진다면.   짜증나지,

Miss Minchin shows her off / when parents come."
민친 교장이 그 애를 자랑하는 방식이   부모들이 올 때마다."

"'Dear Sara must come into the drawing room / and talk
"우리 새라가 거실에 와서   무스그레이브

to Mrs. Musgrave / about India,'" / mimicked Lavinia, /
부인께 말씀 드려야겠네요   인도에 대해,'"   라비니아가 흉내 냈다.

in her most highly flavored imitation / of Miss Minchin.
아주 그럴 듯하게   민친 교장을.

"'Dear Sara must speak French / to Lady Pitkin. Her
"우리 새라가 프랑스어로 말해야겠네요   피트킨 부인께.

accent is so perfect.' She didn't learn her French / at the
그 애의 억양은 매우 완벽하죠.'   그 애는 프랑스어를 배우지 않았잖아

Seminary, / at any rate. And there's nothing so clever /
이 신학교에서,   조금도.   머리가 그렇게 좋아서도 아니고

in her knowing it. She says herself / she didn't learn it at
프랑스어를 알게 된 것이.   그 애가 직접 말하잖아   프랑스어를 전혀 배운 적이 없다고.

all. She just picked it up, / because she always heard / her
단지 주워 들었을 뿐이야.   항상 들었기 때문에

papa speak it. And, / as to her papa, / there is nothing so
아빠가 말하는 것을.   그리고,   그 아이의 아빠에 관해서는, 잘난 것도 없잖아

grand / in being an Indian officer."
인도 장교라는 것이.'"

make such a fuss 법석을 떨다 | show off 자랑하다 | mimic 흉내 내다 | snap 툭 (하고) 부러뜨리다 |
eccentric 괴짜인, 별난, 기이한

"Well," / said Jessie, / slowly, / "he's killed tigers. He
"글쎄,"　　제시가 말했다.　천천히,　"새라 아빠는 호랑이를 죽였대.

killed the one / in the skin / Sara has in her room. That's
그 호랑이를 죽인 거래　가죽으로 된　새라 방에 있는.　　　　그래서

why she likes it so. She lies on it / and strokes its head, /
그 애가 그것을 아주 좋아한대. 그 애는 그 위에서 자고 머리를 쓰다듬으며,

and talks to it / as if it was a cat."
말을 건대　　마치 그것이 고양이인듯."

"She's always doing / something silly," / snapped Lavinia.
"그애는 항상 하지　바보같은 짓을,"　　라비니아가 말을 끊었다.

"My mamma says / that way of hers of pretending things
"우리 엄마가 말했어　그 애가 흉내 내는 방식은

/ is silly. She says / she will grow up eccentric."
어리석다고. 엄마가 말했어　그 애는 자라서 괴짜가 될 거라고."

Key Expression

can't help -ing : ~할 수밖에 없다
can't help -ing는 동명사를 이용한 관용표현으로, '~하지 않을 수 없다, ~할 수 밖에 없다, 어쩔 수 없이 ~하다'라는 뜻입니다. 이 구문에서 help는 '피하다, 막다'의 의미입니다. 같은 의미로 can't but + 동사원형이 있습니다. 또한 'can't help it'은 '어쩔 수 없다'라는 의미를 가진 표현으로 함께 알아두면 좋아요.

ex) I believe I couldn't help being if I had so many fine things and was made such a fuss over.
　　만약 내게 좋은 물건들이 많이 있고 난리법석으로 떠받들어진다면 어쩔 수 없었을 거라고 생각해.

It was quite true / that Sara was never "grand." She was
사실이었다　　　　　　새라는 결코 "거만하지" 않다는 것은.

a friendly little soul, / and shared her privileges and
그녀는 친절한 아이였고,　　　　그녀의 특권과 소유물을 나눠 가졌다

belongings / with a free hand. The little ones, / who were
아낌없이.　　　　　어린 학생들은,

accustomed to / being disdained / and ordered out of the
익숙했던 아이들은　　무시당하고　　　비키라는 명령에

way / by mature ladies / aged ten and twelve, / were never
　　큰 아이들에게　　　열 살에서 열두 살 나이의,

made to cry / by this most envied / of them all. She was
운 적이 없었다　　가장 부러움을 받는 아이 때문에　그들 모두 중.

a motherly young person, / and when people fell down
새라는 엄마같은 아이라서,　　　사람들이 넘어져서

/ and scraped their knees, / she ran and helped them up
무릎을 긁히면,　　　　달려가서 일으켜주고

/ and patted them, / or found in her pocket / a bonbon
쓰다듬어 주거나,　　　주머니에서 찾아주었다

or some other article / of a soothing nature. She never
봉봉 캔디나 다른 것들을　　달래줄 만한.　　　그녀는 절대로 밀치지

pushed them / out of her way / or alluded to their years /
않았고　　　비키라고　　　학년을 언급하며

as a humiliation and a blot / upon their small characters.
창피를 주거나 무시하지도 않았다　　어린 아이들에게.

"If you are four / you are four," / she said severely / to
"네가 네 살이라면　　네 살이야."　　새라는 엄하게 말했다

Lavinia / on an occasion of her having / — it must be
라비니아에게　그녀가 했던 사건에 대해　　　— 그것은 고백해야

confessed — / slapped Lottie / and called her "a brat;" /
할 일이다 —　　로티를 때리고　　　"버릇없는 녀석"이라고 불렀던:

"but you will be five / next year, / and six / the year after
"하지만 넌 다섯 살이 될 거야　　내년에,　　그리고 여섯 살이 되지　그 다음 해에는.

that. And," / opening large, convicting eyes, / "it takes
그리고,"　　눈을 크게 뜨고 단호하게,

sixteen years / to make you twenty."
"16년이 걸리지　　네가 스무 살이 되려면."

"Dear me," / said Lavinia, / "how we can calculate!"
"어머나," 라비니아가 말했다, "어쩜 계산도 잘하네!"

In fact, / it was not to be denied / that sixteen and four
사실, 부인할 수 없는 일이었다 16에 4를 더하면 20이 된다는 걸

made twenty / — and twenty was an age / the most
— 그리고 스무 살은 나이였다

daring were scarcely / bold enough to dream of.
가장 대담한 아이도 좀처럼 함부로 꿈꾸지 못할.

So the younger children adored Sara. More than once /
그래서 어린 아이들은 새라를 좋아했다. 여러 번

she had been known / to have a tea party, / made up of
그녀는 알려졌다 다과회를 열기로,

these despised ones, / in her own room. And Emily had
멸시 받던 아이들로 가득 찬, 그녀의 방에서. 그리고 에밀리도 갖고 놀게

been played with, / and Emily's own tea service used
해 주었고, 에밀리의 찻잔 세트도 쓸 수 있게 했다

/ — the one with cups / which held quite a lot of much-
— 컵이 포함된 세트였다 매우 달콤하고 옅은 차가 굉장히 많이 담겨 있고

sweetened weak tea / and had blue flowers on them. No
그 위에 파란 꽃이 그려진.

one had seen / such a very real doll's tea set / before.
아무도 본 적이 없었다 그렇게 진짜같은 인형 찻잔 세트를 전에는.

From that afternoon / Sara was regarded / as a goddess
그날 오후부터 새라는 여겨졌다 여신이나 여왕으로

and a queen / by the entire alphabet class.
알파벳 반 아이들 전체에 의해.

---

with a free hand 아낌없이 | out of the way (더 이상 방해가 안되도록) 비키어 | bonbon 봉봉 캔디(사탕 속에
부드러운 잼 등이 들어 있음) | allude 암시하다, 넌지시 말하다 | humiliation 굴욕, 굴복, 창피 | blot (인격·명성의)
흠, 오점, 오명 | character 인격, 품성 | slap (손바닥으로) 철썩 때리다, 치다 | brat 버릇없는 녀석 | convict 유죄
판결을 내리다, 단호한 결정을 하다 | daring 대담한, 위험한 | tea party (오후에 하는) 다과회, 티파티 | tea service
찻잔(한 벌)

Lottle Legh worshipped her / to such an extent / that if
로티 레이는 새라를 숭배했다   그런 정도까지

Sara had not been a motherly person, / she would have
새라가 자애로운 사람이 아니었다면,   성가시게 느꼈을 만큼.

found her tiresome. Lottie had been sent to school / by a
                        로티는 학교에 맡겨졌다

rather flighty young papa / who could not imagine / what
다소 변덕이 심한 젊은 아빠에 의해   생각할 수 없었던

else to do with her. Her young mother had died, / and as
딸을 다루는 다른 방법을.   로티의 엄마가 일찍 죽자,

the child had been treated / like a favorite doll / or a very
아이는 다뤄졌기 때문에   좋아하는 인형이나

spoiled pet monkey / or lap dog / ever since the first hour
매우 버릇없는 애완 원숭이나   애완견처럼   태어나면서부터 계속,

of her life, / she was a very appalling little creature. When
                아주 끔찍한 아이가 되었다.

she wanted anything / or did not want anything / she wept
로티는 원하는 것이 있거나   원하지 않는 것이 있으면   울면서 법석을

and howled; / and, / as she always wanted the things / she
떨었다;   그리고,   항상 원했고

could not have, / and did not want the things / that were
가질 수 없는 것을,   하지 않으려 했기 때문에

best for her, / her shrill little voice was usually to be heard
도움이 되는 일은,   그녀의 날카로운 목소리가 늘 들려왔다

/ uplifted in wails / in one part of the house or another.
        격양된 울음 소리에 묻혀   집 안 어디에선가.

Key Expression

make use of : 이용하다

make use of는 동사 use와 같은 의미를 지닌 숙어입니다. 이때 use 앞에 형
용사를 넣어 표현하면 부사적인 의미로 해석하는 것이 자연스러워요.

▶ make good use of : 좋은 일에 이용하다. 잘 이용하다(=use well)
▶ make bad use of : 악용하다(=use badly)
▶ make free use of : 자유롭게 이용하다(=use freely)

ex) So it became her habit to make great use of this knowledge.
    그래서 이 지식을 잘 활용하는 것이 그녀의 습관이 되었다.

Her strongest weapon was that / in some mysterious way
로티의 가장 강력한 무기는   어떤 신기한 방식으로

/ she had found out / that a very small girl / who had lost
알아냈다   여자 아이는

her mother / was a person / who ought to be pitied / and
엄마를 잃은   사람이라는 것을   동정받아야 하고

made much of. She had probably heard / some grown-
중시되어야 할.   아마도 들었을 것이다

up people talking her over / in the early days, / after her
어른들이 자신에 대해 말하는 것을   어렸을 때,

mother's death. So it became her habit / to make great
엄마가 죽고 난 뒤.   그래서 그녀의 습관이 되었다

use of this knowledge.
이 지식을 잘 활용하는 것은.

The first time / Sara took her in charge / was one
처음으로   새라가 로티를 돌보게 된 것은   어느 날 아침이었다

morning / when, / on passing a sitting room, / she heard
그때,   거실을 지나가다가,

both Miss Minchin and Miss Amelia trying to suppress /
민친 교장과 아멜리아 선생이 멈추게 하려고 애쓰는 소리를 들었다

the angry wails of some child / who, / evidently, / refused
어느떤 아이의 화난 울음 소리를   그 아이는, 분명히,

to be silenced. She refused so strenuously / indeed /
조용히 하지 않으려 했다. 아주 완강하게 거부해서   실제로

that Miss Minchin was obliged to almost shout / — in a
민친 교장은 소리를 지를 수밖에 없었다

stately and severe manner — / to make herself heard.
— 위엄 있고 엄격한 태도로 —   자기 목소리를 들리게 하려고.

"What is she crying for?" / she almost yelled.
"왜 우는 거니?"   교장이 소리쳤다.

"Oh — oh — oh!" / Sara heard; / "I haven't got any mam
"아 — 아 — 아!"   새라가 들었다;   "난 엄마가 없어요

/ — ma-a!"
— 엄—마!"

motherly 어머니같은, 자애로운 | tiresome 성가신, 짜증스러운 | flighty 변덕이 심한 | lap dog 애완용 작은 개
| appalling 간담을 서늘케 하는, 끔찍한 | weep 울다, 눈물을 흘리다 | howl 울부짖다, 법석을 떨다 | shrill 새된,
날카로운 | wail 통곡하다, 흐느끼다 | make much of ~을 중시하다 | strenuously 완강하게 | stately 위엄 있는

"Oh, Lottie!" / screamed Miss Amelia. "Do stop, darling!
"아, 로티야!" 아멜리아 선생이 소리쳤다. "그만해, 아가야!

Don't cry! Please don't!"
울지 마! 제발 울지 마!"

"Oh! Oh! Oh! Oh! Oh!" / Lottie howled / tempestuously.
"앙! 앙! 앙! 앙! 앙!" 로티는 울부짖었다 떠들썩하게.

"Haven't — got — any — mam — ma-a!"
"엄마가 — 없-다-고-요!"

"She ought to be whipped," / Miss Minchin proclaimed.
"매를 맞아야겠구나." 민친 교장이 소리쳤다.

"You shall be whipped, / you naughty child!"
"매를 맞을 줄 알아, 이 버릇없는 녀석!"

Lottie wailed / more loudly than ever. Miss Amelia
로티는 울었다 전보다 더 크게. 아멜리아 선생도 울기 시작했다.

began to cry. Miss Minchin's voice rose / until it almost
민친 교장의 목소리가 커졌고 천둥 소리처럼,

thundered, / then suddenly / she sprang up from her chair
그러다 갑자기 의자에서 벌떡 일어나서

/ in impotent indignation / and flounced out of the room, /
주체할 수 없이 화가 나서 여봐란듯이 방 밖으로 나가버렸다,

leaving Miss Amelia to arrange the matter.
아멜리아 선생에게 뒷처리를 맡겨둔 채.

Sara had paused in the hall, / wondering / if she ought to
새라는 복도에 멈춰 섰다. 궁금해 하며 들어가야 하는지

go / into the room, / because she had recently / begun a
방으로, 왜냐하면 최근에 막

friendly acquaintance with Lottie / and might be able to
로티와 친해져서 달랠 수도 있을 것 같았기 때문에.

quiet her. When Miss Minchin came out / and saw her, /
민친 교장이 나와서 새라를 보았을 때,

she looked rather annoyed. She realized / that her voice, /
다소 화가 나 보였다. 그녀는 깨달았다 자신의 목소리가,

as heard from inside the room, / could not have sounded /
방 안에서 들렸던, 들리지 않았을 것이었다고

either dignified or amiable.
위엄 있거나 친절하게.

"Oh, Sara!" / she exclaimed, / endeavoring to produce a
"아, 새라구나!"   그녀가 외쳤다,   적절한 미소를 지으려 애쓰면서.

suitable smile.

tempestuously 떠들썩하게 | whip 채찍질하다 | proclaim 선언하다 | naughty 버릇없는, 말을 안 듣는 |
impotent 무력한 | indignation 분개, 분함 | flounce 여봐란듯이 나가다 | exclaim 외치다 | endeavor to
노력하다

"I stopped," / explained Sara, / "because I knew it was
"멈췄어요," 새라가 설명했다, "로티인 것 같아서요

Lottie / — and I thought, perhaps — / just perhaps, / I
— 제 생각에는, 어쩌면 — 그냥 어쩌면,

could make her be quiet. May I try, Miss Minchin?"
제가 그 애를 달랠 수 있을 것 같아서요. 해 봐도 괜찮나요, 민친 선생님?"

"If you can, / you are a clever child," / answered Miss
"네가 할 수 있다면, 넌 똑똑한 아이니까," 민친 교장이 대답했다,

Minchin, / drawing in her mouth / sharply. Then, /
입술을 내밀며 굳게. 그리고는,

seeing that Sara looked slightly chilled / by her asperity,
새라가 약간 긴장하는 것을 보고 자신의 퉁명스러움에,

/ she changed her manner. "But you are clever / in
태도를 바꾸었다. "하지만 넌 똑똑하잖니

everything," / she said / in her approving way. "I dare
모든 면에서," 그녀가 말했다 호의적인 말투로. "틀림없이 말하

say / you can manage her. Go in." And she left her.
는데 넌 다룰 수 있을 거야. 들어가 보거라." 그리고 그녀는 떠났다.

When Sara entered the room, / Lottie was lying upon
새라가 방에 들어갔을 때, 로티는 바닥에 누워서,

the floor, / screaming / and kicking her small fat legs
소리치며 작고 퉁퉁한 다리를 난폭하게 차고 있었고,

violently, / and Miss Amelia was bending / over her / in
아멜리아 선생은 내려다 보고 있었다 그 아이를

consternation and despair, / looking quite red / and damp
실망스럽고 절망적인 표정으로, 얼굴이 상기된 채 열을 내고 땀을

with heat. Lottie had always found, / when in her own
흘리며. 로티는 늘 알고 있었다, 아기 방에 있을 때

nursery / at home, / that kicking and screaming / would
집에서, 발차고 소리를 지르면

always be quieted / by any means she insisted on. Poor
항상 조용해진다는 것을 자신이 고집 피운 대로.

plump Miss Amelia was trying / first one method, / and
가엾고 퉁퉁한 아멜리아 선생은 시도하는 중이었다 처음에는 한 방법을,

then another.
그리고 다른 방법을.

"Poor darling," / she said / one moment, / "I know / you
"가여운 아가야." 아멜리아는 말했다 이번에는, "나도 알아

haven't any mamma, / poor — " Then in quite another
네가 엄마가 없다는 것을, 가여운 —" 그 다음에는 꽤 다른 목소리로,

tone, / "If you don't stop, / Lottie, / I will shake you.
"멈추지 않으면, 로티, 혼내 줄 테다.

Poor little angel! There — ! You wicked, bad, detestable
가여운 작은 천사! 저기 —! 사악하고, 못되고, 가증스러운 아이같으니라고,

child, / I will smack you! I will!"
두들겨 패 줄 거야! 그럴 거라고!"

Sara went to them / quietly. She did not know at all
새라는 그들에게 다가갔다 조용히. 전혀 알지 못했지만

/ what she was going to do, / but she had a vague
뭘 해야 할지, 하지만 희미하게나마 마음속에

inward conviction / that it would be better not to say /
확신이 있었다 말하지 않는 것이 나을 것 같다는

such different kinds of things / quite so helplessly and
그런 종류의 말들을 저렇게 어쩔 줄 몰라하거나 흥분하는.

excitedly.

"Miss Amelia," / she said / in a low voice, / "Miss
"아멜리아 선생님," 새라가 말했다 낮은 목소리로,

Minchin says / I may try / to make her stop / — may I?"
"민친 선생님이 말했어요 제가 해 봐도 된다고 저 애를 달래는 것을 — 해 볼까요?"

Miss Amelia turned / and looked at her / hopelessly.
아멜리아 선생이 돌아서서 그녀를 보았다 절망적인 얼굴로.

"Oh, do you think you can?" / she gasped.
"아, 할 수 있을 것 같니?" 그녀는 한숨을 쉬었다.

"I don't know / whether I can," / answered Sara, / still in
"모르겠어요 제가 할 수 있을지," 새라가 답했다,

her half-whisper; / "but I will try."
반쯤 속삭이듯 조용히; "하지만 해 볼게요."

---

chilled 차가운, 냉정한 | asperity 퉁명스러움 | consternation 실망 | nursery 아기 방, 보육실 | plump 통통한
| detestable 혐오스러운 | smack (손바닥으로) 때리다

Miss Amelia stumbled up / from her knees / with a
아멜리아 선생은 비틀거리며 일어났고   무릎을 꿇고 있다가

heavy sigh, / and Lottie's fat little legs kicked / as hard as
깊은 한숨을 쉬며,   로티의 통통한 다리는 발버둥쳤다   아주 힘껏.

ever.

"If you will steal / out of the room," / said Sara, "I will
"조용히 빠져 나가시면   방 밖으로."   새라가 말했다,

stay with her."
"제가 그 애 옆에 있을게요."

"Oh, Sara!" / almost whimpered Miss Amelia. "We
"아, 새라야!"   아멜리아 선생은 거의 훌쩍이며 말했다.

never had such a dreadful child / before. I don't believe /
"저렇게 끔찍한 아이는 본 적이 없구나   전에.   내 생각에는

we can keep her."
저 애를 계속 데리고 있지 못할 것 같아."

But she crept out of the room, / and was very much
하지만 그녀는 방 밖으로 빠져 나가며,   매우 안심했다

relieved / to find an excuse for doing it.
나갈 수 있는 구실이 생겨서.

Key Expression

I think vs I don't think

I think[believe/know] ~ 로 시작하는 문장은 '~라고 생각해'라고 해석하
면 자연스러워요.
부정적인 내용을 얘기하는 '~가 아니라고 생각해'라고 말하고 싶을 때 우리말에
서처럼 생각하여 I think + 주어 + not ~으로 표현하지 않는 것에 주의하세요.
영어에서는 I don't think + 주어 + ~로 쓴답니다.
영어에서는 부정하는 말을 앞부분, 즉 주절에 사용하고 종속절을 부정하지 않습
니다.

ex) I don't believe we can keep her.
    나는 저 애를 계속 데리고 있지 못할 것 같아.

stumble 비틀거리다 | whimper 훌쩍이며 말하다 | furious 몹시 화가 난 | coax 구슬리다, 달래다 | shriek
소리를 지르다 | half-hearted 성의가 없는

Sara stood / by the howling furious child / for a few
새라는 서서 울부짖으며 몹시 화가 난 아이 옆에 몇 분 동안,

moments, / and looked down at her / without saying
그 애를 내려다 보았다 아무 말도 하지 않고.

anything. Then she sat down flat / on the floor / beside
그리고는 주저앉아 맨 바닥에 그 애 옆에서

her / and waited. Except for Lottie's angry screams, / the
기다렸다. 로티의 성난 비명 소리 외에,

room was quite quiet. This was a new state of affairs /
방은 아주 조용했다. 이것은 새로운 국면이었다

for little Miss Legh, / who was accustomed, / when she
꼬마 레이 양에게는, 익숙해져 있던,

screamed, / to hear other people protest and implore /
자신이 소리지르면, 다른 사람들이 혼내거나 간청하거나

and command and coax / by turns. To lie and kick and
명령하고 달래는 것을 듣는데 번갈아 가면서. 누워서 발로 차고 소리지르면서,

shriek, / and find the only person near you / not seeming
옆에 있는 유일한 사람이 전혀 신경 쓰지 않는

to mind in the least, / attracted her attention. She opened
것처럼 보이면, 관심을 끄는 법이다.

her tight-shut streaming eyes / to see who this person
로티는 눈물을 흘리느라 굳게 닫고 있던 눈을 떴다 이 사람이 누군지 보려고,

was. And it was only another little girl. But it was the
그런데 그 사람은 겨우 다른 여자 아이일 뿐이었다. 하지만 그 사람이었다

one / who owned / Emily and all the nice things. And
갖고 있는 에밀리와 온갖 멋진 물건들을.

she was looking at her steadily / and as if she was merely
그리고 그 사람은 자신을 계속 보고 있었다 마치 생각만 하고 있는 듯.

thinking. Having paused / for a few seconds / to find
울음을 멈추었다가 잠시 동안 이 사실을 깨닫고,

this out, / Lottie thought / she must begin again, / but the
로티는 생각했다 다시 울기 시작해야 한다고,

quiet of the room / and of Sara's odd, interested face /
하지만 방 안의 고요함과 새라의 이상하고, 흥미로운 얼굴 때문에

made her first howl / rather half-hearted.
로티는 첫 번째 고함을 질렀다 다소 마음이 내키지 않는 듯이.

"I — haven't — / any — ma — ma — ma-a!" / she
"난 — 없어 — 엄 — 마 —가!"

announced; / but her voice was not so strong.
로티가 말했다; 하지만 목소리는 그리 크지 않았다.

Sara looked at her / still more steadily, / but with a sort of
새라는 그 애를 보았다 여전히 조용하게, 하지만 조금 이해한다는 느낌을

understanding / in her eyes.
담아 눈에는.

"Neither have I," / she said.
"나도 없어." 새라가 말했다.

This was so unexpected / that it was astounding. Lottie
이것은 아주 뜻밖이어서 깜짝 놀랄 만한 일이었다.

actually dropped her legs, / gave a wriggle, / and lay and
로티는 실제로 다리를 내리고, 꿈지락거리며, 누워서 쳐다보았다.

stared. A new idea will stop a crying child / when nothing
새로운 생각은 우는 아이를 멈추게 한다 다른 방법이 먹히지 않

else will. Also it was true / that while Lottie disliked Miss
을 때에는. 또한 사실이었다 로티는 민친 교장을 싫어했지만,

Minchin, / who was cross, / and Miss Amelia, / who was
괴팍했기 때문에, 아멜리아 선생도,

foolishly indulgent, / she rather liked Sara, / little as she
바보같이 관대한, 오히려 새라를 좋아했다, 거의 알지 못했기에.

knew her. She did not want / to give up her grievance, /
로티는 원치 않았다 불평하는 것을 그만두기를,

but her thoughts were distracted from it, / so she wriggled
하지만 생각은 다른 곳으로 흘어졌다, 그래서 다시 꿈지락거렸고,

again, / and, / after a sulky sob, / said, / "Where is she?"
그리고, 훌쩍이며 울다가, 말했다, "엄마는 어디 있는데?"

Sara paused a moment. Because she had been told / that
새라는 잠시 가만히 있었다. 그녀는 들어왔기 때문에

her mamma was in heaven, / she had thought a great deal
엄마가 하늘에 계시다고, 많이 생각해 보았다

/ about the matter, / and her thoughts had not been quite /
그 문제에 대해, 그리고 자신의 생각은 많이 달랐다

like those of other people.
다른 사람들의 생각과.

"She went to heaven," / she said. "But I am sure / she
"엄마는 하늘나라에 갔어."   그녀가 말했다. "하지만 난 확신해

comes out sometimes / to see me / — though I don't see
엄마가 이따금 오신다고   날 보러   — 나는 엄마를 볼 수 없지만.

her. So does yours. Perhaps they can both see us / now.
네 엄마도 마찬가지야.   아마 두 분 다 우리를 보고 있을지 몰라   지금.

Perhaps they are both / in this room."
아마도 두 분 다 계실지 모르지   이 방에."

Lottle sat bolt upright, / and looked about her. She was a
로티는 벌떡 일어나 앉더니   주변을 둘러보았다.

pretty, little, curly-headed creature, / and her round eyes
그녀는 예쁘고, 작은, 곱슬머리의 아이였고,   동그란 눈은

were / like wet forget-me-nots. If her mamma had seen her
젖은 물망초 같았다.   로티의 엄마가 그 애를 보았다면

/ during the last half-hour, / she might not have thought /
지난 30분 간,   몰랐을지도 모른다

her the kind of child / who ought to be related to an angel.
그 애가 이런 아이인 줄   천사라고 불릴 만한.

wriggle 꿈틀거리기, 꼼지락거리기 | foolishly 어리석게도, 바보같은 | indulgent 관대한, 하고 싶은 대로 놔두는
| grievance 불만 | sulky 부루퉁한, 골이 난 | sob 흐느낌 | bolt upright 똑바로 서서, 곧장 | forget-me-not
물망초

Sara went on talking. Perhaps / some people might think
새라는 계속 이야기 했다.   아마도   어떤 사람들은 생각할지 모른다

/ that what she said / was rather like a fairy story, / but it
그녀가 말하는 것이   다소 동화 속 이야기같다고,   하지만 그것은

was all so real / to her own imagination / that Lottie began
매우 진짜 같아서   그녀의 상상 속에서   로티는 듣기 시작했다

to listen / in spite of herself. She had been told / that her
자신도 모르게.   로티는 들었으며

mamma had wings and a crown, / and she had been shown
엄마는 날개를 달고 왕관을 쓰고 있다고,   보았다

/ pictures of ladies in beautiful white nightgowns, / who
아름답고 하얀 잠옷을 입은 여자들의 그림을,

were said to be angels. But Sara seemed to be telling / a
천사라고 불리우는.   하지만 새라는 말하는 것 같았다

real story / about a lovely country / where real people were.
진짜 이야기를   이 멋진 나라에 대해   진짜 사람들이 사는.

Key Expression ❢

be made of ~ : ~로 만들어지다

be made of는 동사 make의 수동태 표현으로, of 뒤에 나오는 말은 재료를 의
미합니다. 비슷한 의미로 be made from이 있습니다. 둘 다 '~로 만들어지다'라
는 의미이지만 of는 물리적 변화, from은 화학적 변화일 때 쓰입니다.
이처럼 make가 수동태로 쓰여 '만들어지다'라는 뜻이 될 때 뒤에 오는 전치사에
따라 의미가 달라집니다.
다양한 쓰임새를 구분하여 기억하세요.

▶ A be made of B : A는 B로 만들어진다(B가 재료, 물리적 변화)
▶ A be made from B : A는 B로 만들어진다(B가 재료, 화학적 변화)
▶ A be made into B : A로 B를 만들다(A가 재료)
▶ A be made by B : A는 B에 의해 만들어지다(B는 동작의 주체)

ex) There are walls made of pearl and gold all round the city.
    진주와 금으로 만들어진 벽이 도시를 둘러싸고 있어.

"There are fields and fields of flowers," / she said, / she
"들판과 꽃밭이 있어."
새라가 말했다.

forgetting herself, / as usual, / when she began, / and
자신을 잊어버린듯,   늘 그렇듯이,   시작할 때면,

talking / rather as if she were in a dream, / "fields and
말하면서   마치 꿈을 꾸는 것처럼,

fields of lilies / — and when the soft wind blows over
"백합 가득한 꽃밭이야   — 부드러운 바람이 그 위로 불어오며

them / it wafts the scent of them / into the air — / and
그 향기가 퍼져나가지   공기 중으로 —

everybody always breathes it, / because the soft wind
그래서 누구나 그 향기를 맡을 수 있어,   왜냐하면 가벼운 바람은 항상 불고

is always blowing. And little children run about / in
있거든.   어린 아이들은 뛰놀고

the lily fields / and gather armfuls of them, / and laugh
백합꽃밭에서   한 아름 백합을 모아서,   웃으며

/ and make little wreaths. And the streets are shining.
화환을 만들지.   거리는 빛나고 있어.

And people are never tired, / however far they walk.
사람들은 전혀 지치는 법이 없지,   아무리 멀리 걸어도.

They can float / anywhere they like. And there are walls
사람들은 날아다닐 수 있어   원하는 곳은 어디든지.   그리고 벽이 있는데

/ made of pearl and gold / all round the city, / but they
진주와 금으로 만들어진   도시를 둘러싼,   하지만 그 벽들은

are low enough / for the people / to go and lean on them,
높이가 낮아서   사람들이   가서 기댈 수 있고,

/ and look down on to the earth / and smile, / and send
지구를 내려다 보고   웃으며,

beautiful messages."
아름다운 메시지를 보내는 거야."

---

waft (공중에서) 퍼지다 | armful 한 아름 | wreath 화환

Whatsoever story she had begun to tell, / Lottie would,
새라가 어떤 이야기를 시작했든지,   로티는,

/ no doubt, / have stopped crying, / and been fascinated
틀림없이,   울음을 멈추고,   듣는 것에 열중했을 것이다;

into listening; / but there was no denying / that this story
            하지만 틀림없이   이 이야기가 가장 아름

was prettier / than most others. She dragged herself close
다웠다   그 어떤 이야기보다.   로티는 새라에게 바짝 다가가서

to Sara, / and drank in every word / until the end came
            한 마디 한 마디를 들이마시듯 들었다   이야기가 끝날 때까지

/ — far too soon. When it did come, / she was so sorry /
— 너무 빨리 끝났다.   이야기가 끝나자,   로티는 매우 아쉬워서

that she put up her lip / ominously.
입술을 비죽 내밀었다   기분이 상하여.

"I want to go there," / she cried. "I — haven't any
"나도 거기에 가고 싶어."   로티가 울었다.   "난 — 엄마가 없으니까

mamma / in this school."
            이 학교에."

Sara saw the danger signal, / and came out of her dream.
새라는 위험 신호를 보았고,   꿈에서 깨어났다.

She took hold of the chubby hand / and pulled her close /
새라는 통통한 손을 잡고   로티를 끌어당겼다

to her side / with a coaxing little laugh.
그녀 쪽으로   살짝 웃음으로 달래며.

"I will be your mamma," / she said. "We will play / that
"내가 네 엄마가 될게."   그녀가 말했다.   "역할 놀이를 하는 거야

you are my little girl. And Emily shall be your sister."
넌 내 딸이야.   에밀리는 네 여동생이고."

Lottie's dimples all began to show themselves.
로티의 보조개가 모두 보이기 시작했다.

"Shall she?" / she said.
"그 애가 정말?"   로티가 말했다.

fascinated 매혹된, 마음을 빼앗긴 | ominously 불길하게, 기분 나쁘게 | take hold of ～을 잡다 | trot
종종걸음으로 가다, 빨리 걷다 | majestic 장엄한, 위엄 있는 | authority 권위 | adopted 입양된

"Yes," / answered Sara, / jumping to her feet. "Let us go
"그래." 새라가 대답했다. 벌떡 일어서며. "그 애한테 가서

and tell her. And then / I will wash your face / and brush
말하자. 그리고 나면 네 얼굴을 씻겨 줄게

your hair."
머리도 빗겨 주고."

To which / Lottie agreed quite cheerfully, / and trotted out
그 말에 로티가 신나서 동의했고, 방 밖으로 총총 걸어나가

of the room / and upstairs / with her, / without seeming
위층으로 올라갔다 새라와 함께. 전혀 기억하지 못하는 듯

even to remember / that the whole of the last hour's
지난 한 시간의 비극이 모두

tragedy / had been caused / by the fact / that she had
초래되었다는 것을 사실에 의해

refused to be washed and brushed / for lunch / and Miss
자신이 씻고 빗질하는 것을 거부했던 점심 식사를 위해

Minchin had been called in / to use her majestic authority.
그래서 민친 교장이 들어와서 위엄 있는 권위를 사용했던 것도.

And from that time / Sara was an adopted mother.
그리고 그때부터 새라는 엄마가 되었다.

Key Expression

동격의 that

fact, news, idea와 같은 명사 뒤에 오는 that절이 이 명사를 설명하는 내용일 때 '~라는 (명사)'라고 해석하여 이를 '동격의 that'이라고 부릅니다.
동격의 that은 관계대명사와 해석이 비슷하여 혼동이 될 수 있습니다. 둘을 구별하는 방법은 관계대명사 that이 이끄는 문장은 불완전한 문장이지만, 동격의 that은 접속사이므로 완전한 문장을 이끈다는 점입니다.

▶ the fact   that ~ : ~라는 사실
▶ the news   that ~ : ~라는 뉴스
▶ the idea   that ~ : ~라는 의견
▶ the suggestion   that ~ : ~라는 제안
▶ the feeling   that ~ : ~라는 감정
▶ the possibility   that ~ : ~라는 가능성

ex) The whole of the last hour's tragedy had been caused by the fact that she had refused to be washed and brushed for .
지난 한 시간 동안의 비극이 모두 그녀가 점심 식사를 위해 씻고 빗질하는 것을 거부했던 사실에 의해 초래되었다.

75

A. 다음 문장을 해석해 보세요.

(1) She stared so hard / and bit the ribbon / on her pigtail / so fast / that she attracted the attention of Miss Minchin.
→

(2) Whatsoever she meant, / Ermengarde was sure / it was something delightfully exciting.
→

(3) If she had been a self-opinionated, / domineering child, / she might have become disagreeable / enough to be unbearable / through being so much indulged / and flattered.
→

(4) If her mamma had seen her / during the last half-hour, / she might not have thought / her the kind of child / who ought to be related to an angel.
→

B. 다음 주어진 문구가 알맞은 문장이 되도록 순서를 맞춰 보세요.

(1) 그 애는 공부하도록 시켜야 해요.
(be / learn / must / She / to / made)
→

(2) 그들은 번개처럼 아주 빨라.
(lightning / are / quick / as / They / as)
→

(3) 우리도 '단짝 친구'가 될 수 있으면 좋겠어.
('best friends' / I / could / we / be / wish)
→

A. (1) 어먼가드는 아주 열심히 쳐다보며 땋은 머리의 리본을 매우 빨리 씹어서 민친 교장의 주의를 끌었다. (2) 그녀가 의미하는 것이 무엇이든, 어먼가드는 그것이 뭔가 즐겁게 신나는 일이라고 확신했다. (3) 만약 그녀가 고집 세고, 잘난 체 하는 아이였다면, 아첨에 둘러싸여서 제멋대로이며 참을 수 없을 만큼 무례한 아이가 되었을지 모른

(4) 그래서 그 애가 그것을 그토록 좋아한대.
   (That's / why / she / likes / it / so)
   →

C. 다음 주어진 문장이 본문의 내용과 맞으면 T, 틀리면 F에 동그라미 하세요.

(1) On the first morning, when Sara saw Ermengarde being scolded, she was interested in her.
   (T / F)

(2) Ermengarde wanted Sara to be her 'best friend'.
   (T / F)

(3) Miss Minchin praised Sara for everything because she liked her very much.
   (T / F)

(4) Lottie asked Sara to be her mother.
   (T / F)

D. 의미가 비슷한 것끼리 서로 연결해 보세요.

(1) disdain   ▶   ◀ ① tremble

(2) clasp   ▶   ◀ ② contempt

(3) wobble   ▶   ◀ ③ resentment

(4) indignation   ▶   ◀ ④ grasp

Answer

다. (4) 로티의 엄마가 지난 30분 간 그 애를 보았다면, 천사라고 불릴 만한 아이라고 생각하지 못했을 지도 모른다. | B. (1) She must be made to learn. (2) They are as quick as lightning. (3) I wish we could be 'best friends'. (4)That's why she likes it so. | C. (1) T (2) T (3) F (4) F | D. (1) ② (2) ④ (3) ① (4) ③

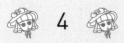

4

Becky
베키

Of course / the greatest power / Sara possessed / and the
물론　　　　가장 위대한 힘과　　　새라가 가진　　　　갖게 한 힘은

one which gained / her even more followers / than her
훨씬 더 많은 추종자를　　　　　호화로운 물건들과

luxuries / and the fact / that she was "the show pupil,"
사실보다　　그녀가 "전시용 학생"이라는,

/ the power / that Lavinia and certain other girls / were
즉 그 힘은　　라비니아와 어떤 다른 여자 아이들이

most envious of, / and at the same time / most fascinated
가장 부러워했고,　　　동시에　　　　가장 매료된

by / in spite of themselves, / was her power / of telling
자신도 모르게,　　　그녀의 힘이었다　　이야기를 들려주고

stories / and of making / everything she talked about /
만들어내는　　　그녀가 말하는 모든 것을

seem like a story, / whether it was one or not.
이야기처럼 보이도록,　　그것이 진짜든 아니든.

Key Expression ❣

not only A but also B : A 뿐만 아니라 B도
not only A but also B는 'A 뿐만 아니라 B도'라는 뜻을 가진 상관접속사 구
문이에요. 이때 A와 B의 자리에는 같은 형태가 와야 합니다.
또한 이 구문이 주어로 쓰일 경우에는 뒤에 오는 B에 동사의 인칭이나 수를 일치
시켜야 합니다.
같은 뜻을 가진 구문으로 as well as 있습니다. 이때는 A와 B의 위치가 바뀌
게 되어 B as well as A와 같이 사용합니다.

ex) Sara not only could tell stories, but she adored telling them.
　　새라는 이야기를 들려줄 뿐만 아니라, 이야기 하는 것을 좋아했다.

---

luxuries 호화로움, 사치품 | in spite of oneself 자신도 모르게 | wonder 경탄, 놀라움 | beseech 간청하다,
애원하다 | relate 이야기 하다, 들려주다 | outskirts (복수형) 변두리, 교외 | midst 중앙, 한가운데 | sway 흔들림,
진동 | dramatic 극적인 | folk 사람 | narrate 이야기를 하다, 들려주다

Anyone who has been at school / with a teller of stories
학교에 다녔던 사람이면 누구나   이야기꾼과 함께

/ knows / what the wonder means / — how he or she is
알고 있다   그 놀라움이 의미하는 바를   — 얼마나 사람들이 따라다니며

followed about / and besought / in a whisper / to relate
간청하는지   속삭이면서   연애 이야기를

romances; / how groups gather round / and hang on the
들려 달라고;   얼마나 많은 집단들이 모여들어   주변을 에워싸고

outskirts / of the favored party / in the hope of being
사랑 받는 친구의   허락해 주기를 바라면서

allowed / to join in and listen. Sara not only could tell
무리에 끼어 이야기를 듣기를.   새라는 이야기를 들려줄 뿐만 아니라,

stories, / but she adored telling them. When she sat or
이야기 하는 것을 좋아했다.   앉거나 서서

stood / in the midst of a circle / and began to invent
둥글게 모인 사람들의 한가운데   놀라운 이야기들을 지어내기 시작하면,

wonderful things, / her green eyes grew big and shining,
그녀의 초록빛 눈은 커지면서 빛났고,

/ her cheeks flushed, / and, / without knowing that she
뺨은 홍조를 띄었으며,   그리고,   자신도 모르는 사이에,

was doing it, / she began to act and made / what she told
움직이면서 만들기 시작했다   자신이 이야기 하는 것을

/ lovely or alarming / by the raising or dropping of her
사랑스럽거나 놀랍게   목소리를 높이거나 낮추면서

voice, / the bend and sway of her slim body, / and the
갸냘픈 몸을 숙이거나 흔들면서.

dramatic movement of her hands. She forgot / that she
또 극적인 손짓을 하면서.   새라는 잊고   자신이 이야기

was talking / to listening children; / she saw and lived
하고 있다는 것을   듣고 있는 아이들에게;   보면서 살고 있었다

/ with the fairy folk, / or the kings and queens / and
요정들이나,   왕과 왕비와

beautiful ladies, / whose adventures / she was narrating.
그리고 아름다운 여인들과,   그리고 그들을 모험담을   들려주고 있었다.

Sometimes / when she had finished her story, / she was
때로는 이야기를 끝냈을 때,

quite out of breath / with excitement, / and would lay her
숨을 몰아 쉬면서 흥분으로, 손을 얹고

hand / on her thin, little, quick-rising chest, / and half
마르고, 작고, 빨리 뛰는 가슴 위에, 반쯤 웃었다

laugh / as if at herself.
마치 자신을 보고 웃는 듯.

"When I am telling it," / she would say, / "it doesn't seem
"내가 이야기 하고 있을 때에는," 그녀는 말하곤 했다. "보이지는 않아

/ as if it was only made up. It seems more real / than you
단지 꾸며낸 이야기처럼. 더 진짜같아 너희들보다

are / — more real than the schoolroom. I feel / as if I
— 교실보다 더 진짜같아. 느껴지는 거야

were all the people / in the story / — one after the other.
마치 내가 모든 사람이 된 것처럼 이야기 속의 — 차례차례로.

It is queer."
신기하지."

She had been at Miss Minchin's school / about two
새라는 민친 교장의 학교에서 지냈고 약 2년 동안

years / when, one foggy winter's afternoon, / as she
그러던 어느 날 안개 낀 겨울의 오후,

was getting out of her carriage, / comfortably wrapped
마차에서 내렸을 때, 편안하게 감싼 채

up / in her warmest velvets and furs / and looking very
가장 따뜻한 벨벳 드레스와 모피 코트로 훨씬 더 우아하게 보이면서

much grander / than she knew, / she caught sight, / as she
자신이 아는 것보다. 그녀는 보았다.

crossed the pavement, / of a dingy little figure standing
길을 건널 때, 지저분하고 작은 아이가 서서

/ on the area steps, / and stretching its neck / so that its
지하실로 내려가는 계단 위에, 목을 빼고 있는 것을

wide-open eyes might peer at her / through the railings.
크게 뜬 눈으로 자신을 엿보기 위해 난간 사이로.

Something / in the eagerness and timidity / of the smudgy
뭔가 때문에　　열망하면서도 겁에 질린 듯한 표정 속에　　그 지저분한 얼굴의

face / made her look at it, / and when she looked / she
새라가 돌아보았고,　　그녀가 보았을 때

smiled / because it was her way / to smile at people.
미소지었다　왜냐하면 그녀의 방식이었으니까　　사람들에게 미소짓는 것은.

But the owner / of the smudgy face / and the wide-open
하지만 그 장본인은　　지저분한 얼굴과　　큰 눈을 가진

eyes / evidently was afraid / that she ought not to have
명백히 두려워했다　　들키면 안 되었기에

been caught / looking at pupils of importance. She dodged
　　중요한 학생을 쳐다보는 것을.　　재빨리 사라졌다

/ out of sight / like a jack-in-the-box / and scurried back
시야 밖으로　　장난감 상자 속의 인형처럼　　허둥대며 돌아갔다

/ into the kitchen, / disappearing so suddenly / that if she
부엌 안으로,　　갑자기 사라져서

had not been such a poor little forlorn thing, / Sara would
만약 그 아이가 그토록 불쌍하고 작고 쓸쓸해 보이는 않았다면,

have laughed / in spite of herself. That very evening, / as
새라는 웃었을 것이다　자신도 모르게.　　바로 그날 저녁,

Sara was sitting / in the midst / of a group of listeners / in
새라가 앉아 있을 때　　한가운데　　청중들의

a corner of the schoolroom / telling one of her stories, /
교실 한 구석의　　이야기를 들려주며,

the very same figure timidly entered the room, / carrying
바로 그 아이가 소심하게 방으로 들어와서,

a coal box / much too heavy for her, / and knelt down /
석탄 상자를 들고　자신에게 너무 무거워 보이는,　　무릎을 꿇었다

upon the hearth rug / to replenish the fire / and sweep up
난로 앞 양탄자 위에　　난로에 땔감을 넣고

the ashes.
재를 쓸어내려고.

out of breath 숨이 가쁜 | one after the other 번갈아, 교대로 | wrap 감싸다 | pavement 인도, 보도 | area
step 지하실로 내려가는 계단 | railing 난간 | eagerness 열의, 열망 | timidity 겁 많음, 수줍음 | smudgy 얼룩이
묻은, 지저분한 | dodge 재빨리 움직이다 | jack-in-the-box 깜짝 장난감 상자(뚜껑을 열면 용수철에 달린 인형
등이 튀어나오도록 되어 있음) | scurry 종종걸음을 치다, 허둥지둥 가다 | forlorn 쓸쓸해 보이는, 황량한 | timidly
소심하게, 소극적으로 | kneel 무릎을 꿇다 | replenish 다시 채우다, 보충하다

She was cleaner / than she had been / when she peeped
그 아이는 더 깨끗했다   지난번보다   엿보았을 때

/ through the area railings, / but she looked just as
계단 난간 사이로.   하지만 똑같이 겁먹은 모습이었다.

frightened. She was evidently afraid / to look at the
그 아이는 확실히 두려워하고 있었다   아이들을 쳐다보거나

children / or seem to be listening. She put on pieces of
듣는 것처럼 보일까 봐.   석탄 조각들을 넣으며

coal / cautiously with her fingers / so that she might
손가락으로 조심스럽게   소음을 내서 방해하지 않으려고,

make no disturbing noise, / and she swept about the fire
난로망 부근을 쓸어냈다

irons / very softly. But Sara saw / in two minutes / that
아주 부드럽게.   하지만 새라는 보았다   잠시 후

she was deeply interested / in what was going on, / and
그 아이가 매우 흥미로워 하고 있으며   진행되는 이야기에,

that she was doing her work / slowly / in the hope of
일을 하고 있다는 것을   천천히   한 단어라도 들으려는 바람으로

catching a word / here and there. And realizing this, / she
여기저기에서.   이 사실을 깨닫자,

raised her voice / and spoke more clearly.
새라는 목소리를 높여서   더 또박또박 말했다.

"The Mermaids swam softly / about in the crystal-green
"인어들은 부드럽게 헤엄치면서   수정처럼 맑은 초록빛 물 속에서,

water, / and dragged after them / a fishing-net / woven
끌고 다녔지   낚시 그물을

of deep-sea pearls," / she said. "The Princess sat / on the
깊은 바다의 진주로 엮은,"   그녀가 말했다.   "공주는 앉아서

white rock / and watched them."
하얀 바위 위에   그들을 쳐다봤어."

It was a wonderful story / about a princess / who was
그것은 멋진 이야기였다   공주에 관한

loved by a Prince Merman, / and went to live with him /
인어 왕자의 사랑을 받고 있으며   그를 따라가서 함께 살았다는

in shining caves / under the sea.
눈부신 동굴에서   바다 속의.

The small drudge / before the grate / swept the hearth once
어린 하녀는　　　　　　　난로 앞에 있던　　　　　난로 바닥을 한 번 쓸고

/ and then swept it again. Having done it twice, / she did
또 쓸었다.　　　　　　　　　　　두 번이나 쓸었지만,

it three times; / and, / as she was doing it the third time,
세 번째로 쓸었다:　　그리고,　　세 번째 쓸고 있을 때에는,

/ the sound of the story so lured her to listen / that she
이야기 소리에 정신을 빼앗겨

fell under the spell / and actually forgot / that she had no
마법에 빠져버린 듯　　　　실제로 잊어버렸다　　　자신에게 권리가 없다는 것을

right / to listen / at all, / and also forgot everything else.
들을 수 있는　　전혀,　　　또한 다른 모든 것도 잊어버렸다.

She sat down upon her heels / as she knelt / on the hearth
아이는 발뒤꿈치 위에 앉았고　　　　　무릎 꿇으면서　　　난로 앞 양탄자 위에,

rug, / and the brush hung idly / in her fingers. The voice
빗자루는 하릴없이 매달려 있었다　　손가락에.

of the storyteller went on / and drew her with it / into
이야기꾼의 목소리가 계속 되면서　　　　그녀를 이끌었다

winding grottos / under the sea, / glowing with soft, clear
바람 부는 작은 동굴로　　바다 속의,　　　부드럽고, 투명한 푸른 빛을 내며,

blue light, / and paved with pure golden sands. Strange
순금 모래가 깔려 있는.

sea flowers and grasses / waved about her, / and far away /
낯선 바다 꽃과 잔디들이　　　　주위에 넘실거렸고,　　　저 멀리에서

faint singing and music echoed.
희미한 노래와 음악 소리가 울려 퍼졌다.

The hearth brush fell / from the work-roughened hand, /
난로 닦는 빗자루가 떨어졌고　　　일하느라 거칠어진 손에서,

and Lavinia Herbert looked round.
그러자 라비니아 허버트가 돌아 보았다.

"That girl has been listening," / she said.
"저 애가 듣고 있었어,"　　　　　그녀가 말했다.

---

evidently 분명히 | coal 석탄 | fire iron 난로용 철물도구 | mermaid 인어 | drudge 힘들고 단조로운 일을
오랫동안 하는 사람 | hearth 난로, 난로 바닥 | lure 유혹하다 | spell 주문 | idly 한가롭게, 우두커니 | grotto (
인공적으로 만든) 작은 동굴 | glow 빛나다, 타오르다 | pave (길을) 포장하다 | faint 희미한 | work-roughened
일을 많이 해서 거칠어진

The culprit snatched up her brush, / and scrambled / to her
그 장본인은 빗자루를 낚아채서, 허둥지둥 움직였다 두 발로.

feet. She caught at the coal box / and simply scuttled / out
석탄 상자를 들고 종종걸음으로 나갔다

of the room / like a frightened rabbit.
방 밖으로 겁먹은 토끼처럼.

Sara felt rather hot-tempered.
새라는 좀 화가 났다.

"I knew / she was listening," / she said. "Why shouldn't
"나도 알았어 그 아이가 듣고 있는 것을," 그녀가 말했다. "왜 들으면 안 되지?"

she?"

Lavinia tossed her head / with great elegance.
라비니아는 고개를 치켜들었다 매우 우아하게.

"Well," / she remarked, / "I do not know / whether your
"글쎄," 그녀가 강조했다, "난 모르겠지만

mamma would like / you to tell stories to servant girls, /
네 엄마는 좋아할지 네가 하녀 아이에게 이야기 해 주는 것을,

but I know / my mamma wouldn't like me / to do it."
하지만 알아 우리 엄마는 싫어하신다는 것을 내가 그런 짓을 하면."

"My mamma!" / said Sara, / looking odd. "I don't believe
"우리 엄마는!" 새라가 말했다, 묘한 표정으로. "내 생각에는

/ she would mind / in the least. She knows / that stories
우리 엄마는 싫어하지 않으실 거야 조금도. 엄마는 알고 계시니까

belong to everybody."
이야기는 모두의 것이라는 것을."

"I thought," / retorted Lavinia, / in severe recollection, /
"내 생각에는," 라비니아가 대꾸했다, 곰곰이 회상하면서,

"that your mamma was dead. How can she know things?"
너희 엄마는 돌아가셨잖아. 어떻게 그것을 알고 계실까?"

"Do you think / she doesn't know things?" / said Sara, /
"넌 생각하니 엄마가 그것을 모른다고?" 새라가 말했다,

in her stern little voice. Sometimes / she had a rather stern
근엄하고 작은 목소리로. 이따금 그녀는 다소 근엄하고 작은

little voice.
목소리로 말할 때가 있었다.

"Sara's mamma knows everything," / piped in Lottie.
"새라의 엄마는 모든 것을 알고 계셔."　　　　　　　　로티가 끼어들었다.

"So does my mamma / — 'cept Sara is my mamma / at
"우리 엄마도 그래　　　　　— 엄마인 새라는 빼고

Miss Minchin's — / my other one knows everything.
민친 학교에서 —　　　진짜 엄마는 모든 것을 알아.

The streets are shining, / and there are fields and fields of
거리가 빛나고,　　　　　　　백합꽃밭이 펼쳐져 있고,

lilies, / and everybody gathers them. Sara tells me / when
　　백합꽃을 꺾어.　　　　새라가 나한테 말해 줬어

she puts me to bed."
날 재울 때."

"You wicked thing," / said Lavinia, / turning on Sara; /
"이 못된 것."　　　　라비니아가 말했다,　　새라를 돌아보며;

"making fairy stories / about heaven."
"이야기를 지어내다니　　천국에 대한."

"There are much more splendid stories / in Revelation,"
"훨씬 멋진 이야기들이 있지　　　　　　　계시록에는,"

/ returned Sara. "Just look and see! How do you know /
새라가 대답했다.　　"찾아서 보시지!　　어떻게 아는 거지

mine are fairy stories? But I can tell you" / — with a fine
내 이야기가 지어낸 이야기라고?　하지만 네게 말해 줄 수 있어"　— 아주 약간

bit / of unheavenly temper — / "you will never find out /
천국과 거리가 먼 모습으로 —　　"넌 절대 못 찾아낼 거야

whether they are or not / if you're not kinder to people /
그것이 지어낸 것인지 아닌지　　네가 사람들에게 더 친절해지지 않는다면

than you are now. Come along, Lottie." And she marched
지금의 너보다.　　　　따라와, 로티."　　　　그리고 그녀는 걸어갔다

/ out of the room, / rather hoping / that she might see the
방 밖으로,　　　　약간 바라면서　그 어린 하녀를 보게 되기를

little servant / again somewhere, / but she found no trace
　　　　　　다시 어딘가에서,　　하지만 어떤 흔적도 찾을 수 없었다

of her / when she got into the hall.
거실로 들어갔을 때.

culprit 범인 | snatch 와락 붙잡다, 잡아채다 | scramble 재빨리 움직이다 | scuttle 종종걸음을 치다, 총총 가다
| hot-tempered 욱하는 성미가 있는, 화를 내는 | toss (고개를) 홱 치켜 들다 | not ~ in the least 전혀 | retort
쏘아붙이다, 대구하다 | stern 근엄한 | pipe 높은 소리로 말하다 | wicked 못된, 짖궂은 | splendid 정말 좋은,
훌륭한 | Revelation 계시록 | unheavenly 천국이 아닌(=not heavenly)

85

"Who is that little girl / who makes the fires?" / she asked
"그 작은 여자애는 누구지 난롯불을 지피는?" 마리에트에게 물었다

Mariette / that night.
그날 밤.

Mariette broke forth / into a flow of description.
마리에트는 말하기 시작했다 긴 설명을.

Ah, indeed, / Mademoiselle Sara might well ask. She was
아, 정말로, 새라 아가씨가 묻는 것이 당연하다고.

a forlorn little thing / who had just taken the place / of
그 아이는 버려진 아이인데 일을 맡고 있는

scullery maid / — though, / as to being scullery maid, /
부엌데기의 — 하지만, 부엌데기로서,

she was everything else / besides. She blacked boots and
그 아이는 만능이었다 게다가, 구두와 난로를 광나게 닦고,

grates, / and carried heavy coal-scuttles / up and down
무거운 석탄 통을 들고 계단을 오르락내리락 하며,

stairs, / and scrubbed floors / and cleaned windows, / and
바닥을 문질러 닦고 창문을 닦고,

was ordered about / by everybody. She was fourteen years
시키는 일을 했다 모두가. 그 애는 열네 살인데,

old, / but was so stunted in growth / that she looked about
성장 발달이 매우 느려서 열두 살로밖에 보이지 않았다.

twelve. In truth, / Mariette was sorry for her. She was so
사실, 마리에트는 그 아이를 가여워 했다. 그 아이는 매우 겁이

timid / that if one chanced to speak to her / it appeared / as
많아서 누군가 말을 걸려고 하면 보였다

if her poor, frightened eyes would jump / out of her head.
불쌍하고, 겁에 질린 눈이 튀어나올 것처럼 얼굴 밖으로.

"What is her name?" / asked Sara, / who had sat by
"이름이 뭐지?" 새라가 물었다. 탁자 옆에 앉아서,

the table, / with her chin on her hands, / as she listened
턱을 손에 괴고, 열중하여 들으면서

absorbedly / to the recital.
설명을.

mademoiselle ~양, 아가씨 (여성을 부르는 프랑스어의 호칭) | may well ~하는 것이 당연하다 | scullery maid
부엌데기 | scuttle 석탄 통 | scrub 문질러 닦다 | stunted 성장을 저해당한 | absorbedly 열중하여 | recital
장황한 설명 | belowstairs (과거 하인들이 거주하던) 아래층에

Her name was Becky. Mariette heard / everyone
그 아이의 이름은 베키였다.   마리에트는 들었다

belowstairs calling, / "Becky, do this," / and / "Becky, do
아래층 사람들이 부르는 것을,   "베키, 이것 해라,"   그리고   "베키, 저것 해라,"

that," / every five minutes / in the day.
라며   5분마다   하루 종일.

Sara sat / and looked into the fire, / reflecting on Becky /
새라는 앉아서 난롯불을 쳐다보았다, 베키에 대해 곰곰이 생각하며

for some time / after Mariette left her. She made up a story
얼마동안 마리에트가 떠난 후. 그녀는 이야기를 지었다

/ of which Becky was the ill-used heroine. She thought
베키가 학대당한 여주인공이라는. 새라는 베키가 보이는 것

she looked / as if she had never had quite enough to eat.
같았다 마치 충분히 먹어본 적이 없는 아이처럼.

Her very eyes were hungry. She hoped / she should see her
베키의 눈은 바로 굶주린 눈이었다. 새라는 바랐지만 다시 베키를 볼 수 있기를,

again, / but though she caught sight / of her carrying things
하지만 보게 되더라도 그 아이가 물건들을 들고

/ up or down stairs / on several occasions, / she always
계단을 오르락내리락 하며 때때로, 항상

seemed in such a hurry / and so afraid of being seen / that
항상 쫓기는 듯 보였고 눈에 띄는 것을 두려워해서

it was impossible / to speak to her.
불가능했다 그 아이에게 말을 거는 것이.

But a few weeks later, / on another foggy afternoon, /
하지만 몇 주 후에, 또 다른 안개 낀 오후에,

when she entered her sitting room / she found herself
새라가 거실에 들어왔을 때 맞닥뜨리게 되었다

confronting / a rather pathetic picture. In her own special
매우 측은한 광경을. 자신이 특히 아끼는 안락의자에

and pet easy-chair / before the bright fire, / Becky / —
환한 난롯불 앞에 있는, 베키가

with a coal smudge / on her nose / and several on her
— 석탄 자국을 묻힌 채 코와 앞치마 여기저기에,

apron, / with her poor little cap / hanging half / off her
허름하고 작은 모자가 반쯤 걸려 있고 머리에서 벗겨져,

head, / and an empty coal box / on the floor / near her / —
빈 석탄 상자를 바닥에 놓아둔 채 그녀의 곁에

sat fast asleep, / tired out / beyond even the endurance / of
— 앉아서 깊이 잠들었다, 완전히 지쳐 감당할 수 없을 만큼

her hard-working young body. She had been sent up / to
고되게 일한 어린 몸이. 그 아이는 올라왔다

put the bedrooms in order / for the evening. There were
침실을 정리하려고   밤을 위해.

a great many of them, / and she had been running about
방은 수없이 많았고,   그 아이는 계속 뛰어다녔다

/ all day. Sara's rooms / she had saved / until the last.
종일.   새라의 방은   남겨두었다   마지막까지.

They were not like the other rooms, / which were plain
그 방은 다른 방들과 달랐기 때문에,   다른 방들은 평범하고 비어

and bare. Ordinary pupils were expected to be satisfied
있었다.   보통 학생들은 만족해야 했다

/ with mere necessaries. Sara's comfortable sitting room
필수품만으로.   새라의 안락한 거실은

/ seemed a bower of luxury / to the scullery maid, /
화려한 안식처 같았다   부엌데기에게는,

though it was, / in fact, / merely a nice, bright little room.
비록, 그 방은,   사실,   그저 깔끔하고, 밝은 작은 방에 불과했지만.

But there were pictures and books / in it, / and curious
하지만 그림과 책들이 있었고   그 방에는,

things from India; / there was a sofa and the low, soft
인도에서 온 신기한 물건들도;   소파와 낮고, 폭신한 의자도 있었다;

chair; / Emily sat / in a chair of her own, / with the air of
에밀리는 앉아 있었고   자신의 의자에,

a presiding goddess, / and there was always a glowing
통솔하는 여신같은 모습으로,   항상 난롯불이 활활 타고 있었으며,

fire / and a polished grate. Becky saved it / until the end
난로는 윤이 났다.   베키는 그 방을 아껴두었다

of her afternoon's work, / because it rested her / to go
오후의 일이 끝날 때까지,   왜냐하면 휴식처였기 때문에   그 안에

into it, / and she always hoped / to snatch a few minutes
들어가는 일은, 베키는 항상 바랐다   잠깐의 시간을 내어서

---

ill-used 학대당한 | heroine (소설·영화 등의) 여자 주인공 | on occasions 때로는 | confront 맞서다, 직면하다
| pathetic 불쌍한, 애처로운 | fall asleep 깊이 잠들다 | endurance 인내(력), 참을성 | bare 벌거벗은, 텅 빈 |
necessaries (복수형) 필수품들 | bower 나무 그늘(의 휴식 장소), 정자 | presiding 통솔하는, 수석의

/ to sit down / in the soft chair / and look about her, / and
앉아　　　　　　푹신한 의자에　　　　　주변을 돌아보며,

think about / the wonderful good fortune / of the child /
생각해 보는 일을　놀랍고 멋진 행운에 대해　　　　이 아이의

who owned such surroundings / and who went out / on the
그 모든 환경을 소유했으며　　　　　　　외출하는

cold days / in beautiful hats and coats / one tried to catch a
추운 날이면　아름다운 모자를 쓰고 코트를 입은 채　누구나 살짝 엿보고 싶어 할 만큼

glimpse of / through the area railing.
　　　　　계단 난간 사이로.

On this afternoon, / when she had sat down, / the sensation
이날 오후에,　　　　　베키가 앉았을 때,　　　　놀라운 안도감이

of relief / to her short, aching legs / had been so wonderful
　　　　　그 작고 아픈 다리가 느낀

and delightful / that it had seemed to soothe / her whole
매우 놀랍고 기뻐서　　　달래주는 듯 했고　　　　　몸 전체를,

body, / and the glow of warmth and comfort / from the fire
　　　따뜻하고 아늑한 불빛이　　　　　　　난롯불의

/ had crept over her / like a spell, / until, / as she looked at
　그 아이의 몸에 스며들었다　마법처럼,　　그러자,　붉게 타오르는 석탄을 바라보

the red coals, / a tired, slow smile stole over / her smudged
고 있을 때,　　　지치고, 느긋한 미소가 번졌고　　　얼룩진 얼굴 위로,

face, / her head nodded forward / without her being aware
고개가 앞으로 수그러지더니　　　　자신도 모르게,

of it, / her eyes drooped, / and she fell fast asleep. She had
눈이 감기면서,　　　　깊이 잠들어 버렸다.

really been only about ten minutes / in the room / when
실제로 10분 정도 지났을 뿐이었다　　　　그 방에서

Sara entered, / but she was in as deep a sleep as / if she had
새라가 들어왔을 때,　　하지만 그 아이는 깊이 잠들었다　　　마치 자신이,

been, / like the Sleeping Beauty, / slumbering for a hundred
　　　잠자는 숲 속의 공주가 된 듯이,　　　100년 동안 잠들어 있었던.

years. But she did not look / — poor Becky — / like a
하지만 그 모습은 달랐다　　　— 가엾은 베키는 —

glimpse 힐끗 봄 | aching 쑤시는, 아픈 | slumber 잠을 자다 | attired ~한 복장의 | diaphanous 천이 아주
얇은, 속이 비치는

Sleeping Beauty / at all. She looked / only like an ugly,
잠자는 숲 속의 공주와는　전혀.　그 아이는 보였다

stunted, worn-out little scullery drudge.
그저 못생기고, 덜 자란, 지쳐버린 어린 부엌데기로.

Sara seemed as much unlike her / as if she were a
새라는 그 아이와 전혀 달라 보였다　　마치 존재인 듯

creature / from another world.
　　다른 세상에서 온.

On this particular afternoon / she had been taking
이 특별한 오후에　　　　　새라는 무용 수업을 받았는데,

her dancing lesson, / and the afternoon / on which the
　　　　　그날 오후는　　　무용 선생이 등장한

dancing master appeared / was rather a grand occasion
　　　　　　　　꽤 대단한 사건이었다

/ at the seminary, / though it occurred every week. The
　신학교에서는,　　매주 있는 일이긴 했지만.

pupils were attired / in their prettiest frocks, / and as
학생들은 차려 입었고　가장 예쁜 드레스로,

Sara danced particularly well, / she was very much
그리고 새라는 특별히 춤을 잘 춰서,　　휠씬 앞쪽으로 섰기 때문에,

brought forward, / and Mariette was requested / to make
　　　　마리에트는 지시를 받았다　　　　새라를 꾸며

her / as diaphanous and fine / as possible.
주라고　하늘하늘하고 멋지게　　가능한 한.

Key Expression ♀

as~as possible : 가능한 한 ~하게

as~as possible은 '가능한 한 ~하게'라는 의미를 가지고 있어요.
이때 as와 as 사이에는 형용사나 부사가 들어가며 possible 대신 주어 + can
으로 바꾸어 쓸 수 있습니다.

ex) Mariette was requested to make her as diaphanous and fine as possible.
　　　　　　　　　　　　　　　　　　　　　　　　(ㄴ =she could)
　마리에트는 그녀를 가능한 한 하늘하늘하고 멋지게 꾸며 주라는 지시를 받았다.

Today / a frock the color of a rose / had been put on her,
이날   장밋빛 드레스를   새라에게 입혔고,

/ and Mariette had bought some real buds / and made
   마리에트는 진짜 꽃봉오리를 사 와서   화관을 만들어주었다

her a wreath / to wear on her black locks. She had been
검은 머리 위에 씌울.   새라는 배우는 중이었다

learning / a new, delightful dance / in which she had
          새롭고, 즐거운 춤을   스치듯 지나가며

been skimming / and flying about the room, / like a large
              방을 나는 듯 돌아다니는,

rose-colored butterfly, / and the enjoyment and exercise /
커다란 장밋빛 나비처럼,   그리고 즐거움과 흥분으로

had brought a brilliant, happy glow / into her face.
환하고, 행복하게 빛났다   그녀의 얼굴은.

When she entered the room, / she floated in / with a few
새라는 방으로 들어올 때,   떠다니듯 들어왔다

of the butterfly steps / — and there sat Becky, / nodding
나비같은 발걸음으로,   — 그리고 베키가 앉아 있었다,   모자를 끄떡거

her cap / sideways off her head.
리며   머리에 비스듬히 얹혀진.

Key Expression

to tell the truth : 사실을 말하자면

to tell the truth는 '사실은, 사실을 말하자면, 솔직히 말하면'이라는 뜻을 가진 대표적인 독립부정사입니다.
독립부정사란 독립적으로 쓰이며 문장 전체를 수식하는 to 부정사구를 일컫는 용어입니다.
to tell the truth는 to be honest나 to be frank with you, 그리고 동명사를 사용한 숙어 frankly speaking와도 같은 의미로 쓰입니다.

ex) To tell the truth, she was quite glad to find it there.
　　사실을 말하자면, 그녀는 그곳에서 그 장면을 보게 되어 매우 기뻤다.

"Oh!" / cried Sara, / softly, / when she saw her. "That
"아!"　새라가 소리쳤다, 부드럽게. 그 아이를 보았을 때.

poor thing!"
"참 불쌍한 아이구나!"

It did not occur to her to feel cross / at finding her pet
화가 나는 감정은 일어나지 않았다　　자신이 아끼는 의자에

chair / occupied by the small, dingy figure. To tell the
작고, 지저분한 아이가 앉아 있는 것을 보고.　사실을 말하자면,

truth, / she was quite glad / to find it there. When the ill-
새라는 매우 기뻤다　그곳에서 그 장면을 보게 되어.

used heroine / of her story / wakened, / she could talk to
학대 받는 여주인공이　그녀 이야기의　깨어났을 때,　말을 걸 수 있을테니.

her. She crept toward her / quietly, / and stood looking at
그녀는 그 애한테 가서　조용히,　서서 바라보았다.

her. Becky gave a little snore.
베키는 가볍게 코를 골고 있었다.

"I wish she'd waken herself," / Sara said. "I don't like
"이 아이가 스스로 깨어났으면 좋겠어,"　새라가 말했다.　"저 애를 깨우고 싶지

to waken her. But Miss Minchin would be cross / if she
않아.　하지만 민친 교장이 화를 낼 텐데

found out. I'll just wait / a few minutes."
만약 발견하면.　기다려 보자　조금만.

She took a seat / on the edge of the table, / and sat /
새라는 걸터 앉아서　탁자 끝에,　앉아 있었다

swinging her slim, rose-colored legs, / and wondering /
가냘픈, 장밋빛 다리를 흔들며,　궁금해 하면서

what it would be best to do. Miss Amelia might come in
무엇이 최선인지를.　아멜리아 선생이 들어올지 몰랐고

/ at any moment, / and if she did, / Becky would be sure /
언제든지,　만약 그러면,　베키는 분명히

to be scolded.
야단맞을 것이다.

"But she is so tired," / she thought. "She is so tired!"
"하지만 저 애는 아주 지쳐 있어,"　그녀는 생각했다.　"저 애는 아주 지쳐 있다고!"

skim 스치듯 지나가다 | sideways 옆으로 | occupied 점유당한 | snore 코를 골다

93

A piece of flaming coal / ended her perplexity for her /
불타는 석탄 한 조각이 　　　　　　　　　새라의 당혹감을 해결해 주었다

that very moment. It broke off from a large lump / and fell
바로 그 순간. 　　　　큰 석탄 덩어리가 깨지면서 　　　　　떨어졌다

on / to the fender. Becky started, / and opened her eyes /
난로 칸막이로. 　　베키는 흠칫 놀라, 　　　눈을 떴다

with a frightened gasp. She did not know / she had fallen
겁에 질려 숨을 헐떡이며. 　　몰랐던 것이다 　　　자신이 깊이 잠들었던 것을.

asleep. She had only sat down / for one moment / and felt
그냥 앉아 있었을 뿐이었다 　　　잠시 동안

the beautiful glow / — and here / she found herself staring
아름다운 불빛을 느끼며 　　— 그리고 여기에서 　베키는 보게 되었다

in wild alarm / at the wonderful pupil, / who sat perched /
깜짝 놀라며 　　그 굉장한 학생을, 　　　　　앉아 있는

quite near her, / like a rose-colored fairy, / with interested
자신의 바로 옆에, 　　장밋빛 요정처럼, 　　　　흥미로운 눈으로.

eyes.

She sprang up / and clutched at her cap. She felt it dangling
그녀는 벌떡 일어나 　모자를 움켜쥐었다. 　　　　모자가 걸려 있음을 느끼고

/ over her ear, / and tried wildly / to put it straight. Oh, /
귀에, 　　무작정 애썼다 　똑바로 하려고. 　　아,

she had got herself into trouble / now / with a vengeance!
곤경에 빠져 버렸구나 　　　이제 　호되게!

To have impudently / fallen asleep / on such a young lady's
건방지게 　　　　잠이 들어 버리다니 　저 어린 숙녀의 의자 위에서!

chair! She would be turned / out of doors / without wages.
내쫓기고 말 상황이었다 　문 밖으로 　　월급도 못 받고!

She made a sound / like a big breathless sob.
베키는 소리 내었다 　숨막히도록 크게 우는 듯이.

"Oh, miss! Oh, miss!" / she stuttered. "I arst yer pardon,
"아, 아가씨! 　아, 아가씨!" 　더듬거리며 말했다. 　"제발 부탁이에요, 아가씨!

miss! Oh, I do, miss!"
아, 부탁이에요, 아가씨!"

Sara jumped down, / and came quite close / to her.
새라는 뛰어 내려, 　　가까이 다가갔다 　　그 아이에게.

"Don't be frightened," / she said, / quite as if she had
"두려워하지 마." 새라가 말했다. 마치 말하고 있는 것처럼

been speaking / to a little girl / like herself. "It doesn't
여자 아이에게 자신과 같은. "그것은 중요하지 않아

matter / the least bit."
조금도."

"I didn't go to do it, / miss," / protested Becky. "It was
"그러려고 한 것이 아니었어요, 아가씨." 베키가 항변했다. "그것은

the warm fire / — an' me bein' so tired. It — it wasn't
"따뜻한 난롯불이어서 — 그리고 제가 아주 피곤해서. 그것은 — 건방진 생각으로

imperence!"
한 것은 아니었어요!"

Sara broke into a friendly little laugh, / and put her hand
새라는 다정한 웃음을 살짝 터뜨리고, 손을 올려 놓았다

/ on her shoulder.
베키의 어깨에.

Key Expression 🍎

'find oneself~' 표현의 해석

find oneself는 '(자신이 어떤 장소, 상태에 있음을) 알다'라는 의미를 가진 숙어입니다. 뒤에는 형용사, 현재분사, 과거분사, 장소의 부사구가 옵니다.
하지만 이 표현을 사용한 문장은 직역하기 보다는 be동사 역할로 해석하는 것이 자연스러워요. 특히 문학작품 속에서는 be동사 대신 이 표현을 쓰는 경우가 많답니다.

ex) She found herself staring in wild alarm at the wonderful pupil.
그녀는 깜짝 놀라며 그 굉장한 학생을 바라보았다.
She found herself confronting a rather pathetic picture.
그녀는 매우 측은한 광경을 맞닥뜨리게 되었다.

---

flaming 불타는 | perplexity 당혹감 | fender (벽난로 앞에 세워 두는) 난로망 | perched ~에 앉아 있는 | with a vengeance 호되게, 맹렬히 | impudently 건방지게, 경솔하게 | matter 중요하다 | imperence 뻔뻔스러움, 무례함

"You were tired," / she said; / "you could not help it. You
"넌 피곤했잖니,"　　　그녀가 말했다;　"너도 어쩔 수 없었잖아.

are not really awake yet."
아직도 완전히 깨어나지 못했네."

How poor Becky stared at her! In fact, / she had never
너무도 가엾은 베키가 그녀를 바라보았다!　사실,　한 번도 들은 적이 없었다

heard / such a nice, friendly sound / in anyone's voice
그렇게 상냥하고, 친절한 소리를　어느 누구에게도

/ before. She was used to / being ordered about / and
전에.　베키는 익숙했다　명령 받거나

scolded, / and having her ears boxed. And this one / —
꾸중을 듣고,　따귀를 맞는 것에.　그런데 이 사람은

in her rose-colored dancing afternoon splendor — / was
— 장밋빛의 화려한 댄스복을 입은 —

looking at her / as if she were not a culprit / at all / — as
보고 있었다　마치 자신은 죄인이 아닌 것처럼　전혀

if she had a right / to be tired — / even to fall asleep!
— 마치 권리가 있는 듯　피곤해도 되는 —　심지어 잠이 들 수도 있는!

Key Expression ❓

be used to -ing : ~하는 데 익숙하다

be used to는 '~에 익숙하다'라는 뜻의 숙어인데, 여기에서 to는 전치사이므
로 뒤에는 동명사가 와야 합니다. 같은 뜻의 표현으로 be accustomed to
-ing가 있습니다.
또한 be 동사 대신 get를 쓰기도 하는데, 이 경우에는 '익숙해지다'라는 의미
가 강조됩니다.

ex) She was used to being ordered about and scolded, and having her ears
boxed.
그녀는 명령 받거나 꾸중을 듣고 따귀를 맞는 데 익숙했다.

---

splendor 화려함, 광채 | woeful 몹시 슬픈, 비통한 | smutted 검댕이 묻은 | grasp 움켜잡다, 이해하다 | run
over 차로 치다

The touch of the soft, slim little paw / on her shoulder /
부드럽고, 가녀린 작은 손길이　　　　　　　그녀의 어깨 위에 얹혀진

was the most amazing thing / she had ever known.
가장 놀라운 것이었다　　　　　　알고 있던.

"Ain't — ain't yer angry, / miss?" / she gasped. "Ain't
"저기 — 화 안 나세요,　　　　아가씨?"　베키가 숨을 내쉬었다.

yer goin' to tell the missus?"
"마님께 말하지 않으실 거예요?"

"No," / cried out Sara. "Of course / I'm not."
"안 해,"　　새라가 외쳤다.　　"물론　　안 할 거야."

The woeful fright / in the coal-smutted face / made her
애달픈 두려움이　　　석탄재가 묻은 얼굴에 떠오른

suddenly so sorry / that she could scarcely bear it. One
매우 가엾게 느껴져서　　　좀처럼 참을 수 없었다.

of her queer thoughts / rushed into her mind. She put her
신기한 생각 중 하나가　　　마음속에 급히 떠올랐다.　　새라는 손을 얹었다

hand / against Becky's cheek.
　　　베키의 뺨에.

"Why," / she said, / "we are just the same / — I am only
"저기,"　　그녀가 말했다,　"우리는 똑같아　　　— 나도 그냥 어린

a little girl / like you. It's just an accident / that I am not
여자 아이야　　너처럼.　그냥 사고일 뿐이지　　내가 네가 아니고,

you, / and you are not me!"
네가 내가 아닌 것은!"

Becky did not understand / in the least. Her mind could
베키는 이해할 수 없었다　　　조금도.　　베키의 생각으로는 이해할 수

not grasp / such amazing thoughts, / and "an accident" /
없었다　　그런 놀라운 생각들을,　　　그리고 "사고"라는 것은

meant to her a calamity / in which someone was run over
그녀에게 재앙을 의미했다　　　누군가 차에 치였거나

/ or fell off a ladder / and was carried to "the 'orspital."
사다리에서 떨어졌거나　　"병원"으로 옮겨지는 것과 같은.

"A' accident, / miss," / she fluttered / respectfully. "Is it?"
"사고라고요,　　아가씨,"　심장이 팔딱거렸다　공손히.　　　"그게요?"

"Yes," / Sara answered, / and she looked at her / dreamily /
"맞아," 새라가 대답했다. 그리고 그녀를 보았다 꿈꾸듯이

for a moment. But the next / she spoke / in a different tone.
잠시 동안. 하지만 다음 순간 말했다 다른 말투로.

She realized / that Becky did not know / what she meant.
그녀는 깨달았다 베키가 모른다는 것을 자신이 의미하는 바를.

"Have you done your work?" / she asked. "Dare you stay
"넌 일을 다 끝냈니? 그녀가 물었다. "혹시 여기 머무를 수 있니

here / a few minutes?"
몇 분간?"

Becky lost her breath / again.
베키는 숨을 멈췄다 다시.

"Here, miss? Me?"
"여기예요, 아가씨? 제가요?"

Sara ran to the door, / opened it, / and looked out / and
새라는 문으로 달려가서, 문을 열고, 밖을 살피며

listened.
귀 기울였다.

"No one is anywhere / about," / she explained. "If your
"아무도 없어 근처에," 그녀가 설명했다.

bedrooms are finished, / perhaps / you might stay / a tiny
"만약 침실 정리가 끝났으면, 아마도 머무를 수 있을 거야

while. I thought / — perhaps — / you might like a piece of
잠시 동안. 내 생각에 — 아마도 — 넌 케이크를 좋아할 것 같은데."

cake."

The next ten minutes / seemed to Becky / like a sort of
다음 10분 동안은 베키에게 보였다 마치 일종의 망상처럼.

delirium. Sara opened a cupboard, / and gave her / a thick
새라는 찬장을 열어서, 베키에게 주었다 두툼한 케이

slice of cake. She seemed to rejoice / when it was devoured
크 한 조각을. 새라는 기뻐 보였다 베키가 걸신 들린 듯 먹어 치울 때

---

delirium 망상, 헛소리 | rejoice 크게 기뻐하다 | devour 걸신 들린 듯 먹다 | boldness 대담함 | longingly
갈망하며, 간절한 마음으로 | swell 명사(名士), 멋쟁이 | cloak 망토

/ in hungry bites. She talked / and asked questions, /
배고파서 덥석.　　　　새라는 말을 걸고　　질문을 했으며,

and laughed / until Becky's fears actually began to calm
웃었다　　　　베키의 두려움이 실제로 잠잠해질 때까지,

themselves, / and she once or twice gathered boldness /
그리고 베키는 한두 번 용기를 내었다

enough to ask a question or so / herself, / daring / as she
질문 한두 개를 할 만큼　　　　　　스스로,　　감히

felt it to be.
그래도 될까 생각하며.

"Is that — " / she ventured, / looking longingly / at the
"저기 —"　　베키가 조심스레 말했다,　　갈망하듯 보면서

rose-colored frock. And she asked it / almost in a whisper.
장밋빛 드레스를.　　　　그리고 그녀는 물었다　　거의 속삭이듯이.

"Is that there your best?"
"그 옷이 가장 좋은 건가요?"

"It is one of my dancing-frocks," / answered Sara. "I like
"이것은 내 무용복 중 하나야,"　　　　새라가 대답했다.　　"난 이것이

it, / don't you?"
좋아, 그렇지 않니?"

For a few seconds / Becky was almost speechless / with
잠시 동안　　　　베키는 거의 할 말을 잃었다

admiration. Then she said / in an awed voice, / "Onct /
감탄하면서.　　그리고 말했다　　겁먹은 목소리로,　　"언젠가

I see a princess. / I was standin' / in the street / with the
공주님을 봤어요.　　난 서 있었어요　　거리에　　군중들과 함께

crowd / outside Covin' Garden, / watchin' the swells / go
코빈 가든 밖에,　　　　멋진 사람들을 보면서

inter the operer. An' there was one / everyone stared at /
오페라 극장으로 들어가는. 그리고 한 명이 있었죠　　모두 쳐다보는

most. They ses to each other, / 'That's the princess.' She
가장 많이. 그들은 서로에게 말했어요,　　'저분이 공주님이야.'

was a growed-up young lady, / but she was pink all over
그녀는 다 자란 젊은 숙녀였는데,　　　　모두 분홍색이었어요

/ — gownd / an' cloak, / an' flowers / an' all. I called her /
— 외투와　　망토와,　　꽃도　　모든 것이. 난 그녀가 생각났어요

99

to mind / the minnit I see you, / sittin' there / on the table, /
마음속에 아가씨를 본 순간, 저기 앉아 있는 탁자 위에,

miss. You looked like her."
아가씨. 아가씨는 그 공주님같아요."

"I've often thought," / said Sara, / in her reflecting voice, /
"난 종종 생각했었지," 새라가 말했다. 생각에 잠긴 목소리로,

"that I should like to be a princess; / I wonder / what it feels
"나도 공주가 되고 싶다고; 궁금해 그것이 어떤 느낌일지.

like. I believe / I will begin pretending / I am one."
생각해 그런 척 해 보려고 내가 공주라고."

Becky stared at her / admiringly, / and, / as before, / did
베키는 그녀를 보았다 존경의 눈빛으로, 그리고. 전처럼,

not understand her / in the least. She watched her / with a
그녀를 이해할 수 없었다 조금도. 베키는 그녀를 보았다

sort of adoration. Very soon / Sara left her reflections / and
흠모하듯. 곧바로 새라는 정신을 차리고

turned to her / with a new question.
베키를 돌아보았다 새로운 질문을 하며.

"Becky," / she said, / "weren't you listening / to that story?"
"베키," 그녀가 말했다. 듣고 있었지 그 이야기를?"

"Yes, miss," / confessed Becky, / a little alarmed / again.
"네, 아가씨," 베키가 고백했다. 약간 놀라며 다시.

"I knowed I hadn't orter, / but it was that beautiful / I — I
"제가 그러면 안 되는 것을 알아요. 하지만 이야기가 멋져서 전 — 어쩔 수 없었어요."

couldn't help it."
전 — 어쩔 수 없었어요."

"I liked you to listen to it," / said Sara. "If you tell stories,
"네가 그 이야기를 들어줘서 좋았어," 새라가 말했다. "이야기를 하는 사람은,

/ you like nothing so much / as to tell them / to people who
가장 좋아하거든 이야기를 들려주는 것을 듣고 싶어 하는 사람에게.

want to listen. I don't know why it is. Would you like to
왜 그런지는 모르겠어. 나머지를 듣고 싶니?"

hear the rest?"

Becky lost her breath / again.
베키는 숨을 멈췄다 다시.

"Me hear it?" / she cried. "Like as if I was a pupil, /
"제가 들어도 되나요?   베키는 소리쳤다. "제가 학생처럼,

miss! All about the Prince / — and the little white Mer-
아가씨! 왕자에 대한 모든 것을   — 그리고 작고 하얀 인어 아기들 이야기를

babies / swimming about laughing / — with stars / in
웃으며 헤엄치는   — 별을 달고

their hair?"
머리에는?"

Sara nodded.
새라가 끄덕였다.

"You haven't time to hear it / now, / I'm afraid," / she
"그 이야기를 들을 시간은 없어   지금,   유감이지만."   새라가

said; "but if you will tell me / just what time you come /
말했다: "하지만 네가 나한테 알려 주면   네가 오는 시간을

to do my rooms, / I will try to be here / and tell you a bit
내 방을 정리하러.   내가 여기에 있으면서   조금씩 말해 줄게

of it / every day / until it is finished. It's a lovely long one
그것에 대해   매일   이야기가 끝날 때까지.   그것은 아름답고 긴 이야기야

/ — and I'm always putting new bits / to it."
— 그리고 난 항상 새로운 이야기를 집어 넣지   거기에."

Key Expression ♥

부정 의문문에 대답하기

부정의 의미를 담아 질문 했을 경우 우리말 식으로 생각하여 헷갈리는 경우가 많죠. 따라서 부정의문문에서 not을 빼고 해석하면 질문과 대답이 모두 자연스럽게 해석이 됩니다.

영어의 경우 의문문에 대한 대답은 질문에 상관없이 긍정의 대답이면 Yes, 부정의 대답이면 No를 사용합니다.

ex) A: Becky, weren't you listening to that story?
    베키, 너 그 이야기를 듣고 있었지?
    B : Yes, miss.
    네, 아가씨.

---

admiringly 감탄하여 | adoration 흠모, 경배 | reflection 거울에 비친 모습, (깊은) 생각

"Then," / breathed Becky, / devoutly, / "I wouldn't mind
"그러면," 베키가 숨을 쉬며 말했다, 간곡히, "난 괜찮을 거예요

/ how heavy the coal boxes was / — or what the cook
석탄 상자가 아무리 무거워도 — 아니면 요리사가 무슨 짓을 해도,

done to me, / if — if I might have that / to think of."
만약 — 만약 내가 그것을 듣게 된다고 생각하면."

"You may," / said Sara. "I'll tell it all / to you."
"넌 듣게 될 거야," 새라가 말했다. "내가 모두 말해 줄게 네게."

When Becky went downstairs, / she was not the same
베키가 아래층에 내려갔을 때, 그녀는 예전의 베키가 아니었다

Becky / who had staggered up, / loaded down / by the
비틀거렸던, 짐을 지고

weight of the coal scuttle. She had an extra piece of cake /
무거운 석탄통의. 베키는 케이크 한 조각을 더 갖고 있었다

in her pocket, / and she had been fed / and warmed, / but
주머니에, 그리고 배가 부르고 따뜻했다.

not only by cake and fire. Something else / had warmed
단지 케이크와 난롯불 때문이 아니었다. 다른 뭔가가 그 아이를 따뜻하고 배

and fed her, / and the something else was Sara.
부르게 해 주었다. 그 다른 뭔가는 바로 새라였다.

When she was gone / Sara sat / on her favorite perch / on
베키가 떠나자 새라는 앉았다 가장 좋아하는 자리에

the end of her table. Her feet were on a chair, / her elbows
탁자의 끝에 있는. 다리를 의자 위에 두고,

on her knees, / and her chin in her hands.
팔꿈치를 무릎에 대고, 뺨은 두 손으로 받쳤다.

"If I was a princess / — a real princess," / she murmured,
"내가 공주라면 — 진짜 공주라면," 그녀는 중얼거렸다,

/ "I could scatter largess / to the populace. But even if I
"선물을 아낌없이 나눠줬을 텐데 백성들에게.

am only a pretend princess, / I can invent / little things to
하지만 내가 가짜 공주라 하더라도, 난 만들 수 있어 할 수 있는 작은 일을

do / for people. Things like this. She was just as happy as
사람들을 위해. 이와 같은 이야기들을. 그 아이는 기뻐했어

/ if it was largess. I'll pretend that / to do things people
마치 그것이 선물인 듯. 난 그런 척 하겠어 사람들이 좋아하는 일은

like / is scattering largess. I've scattered largess."
선물을 베푸는 것이라고. 난 많은 것을 베풀었잖아."

devoutly 진심으로, 간곡히 | stagger 비틀거리다 | murmur 속삭이다, 중얼거리다 | scatter 뿌리다 | largess
아낌없이 줌, (아낌없이 주어진) 선물 | populace 대중들, 사람들

103

A. 다음 문장을 해석해 보세요.

(1) Anyone who has been at school / with a teller of stories / knows / what the wonder means.
→

(2) As she was doing it the third time, / the sound of the story so lured her to listen / that she fell under the spell / and actually forgot / that she had no right / to listen / at all.
→

(3) I do not know / whether your mamma would like / you to tell stories to servant girls, / but I know / my mamma wouldn't like me / to do it.
→

(4) She took a seat / on the edge of the table, / and sat / swinging her slim, rose-colored legs, / and wondering / what it would be best to do.
→

B. 다음 주어진 문장이 되도록 빈칸에 써 넣으세요.

(1) 새라 아가씨가 묻는 것이 당연하다.

→

(2) 마리에트는 새라를 가능한 한 하늘하늘하고 멋지게 꾸며 주라고 지시받았다.

Mariette was requested [   ]
[   ].

(3) 사실을 말하자면, 그녀는 그곳에서 그 장면을 보게 되어 매우 기뻤다.

[   ], she was quite glad to find it there.

A. (1) 이야기꾼과 함께 학교에 다녔던 사람이면 누구나 그 놀라움이 의미하는 바를 알고 있다. (2) 그녀는 세 번째 쓸고 있을 때에는, 마법에 빠져버린 듯 이야기 소리에 정신이 빼앗겨 자신에게는 들을 수 있는 권리가 전혀 없다는 것을 실제로 잊어버렸다. (3) 네 엄마는 네가 하녀 아이에게 이야기 해 주는 것

(4) 베키는 명령 받거나 꾸중을 듣는 데 익숙했다.

→

C. 다음 주어진 문구가 알맞은 문장이 되도록 순서를 맞춰 보세요.

(1) 새라는 <u>이야기를 들려줄 뿐만 아니라, 이야기 하는 것을 좋아했다.</u>
(only / stories, / but / them / not / telling / adored / she /
could tell / Sara)
→

(2) 그녀는 매우 측은한 광경을 맞닥뜨리게 되었다.
(herself / found / picture / She / rather / pathetic / a
/ confronting)
→

(3) 그것은 조금도 중요하지 않아.
(least / doesn't / It / bit / the / matter)
→

(4) 그것이 어떤 느낌일지 궁금해.
(it / like / wonder / I / feels / what)
→

D. 다음 단어에 대한 맞는 설명과 연결해 보세요.

(1) dodge   ▶   ◀ ① reply angrily to someone

(2) retort   ▶   ◀ ② eat quickly and eagerly

(3) perplexity   ▶   ◀ ③ move suddenly

(4) devour   ▶   ◀ ④ being confused and frustrated

5

In the Attic
다락방에서

The first night / she spent in her attic / was a thing / Sara
첫날 밤은　　　　그녀가 다락방에서 보낸　　　것이었다　　　새라가

never forgot. During its passing / she lived through / a
절대 잊을 수 없는.　그 시간이 지나는 동안　　사라는 겪었다　　　어린 아이

wild, unchildlike woe / of which she never spoke / to
에게 어울리지 않는 끔찍한 고통을　　절대 이야기 하지 않은

anyone / about her. There was no one / who would have
누구에게도　그녀 주변의.　아무도 없었다　　　이해해 줄 사람은.

understood. It was, / indeed, / well for her / that as she lay
　　　　　그것은,　　진짜로,　　그녀에게 다행이었다　눈뜬 채 누워 있는 동안

awake / in the darkness / her mind was forcibly distracted,
깨어　　　어둠 속에서　　　마음이 매우 산만해진 것은,

/ now and then, / by the strangeness of her surroundings.
이따금,　　　　　이 낯선 환경에.

It was, / perhaps, / well for her / that she was reminded /
그것은,　　아마도,　　그녀에게는 다행이었다　기억하는 것은

by her small body / of material things. If this had not been
그녀의 작은 몸이　　　　물질적인 고통을.　　그렇지 않았다면,

so, / the anguish of her young mind / might have been too
　　새라의 어린 마음의 고통은　　　　　너무 컸을 것이다

great / for a child to bear. But, / really, / while the night
아이가 견뎌내기에는.　　하지만,　사실,　　그 밤이 지나는 동안

was passing / she scarcely knew / that she had a body at
　　　　그녀는 거의 몰랐거나　　자신의 몸에 대해서나

all / or remembered / any other thing than one.
　　생각하지 못했다　　한 가지 사실 외에는.

"My papa is dead!" / she kept whispering to herself. "My
"아빠가 돌아가셨어!"　　　　새라는 계속 중얼거렸다.

papa is dead!"
"우리 아빠가 돌아가셨어!"

---

attic 다락방 | unchildlike 아이에게 맞지 않는 | woe 비통, 비애 | distracted 정신이 산만해진 | anguish (극심한)
괴로움, 비통 | scuffling 획획 (움직이는 소리) | scratching 긁는 소리 | squeaking 찍 하는 소리 | skirting board
굽도리 널 | rat 쥐 | mouse 생쥐 | recall 기억해내다 | bedclothes 이부자리 | gradually 서서히

It was not until long / afterward / that she realized / that
머지않아   그 이후   새라는 깨달았다

her bed had been so hard / that she turned over and over
침대가 너무 딱딱해서   몸을 계속 뒤척이고 있다는 것이나

/ in it / to find a place to rest, / that the darkness seemed
침대에서 편하게 쉴 곳을 찾으려고.   어둠은 더 깊어 보인다는 것이나

more intense / than any she had ever known, / and that the
                자신이 알고 있던 어떤 어둠보다도,   바람 소리가 울부짖는

wind howled / over the roof / among the chimneys / like
소리로 들린다는 것을   지붕 위에서   굴뚝 사이의

something which wailed aloud. Then / there was something
뭔가 크게 울부짖는 것처럼.   그리고   더욱 끔찍한 것이 있었다.

worse. This was certain scufflings and scratchings / and
이것은 바로 휙휙하고며 박박 긁는 소리와

squeakings / in the walls and behind the skirting boards.
찍찍거리는 소리였다   벽 안쪽과 굽도리 널 뒤쪽에서.

She knew / what they meant, / because Becky had described
새라는 알고 있었다 그것이 무슨 소리인지.   베키가 그것을 설명해 줬기 때문에.

them. They meant rats and mice / who were either fighting
그것은 쥐와 생쥐들이었다   싸우거나

/ with each other / or playing together. Once or twice / she
서로   함께 놀고 있는.   한두 번은

even heard / sharp-toed feet / scurrying across the floor,
들리기도 했다   날카로운 발톱이 달린 발이 마룻바닥을 지나 총총 뛰어다니는 소리가.

/ and she remembered in those / after days, / when she
새라는 그것들을 기억해냈다   며칠 후,

recalled things, / that when first she heard them / she started
그것들을 회상했을 때,   처음 그 소리를 들었던 때   깜짝 놀라 침대에

up in bed / and sat trembling, / and when she lay down
서 일어나서   벌벌 떨며 앉아 있다가,   다시 누웠을 때를

again / covered her head with the bedclothes.
          이불을 머리 끝까지 뒤집어 쓴 채.

The change / in her life / did not come about gradually, / but
변화는   그녀의 삶의   서서히 온 것이 아니라,

was made / all at once.
변해 버렸다   갑자기.

"She must begin / as she is to go on," / Miss Minchin
"그 애는 시작해야 해   계속 있겠다면,"   민친 교장이 말했다

said / to Miss Amelia. "She must be taught / at once /
아멜리아 선생에게.   "그 애는 배워야 해   당장

what she is to expect."
하게 될 일들을."

Mariette had left the house / the next morning. The
마리에트는 그 집을 떠났다   다음 날 아침.

glimpse / Sara caught of her sitting room, / as she passed
잠깐의 광경은   새라가 자신의 거실을 얼핏 보았을 때,   열린 문을 지나가면서,

its open door, / showed her / that everything had been
보여 줬다   모든 것이 바뀌어 버렸음을.

changed. Her ornaments and luxuries had been removed,
새라의 장식품들과 호화로운 물건들은 사라졌고,

/ and a bed had been placed / in a corner / to transform it
침대 하나가 놓여 있었다   구석에   그 방을 바꾸기 위해

/ into a new pupil's bedroom.
새 학생의 침실로.

Key Expression 🎔

전치사 into의 의미

'~로'의 뜻을 가진 전치사 into은 변화나 방향의 뜻을 지니고 있습니다.
change, transform, translate 등 변화를 의미하는 동사와 함께 A
into B의 형태로 쓰이면 'A를 B로', go, come 등 이동을 의미하는 동사와 함께
쓰이면 '~ 안으로'라는 뜻이 됩니다.

ex) Her ornaments and luxuries had been removed, and a bed had been placed
in a corner to transform it into a new pupil's bedroom.
그 방을 새 학생의 침실로 바꾸기 위해 새라의 장식품들과 호화로운 물건들은
사라지고 구석에 침대 하나가 놓여 있었다. (변화의 into)
She grudgingly allowed to go into the deserted schoolroom.
그녀는 버려진 교실로 들어가는 것을 겨우 허락 받았다. (방향의 into)

---

ornament 장식품 | transform 완전히 바꿔 놓다 | behave well 예의 바르게 행동하다 | from day to day
나날이 | errand 심부름 | neglect 방치하다, (해야 할 일을) 하지 않다

When she went down / to breakfast / she saw / that her seat
새라가 내려갔을 때 / 아침을 먹으러 / 보았다 / 자신의 자리에

/ at Miss Minchin's side / was occupied by Lavinia, / and
민친 교장의 옆의 / 라비니아가 앉아 있는 것을,

Miss Minchin spoke to her / coldly.
그리고 민친 교장이 말했다 / 냉정하게.

"You will begin your new duties, / Sara," / she said, / "by
"넌 네 새로운 일을 시작해야 해, / 새라," / 교장이 말했다, / "

taking your seat / with the younger children / at a smaller
"자리에 앉아서 / 어린 학생들과 / 더 작은 테이블에.

table. You must keep them quiet, / and see that they behave
그 애들을 조용히 시켜야 해 / 그리고 예절 바르게 행동하는지 보고

well / and do not waste their food. You ought to have been
음식을 흘리지 않게 해라. / 좀 더 일찍 내려왔어야 했어.

down earlier. Lottie has already upset her tea."
로티가 이미 차를 엎질렀잖니."

That was the beginning, / and from day to day / the duties
그것은 시작이었다. / 그리고 나날이 / 새라에게 주어진

given to her / were added to. She taught the younger
임무가 / 늘어났다. / 어린 아이들에게 프랑스어를 가르쳤고

children French / and heard their other lessons, / and these
어린 학생들의 다른 수업도 들었다, / 그리고 이것들은

were the least / of her labors. It was found / that she could
가장 작은 것이었다 / 그녀의 노동 중에. / 알고 보니

be made use of / in numberless directions. She could be
새라는 쓸모 있었다 / 수많은 곳에.

sent on errands / at any time / and in all weathers. She
심부름을 보낼 수 있었다 / 언제든지 / 어떤 날씨에도.

could be told to do / things other people neglected. The
하라고 시킬 수 있었다 / 다른 사람들이 내버려둔 일을.

cook and the housemaids / took their tone from Miss
요리사와 하녀들은 / 민친 교장을 말투를 흉내 내며,

Minchin, / and rather enjoyed ordering / about the "young
명령하는 걸 꽤 즐겼다 / 그 "어린 아이"에게

one" / who had been made so much fuss / over for so long.
야단법석을 떨게 만들었던 / 매우 오랫동안.

109

They were not servants of the best class, / and had
그들은 훌륭한 계급의 하인이 아니었고,

neither good manners / nor good tempers, / and it was
좋은 매너도   좋은 성격도 갖지 못했다,

frequently convenient / to have at hand / someone / on
그래서 종종 편리했다   가까이 두는 것이   누군가를

whom blame could be laid.
잘못을 뒤집어 씌울 수 있는.

During the first month or two, / Sara thought / that her
한두 달 동안,   새라는 생각했다

willingness to do things / as well as she could, / and her
기꺼이 일을 하고   최선을 다해,

silence under reproof, / might soften / those who drove
꾸중을 들을 때도 침묵하며 참으면,   누그러뜨릴지 모른다고 자신을 아주 힘들게 몰아가는

her so hard. In her proud little heart / she wanted them
사람들을.   자존심 강한 어린 마음 속에서   새라는 그들이 봐 줬으면 했다

to see / that she was trying / to earn her living / and not
그녀가 노력하는 것을   밥벌이를 하려고

accepting charity. But the time came / when she saw /
동정 받지 않고.   하지만 시간이 흘러   새라는 알게 되었다

that no one was softened / at all; / and the more willing /
아무도 누그러들지 않는다는 사실을   전혀;   그리고 기꺼이 하면 할수록

she was to do / as she was told, / the more domineering
새라가   명령대로,   더 위세를 떨며 까다롭게 굴면서

and exacting / careless housemaids became, / and the
경솔한 하녀들은,   더욱 준비를 갖출

more ready / a scolding cook was / to blame her.
뿐이었다   잔소리가 심한 요리사는   그녀를 꾸짖으려고.

If she had been older, / Miss Minchin would have given
만약 새라가 좀 더 나이가 많았다면,   민친 교장은 그녀에게 시키고

her / the bigger girls to teach / and saved money / by
더 큰 여자애들을 가르치라고   돈을 절약했을 것이다

---

* h로로 시작하는 단어의 h음을 빼고 발음하는 것은 런던 사투리의 특징이다.

willingness 자진하여 하기, 기꺼이 함 | reproof 책망, 꾸지람 | earn one's living 입에 풀칠하다 | charity
자선, 너그러움, 관용 | domineering 위세 떠는, 지배하려 드는 | exacting 힘든, 까다로운 | scolding 잔소리가
심한 | dismiss 해고하다 | instructress 여교사 | reliable 믿을 수 있는 | combine (두 가지 이상의 일을)
병행하다 | grudgingly 마지못해, 억지로 | deserted 버려진, 황량한

dismissing an instructress; / but while she remained and
교사를 해고함으로써; 하지만 새라가 아이 모습으로 남아있는 동안,

looked like a child, / she could be made more useful /
그녀는 더 유용했다

as a sort of little superior errand girl / and maid of all
훌륭한 심부름꾼으로나 모든 일을 시키는 하녀로.

work. An ordinary errand boy / would not have been so
보통의 심부름꾼 아이는 그렇게 똑똑하고 믿음직스럽지 못할

clever and reliable. Sara could be trusted / with difficult
것이었다. 새라는 믿음이 갔다 어려운 임무나

commissions / and complicated messages. She could even
복잡한 전갈을 맡겨도. 그녀는 가서 돈을 지불할

go and pay bills, / and she combined with this / the ability
수도 했고, 이 일과 병행했다

to dust a room well / and to set things in order.
방을 청소하거나 물건들을 정리하는 일도.

Her own lessons / became things of the past. She was
새라의 공부는 과거의 일이 되어버렸다. 그녀는 아무것도

taught nothing, / and only after long and busy days / spent
배우지 못했고, 길고 바쁜 하루가 끝난 후에야

in running here and there / at everybody's orders / was she
여기저기를 뛰어다니며 보낸 모든 사람의 명령을 받으며

grudgingly allowed / to go into the deserted schoolroom, /
겨우 허락 받았다 버려진 교실로 들어가서,

with a pile of old books, / and study alone / at night.
낡은 책들 한 무더기를 갖고, 혼자 공부하는 것을 밤에.

"If I do not remind myself / of the things I have learned,
"내가 스스로 기억하지 못하면 내가 배웠던 것들을,

/ perhaps I may forget them," / she said to herself. "I am
아마 난 다 잊어버릴지 몰라." 그녀는 혼잣말을 했다.

almost a scullery maid, / and if I am a scullery maid / who
"난 거의 부엌데기야. 그리고 내가 부엌데기가 되면

knows nothing, / I shall be like poor Becky. I wonder / if
아무것도 모르는, 불쌍한 베키처럼 되고 말 거야. 어쩌면

I could quite forget / and begin to / *drop my h's / and not
다 잊어버리게 될지도 h음을 빼먹기 시작하고 기억하지 못할

remember / that Henry the Eighth had six wives."
지도 몰라 헨리 8세에게 여섯 명의 부인이 있었다는 것도."

111

One of the most curious things / in her new existence /
가장 흥미로운 일 중 하나는   새라의 새로운 삶에서

was her changed position / among the pupils. Instead of
그녀의 바뀐 위치였다   학생들 사이에서.

being a sort of small royal personage / among them, /
어린 왕족이 되는 대신에   그들 사이에서,

she no longer seemed / to be one of their number / at all.
그녀는 더 이상 보이지 않았다   그들의 무리 중 하나로   전혀.

She was kept so constantly at work / that she scarcely
새라는 쉴새없이 일하느라   좀처럼 기회가 없었고

ever had an opportunity / of speaking / to any of them,
                      말할   그들 중 누구에게도,

/ and she could not avoid seeing / that Miss Minchin
그리고 알 수밖에 없었다   민친 교장이 원한다는 사실을

preferred / that she should live a life / apart from that of
          새라가 살아야 한다고   학생들과 떨어져서

the occupants / of the schoolroom.
              교실의.

"I will not have / her forming intimacies and talking
"난 내버려두지 않겠어   그 애가 친해지고 이야기 나누도록

/ to the other children," / that lady said. "Girls like a
다른 아이들과."   교장은 말했다.   "여자 아이들은 불평하기를

grievance, / and if she begins to tell / romantic stories
좋아하니까   만약 저 애가 말하기 시작하면

about herself, / she will become an ill-used heroine, /
자신에 대한 이야기를,   그 애는 학대 받는 여주인공이 될 것이고,

and parents will be given a wrong impression. It is better
부모들은 안 좋은 인상을 받겠지.   훨씬 낫지

/ that she should live a separate life / — one suited to
저 애가 격리된 삶을 사는 것이   — 저 애 환경에 맞는.

her circumstances. I am giving her a home, / and that is
          난 저 애에게 집을 주고 있으니,   그것은 그 이상이야

more than / she has any right to expect from me."
          저 애가 내게서 기대할 수 있는 권리보다.

existence 존재 | personage 저명인사 | constantly 끊임없이 | intimacy 친밀함 | grievance 불만, 고충 (사항)
| awkward 어색한, 불편한 | matter-of-fact (감정 표현 없이) 사무적인 | accustomed 익숙한 | shabby 허름한,
해진 | established 인정받는, 확실히 자리잡은 | under servant 잔심부름꾼, 잔심부름하는 하녀

Sara did not expect much, / and was far too proud / to try
새라는 많은 것을 기대하지 않았고,　자존심이 너무 세서　계속 친하게

to continue to be intimate / with girls / who evidently felt
지내려고 애쓰지도 않았다　여자애들과　느낄 것이 뻔한

/ rather awkward and uncertain about her. The fact was
자신에 대해 어색하고 불확실하게.　사실은

/ that Miss Minchin's pupils were / a set of dull, matter-
민친 교장의 학생들은　둔감하고 감정을 드러내지 않는

of-fact young people. They were accustomed to / being
아이들이었다.　그들은 익숙했다　부유하고

rich / and comfortable, / and as Sara's frocks grew shorter
편안한 것에,　그래서 새라의 드레스가 점점 더 짧아지고

/ and shabbier / and queerer-looking, / and it became an
더 초라해져서　이상하게 변하자,　기정 사실이 되어버렸다

established fact / that she wore shoes with holes in them /
사라가 구멍 난 신발을 신고

and was sent out / to buy groceries and carry them / through
밖으로 나가서　식료품을 사 오는 것이

the streets / in a basket / on her arm / when the cook wanted
거리를 지나　바구니를 들고　한쪽 팔에　요리사가 시킬 때면 언제나

them / in a hurry, / they felt rather / as if, / when they spoke
서둘러,　그들은 다소 느꼈다　마치,　자신들이 새라에게 말을 걸면,

to her, / they were addressing an under servant.
잔심부름꾼한테 말하는 것이라고.

Key Expression

부정의 의미를 지닌 부사의 위치

hardly, scarcely, seldom, rarely 등 부정의 의미를 지닌 부사는 빈도부사처럼 be 동사 앞, 조동사 뒤, 일반동사 앞에 위치합니다.

▶ hardly (ever), scarcely (ever), barely : 거의 ~않다(정도, 양)
▶ seldom, rarely : 좀처럼 ~않다(횟수)

ex) She scarcely ever had an opportunity of speaking to any of them.
　　그녀는 좀처럼 그들 중 누구에게도 말할 기회가 없었다.

"To think / that she was the girl with the diamond mines,"
"생각했다니   저 애가 다이아몬드 광산을 가진 아이라고."

/ Lavinia commented. "She does look an object. And she's
라비니아가 말했다.   "참 볼 만 하지.

queerer than ever. I never liked her much, / but I can't bear
예전보다 더 이상해졌어.   난 그 아이를 절대 좋아하지 않았지만,   그런데 참을 수 없어

/ that way she has now / of looking at people / without
저 애가 요즘 하는 방식이   사람을 쳐다보는

speaking / — just as if she was finding them out."
말없이   — 마치 그들에 대해 알아내려고 하듯."

"I am," / said Sara, / promptly, / when she heard of this.
"맞아,"   새라가 말했다,   즉시,   이 말을 들었을 때.

"That's what I look at some people for. I like to know /
"그것이 바로 내가 사람들을 쳐다보는 이유야.   난 알고 싶어

about them. I think them over / afterward."
사람들에 대해.   그에 대해 곰곰히 생각하지   나중에."

Key Expression ♪

비교급 + 비교급 : 점점 더 ~한

비교급 + 비교급은 '점점 더 ~한'이라는 의미를 가진 관용표현입니다.
become, grow, get가 같은 상태 변화를 나타내는 2형식 동사 뒤에 쓰이면
'점점 더 ~해지다'라는 뜻이 됩니다.

ex) As Sara's frocks grew shorter and shabbier and queerer-looking, and it
    became an established fact.
    새라의 드레스가 점점 더 짧아지고 초라해져서 이상하게 변하자, 그것이 기정 사
    실이 되어버렸다.
    She became shabbier and more forlorn-looking.
    그녀는 점점 더 초라해지고 쓸쓸해 보였다.

---

* 여기에서는 하녀들이 있는 곳을 가리킴

annoyance 골칫거리 | keep an eye on ~을 계속 지켜보다 | mischief 장난, (평판에 대한) 피해 | tramp
터벅터벅 걷다 | parcel 소포, 꾸러미 | sore 아픈, 따가운

The truth was / that she had saved herself annoyance /
사실은　　　　그녀는 자신을 말썽으로부터 구한 적이 있었다

several times / by keeping her eye / on Lavinia, / who
여러 번　　　계속 지켜봄으로써　　　라비니아를,

was quite ready to make mischief, / and would have been
라비니아는 항상 사람들을 괴롭혔고,　　　기뻐하곤 했다

rather pleased / to have made it / for the ex-show pupil.
　　　못된 짓을 하고는　　　과거의 자랑거리였던 학생에게.

Sara never made any mischief herself, / or interfered
새라는 절대 말썽을 피우지 않았고,　　　누구도 방해하지 않았다.

with anyone. She worked / like a drudge; / she tramped
그녀는 일했고　　허드렛일꾼처럼;　　　저벅저벅 걸었다

/ through the wet streets, / carrying parcels and baskets;
질척이는 거리를,　　　짐 꾸러미와 바구니를 들고서;

/ she labored with the childish inattention / of the little
철부지 학생들을 돌보느라 열심이었다

ones' French lessons; / as she became shabbier / and more
초급 프랑스어 수업 시간에;　　　그래서 새라가 점점 더 초라해지고

forlorn-looking, / she was told / that she had better take
더 쓸쓸해 보이자,　　말도 들었다　　　식사를 하는 편이 더 낫겠다고

her meals / *downstairs; / she was treated / as if she was
　　　아래층에서;　　　그녀는 취급받았다　　　마치 아무도 관심을

nobody's concern, / and her heart grew proud and sore, /
두지 않는 듯,　　　그래서 그녀의 마음은 자존심이 상했지만,

but she never told anyone / what she felt.
아무에게도 말하지 않았다　　　자신이 느낀 것을.

"Soldiers don't complain," / she would say / between her
"군인들은 불평하지 않아."　　　그녀는 말하곤 했다　　작은 입을 꽉 다물고,

small, shut teeth, / "I am not going to do it; / I will pretend
　　　"나도 불평하지 않을 거야;　　　척 할 거야

/ this is part of a war."
지금은 전쟁 중이라고."

But there were hours / when her child heart might almost
하지만 때가 있었다　　　그녀의 어린 마음이 부서졌을지도 모를

have broken / with loneliness / but for three people.
　　　외로움으로　　　세 사람이 없었다면.

The first, / it must be owned, / was Becky / — just Becky.
첫째는, 당연히 첫째를 차지하는 건, 베키였다 — 베키뿐이었다.

Throughout all that first night / spent in the garret, /
첫날 밤 내내 다락방에서 보낸,

she had felt a vague comfort / in knowing / that on the
모호한 편안함을 느꼈었다 알았을 때 반대편에서

other side / of the wall / in which the rats scuffled / and
벽의 쥐가 획획 다니며

squeaked / there was another young human creature. And
찍찍 대는 또 다른 어린 친구가 있다는 것을.

during the nights that followed / the sense of comfort
그리고 그 이후 밤마다 안도감은 점점 커졌다.

grew. They had little chance / to speak to each other /
두 사람은 기회가 거의 없었다 서로에게 말을 걸

during the day. Each had her own tasks / to perform,
낮 동안에는. 각자 자신의 일이 있었고 해야 할,

/ and any attempt at conversation / would have been
대화하려는 어떤 시도는 여겨질 수 있었다

regarded / as a tendency / to loiter and lose time. "Don't
의도로 어슬렁거리며 시간을 낭비하려는. "언짢아하지

mind me, / miss," / Becky whispered / during the first
마세요, 아가씨." 베키가 속삭였다 첫날 아침에,

morning, / "if I don't say nothin' polite. *Some un'd be
"제가 공손하게 말하지 않아도. 누군가 싫어할 테니까요

down on us / if I did. I means 'please' an' 'thank you' an'
제가 그렇게 하면. 전 '부디', '고맙습니다', '간청컨대'라고 말하려는 것이지만,

'beg pardon,' / but I dassn't to take time / to say it."
시간도 없고요 그렇게 말할."

But before daybreak / she used to slip / into Sara's attic
하지만 동트기 전에 베키는 살짝 들어오곤 했다 새라의 다락방으로

/ and button her dress / and give her such help / as she
옷의 단추를 채워주고 도움을 주러 새라가 필요로

required / before she went downstairs / to light the
하는 아래층으로 내려가기 전에 부엌에 불을 지피기 위해.

kitchen fire. And when night came / Sara always heard
밤이 오면 새라는 항상 들었다

/ the humble knock / at her door / which meant / that
작은 노크 소리를   그녀의 문에서   그것은 의미했다

her handmaid was ready / to help her again / if she was
하녀가 대기 중이라는 것을   자신을 다시 돕기 위해

needed. During the first weeks of her grief / Sara felt / as
필요하면.   슬펐던 처음 몇 주 동안   새라는 느꼈다

if she were too stupefied to talk, / so it happened / that
너무 얼이 빠져서 아무 말도 못할 것처럼,   그래서 그런 일이 일어났다

some time passed / before they saw each other much / or
어느 정도 시간이 지난 후에야   두 사람은 서로 찾아가며

exchanged visits. Becky's heart told her / that it was best /
서로를 방문했다.   베키의 진심이 말해 줬다   그것이 최선이라고

that people in trouble / should be left alone.
곤경에 빠진 사람은   혼자 두어야 하는 것이.

Key Expression

과거의 습관을 나타내는 used to

used to은 '~하곤 했었다'라는 의미로 과거의 습관이나 상태를 표현하는 조동
사입니다. 여기에는 지금은 그렇지 않다는 의미가 함축되어 있습니다.
또한 used는 다음과 같은 세 가지로 사용될 수 있으므로 의미의 구별이 필요합
니다.

▶ used to + 동사원형 : ~하곤 했다 (조동사 used to)
▶ be used to -ing : ~에 익숙하다
▶ be used (by) : 사용되다, 쓰이다(use의 수동태)

ex) Before daybreak she used to slip into Sara's attic and button her dress and
give her such help as she required.
동트기 전에 그녀는 새라의 다락방으로 살짝 들어와 옷의 단추를 채워주고 새라
가 필요로 하는 도움을 주곤 했다.

---

* Some un'd = Someone would

garret 다락방 | vague 모호한, 애매한 | scuffle 실랑이를 벌이다. 휙 움직이다 | tendency 경향 | loiter
어슬렁거리다 | be down on ~을 미워하다, ~에 반대하다 | handmaid 하녀, 잔심부름꾼 | stupefied 얼이 빠진

117

The second / of the trio of comforters / was Ermengarde,
두 번째는   세 명의 위로가 되는 사람 중   어먼가드였다,

/ but odd things happened / before Ermengarde found her
하지만 이상한 일이 생겼다   어먼가드가 두 번째 자리를 찾기 전에.

place.

When Sara's mind / seemed to awaken again / to the life
새라의 마음이   다시 깨어난 듯 보였을 때   주변의 삶에 대해,

about her, / she realized / that she had forgotten / that
          그녀는 깨달았다   자신이 잊고 있었다는 것을

an Ermengarde lived / in the world. The two had always
어먼가드가 살고 있다는 사실을   이 세상에.   그 둘은 항상 친구였지만,

been friends, / but Sara had felt / as if she were years the
          새라는 느꼈다   자신이 몇 살 많은 언니인 듯.

older. It could not be contested / that Ermengarde was
두말할 나위 없이   어먼가드가 둔한 아이였다

as dull / as she was affectionate. She clung to Sara / in
다정한 만큼.   어먼가드는 새라한테 매달렸다

a simple, helpless way; / she brought her lessons to her /
순전히, 속수무책으로;   자기 수업에 새라를 데려가서

that she might be helped; / she listened to her every word
도와달라고 했고;   새라의 말은 모조리 귀기울였으며

/ and besieged her with requests / for stories. But she
계속 요청했다   이야기 해 달라고.

had nothing interesting to say herself, / and she loathed
하지만 그녀 자신은 아무 할 말도 없었고,   책을 혐오했다

books / of every description. She was, / in fact, / not a
온갖 종류의.   그녀는,   사실,

person one would remember / when one was caught / in
기억할 만한 사람이 아니었다   누군가 빠져 있을 때

the storm of a great trouble, / and Sara forgot her.
엄청난 곤경의 소용돌이에,   그래서 새라는 그녀를 잊었다.

comforter 위안을 주는 것, 위로가 되는 사람 | affectionate 다정한, 애정 어린 | cling to ~을 고수하다, ~에
매달리다 | helpless 무력한, 속수무책인 | besiege 퍼붓다 | loathe 혐오하다 | encounter 마주치다 | corridor
복도, 회랑 | garment 옷, 의류 | mend 수리하다, 꿰매다 | attired (특정한) 복장의 | outgrown 너무 커져 맞지
않게 된 | be equal to 같다, 거뜬히 해내다 | miserable 비참하게 만드는 | hysterical 히스테리 상태의, 발작적인
| aimlessly 목적 없이

It had been all the easier / to forget her / because she had
더욱 쉬웠던 이유는   어먼가드를 잊는 것이

been suddenly called home / for a few weeks. When she
그녀가 갑자기 집에 갔기 때문이었다   몇 주 동안.   어먼가드가 돌아

came back / she did not see Sara / for a day or two, / and
왔을 때   새라를 보지 못했다   하루 이틀 동안은,

when she met her / for the first time / she encountered
그리고 새라를 만났을 때   처음으로   마주쳤다

/ her coming down a corridor / with her arms full of
새라가 복도를 내려오는 모습과   두 팔에 옷가지를 가득 들고

garments / which were to be taken downstairs / to be
            아래층으로 가져가야 할

mended. Sara herself had already been taught / to mend
수선을 위해.   새라는 스스로 이미 터득하고 있었다   옷을 수선하는

them. She looked pale / and unlike herself, / and she was
방법을.   새라는 창백해 보였고   그녀같지 않았다,   그리고 이상한 옷을

attired in the queer, / outgrown frock / whose shortness
입고 있었다.   몸에 비해 너무 작았고   옷이 짧아서

showed / so much thin black leg.
          아주 가냘프고 까만 다리가 보였다.

Ermengarde was too slow a girl / to be equal / to such a
어먼가드는 너무 둔한 아이라서   대처할 수 없었다

situation. She could not think / of anything to say. She
그런 상황에.   생각할 수 없었다   할 말을.   알고

knew / what had happened, / but, / somehow, / she had
있었지만   무슨 일이 생겼는지,   하지만, 어쨌든,

never imagined / Sara could look like this / — so odd
상상할 수 없었다   새라가 이렇게 보일 수 있다는 것을   — 아주 이상하고

and poor / and almost like a servant. It made her quite
불쌍하게   그래서 거의 하인처럼.   그 모습이 아주 불쌍해서.

miserable, / and she could do nothing / but break into a
            아무것도 할 수 없었다   갑자기 짧은 웃음을 터뜨리는

short hysterical laugh / and exclaim / — aimlessly / and
것 외에는   그리고 소리쳤다   — 뜻하지 않게

as if without any meaning, / "Oh, Sara, is that you?"
어떤 의미도 없는 양,   "아, 새라, 너 맞니?"

"Yes," / answered Sara, / and suddenly a strange thought
"그래," 새라가 답했다. 그리고 갑자기 이상한 생각이

/ passed through her mind / and made her face flush. She
그녀의 마음을 지나갔고 얼굴이 붉어졌다.

held the pile of garments / in her arms, / and her chin
새라는 옷 더미를 들고 두 팔에, 턱으로 누르고 있었다

rested / upon the top of it / to keep it steady. Something /
그 꼭대기를 그것을 잘 받치려고. 뭔가

in the look of her straight-gazing eyes / made Ermengarde
그녀가 똑바로 쳐다보는 시선 속의 어먼가드를 당황하게 만들었다

lose her wits / still more. She felt / as if Sara had changed
더더욱. 그녀는 느꼈다 새라가 변해 버렸으며

/ into a new kind of girl, / and she had never known her /
다른 여자 아이로, 그녀를 전혀 모르는 것처럼

before. Perhaps / it was because she had suddenly grown
전에. 아마도 그것은 새라가 갑자기 가난해져서

poor / and had to mend things / and work like Becky.
옷을 수선해야 하고 베키처럼 일하기 때문인 것 같았다.

"Oh," / she stammered. / "How — how are you?"
"아," 어먼가드는 더듬거렸다. "어떻게 — 잘 지내?"

"I don't know," / Sara replied. "How are you?"
"난 잘 모르겠어," 새라가 대답했다. "넌 잘 지내니?"

"I'm — I'm quite well," / said Ermengarde, / overwhelmed
"난 — 난 아주 잘 지내," 어먼가드가 말했다. 수줍음에 압도되어.

with shyness. Then spasmodically / she thought of /
그리고 갑자기 생각해 냈다

something to say / which seemed more intimate. "Are you
할 말을 더 친근해 보이는.

— are you very unhappy?" / she said / in a rush.
"넌 — 넌 아주 불행하니?" 그녀는 말했다 서둘러.

---

overwhelmed 압도된 | spasmodically 발작적으로, 갑자기 | injustice 불평등, 부당 | swell 부어 오르다 | in
course of time 머지않아, 이윽고 | wretchedness 비참, 불행 | blame 비난하다 | over-sensitive 지나치게
민감한

Then / Sara was guilty / of an injustice. Just at that moment
그러자   새라는 죄책감이 들었다   부당함에 대해.   바로 그때

/ her torn heart swelled / within her, / and she felt / that
새라의 상처 받은 마음은 부풀었고   그녀 안에서,   느꼈다

if anyone was as stupid as that, / one had better get away
저렇게 바보같은 아이라면.   멀리 하는 것이 낫다고.

from her.

"What do you think?" / she said. "Do you think / I am very
"넌 어떻게 생각해?"   새라가 말했다.   "넌 생각하니   내가 아주

happy?" And she marched past her / without another word.
행복하다고?" 그리고 어먼가드를 지나쳐 걸어갔다   더 이상 아무 말없이.

In course of time / she realized / that if her wretchedness
머지않아   새라는 깨달았다   자신의 비참함으로 인해

had not made / her forget things, / she would have known /
자신이 잊어버리지 않았다면,   알았을 것이라고

that poor, dull Ermengarde was not to be blamed / for her
불쌍하고, 둔한 어먼가드가 비난 받아서는 안 된다는 것을

unready, awkward ways. She was always awkward, / and
준비되지 않은, 어색한 태도 때문에.   어먼가드는 항상 서툴렀고,

the more she felt, / the more stupid she was given to being.
더 그렇게 느낄수록,   더 바보같이 되어버렸다.

But the sudden thought / which had flashed upon her / had
하지만 갑작스런 생각이   새라에게 번뜩 스치면서

made her over-sensitive.
그녀를 과민하게 만든 것이다.

"She is like the others," / she had thought. "She does not
"그 애도 다른 사람과 같아,"   그녀는 생각했다.   "그 애도 사실은 원치

really want / to talk to me. She knows no one does."
않을 거야   내게 말 거는 것을.   아무도 그러지 않는다는 것을 알고 있을테니."

So for several weeks / a barrier stood / between them.
그래서 몇 주 동안   장벽이 있었다   둘 사이에.

When they met / by chance / Sara looked the other way, /
그들이 만나게 되면   우연히   새라는 다른 쪽을 보았고,

and Ermengarde felt too stiff / and embarrassed / to speak.
어먼가드는 너무 경직되고   당황해서   말할 수 없었다.

Sometimes / they nodded to each other / in passing, / but
때때로   그들은 서로에게 고개를 끄덕였다   지나가면서,

there were times / when they did not even exchange a
하지만 많은 경우   인사조차 교환하지 않았다.

greeting.

"If she would rather not talk to me," / Sara thought, / "I
"만약 그 애가 나한테 말을 걸고 싶어 하지 않는다면,"   새라는 생각했다,

will keep out of her way. Miss Minchin makes / that easy
"내가 피하면 돼.   민친 교장이 만들어 줄 거야

enough."
아주 쉽게."

Miss Minchin made it so easy / that at last / they scarcely
민친 교장은 쉽게 만들어 주었고   마침내   두 사람은 보지 않았다

saw / each other / at all. At that time / it was noticed /
서로를   전혀.   그때는   보였다

that Ermengarde was more stupid / than ever, / and that
어먼가드가 가장 멍청하게   어느 때보다,

she looked / listless and unhappy. She used to sit / in
그리고 보였다   무기력하고 불행하게.   그녀는 앉아 있곤 했다

the window-seat, / huddled in a heap, / and stare out of
창가 자리에,   몸을 웅크린 채,   창 밖을 응시하며

the window / without speaking. Once Jessie, / who was
창문   아무 말 없이.   한 번은 제시가,   지나가다가,

passing, / stopped to look at her / curiously.
멈춰서 그녀를 쳐다보았다   의아하게.

Key Expression

전치사로 쓰이는 but

but이 전치사로 쓰일 경우에는 '~외에'라고 뜻으로, except와 같은 의미가 됩니다.

ex) Nobody goes there but myself.
나 외에 아무도 그곳에 가지 않아.
No one but Sara could have done it.
새라 외에 아무도 그것을 할 수 없었을 것이다.

"What are you crying for, Ermengarde?" / she asked.
"왜 울고 있니, 어먼가드?"
제시가 물었다.

"I'm not crying," / answered Ermengarde, / in a muffled,
"우는 게 아니야,"
어먼가드가 대답했다,
잘 들리지 않고, 떨리는

unsteady voice.
목소리로.

"You are," / said Jessie. "A great big tear just rolled down /
"울고 있잖아,"
제시가 말했다.
"커다란 눈물 방울이 굴러 내려와서

the bridge of your nose / and dropped off / at the end of it.
콧날을 타고
똑 떨어졌어
코 끝에서.

And there goes another."
그리고 또 떨어지네."

"Well," / said Ermengarde, / "I'm miserable / — and no
"음,"
어먼가드가 말했다,
"난 괴로우니까
— 아무도 방해하지

one need interfere." And she turned her plump back / and
말아줘."
그리고 통통한 등을 돌려

took out her handkerchief / and boldly hid her face / in it.
손수건을 꺼내고
얼굴을 대놓고 숨겼다
그 안에.

That night, / when Sara went to her attic, / she was later
그날 밤,
새라가 다락방에 갔을 때,
평소보다 늦었다.

than usual. She had been kept at work / until after the hour
그녀는 일을 계속 했고
한 시간 후까지

/ at which the pupils went to bed, / and after that / she had
학생들이 잠자리에 들고 난,
그 후에는

gone to her lessons / in the lonely schoolroom. When she
공부하러 갔다
쓸쓸한 교실로.

reached the top of the stairs, / she was surprised / to see a
계단 꼭대기에 다다랐을 때,
새라는 놀랐다

glimmer of light / coming from under the attic door.
희미한 불빛을 보고
다락방 문 아래에서 나오는.

"Nobody goes there / but myself," / she thought quickly, /
"아무도 그곳에 가지 않는데
나 외에는,"
그녀는 얼른 생각했다,

"but someone has lighted a candle."
"하지만 누군가 촛불을 켜 놨네."

listless 무기력한 | heap 무더기 | muffled 소리가 잘 들리지 않게 낮춘 | unsteady 불안정한, 떨리는 | the
bridge of the nose 콧대 | boldly 대담하게, 뚜렷이 | glimmer 깜빡이는 빛, 희미한 기미

Someone had, / indeed, / lighted a candle, / and it was not
누군가,   정말로,   촛불을 켰다.   그런데 초는 타고 있는 것이

burning / in the kitchen candlestick / she was expected
아니었고   부엌에서 쓰는 촛대에서   자신이 사용해야 할,

to use, / but in one of those / belonging to the pupils'
촛대에서 타고 있었다   학생들의 침실에서 쓰는.

bedrooms. The someone was sitting / upon the battered
누군가 앉아 있었는데   낡은 의자에,

footstool, / and was dressed / in her nightgown / and
          입고 있었다   잠옷을

wrapped up in a red shawl. It was Ermengarde.
빨간 숄을 두른 채.   그것은 어먼가드였다.

"Ermengarde!" / cried Sara. She was so startled / that she
"어먼가드!"   새라가 소리쳤다. 그녀는 매우 놀라서

was almost frightened. "You will get into trouble."
거의 공포에 질려 있었다.   "큰일날 거야."

Ermengarde stumbled up / from her footstool. She shuffled
어먼가드는 비틀거리며 일어났다   의자에서.   발을 끌며 걸어왔는데

/ across the attic / in her bedroom slippers, / which were too
   다락방을 가로질러   침실 슬리퍼를 신고,   슬리퍼는 너무 컸다

large / for her. Her eyes and nose were pink / with crying.
     그녀에게.   눈과 코는 분홍빛이 되어 있었다   울어서.

Key Expression ❣

It is ~ that 강조구문

It is와 that 사이에 강조하고 싶은 말을 넣어 '~한 것은 바로 ~이다'라는 의
미를 나타낼 수 있습니다. 이때 강조하는 자리에 들어갈 수 있는 것은 주어, 목적
어, 부사구입니다.
또한 강조하는 말이 사람일 경우에는 that 대신 who를 사용할 수 있습니다.

ex) It was you who were different!"
    변한 사람은 바로 너야!"

"I know / I shall / — if I'm found out." / she said. "But I
"나도 알아   큰일난다는 것을 — 발각되면."   그녀가 말했다. "하지만 난

don't care / — I don't care a bit. Oh, Sara, / please tell me.
상관없어   — 난 조금도 상관 없어.   아, 새라,   나한테 말해 줘.

What is the matter? Why don't you like me / any more?"
뭐가 문제야?   왜 날 좋아하지 않지   더 이상?"

Something in her voice / made the familiar lump rise /
어먼가드의 목소리 때문에   익숙한 응어리가 올라왔다

in Sara's throat. It was so affectionate and simple / — so
새라의 목에서.   그것은 아주 다정하고 순진한 목소리였다

like the old Ermengarde / who had asked her / to be "best
— 예전의 어먼가드와 똑같은   자신에게 간청했던   "단짝"이 되자고.

friends." It sounded / as if she had not meant / what she
그 소리는 들렸다   마치 자신이 의도한 일이 아니었다는 듯이

had seemed to mean / during these past weeks.
그렇게 보였던 것들이   지난 몇 주 동안.

"I do like you," / Sara answered. "I thought / — you see,
"난 널 정말 좋아해,"   새라가 답했다.   "난 생각했어   — 있잖아,

/ everything is different / now. I thought / you — were
모든 것이 변했다고   이제는. 난 생각했어   너도

different."
너도 — 변했다고."

Ermengarde opened her wet eyes / wide.
어먼가드는 젖은 눈을 떴다   크게.

"Why, / it was you / who were different!" / she cried.
"아니,   바로 너야   변한 사람은!"   어먼가드는 울먹였다.

"You didn't want to talk to me. I didn't know / what to do.
"넌 나랑 말하고 싶어 하지 않았잖아.   난 모르겠어   뭘 해야 할지.

It was you / who were different / after I came back."
바로 너야   달라진 사람은   내가 돌아온 후."

Sara thought / a moment. She saw / she had made a
새라는 생각했다   잠시.   그녀는 알았다   자기가 실수했다는 것을.

mistake.

---

candlestick 촛대 | battered 낡은, 닳은 | footstool 발을 얹는 받침 | shawl 숄 | shuffle 발을 끌며 걷다

"I am different," / she explained, / "though not in the way
"난 달라졌어." 새라가 설명했다, "방식은 아니지만

/ you think. Miss Minchin does not want / me to talk to
네가 생각한. 민친 교장은 원하지 않아 내가 애들한테 말하는 것을.

the girls. Most of them don't want / to talk to me. I thought
아이들도 대부분 원하지 않아 내게 말하는 것을. 난 생각했어

/ — perhaps — / you didn't. So I tried / to keep out of your
— 아마도 — 너도 원치 않는다고. 그래서 난 노력했어

way."
일부러 널 피하려고.

"Oh, Sara," / Ermengarde almost wailed / in her reproachful
"아, 새라." 어먼가드는 거의 울먹였다 원망스럽고 실망스러운

dismay. And then / after one more look / they rushed /
마음에. 그리고 나서 한 번 더 바라본 후 그들은 달려갔다

into each other's arms. It must be confessed / that Sara's
서로의 팔 안으로. 말해야겠다 새라의 작고 까만

small black head lay / for some minutes / on the shoulder /
머리가 놓여졌다는 것을 몇 분 동안 어깨에

covered by the red shawl. When Ermengarde had seemed to
빨간 숄로 덮힌. 어먼가드가 자신을 버린 듯 보였을 때,

desert her, / she had felt horribly lonely.
새라는 끔찍하게 외로웠다.

Afterward / they sat down / upon the floor / together, / Sara
그 후에 그들은 앉았다 바닥에 함께,

clasping her knees / with her arms, / and Ermengarde rolled
새라는 무릎을 껴안고 두 팔로, 어먼가드는 돌돌 말고서

up / in her shawl. Ermengarde looked / at the odd, big-eyed
숄로. 어먼가드는 보았다 묘하고, 큰 눈을 가진 작은 얼굴을

little face / adoringly.
사랑스럽게.

"I couldn't bear it / any more," / she said. "I dare say / you
"난 참을 수 없어 더 이상." 그녀가 말했다. "분명히

could live / without me, / Sara; / but I couldn't live / without
넌 살 수 있겠지 나 없이도, 새라; 하지만 난 살 수 없어 너 없이.

you. I was nearly dead. So tonight, / when I was crying /
난 거의 죽을 지경이야. 그래서 오늘 밤, 울고 있다가

under the bedclothes, / I thought / all at once / of creeping
이불 속에서, 난 생각했어 갑자기 여기로 올라와서

up here / and just begging you / to let us be friends again."
네게 간청해 보겠다고 우리 다시 친구 하자고."

"You are nicer than I am," / said Sara. "I was too proud
"네가 나보다 더 착하구나." 새라가 말했다. "난 자존심이 너무 세서

/ to try and make friends. You see, / now that trials have
친해지려고 하지도 못했어. 있잖아, 시련들이 왔기 때문에,

come, / they have shown / that I am not a nice child. I was
드러났어 난 착한 아이는 아니라는 사실이.

afraid they would. Perhaps" / — wrinkling her forehead /
그런 것 같아. 아마도" — 이마를 찡그리며

wisely — / "that is / what they were sent for."
생각하듯이 — "그것이 바로 그 시련들이 보내진 이유야."

"I don't see any good in them," / said Ermengarde / stoutly.
"난 그 시련들의 좋은 점을 모르겠어." 어먼가드는 말했다 완강히.

"Neither do I / — to speak the truth," / admitted Sara, /
"나도 그래 — 사실을 말하자면," 새라가 인정했다,

frankly. "But I suppose / there might be good / in things,
솔직하게. "하지만 어쩌면 좋은 것이 있을지도 몰라 시련에,

/ even if we don't see it. There might" / — doubtfully — /
우리가 볼 수 없더라도. 있을 거야" — 의심스럽게 —

"be good / in Miss Minchin."
"좋은 점이 민친 교장선생님에도."

Ermengarde looked / round the attic / with a rather
어먼가드는 보았다 다락방 주위를

fearsome curiosity.
두려워하면서도 호기심 어린 표정으로.

"Sara," / she said, / "do you think you can bear / living
"새라," 그녀는 말했다, "견딜 수 있을 것 같니

here?"
여기에서 사는 것을?"

Sara looked round / also.
새라도 주변을 보았다 역시.

---

reproachful 비난하는, 원망하는 | dismay 실망 | adoringly 숭배하여, 흠모하여 | wrinkle 주름살 지다,
구겨지다 | stoutly 용감하게, 완강하게 | fearsome 무시무시한

"If I pretend it's quite different, / I can," / she answered;
"만약 여기가 아주 다른 척 하면, 살 수 있어," 그녀는 대답했다;

/ "or if I pretend / it is a place / in a story."
"아니면 그런 척 하면 이곳이 장소라고 이야기 속의."

She spoke / slowly. Her imagination / was beginning to
새라는 말했다 천천히. 그녀의 상상력이 발휘되기 시작했다.

work for her. It had not worked for her / at all / since her
그것은 발휘되지 않았었다 전혀

troubles had come / upon her. She had felt / as if it had
시련이 닥친 이후로 그녀에게. 새라는 느꼈다 마치 기절한 것처럼.

been stunned.

"Other people have lived / in worse places. Think of the
"다른 사람들은 살고 있어 더 나쁜 환경에서도. 몬테 크리스토 백작을

Count of Monte Cristo / in the dungeons / of the Chateau
생각해 봐 지하 감옥에 있는 디프 성의.

d'If. And think of the people / in the Bastille!"
그리고 사람들을 생각해 봐 바스티유 감옥에 있는!"

"The Bastille," / half whispered Ermengarde, / watching
"바스티유 감옥," 어먼가드가 반쯤 중얼거렸다. 그녀를 보면서

her / and beginning to be fascinated. She remembered
매료되기 시작하면서. 그녀는 이야기들을 기억해냈다

stories / of the French Revolution / which Sara had been
프랑스 혁명에 대한 새라가 심어 주었던

able to fix / in her mind / by her dramatic relation / of
마음속에 극적인 이야기로 그것에

them. No one / but Sara / could have done it.
대한. 아무도 새라 말고는 그렇게 할 수 없었다.

A well-known glow / came into Sara's eyes.
친숙한 감정이 새라의 눈에 나타났다.

---

stun 기절시키다 | dungeon (과거 성 안에 있던) 지하 감옥 | Chateau (프랑스 시골의) 대저택, 성 | Bastille (파리의)
바스티유 감옥 | prisoner 죄수 | jailer 교도소장 | cell 감방 | enrapture 황홀하게 만들다, 도취시키다 | adversity
역경

"Yes," / she said, / hugging her knees, / "that will be a
"맞아," 새라가 말했다. 무릎을 껴안으며, "그것이 좋은 장소겠다

good place / to pretend about. I am a prisoner / in the
그런 척 하는데. 난 죄수야 바스티유 감옥에

Bastille. I have been here / for years and years / — and
있는. 난 여기 있었어 수년 동안 — 또 수년

years; / and everybody has forgotten / about me. Miss
동안을; 모두 다 잊었지 나에 대해.

Minchin is the jailer / — and Becky" — / a sudden light
민친 교장은 교도소장이고 — 베키" — 갑자기 환한 빛이 더해졌다

adding itself / to the glow / in her eyes — / "Becky is the
그 감정에 그녀의 눈에 담긴 — "베키는 죄수야

prisoner / in the next cell."
옆 감방에 있는."

She turned to Ermengarde, / looking quite like the old
새라는 어먼가드를 돌아보았다. 예전의 새라와 똑같은 표정으로.

Sara.

"I shall pretend that," / she said; / "and it will be a great
"난 그런 척 할 거야." 그녀가 말했다; "그러면 훨씬 편해질 거야."

comfort."

Ermengarde was / at once / enraptured and awed.
어먼가드는 즉시 사로잡혔고 경이로워 했다.

"And will you tell me all / about it?" / she said. "May I
"그럼 나한테 모두 얘기해 줄래 그것에 대해?" 그녀가 말했다. "올라와도 돼

creep up / here at night, / whenever it is safe, / and hear the
밤에 이곳으로 안전할 때마다. 그리고 이야기를 들

things / you have made up / in the day? It will seem / as if
어도 될까 네가 지어낸 낮 동안? 될 수 있을 것 같구나

we were more 'best friends' / than ever."
우리는 더 가까운 '단짝'인 것처럼 어느 때보다."

"Yes," / answered Sara, / nodding. "Adversity tries people,
"그래." 새라가 대답했다. 고개를 끄덕이며. "역경은 사람들을 시험하지.

/ and mine has tried you / and proved / how nice you are."
그리고 내 역경은 널 시험했고 증명했어 네가 얼마나 착한지."

129

 mini test 4

A. 다음 문장을 해석해 보세요.

(1) It was not until long / afterward / that she realized / that her bed had been so hard / that she turned over and over / in it / to find a place to rest.
→

(2) If she had been older, / Miss Minchin would have given her / the bigger girls to teach / and saved money / by dismissing an instructress.
→

(3) As she became shabbier / and more forlorn-looking, / she was told / that she had better take her meals / downstairs.
→

(4) She realized / that if her wretchedness had not made / her forget things, / she would have known / that poor, dull Ermengarde was not to be blamed / for her unready, awkward ways.
→

B. 다음 주어진 문구가 알맞은 문장이 되도록 순서를 맞춰 보세요.

(1) 그녀는 좀처럼 그들 중 누구에게도 말할 기회가 없었다.
(scarcely / She / ever / of speaking / had / to any of them / an opportunity)
→

(2) 어먼가드는 항상 서툴렀고, 더 그렇게 느낄수록, 더 바보같이 되어버렸다.
(she felt, / stupid / the more / the more / she was / being / given to)
She was always awkward, and [   ]

[   ] .

 Answer

A. (1) 그 이후 머지않아 그녀는 침대가 너무 딱딱해서 편하게 쉴 곳을 찾으려고 몸을 계속 뒤척이고 있다는 것을 깨달았다. (2) 만약 새라가 좀 더 나이가 많았다면, 민친 교장은 그녀에게 더 큰 여자애들을 가르치라고 시키고 교사를 해고함으로써 돈을 절약했을 것이다. (3) 그녀가 점점 더 초라해지고 더 쓸쓸해 보이자, 아래층에서 식사를 하

(3) 나 외에는 아무도 그곳에 가지 않아.
   (goes / there / Nobody / myself / but)
   →

(4) 변한 사람은 바로 너야!
   (who / different / was / It / you / were)
   →

C. 다음 주어진 문장이 본문의 내용과 맞으면 T, 틀리면 F에 동그라미 하세요.

(1) The change in Sara's life gradually came to her.
   (T / F)

(2) Sara was in charge of teaching the younger children French and taking care of them.
   (T / F)

(3) Sara was not allowed to study at all.
   (T / F)

(4) Sara and Ermengarde became 'best friend' again.
   (T / F)

D. 의미가 비슷한 것끼리 서로 연결해 보세요.

(1) anguish   ▶   ◀ ① hate

(2) reproof   ▶   ◀ ② reluctantly

(3) grudgingly   ▶   ◀ ③ suffering

(4) loathe   ▶   ◀ ④ scolding

는 편이 낫겠다는 말을 들었다. (4) 새라는 자신의 비참함 때문에 잊어버리지 않았다면, 불쌍하고, 둔한 어떤 가드가 준비되지 않은 어색한 태도 때문에 비난 받아서는 안 된다는 것을 알았을 것이라고 깨달았다. | B. (1) She scarcely ever had an opportunity of speaking to any of them. (2) the more she felt, the more stupid she was given to being (3) Nobody goes there but myself. (4) It was you who were different! | C. (1) F (2) T (3) F (4) T | D. (1) ③ (2) ④ (3) ② (4) ①

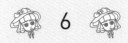

6

Melchisedec
멜기세덱

The third person / in the trio / was Lottie. She was a
세 번째 사람은   세 명 중   로티였다.   로티는 어린 아이라서

small thing / and did not know / what adversity meant, /
몰랐고   역경이 뭔지,

and was much bewildered / by the alteratio she saw / in
무척 어리둥절 했다   변화를 보면서

her young adopted mother. She had heard / it rumored
어린 양엄마의.   들었지만   소문이 도는 것을

/ that strange things had happened / to Sara, / but she
이상한 일이 발생했다는   새라에게,

could not understand / why she looked different / —
이해할 수 없었다   왜 새라가 달라졌는지

why she wore / an old black frock / and came into the
— 왜 입고 있는지   낡고 검은 드레스를   그리고 교실에 들어와서

schoolroom / only to teach / instead of to sit / in her
가르치기만 하고   앉지 않고

place of honor / and learn lessons herself. There had
명예로운 자신의 자리에   공부하지 않는지.

been much whispering / among the little ones / when it
수군거림이 들려왔다   어린 아이들 사이에서

had been discovered / that Sara no longer lived / in the
알려졌을 때   새라가 더 이상 살지 않는다는 것이

rooms / in which Emily had so long sat / in state. Lottie's
그 방에서   에밀리가 그토록 오래 앉아 있었던   당당하게.

chief difficulty was / that Sara said so little / when one
로티의 가장 힘든 점은   새라가 거의 말을 하지 않는다는 점이었다

asked her questions. At seven / mysteries must be made
누군가 질문을 하면.   일곱 살 아이에게   수수께끼란 풀리는 법이다

very clear / if one is to understand them.
누군가 이해할 수 있게 해 주어야.

bewildered 어리둥절한 | alteration 변화, 개조 | rumor 소문, 소문 내다 | in state 위엄을 갖추고, 당당하게 |
mystery 수수께끼, 미스터리 | confidentially 은밀하게 | take charge of ~을 맡다, ~의 책임을 지다 | thrust
밀치다, 쑤셔넣다 | console 위로하다, 위안을 주다 | courageously 용감하게

"Are you very poor now, / Sara?" / she had asked /
"이제 아주 가난해진 거야, 새라?" 로티가 물었었다

confidentially / the first morning / her friend took
몰래 첫날 아침 자신의 친구가 맡았을 때

charge / of the small French class. "Are you as poor as
초급 프랑스어 수업을. "거지처럼 가난해진 거야?"

a beggar?" She thrust a fat hand into the slim one / and
로티는 통통한 손을 가냘픈 손에 쑤셔넣고

opened round, tearful eyes. "I don't want / you to be as
눈물이 고인 눈을 동그랗게 떴다. "난 싫어 새라가 가난한 건

poor / as a beggar."
거지처럼."

She looked / as if she was going to cry. And Sara
로티는 보였다 마치 울음을 터뜨릴 것처럼.

hurriedly consoled her.
그래서 새라는 서둘러 달랬다.

"Beggars have nowhere to live," / she said /
"거지는 살 곳이 없잖아." 새라가 말했다

courageously. "I have a place to live in."
용기 있게. "난 살 곳이 있는 걸."

"Where do you live?" / persisted Lottle. "The new girl
"어디 사는데?" 로티가 고집을 피웠다. "새로 온 여자애가 자고

sleeps / in your room, / and it isn't pretty any more."
있던데 새라의 방에서, 그 방은 더 이상 예쁘지 않아."

"I live in another room," / said Sara.
"난 다른 방에서 살아." 새라가 말했다.

"Is it a nice one?" / inquired Lottie. "I want to go and see
"거기는 예쁜 방이야?" 로티가 물었다. "나도 가서 보고 싶어."

it."

"You must not talk," / said Sara. "Miss Minchin is
"그만 얘기해." 새라가 말했다. "민친 교장이 우리를 보고 있어.

looking at us. She will be angry with me / for letting you
나한테 화내실 거야 네가 떠드는 것을 내버

whisper."
려 둔다고."

She had found out already / that she was to be held
새라는 이미 알고 있었다   책임을 떠맡게 된다는 것을

accountable / for everything / which was objected to. If the
              모든 일에 대해   거스르는.

children were not attentive, / if they talked, / if they were
아이들이 산만해지거나,   떠들거나,   얌전히 있지 않으면,

restless, / it was she / who would be reproved.
          바로 그녀였다   혼나는 사람은.

But Lottie was a determined little person. If Sara would
하지만 로티는 고집 센 아이였다.   새라가 말해 주지 않는다면

not tell her / where she lived, / she would find out / in
어디 사는지,   알아낼 것이었다

some other way. She talked to her small companions / and
다른 방법으로.   어린 친구들한테 말을 걸고

hung about the elder girls / and listened / when they were
언니들의 주변을 어슬렁거리며   귀담아 들었다   소문을 이야기 할 때;

gossiping; / and acting upon certain information / they had
            어떤 정보에 따라

unconsciously let drop, / she started / late one afternoon /
그들이 무심코 흘려 말한,   로티는 시작했다   어느 날 저녁

on a voyage of discovery, / climbing stairs / she had never
탐험의 여정을,   계단을 여러 개 올라   전혀 알지 못했던

known / the existence of, / until she reached the attic floor.
        그것이 있다는 것조차,   마침내 다락방이 있는 층에 도착했다.

Key Expression 🎯

be to 부정사 용법
be to 부정사는 to 부정사의 특수한 형태입니다. be to 부정사는 다음과 같이
다양한 의미를 지니고 있어 문맥에 따라 해석해야 합니다.

▶ 예정 : ~할 예정이다(=will) → 미래를 나타내는 부사/부사구와 함께
▶ 의무 : ~해야 한다(=should)
▶ 가능 : ~할 수 있다(=can) → 주로 수동태로 쓰임
▶ 운명 : ~할 운명이다(=be destined to)
▶ 의도 : ~하고자 한다(=intend to)
▶ 가정 : ~한다면 → 가정법에서 절대 불가능한 가정을 표현할 때

ex) She had found out already that she was to be held accountable for
    everything which was objected to.
    새라는 거스르는 모든 일에 대해 책임을 떠맡게 된다는 것을 이미 알고 있었다.

There she found two doors / near each other, / and
거기에는 문이 두 개 있었다   가까이 붙어있는,

opening one, / she saw / her beloved Sara / standing
하나를 열자,   보였다   사랑하는 새라가

upon an old table / and looking out of a window.
낡은 탁자 위에 서서   창 밖을 내다보는 모습이.

"Sara!" / she cried, / aghast. "Mamma Sara!" She was
"새라!"   로티가 소리쳤다.   몹시 놀라서.   "새라 엄마!"   로티는 깜짝 놀랐다

aghast / because the attic was / so bare and ugly / and
왜냐하면 다락방이   텅 비어 있는 데다가 보기 흉해서

seemed so far away / from all the world. Her short legs /
멀리 떨어진 곳 같았기 때문이다   모든 세상으로부터.   로티의 짧은 다리는

had seemed to have been mounting / hundreds of stairs.
올라온 듯 했다   수백 개의 계단을.

Sara turned round / at the sound of her voice. It was her
새라는 돌아보았다   로티의 목소리를 듣고.

turn to be aghast. What would happen now? If Lottie
돌아보고는 깜짝 놀랐다.   지금 무슨 일이 일어난 거지?   로티가 울음을

began to cry / and any one chanced to hear, / they were
터뜨려서   누군가 우연히 듣기라도 하면,   둘 다 끝장이었다.

both lost. She jumped down / from her table / and ran to
새라는 뛰어 내려   탁자에서

the child.
그 아이에게 달려갔다.

"Don't cry / and make a noise," / she implored. "I shall
"울지 말고   소리도 내지 마."   그녀가 간청하듯 말했다.

be scolded / if you do, / and I have been scolded / all day.
"혼나고 말 거야   만약 네가 운다면,   계속 혼났으니까   하루 종일.

It's — it's not such a bad room, / Lottie."
여긴 — 여긴 그렇게 나쁜 방은 아니야,   로티."

accountable 책임이 있는 | be objected to ~에 반대되다 | attentive 배려하는 | restless 가만히 못 있는 |
reprove 나무라다 | determined 단호한, 고집 센 | hang about 어슬렁거리다, 배회하다 | gossip (소문이나
험담을) 이야기 하다 | unconsciously 무의식적으로, 무심결에 | beloved 사랑하는 | aghast 경악한, 겁에 질린 |
bare 발가벗은, 텅빈 | mount 올라가다 | implore 애원하다, 간청하다 | scold 꾸짖다

135

"Isn't it?" / gasped Lottie, / and as she looked round it /
"아니라고?" 로티가 훌쩍거리다가, 그리고 주변을 돌아보면서

she bit her lip. She was a spoiled child / yet, / but she was
입을 꽉 다물었다. 로티는 버릇없는 아이였지만 여전히,

fond enough of her adopted parent / to make an effort
양엄마를 무척 좋아했기에 노력했다

/ to control herself / for her sake. Then, / somehow, / it
참으려고 엄마를 위해. 그리고는, 어쨌든,

was quite possible / that any place / in which Sara lived
충분히 가능했다 어느 곳이든 새라가 사는 곳이면

/ might turn out to be nice. "Why isn't it, Sara?" / she
좋은 곳이 될 수 있을 것이. "왜 아닌데, 새라?"

almost whispered.
거의 속삭이듯 말했다.

Sara hugged her close / and tried to laugh. There was a
새라는 로티를 바짝 끌어안고 웃으려고 애썼다.

sort of comfort / in the warmth / of the plump, childish
위로가 느껴졌다 따뜻함 속에서 통통한 아이의 몸이 주는.

body. She had had a hard day / and had been staring / out
새라는 힘든 하루를 보냈고 보고 있던 중이었다

of the windows / with hot eyes.
창 밖을 뜨거워진 눈으로.

"You can see all sorts of things / you can't see
"온갖 종류의 것들을 볼 수 있거든 아래층에서 볼 수 없었던,"

downstairs," / she said.
그녀가 말했다.

"What sort of things?" / demanded Lottie, / with that
"뭔데?" 로티가 따져 물었다, 호기심으로

curiosity / Sara could always awaken / even in bigger
새라가 항상 불러 일으켰던 더 큰 여자애들에게도.

girls.

---

turn out 나타나다, ~로 밝혀지다 | plump 통통한 | chimney 굴뚝 | curl up 동그랗게 말리다 | sparrow 참새 |
pop out 튀어 나오다 | lean 기대다 | edge 끝, 모서리 | flat window 평평한 지붕 창문

"Chimneys / — quite close to us — / with smoke /
"굴뚝이랑   — 아주 가까이 있는 —   연기가

curling up in wreaths and clouds / and going up into the
고리 모양으로 구름처럼 동그랗게 말려서   하늘로 올라가는

sky / — and sparrows / hopping about / and talking to
— 참새들이랑   주위를 뛰어다니며   서로 이야기 하는

each other / just as if they were people — / and other
      사람인 양 —   그리고 다른 다락방

attic windows / where heads may pop out / any minute /
창문들도   머리가 튀어나올지 모르는   어느 때든

and you can wonder / who they belong to. And it all feels
그리고 상상해 볼 수 있어   거기에 누가 사는지.   그래서 높이 올라온 기분

as high up / — as if it was another world."
이 들어   — 마치 다른 세상인 것처럼.

"Oh, let me see it!" / cried Lottie. "Lift me up!"
"와, 나도 볼래!"   로티가 소리쳤다.   "날 올려줘!"

Sara lifted her up, / and they stood / on the old table /
새라는 로티를 올려줬고,   그들은 서서   낡은 탁자 위에

together / and leaned on the edge / of the flat window in
함께   모서리에 기대어   지붕 창문의,

the roof, / and looked out.
            내다 보았다.

Key Expression ♥

for one's sake : ~을 위해

for one's sake는 '~를 위해'라는 의미의 숙어입니다.
소유격 대신 for the sake of ~로 바꾸어 쓰기도 합니다. 사람일 경우에는 소
유격을, 사물일 경우에는 후자를 쓰는 경우가 많습니다.

ex) She was fond enough of her adopted parent to make an effort to control
herself for her sake.
그녀는 양엄마를 무척 좋아했기에 엄마를 위해 참으려고 노력했다.

Anyone who has not done this / does not know / what a
이런 일을 해 보지 않은 사람은   모른다

different world they saw. The slates spread out / on either
세상이 얼마나 다르게 보이는지.   슬레이트 지붕이 펼쳐져 있고

side of them / and slanted down / into the rain gutter-pipes.
양쪽으로   비스듬하게 기울어져 있었다   빗물받이 홈통 쪽으로.

The sparrows, / being at home there, / twittered and hopped
참새들은,   그곳에서 살고 있는,   재잘거리며 뛰놀았다

about / quite without fear. Two of them perched / on the
         겁도 없이.   그 중 두 마리는 앉아 있다가

chimney top nearest / and quarrelled with each other /
가장 가까운 굴뚝 꼭대기에   서로 싸우더니

fiercely / until one pecked the other / and drove him away.
사납게   한 놈이 다른 놈을 쪼아대며   쫓아버렸다.

The garret window / next to theirs / was shut / because the
다락방의 창문은   그 옆에 있는   닫혀 있었다

house next door was empty.
옆집은 비어 있었기 때문에.

Key Expression ♥

how와 what으로 시작하는 감탄문

영어의 감탄문은 how와 what으로 시작하는 두 가지가 있어요.
how는 형용사나 부사의 문장에, what은 명사가 있는 문장에 쓰이는데 각각의
어순이 다르므로 잘 기억하세요.

▶ How + 형용사/부사 + (주어 + 동사)!
▶ What + (a/an) + 형용사 + 명사 + (주어 + 동사)!

ex) Anyone who has not done this does not know what a different world they
    saw.
    이런 일을 해 보지 않은 사람이라면 세상이 얼마나 다르게 보이는지 모른다.
    Just think how nice it would be
    그것이 얼마나 멋질지 생각해 봐.

---

slate 점판암, 슬레이트(과거 지붕의 재료로 많이 사용되었음) | slant 기울어지다 | gutter (지붕의) 홈통 | perch (새가) 앉아 있다 | fiercely 사납게, 맹렬하게 | peck 쪼다 | enchanted 황홀해 하는 | chimney pot 굴뚝 꼭대기의 통풍관 | crumb 빵 부스러기 | bun 둥근 빵

"I wish someone lived there," / Sara said. "It is so close /
"저곳에 누군가 살고 있으면 좋을텐데." 새라가 말했다. "아주 가까워서

that if there was a little girl / in the attic, / we could talk to
만약 여자 아이가 산다면 저 다락방에, 서로 이야기 할 수도 있고

each other / through the windows / and climb over to see /
창문을 통해 타고 넘어가서 만날 수도 있을 거야

each other, / if we were not afraid of falling."
서로, 떨어질 염려만 없다면.'

The sky seemed so much nearer / than when one saw it /
하늘은 훨씬 가깝게 보여서 봤을 때보다

from the street, / that Lottie was enchanted. From the attic
거리에서, 로티는 황홀해 했다. 다락방 창문에서 보면,

window, / among the chimney pots, / the things which
굴뚝 꼭대기의 통풍관 사이로, 일어나고 있는 일들이

were happening / in the world below / seemed almost
저 아래 세상에서 거의 비현실적으로 보였다.

unreal. One scarcely believed / in the existence / of Miss
믿을 수 없었고 존재를 민친 교장과 아멜리아 선생과

Minchin and Miss Amelia / and the schoolroom, / and the
교실의, 바퀴가 굴러가는 소리도

roll of wheels / in the square / seemed a sound / belonging
광장에서 들리는 것 같았다

to another existence.
다른 세상의 소리처럼.

"Oh, Sara!" / cried Lottie, / cuddling in her guarding arm.
"와, 새라!" 로티가 소리쳤다, 새라가 붙잡고 있는 팔에 안겨.

"I like this attic / — I like it! It is nicer / than downstairs!"
"난 이 다락방이 좋아 — 정말 좋아! 더 멋져 아래층보다!"

"Look at that sparrow," / whispered Sara. "I wish / I had
"저 참새 좀 봐," 새라가 속삭였다. "좋겠는데

some crumbs / to throw to him."
빵 부스러기가 있었으면 쟤한테 던져 줄.'

"I have some!" / came in a little shriek / from Lottie. "I
"나한테 있어!" 작은 외침 소리가 들려왔다 로티로부터.

have part of a bun / in my pocket; / I bought it / with my
"나한테 빵 조각이 있어 주머니에; 내가 샀는데

penny / yesterday, / and I saved a bit."
내 돈으로 어제, 조금 남겨뒀지.'

139

When they threw out / a few crumbs / the sparrow
그들이 던져주자   빵부스러기를   참새는 폴짝 뛰더니

jumped / and flew away / to an adjacent chimney top. He
날아가 버렸다   가까운 굴뚝 꼭대기로.

was evidently not accustomed / to intimates in attics, /
분명히 익숙지 않은 듯 했고   다락방의 친구들이,

and unexpected crumbs startled him. But when Lottie
갑작스런 빵부스러기에 깜짝 놀란 모양이었다.

remained quite still / and Sara chirped very softly / —
하지만 로티가 가만히 있고   새라가 아주 부드럽게 짹짹 소리를 내자

almost as if she were a sparrow herself — / he saw /
— 마치 자기가 참새인 듯 —   참새는 알았다

that the thing / which had alarmed him / represented
물건이   자신을 놀라게 했던   환대의 표시임을,

hospitality, / after all. He put his head on one side, / and
결국.   참새는 고개를 한 쪽으로 까닥거리며,

from his perch / on the chimney / looked down at the
앉은 곳에서   굴뚝 위에   빵부스러기를 쳐다봤다

crumbs / with twinkling eyes. Lottie could scarcely keep
빛나는 눈으로.   로티는 더 이상 가만히 있을 수 없었다.

still.

"Will he come? Will he come?" / she whispered.
"저것이 올까?   올려나?   그녀는 속삭였다.

"His eyes look as if he would," / Sara whispered back.
"올 것처럼 보이는 눈빛인데,"   새라가 속삭이며 대답했다.

"He is thinking and thinking / whether he dare. Yes, he
"곰곰이 생각하는 중인 거야   용기를 낼지 말지.   맞아, 올 거야!

will! Yes, he is coming!"
그래, 오고 있어!"

---

adjacent 인접한, 가까운 | startle 놀라게 하다 | chirp 짹짹거리다 | hospitality 환대 | twinkling 반짝이는 |
dare 감히 ~하다, ~한 용기를 내다 | reflecting on 곰곰이 생각하다 | dart 쏜살같이 움직이다 | seize 꽉 붙잡다 |
relative 친척, 동족 | hearty 다정한, 푸짐한 | chatter 수다 떨다, 재잘거리다

He flew down / and hopped / toward the crumbs, / but
참새가 날아오더니 뛰어갔지만 빵부스러기를 향해,

stopped / a few inches away from them, / putting his head
멈췄다 몇 인치 떨어져서, 고개를 까닥거리면서

on one side / again, / as if reflecting on the chances / that
다시, 가능성을 생각하는 듯이

Sara and Lottie might turn out / to be big cats / and jump
새라와 로티가 돌변하여 큰 고양이로 자신을 덮칠.

on him. At last / his heart told him / they were really nicer
마침내 마음으로 느꼈는지 그 사람들은 정말 더 착하다고

/ than they looked, / and he hopped / nearer and nearer,
보기보다, 뛰어가더니 점점 더 가까이,

/ darted at the biggest crumb / with a lightning peck, /
가장 큰 부스러기를 향해 돌진했고 번개처럼 쪼면서,

seized it, / and carried it / away to the other side / of his
그것을 물더니, 가져갔다 멀리 반대편으로

chimney.
굴뚝의.

"Now he knows," / said Sara. "And he will come back / for
"이제 아는 거야." 새라가 말했다. "그리고 돌아올 거야

the others."
다른 친구들을 위해."

He did come back, / and even brought a friend, / and the
참새는 정말로 돌아왔고, 친구까지 데려왔다,

friend went away / and brought a relative, / and among
그리고 그 친구가 가서 또 동료를 데려와서, 그들 속에서

them / they made a hearty meal / over which they twittered
배불리 먹었다 지저귀고 짹짹거리며 소리를 지르며,

and chattered and exclaimed, / stopping every now and
그리고 이따금 먹는 것을 멈추고

then / to put their heads on one side / and examine Lottie
고개를 한 쪽으로 기울여 로티와 새라를 살펴보았다.

and Sara. Lottie was so delighted / that she quite forgot /
로티는 아주 기뻐서 완전히 잊었다

her first shocked impression / of the attic. In fact, / when
처음의 충격적인 인상을　　　　　　　　　다락방의.　　　사실,

she was lifted down / from the table / and returned to
로티를 내려놓고　　　　　　탁자에서　　　　현실로 돌아오자,

earthly things, / as it were, / Sara was able to point out / to
　　　　　　　　　말하자면,　　　새라는 알려 줄 수 있게 되었다

her many beauties / in the room / which she herself would
많은 멋진 것들에 대해　　　방에 있는　　　그녀 자신도 생각하지 못했던

not have suspected / the existence of.
　　　　　　　　　그 존재에 대해.

"It is so little / and so high / above everything," / she said, /
"여기는 아주 작고　　매우 높아　　모든 것보다,"　　　새라가 말했다,

"that it is almost like a nest / in a tree. The slanting ceiling
"그래서 거의 둥지같지　　　나무에 있는.　비스듬한 천장은 아주 재미있어.

is so funny. See, / you can scarcely stand up / at this end of
　　봐,　　서 있을 수도 없잖아　　　　　　방의 이쪽 끝에서는:

the room; / and when the morning begins to come / I can
　　　　　그리고 아침이 오기 시작하면

lie in bed / and look right up into the sky / through that flat
난 침대에 누워서　하늘을 바로 쳐다볼 수 있어　　저 평평한 창문을 통해

window / in the roof. It is like / a square patch of light. If
　　　　지붕에 있는.　창문은 마치　네모난 햇빛 조각같아.

the sun is going to shine, / little pink clouds float about, /
해가 비추기 시작하면,　　　　　작은 분홍색 구름들이 떠다니고,

and I feel / as if I could touch them. And if it rains, / the
느껴지지　　마치 만질 수 있을 것처럼.　　그리고 비가 오면,

drops patter and patter / as if they were saying / something
빗방울이 후두둑 후두둑 떨어지지　　말하는 듯　　　　　뭔가 멋진 걸.

nice. Then / if there are stars, / you can lie / and try to
　　　그리고는　별이 뜨면,　　　누워서　　셀 수 있어

count / how many go into the patch. It takes such a lot.
　　　얼마나 많은 별이 그 조각 안에 들어가는지.　엄청 많이 들어가지.

---

earthly 현세의, 세속적인 | as it were 말하자면 | point out 가리키다, 알려 주다 | suspect 의심하다 | nest 둥지
| patch 부분, 조각 | float 떠 다니다 | patter 후닥닥 달리다 | rusty 녹슨

And just look at that tiny, rusty grate / in the corner. If it was
저 작고, 녹슨 벽난로를 봐   구석에 있는.   난로를 윤이

polished / and there was a fire in it, / just think / how nice it
나게 닦아   그 안에 불을 피운다면,   생각해 봐   얼마나 멋질지.

would be. You see, / it's really a beautiful little room."
있잖아,   여기는 정말 멋진 작은 방이야."

She was walking / round the small place, / holding Lottie's
새라는 걸어 다녔다   작은 방 주위를,   로티의 손을 잡고

hand / and making gestures / which described / all the
몸짓을 하며   설명하는   아름다운 모든 것

beauties / she was making herself see. She quite made
들을   자신이 보고 있는.   새라는 로티에게도 볼 수 있게

Lottie see them, / too. Lottie could always believe / in the
했다,   역시.   로티는 항상 믿을 수 있었다

things / Sara made pictures of.
것들을   새라가 그려내는.

"You see," / she said, / "there could be a thick, soft blue
"보이지,"   새라가 말했다,   "두껍고, 부드러운 푸른색 인도산 양탄자가 있을 거야

Indian rug / on the floor; / and in that corner / there could
바닥에는;   그리고 저 구석에는

be a soft little sofa, / with cushions / to curl up on; / and
푹신하고 작은 소파가 있을 테고,   쿠션이 있는   몸을 기댈;

just over it / could be a shelf / full of books / so that one
그 바로 위에는   책장이 있지   책으로 가득 찬

could reach them / easily; / and there could be a fur rug
손이 닿을 수 있도록   쉽게;   모피로 된 양탄자도 있어

/ before the fire, / and hangings on the wall / to cover up
모닥불 앞에는,   벽에는 벽걸이가 있어서   회칠을 가려주고,

the whitewash, / and pictures. They would have to be little
그림들도.   벽걸이나 그림은 작은 것이겠지만,

ones, / but they could be beautiful; / and there could be
그래도 멋질 거야;   그리고 전등이 있어

a lamp / with a deep rose-colored shade; / and a table in
짙은 장밋빛 전등갓을 씌운;   가운데에는 탁자가 있어,

the middle, / with things to have tea with; / and a little fat
찻잔 세트가 놓여 있는;

copper kettle singing / on the hob; / and the bed could be
작고 두툼한 구리 주전자가 노래하고 벽난로 선반에서;

quite different. It could be made soft / and covered with a
침대는 아주 달라질 거야. 푹신해질 거고   예쁜 실크 침대보에 덮여 있는 거야.

lovely silk coverlet. It could be beautiful. And perhaps / we
멋지겠지.   그리고 어쩌면

could coax the sparrows / until we made such friends with
참새들을 구슬릴 수도 있지   마침내 참새들과 친구가 되어

them / that they would come / and peck at the window /
이쪽으로 와서   창문을 쪼아대며

and ask to be let in."
들어보내 달라고 조를지도 몰라.'

"Oh, Sara!" / cried Lottie. "I should like to live here!"
"와, 새라!"   로티가 소리쳤다.   "난 여기에 살고 싶어!"

When Sara had persuaded her / to go downstairs again,
새라가 로티를 설득하여   다시 아래층으로 가도록 했고,

/ and, / after setting her on her way, / had come back
그리고,   다시 돌아온 후,   다락방으로 돌아오자,

to her attic, / she stood in the middle of it / and looked
방 한가운데 서서   주변을 둘러보았다.

about her. The enchantment of her imaginings / for
상상 속의 황홀했던 장면은   로티를 위한

Lottie / had died away. The bed was hard / and covered
사라져 버렸다.   침대는 딱딱했고

with its dingy quilt. The whitewashed wall / showed its
더러운 누비이불로 덮여 있었다.   회칠한 벽은

broken patches, / the floor was cold and bare, / the grate
깨진 조각들이 드러났고,   바닥은 차갑고 낡았으며,

was broken and rusty, / and the battered footstool, / tilted
벽난로는 망가지고 녹슬었고,   낡아빠진 의자는,

sideways on its injured leg, / the only seat / in the room.
다리가 망가져 기울어진,   유일한 의자였다   방 안에 있는.

She sat down on it / for a few minutes / and let her head
새라는 그 위에 앉아서   잠시 동안   고개를 숙여

drop / in her hands. The mere fact / that Lottie had come
손에 묻었다.   그 단순한 사실이   로티가 왔다가

/ and gone away again / made things seem a little worse
다시 떠났다는 것 뿐인데   상황을 더욱 악화시킨 것 같았다

/ — just as perhaps prisoners feel / a little more desolate
— 마치 죄수들이 느끼는 것처럼   더 외롭게

/ after visitors come and go, / leaving them behind.
방문객들이 왔다 간 후,   남겨졌을 때.

whitewash (초크나 석회로 만든) 백색 도료 | shade (전등) 갓 | fat 두툼한, 넓은 | copper 구리 | kettle 주전자 |
hob 벽난로 안의 (냄비를 올려 놓는) 시렁 | coverlet 침대보 | coax 구슬리다, 달래다 | persuade 설득하다 | quilt
퀼트, 누비이불 | battered 낡은, 닳은 | tilt 기울다 | injured 상처 입은 | desolate 너무나 외로운, 적막한

145

"It's a lonely place," / she said. "Sometimes / it's the
"여기는 외로운 곳이야," 새가 말했다. "때때로

loneliest place / in the world."
가장 외로운 곳이지 세상에서."

She was sitting / in this way / when her attention was
새라는 앉아 있었다 이런 식으로 그때 주목을 끌었다

attracted / by a slight sound / near her. She lifted her
작은 소리가 그녀 옆에서. 새라는 고개를 들고 보았다

head to see / where it came from, / and if she had been
그 소리가 어디에서 나는지, 만약 겁을 잘 먹는 아이였다면

a nervous child / she would have left her seat / on the
자리를 떠났을지 모른다

battered footstool / in a great hurry. A large rat was
그 낡은 의자에서 아주 서둘러서. 큰 쥐가 앉아 있었다

sitting / up on his hind quarters / and sniffing the air /
뒷다리로 선 채 허공에 코를 벌름거리면서

in an interested manner. Some of Lottie's crumbs had
흥미롭다는 태도로. 로티의 빵부스러기들이 떨어져 있었고

dropped / upon the floor / and their scent had drawn him
바닥에 그 냄새가 그를 끌어낸 것이었다

/ out of his hole.
구멍 밖으로.

He looked so queer / and so like a gray-whiskered dwarf
그 쥐는 매우 신기해 보였고 잿빛 구레나룻을 기른 난장이나 도깨비같아서

or gnome / that Sara was rather fascinated. He looked
새라는 몹시 마음이 끌렸다. 쥐는 새라를 쳐다보았다

at her / with his bright eyes, / as if he were asking a
눈을 빛내며, 마치 질문을 하는 듯이.

question. He was evidently so doubtful / that one of the
분명 망설이는 듯 보였고

child's queer thoughts / came into her mind.
그래서 새라의 신기한 생각 중 하나가 머리 속에 떠올랐다.

slight 약간의, 작은 | nervous 신경이 과민한, 겁을 잘 먹는 | hind quarters (짐승의 두 뒷다리를 포함하는)
후 반신 | sniff 코를 킁킁거리다, 냄새를 맡다 | whiskered 구레나룻을 기른 | dwarf 난장이 | gnome 난장이,
아기도깨비 | muse (사색에 잠긴 채) 혼잣말을 하다 | pounce 덮치다, 덤비다 | frightfully 몹시, 대단히 |
cautiously 조심스럽게

"I dare say / it is rather hard / to be a rat," / she mused.
"분명히　　　　꽤 힘들 거야　　　　쥐가 되는 것을,"　　새라는 혼잣말을 했다.

"Nobody likes you. People jump / and run away / and
"아무도 좋아하지 않지.　　　사람들은 펄쩍 뛰어　　도망가며

scream out, / 'Oh, a horrid rat!' I shouldn't like / people
소리지르지,　　　'아, 징그러운 쥐!'라며.　　난 좋아하지 않겠지

to scream and jump and say, / 'Oh, a horrid Sara!' / the
사람들이 소리지르고 펄쩍 뛰며 말한다면,　　'아, 징그러운 새라!'라고

moment they saw me. And set traps for me, / and pretend
날 봤을 때.　　　　그리고 잡으려는 덫을 놓잖아,　　　꾸며서

/ they were dinner. It's so different / to be a sparrow. But
저녁 식사인 척.　　　아주 달라　　　참새가 되는 것과는.

nobody asked this rat / if he wanted to be a rat / when
하지만 누구도 이 쥐에게 묻지 않았어　쥐가 되고 싶었냐고

he was made. Nobody said, / 'Wouldn't you rather be a
처음 생겼을 때.　　아무도 말하지 않았지,　'넌 참새가 되는 것이 낫지 않겠니?'라고."

sparrow?'"

She had sat so quietly / that the rat had begun to take
새라가 아주 조용히 앉아 있으니까　　쥐는 용기를 내기 시작했다.

courage. He was very much afraid of her, / but perhaps
쥐는 새라를 매우 두려워 했지만,　　　　　아마도

/ he had a heart / like the sparrow / and it told him /
마음을 갖고 있어서　　참새와 같은　　　그 마음이 말했는지도 몰랐다

that she was not a thing / which pounced. He was very
그녀는 그런 사람이 아니라고　　확 덮칠.　　　쥐는 매우 배고팠다.

hungry. He had a wife and a large family / in the wall,
아내와 많은 가족도 있었고　　　　벽 속에,

/ and they had had frightfully bad luck / for several
그리고 몹시도 운이 나빴다　　　　며칠 동안.

days. He had left the children / crying bitterly, / and felt
아이들을 두고 왔고　　　비통하게 우는,　　　생각했다

/ he would risk a good deal / for a few crumbs, / so he
위험을 감수하겠다고　　빵부스러기를 갖기 위해,

cautiously dropped upon his feet.
그래서 조심스럽게 발을 내렸다.

147

"Come on," / said Sara; / "I'm not a trap. You can have
"이리와," 새라가 말했다; "난 쥐덫이 아니야. 그것을 가져가도 돼,

them, / poor thing! Prisoners in the Bastille / used to make
가엾은 것! 바스티유 감옥의 죄수들은 친하게 지내곤 했지

friends / with rats. Suppose I make friends with you."
쥐들과. 난 너랑 친하게 지낼 수 있을 것 같아."

How it is that / animals understand things / I do not know,
도대체 어떻게 동물들이 이해하는지는 나도 모른다,

/ but it is certain / that they do understand. Perhaps /
하지만 확실하다 그들이 정말 이해한다는 사실은. 아마도

there is a language / which is not made of words / and
언어가 있을지 모른다 말의 형태로 만들어지지는 않아도

everything in the world / understands it. Perhaps / there
세상에 모든 것이 이해할 수 있는. 아마도 숨겨진 영혼

is a soul hidden / in everything / and it can always speak,
이 있을지 모른다 모든 것에 그래서 언제나 대화할 수 있는 것이다,

/ without even making a sound, / to another soul. But
소리조차 내지 않고, 다른 영혼에게.

whatsoever was the reason, / the rat knew / from that
하지만 이유가 무엇이든, 쥐는 알았다 그 순간부터

moment / that he was safe / — even though he was a
안전하다는 것을 — 그가 쥐일지라도.

rat. He knew / that this young human being / sitting on
쥐는 알았다 이 어린 사람은

the red footstool / would not jump up / and terrify him /
빨간 의자 위에 앉아 있는 뛰어 오르거나 겁을 주지 않을 거라고

with wild, sharp noises / or throw heavy objects / at him
거칠고, 날카로운 비명을 지르거나 무거운 물건들을 던져서 그에게

/ which, / if they did not fall and crush him, / would send
그 물건이, 떨어져 자신을 뭉개버리지 않더라도 절뚝거리며 가게 만

him limping / in his scurry / back to his hole. He was
들 것이었다 종종 걸음으로 쥐구멍으로 돌아가도록.

really a very nice rat, / and did not mean / the least harm.
그는 정말 착한 쥐였고, 의도하지 않았다 조금도 해로운 것을.

terrify 겁먹게 하다 | crush 으스러뜨리다 | limp 절뚝거리다 | scurry 종종걸음을 치다 | apologetic 미안해
하는, 사과하는 | evident 분명한

When he had stood / on his hind legs / and sniffed the air, /
쥐가 서서   뒷다리로   허공에 킁킁 대고 있을 때,

with his bright eyes fixed on Sara, / he had hoped / that she
빛나는 눈은 새라에게 고정한 채,   쥐는 바랐던 것이다

would understand this, / and would not begin by hating him
새라가 이것을 이해하기를,   그리고 자신을 미워하지 않기를

/ as an enemy. When the mysterious thing / which speaks
적으로.   신비스러운 존재가

without saying any words / told him / that she would not, /
말을 하지 않고 말을 거는   쥐에게 말하자   그녀는 그러지 않을 거라고,

he went softly / toward the crumbs / and began to eat them.
쥐는 조용히 다가가서   빵부스러기 쪽으로   그것을 먹기 시작했다.

As he did it / he glanced / every now and then / at Sara, /
그러면서   쳐다보았다   이따금씩   새라를,

just as the sparrows had done, / and his expression was so
참새가 그랬듯이,   쥐의 표정이 매우 미안해 하는 듯하여

very apologetic / that it touched her heart.
       새라의 심금을 울렸다.

She sat / and watched him / without making any movement.
새라는 앉아서 쥐를 보았다   전혀 움직이지 않고.

One crumb was very much larger / than the others / — in
한 부스러기가 훨씬 컸다   다른 것보다

fact, / it could scarcely be called a crumb. It was evident
— 사실,   부스러기라고 부를 수도 없었지만.   분명히

/ that he wanted that piece / very much, / but it lay / quite
그 조각을 원했지만   아주 많이,   그 조각은 놓여 있어서

near the footstool / and he was still rather timid.
의자에 아주 가까이   쥐는 여전히 겁을 냈다.

"I believe / he wants it to carry / to his family / in the wall,"
"내 생각에   그 조각을 가져가고 싶은 것 같아   가족에게   벽 속에 있는,"

/ Sara thought. "If I do not stir at all, / perhaps he will come
새라는 생각했다.   "만약 내가 전혀 움직이지 않으면,   아마 다가와서

/ and get it."
그것을 가져갈 거야."

She scarcely allowed herself to breathe, / she was so deeply
새라는 숨도 거의 쉬지 않았고, 아주 깊이 흥미로워 했다.

interested. The rat shuffled / a little nearer / and ate a few
쥐는 발을 질질 끌며 와서 좀 더 가까이 몇 조각을 더 먹었고,

more crumbs, / then he stopped / and sniffed delicately, /
그리고는 멈춰서 면밀히 냄새를 맡았다,

giving a side glance / at the occupant of the footstool; / then
곁눈질로 살피며 의자에 앉아 있는 사람을; 그리고는

/ he darted at the piece of bun / with something very like
빵 조각으로 돌진했다 똑같이 갑작스럽고 대담하게

the sudden boldness / of the sparrow, / and the instant he
참새가 했던 것처럼, 그리고 그 조각을 갖자마자

had possession of it / fled back to the wall, / slipped down a
쏜살같이 벽으로 돌아가, 갈라진 틈으로 미끄러져

crack / in the skirting board, / and was gone.
들어가더니 굽도리 널에 나 있는, 그리고 사라졌다.

"I knew / he wanted it / for his children," / said Sara. "I do
"난 알았어 그것을 원했다는 것을 아이들을 위해." 새라가 말했다.

believe / I could make friends with him."
"난 믿어 그 쥐랑 친하게 지낼 수 있다고."

A week or so afterward, / on one of the rare nights / when
일주일 정도 후에, 드물었던 어느 밤에

Ermengarde found it safe / to steal up to the attic, / when
어먼가드가 안전하다고 판단한 다락방에 몰래 가는 것이,

she tapped on the door / with the tips of her fingers / Sara
어먼가드가 문을 두드렸을 때 손 끝으로

did not come to her / for two or three minutes. There
새라는 나오지 않았다 2~3분 동안.

was, / indeed, / such a silence / in the room / at first / that
있었다, 실제로, 적막이 방 안에 처음에는

Ermengarde wondered / if she could have fallen asleep.
어먼가드는 궁금했다 새라가 잠이 든 것은 아닌지.

Then, / to her surprise, / she heard/ her utter a little, low
그리고는, 놀랍게도, 들렸다 새라가 작은 소리로 낮게 웃으면서

laugh / and speak coaxingly / to someone.
달래면서 말하는 것이 누군가에게.

"There!" / Ermengarde heard her say. "Take it and go
"자!" 어먼가드는 그녀가 말하는 것을 들었다. "그것을 갖고 집으로 가,

home, / Melchisedec! Go home / to your wife!"
멜기세덱! 집에 가 부인에게로!"

Almost immediately / Sara opened the door, / and when
거의 동시에 새라가 문을 열었고,

she did so / she found Ermengarde standing / with
그렇게 했을 때 어먼가드가 서 있는 것을 발견했다

alarmed eyes / upon the threshold.
놀란 눈으로 문지방 위에.

"Who — who are you talking to, Sara?" / she gasped
"누구 — 누구랑 얘기하는 거야, 새라?" 숨 넘어가는 소리로

out.
말했다.

Sara drew her in cautiously, / but she looked / as if
새라는 어먼가드를 조심스럽게 잡아끌었는데, 하지만 보였다

something pleased and amused her.
마치 뭔가 즐겁고 기쁜 듯이.

"You must promise / not to be frightened / — not to
"약속해야 해 겁내지 않겠다고

scream the least bit, / or I can't tell you," / she answered.
— 조금도 소리지르지 않겠다고, 안 그러면 말 안 할 거야," 새라가 대답했다.

Ermengarde felt almost inclined to scream / on the spot, /
어먼가드는 거의 소리를 지를 것 같았지만 그곳에서,

but managed to control herself. She looked all round the
겨우 참았다. 그녀는 다락방 주위를 모두 보았고

attic / and saw no one. And yet / Sara had certainly been
아무도 없었다. 하지만 새라는 분명히 말하고 있었다

speaking / to someone. She thought of ghosts.
누군가에게. 어먼가드는 유령이라고 생각했다.

"Is it / — something that will frighten me?" / she asked /
"그것이 — 날 무섭게 하는 거야?" 그녀가 물었다

timorously.
무서워하며.

delicately 섬세하게 | glance 흘낏 봄 | instant 순간 | crack (갈라진) 금, 틈 | rare 드문 | utter 입 밖에 내다,
말하다 | threshold 문지방 | gasp out 숨 넘어가는 소리로 말하다 | manage to 가까스로 ~하다 | timorously
무서워하여, 소심하게

151

"Some people are afraid / of them," / said Sara. "I was at
"어떤 사람들은 무서워 해   그들을."   새라가 말했다.   "나도 처음에는

first / — but I am not now."
그랬어   — 하지만 지금은 안 그래."

"Was it / — a ghost?" / quaked Ermengarde.
"그것   — 유령이니?"   어먼가드가 몸을 떨었다.

"No," / said Sara, / laughing. "It was my rat."
"아니,"   새라가 말했다.   웃으며.   "그것은 내 쥐야."

Ermengarde made one bound, / and landed / in the
어먼가드는 펄쩍 뛰더니.   올라섰다

middle of the little dingy bed. She tucked her feet / under
작고 더러운 침대 한가운데에.   그녀는 다리를 끌어당겼다

her nightgown / and the red shawl. She did not scream, /
잠옷과   빨간 숄 아래로.   소리를 지르지는 않았지만,

but she gasped / with fright.
숨도 제대로 쉬지 못했다 공포로.

"Oh! Oh!" / she cried / under her breath. "A rat! A rat!"
"아!   아!"   그녀가 외쳤다 작은 소리로.   "쥐! 쥐라고!"

"I was afraid you would be frightened," / said Sara. "But
"네가 겁낼 것 같았어,"   새라가 말했다.

you needn't be. I am making him tame. He actually
"하지만 그럴 필요 없어. 내가 길들이는 중이거든.   정말로 날 알고 있어서

knows me / and comes out / when I call him. Are you
밖으로 나오지   내가 부르면.

too frightened / to want to see him?"
넌 너무 무서워서   보고 싶지 않지?"

The truth was that, / as the days had gone on / and, /
사실은 그랬다,   며칠이 지나는 동안   그리고,

with the aid of scraps / brought up from the kitchen, / her
먹다 남은 음식들로   부엌에서 가져온,

curious friendship had developed, / she had gradually
새라의 희한한 우정이 생겨났고,   서서히 잊어버렸다

forgotten / that the timid creature / she was becoming
그 소심한 동물이   자신이 익숙해지고 있는

familiar with / was a mere rat.
단지 쥐라는 사실을.

At first / Ermengarde was too much alarmed / to do
처음에   어먼가드는 너무 놀라서   아무것도

anything / but huddle in a heap / upon the bed / and
하지 않고   몸을 웅크리고 앉아   침대 위에서   다리를

tuck up her feet, / but the sight of Sara's composed
끌어안고 있기만 했다,   하지만 새라의 침착한 표정을 보고

little countenance / and the story of Melchisedec's first
                      멜기세덱의 처음 모습에 대한 이야기를 듣자

appearance / began at last to rouse her curiosity, / and
              마침내 호기심이 일어나기 시작했다.

she leaned forward / over the edge of the bed / and
그래서 앞으로 기대고   침대 모서리 위로

watched / Sara go and kneel down / by the hole / in the
보았다   새라가 가서 무릎을 꿇고 앉는 것을   구멍 옆에

skirting board.
굽도리 널에 있는.

"He — he won't run out / quickly / and jump on the bed,
"그 애는 — 뛰어나오거나   재빨리   침대로 뛰어올라가지 않을까,

/ will he?" / she said.
   그럴까?"   어먼가드가 말했다.

Key Expression

I'm afraid의 의미

afraid는 원래 '두려워하는, 걱정하는, 염려하는'이라는 의미의 형용사입니다.
하지만 회화체에서는 부정적인 내용을 말할 때 덧붙이는 표현으로 쓰여, '~인
것 같다, (유감이지만) ~이다'와 같은 뜻을 나타내는 경우가 많습니다. 이런 때에
는 I think에 부정적인 내용이 따라올 때 완곡하게 표현하는 말로 해석하는 것
이 자연스러워요.

ex) I was afraid you would be frightened.
    네가 겁낼 것 같았어.

---

quake 몸을 떨다, 전율하다 | under one's breath 속삭이며, 작은 소리로 | tame 길들여진 | scrap 먹다 남은 음식,
찌꺼기 | timid 겁먹은 | composed 침착한, 차분한 | countenance 얼굴, 표정

"No," / answered Sara. "He's as polite as we are. He is just
"전혀," 새라가 대답했다. "그 애는 우리처럼 예의 바르니까.

like a person. Now watch!"
사람하고 똑같아. 이제 봐!"

She began to make a low, whistling sound / — so low and
새라는 낮은, 휘파람 소리를 내기 시작했다 — 아주 낮게 달래는 듯

coaxing / that it could only have been heard / in entire
한 소리라서 겨우 들을 수 있었다 완전히 조용해야,

stillness. She did it / several times, / looking entirely
새라는 그렇게 했다 여러 번, 그 일에 완전히 몰두한 듯이.

absorbed in it. Ermengarde thought / she looked / as if she
어먼가드는 생각했다 그녀가 보인다고

were working a spell. And at last, / evidently in response
마치 주문을 거는 것처럼. 그리고 마침내, 정말 소리에 반응하여,

to it, / a gray-whiskered, / bright-eyed head peeped / out of
회색 구레나룻이 있는, 밝게 빛나는 눈을 가진 머리가 살짝 보였다

the hole. Sara had some crumbs / in her hand. She dropped
구멍 밖으로. 새라는 빵부스러기를 가지고 있었다 손 안에. 그것을 떨어뜨리자,

them, / and Melchisedec came quietly forth / and ate them.
멜기세덱은 조용히 앞으로 나와서 그것들을 먹었다.

A piece of larger size / than the rest / he took and carried /
더 큰 조각은 다른 것보다 집어서 갖고 갔다

in the most businesslike manner / back to his home.
완전히 업무에 충실한 태도로 집으로 다시.

"You see," / said Sara, / "that is for his wife and children.
"있잖아," 새라가 말했다. "그것은 아내와 아이들을 위한 거야.

He is very nice. He only eats the little bits. After he
그는 아주 착해. 작은 조각들만 먹어. 돌아간 후

goes back / I can always hear / his family squeaking for
항상 들을 수 있어 가족들이 기뻐서 찍찍거리는 것을.

joy. There are three kinds of squeaks. One kind is the
세 종류의 찍찍거리는 소리가 있어. 하나는 아이들이고,

children's, / and one is Mrs. Melchisedec's, / and one is
하나는 멜기세덱 부인이고,

Melchisedec's own."
또 하나는 멜기세덱 자신이지."

Ermengarde began to laugh.
어먼가드는 웃기 시작했다.

"Oh, Sara!" / she said. "You are queer / — but you are
"아, 새라!" 그녀가 말했다. "넌 정말 희한해 — 하지만 넌 착해"

nice."

"I know / I am queer," / admitted Sara, / cheerfully; /
"나도 알아 내가 희한하다는 것을." 새라는 인정했다, 즐겁게;

"and I try to be nice." She rubbed her forehead / with
"그리고 난 착해지려고 노력해." 그녀는 이마를 문질렀고

her little brown paw, / and a puzzled, tender look / came
작은 갈색 손으로, 어리둥절하고, 다정한 표정이

into her face. "Papa always laughed / at me," / she said;
얼굴에 나타났다. "아빠는 항상 웃었어 날 보고," 그녀가 말했다;

/ "but I liked it. He thought / I was queer, / but he liked /
"하지만 난 그것이 좋았어. 아빠는 생각했어 내가 희한하다고, 하지만 아빠는 좋아했어

me to make up things. I — I can't help making up things.
내가 이야기를 지어내는 것을. 난 — 난 이야기를 지어낼 수밖에 없어.

If I didn't, / I don't believe I could live." She paused and
내가 하지 않으면, 살 수 있을 것 같지 않아." 그녀는 말을 멈추고 보았다

glanced / around the attic. "I'm sure / I couldn't live
다락방 주위를. "분명히 여기에서 살 수 없을 거야,"

here," / she added / in a low voice.
그녀는 덧붙였다 낮은 목소리로.

Key Expression

as ~ as 동등비교

A = B 일때 쓰이는 비교급 표현를 원급비교 혹은 동등비교라고 부르며, as + 형용
사/부사 원급 +as…의 형태로 사용합니다. 이때 '…만큼 ~한'이라고 해석하지요.
반대로 as의 앞에 not을 붙여 not as(so) + ~ +as…가 되면 '…만큼 ~하지
않은'으로, A < B라는 비교의 의미를 나타내게 됩니다.

ex) He's as polite as we are.
그 애는 우리처럼 예의 바르지.

---

whistling 휘파람을 부는 | peep 엿보다 | businesslike 효율적인, 업무에 충실한 | squeak 꽥 소리치다 | rub
문지르다 | paw (동물의) 발, (사람의) 손 | puzzled 어리둥절해 하는, 얼떨떨한 | tender 상냥한 | can't help ~ing
할 수 없이 ~하다

eagerly 열망하여; 열심히; 간절히

Ermengarde was interested, / as she always was. "When
어먼가드는 흥미로웠다.   항상 그랬듯이.

you talk about things," / she said, / "they seem as if they
"네가 뭔가를 이야기할 때,"   그녀가 말했다,   "그것이 진짜처럼 보여.

grew real. You talk about Melchisedec / as if he was a
멜기세덱에 대해 말하고 있잖아

person."
사람인 것처럼."

"He is a person," / said Sara. "He gets hungry and
"그는 사람이야,"   새라가 말했다.   "배가 고프기도 하고 겁내기도 해,

frightened, / just as we do; / and he is married / and has
꼭 우리처럼;   그리고 결혼했고

children. How do we know / he doesn't think things, /
아이들도 있어. 어떻게 알지   그 애가 생각하지 않는다고,

just as we do? His eyes look as if he was a person. That
꼭 우리처럼?   눈빛도 마치 사람처럼 보여.

was why I gave him a name."
그래서 그에게 이름을 붙여준 거야."

She sat down / on the floor / in her favorite attitude, /
그녀는 앉았다   바닥에   그녀가 가장 좋아하는 자세로,

holding her knees.
무릎을 껴안고서.

"Besides," / she said, / "he is a Bastille rat / sent to be
"게다가,"   그녀가 말했다,   "그는 바스티유 감옥의 쥐야

my friend. I can always get a bit of bread / the cook has
내 친구로 보내진. 난 항상 빵 조각을 가져올 수 있고   요리사가 버린,

thrown away, / and it is quite enough / to support him."
그것으로 충분해   그를 먹여 살리기에는."

"Is it the Bastille yet?" / asked Ermengarde, / eagerly.
"여기가 아직 바스티유 감옥이야?"   어먼가드가 물었다,   간절하게.

"Do you always pretend / it is the Bastille?"
"넌 항상 그런 척 하는 거야   여기가 바스티유 감옥이라고?"

"Nearly always," / answered Sara. "Sometimes / I try to
"거의 항상,"   새라가 대답했다.   "가끔은

pretend it is another kind of place; / but the Bastille is
여기가 다른 장소인 척 해 보지;   하지만 바스티유 감옥이 보통

generally easiest / — particularly when it is cold."
가장 편해   — 특히 추울 때는."

Just at that moment / Ermengarde almost jumped off the
바로 그때   어먼가드는 침대 밖으로 뛰어내릴 뻔 했다.

bed, / she was so startled / by a sound she heard. It was
       매우 놀랐다   소리가 들려서.

like two distinct knocks / on the wall.
그건 두 번의 뚜렷한 노크 소리였다   벽에서 나는.

"What is that?" / she exclaimed.
"저것은 뭐야?"   그녀가 외쳤다.

Sara got up / from the floor / and answered quite
새라가 일어나서   바닥에서   연극조로 대답했다:

dramatically:

"It is the prisoner / in the next cell."
"그것은 죄수야   옆 감방에 있는."

"Becky!" / cried Ermengarde, / enraptured.
"베키!"   어먼가드가 소리쳤다,   들떠서.

"Yes," / said Sara. "Listen; / the two knocks meant, /
"맞아,"   새라가 말했다.   "잘 들어;   두 번의 노크는 의미해,

'Prisoner, are you there?'"
'죄수야, 거기 있지?'"

She knocked three times / on the wall / herself, / as if in
그녀는 세 번 노크했다   벽에   직접,

answer.
마치 대답하는 듯.

"That means, / 'Yes, I am here, / and all is well.'"
"그것은 의미해,   '그래, 나 여기 있어,   그리고 모든 것이 괜찮아.'"

Four knocks came / from Becky's side / of the wall.
네 번 노크 소리가 들려왔다   베키 쪽에서   벽의.

"That means," / explained Sara, / "'Then, / fellow-
"그것은 의미해,"   새라가 설명했다,   "'그럼,   동병상련 친구,

sufferer, / we will sleep in peace. Good night.'"
            편히 자자.   잘 자.'"

Ermengarde quite beamed / with delight.
어먼가드는 아주 활짝 웃었다   기쁨으로.

---

distinct 뚜렷한, 분명한 | enraptured 황홀해서, 도취되어 | fellow-suffer 동병상련 | beam 활짝 웃다

"Oh, Sara!" / she whispered joyfully. "It is like a story!"
"오, 새라!"　　　그녀는 기뻐서 속삭였다.　　　"그것은 이야기같아!"

"It is a story," / said Sara. "Everything's a story. You are
"그것은 이야기야,"　　　새라가 말했다.　　"모든 것이 이야기지.　　　너도 이야기

a story / — I am a story. Miss Minchin is a story."
이고　　　— 나도 이야기야.　　민친 교장도 이야기지."

And she sat down again / and talked / until Ermengarde
그리고 새라는 다시 앉아서　　　　말했다　　　어먼가드가 잊을 때까지

forgot / that she was a sort of escaped prisoner herself,
　　　그녀 자신이 도망친 죄수라는 것을.

/ and had to be reminded by Sara / that she could not
　그리고 새라는 일깨워 줘야 했다　　　　남아 있을 수 없고

remain / in the Bastille / all night, / but must steal
　　　바스티유 감옥에　　　밤새,

noiselessly downstairs / again / and creep back / into her
아래층으로 몰래 가야 한다는 것을　　　다시　　　그리고 나서 기어 들어갔다

deserted bed.
황량한 침대 속으로.

A. 다음 문장을 해석해 보세요.

(1) She was a small thing / and did not know / what adversity meant, / and was much bewildered / by the alteration she saw / in her young adopted mother.
→

(2) She was fond enough of her adopted parent / to make an effort / to control herself / for her sake.
→

(3) The mere fact / that Lottie had come / and gone away again / made things seem a little worse / ? just as perhaps prisoners feel / a little more desolate / after visitors come and go, / leaving them behind.
→

(4) The truth was that, / as the days had gone on / and, / with the aid of scraps / brought up from the kitchen, / her curious friendship had developed, / she had gradually forgotten / that the timid creature / she was becoming familiar with / was a mere rat.
→

B. 다음 주어진 문장이 되도록 빈칸에 써서 넣으세요.

(1) 난 새라가 거지처럼 가난한 건 싫어.

→

(2) 로티가 울음을 터뜨려서 누군가 우연히 듣기라도 하면, 둘 다 끝장이었다.

If Lottie began to cry and any one chanced to hear,

.

(3) 이런 일을 해 보지 않은 사람은 세상이 얼마나 다르게 보이는지 모른다.

A. (1) 로티는 어린 아이라서 역경이 뭔지 몰랐고, 어린 양엄마의 변화를 보면서 무척 어리둥절 했다. (2) 로티는 여전히 버릇없는 아이였지만, 양엄마를 무척 좋아했기에 엄마를 위해 참으려고 노력했다. (3) 그저 로티가 왔다가 다시 떠났다는 사실만으로 상황은 더욱 나빠진 것 같았다 ― 마치 방문객들이 왔다 간 후 남

Anyone who has not done this does not know

(4) 그래서 그에게 이름을 붙여준 거야.
→

C. 다음 주어진 문구가 알맞은 문장이 되도록 순서를 맞춰 보세요.

(1) 그것이 얼마나 멋질지 생각해 봐.
(Just / think / how / nice / it / would / be)
→

(2) 도대체 어떻게 동물들이 이해하는지는 나도 모른다.
(must / You / not / be / promise / frightened / to)
                                                           I do not know.

(3) 겁내지 않겠다고 약속해야 해.
(must / You / not / be / promise / frightened / to)
→

(4) 그 애는 우리만큼 예의가 바르지.
(as / He's / as / are / polite / we)
→

D. 다음 단어에 대한 맞는 설명과 연결해 보세요.

(1) console   ▶   ◀ ① speak angrily

(2) reprove   ▶   ◀ ② make someone feel more
                                     cheerful

(3) plump   ▶   ◀ ③ make a short and loud cry

(4) shriek   ▶   ◀ ④ rather fat or rounded

겨졌을 때 죄수들이 더 외롭게 느끼는 것처럼. (4) 사실은 며칠이 지나는 동안 부엌에서 가져온 먹다 남은 음식들로. 새와의 희한한 우정이 생겨났고, 자신이 익숙해지고 있는 그 소심한 동물이 단지 쥐라는 사실을 서서히 잊어버렸다. | B. (1) I don't want you to be as poor as a beggar. (2) they were both lost (3) what a different world they saw (4) That was why I gave him a name. | C. (1) Just think how nice it would be. (2) How it is that animals understand things (3) You must promise not to be frightened. (4) He's as polite as we are. | D. (1) ② (2) ① (3) ④ (4) ③

161

7

The Indian Gentleman
인도 신사

But it was a perilous thing / for Ermengarde and Lottie / to
하지만 아주 위험한 일이었다   어먼가드와 로티가

make pilgrimages / to the attic. They could never be quite
순례를 떠나는 것은   다락방으로.   그들은 확신할 수 없었다

sure / when Sara would be there, / and they could scarcely
새라가 언제 그곳에 있을지를.   그리고 좀처럼 확신할 수 없었다

ever be certain / that Miss Amelia would not make a tour
아멜리아 선생이 돌아다니지 않을지

/ of inspection / through the bedrooms / after the pupils
감시하러   침실을 둘러보면서   학생들의

were supposed to be asleep. So their visits were rare ones,
취침 시간 이후에.   그래서 그들의 방문은 드문 일이었고,

/ and Sara lived / a strange and lonely life. It was a lonelier
새라는 살았다   낯설고 외로운 삶을.   더 외로운 삶이었다

life / when she was downstairs / than when she was in her
아래층에 있을 때에는   다락방에 있을 때보다도.

attic. She had no one / to talk to; / and when she was sent
그녀에게는 아무도 없었다   말을 걸 수 있는;   그리고 심부름으로 바깥에 나가

out on errands / and walked through the streets, / a forlorn
거리를 걸어갈 때면,

little figure / carrying a basket or a parcel, / trying to hold
외로운 아이는   바구니나 소포꾸러미를 든 채,   모자를 잡으려 애쓰거나

her hat on / when the wind was blowing, / and feeling
바람이 불 때면,   물이 스며드는 것을 느끼며

the water soak / through her shoes / when it was raining,
신발을 통해   비가 올 때면,

/ she felt / as if the crowds hurrying past her / made her
새라는 느꼈다   마치 그녀를 바삐 지나치는 군중들이   외로움을 더 크게

loneliness greater. When she had been the Princess Sara,
만드는 것처럼.   그녀가 새라 공주였을 때는,

perilous 아주 위험한 | pilgrimage 순례, 성지 참배 | soak 스며, 배어 들다 | brougham 사륜마차 | attend
수행하다, 시중들다 | eager 열렬한, 간절히 바라는, 열심인 | picturesque 그림같은 | plain 소박한, 꾸밈 없는 |
remnants (복수형) 나머지, 자투리 천

/ driving through the streets / in her brougham, / or
거리를 지나가거나 사륜마차를 타고,

walking, / attended by Mariette, / the sight of her bright,
또는 걸어갈 때, 마리에트의 시중을 받으며, 그녀의 밝고, 열망하는 작은 얼굴과

eager little face / and picturesque coats / and hats / had
그림같이 아름다운 외투와 모자로 인해

often caused people to look after her. A happy, beautifully
종종 사람들이 그녀를 보곤 했었다. 행복하고, 예쁘게 키워진

cared / for little girl / naturally / attracts attention. Shabby,
어린 소녀는 자연스럽게 주목을 끄는 법이다. 초라하고,

poorly dressed children / are not rare enough / and pretty
보잘 것 없게 옷을 입은 아이들은 그리 드물지 않고 예쁘지도 않다

enough / to make people turn around / to look at them /
사람들이 돌아서서 그들을 보고

and smile. No one looked at Sara / in these days, / and no
미소 지을 만큼. 아무도 새라를 보지 않았다 이 시절에는,

one seemed to see her / as she hurried / along the crowded
그리고 아무도 보는 것 같지 않았다 서둘러 가는 동안 사람들이 북적거리는 도로를

pavements. She had begun to grow very fast, / and, as she
따라. 그녀는 매우 빠르게 성장하기 시작했고,

was dressed only in such clothes / as the plainer remnants
그런 옷들만 입게 되었기 때문에 허름한 천조각같은

/ of her wardrobe would supply, / she knew / she looked
옷장에 남아있는, 그녀는 알았다 자신이 아주 이상해

very queer, / indeed. All her valuable garments had been
보인다는 것을, 정말로. 값비싼 옷들은 모두 처분되었고,

disposed of, / and such as had been left / for her use / she
남겨진 옷들은 사용할 수 있게

was expected to wear / so long as she could put them on at
입어야만 했다 입을 수 있는 한 최대한 오랫동안.

all. Sometimes, / when she passed a shop window / with
이따금, 가게 창문을 지날 때면

a mirror in it, / she almost laughed outright / on catching
안에 거울이 있는, 거의 웃음을 터뜨릴 뻔 했다

a glimpse of herself, / and sometimes / her face went red /
자신을 언뜻 보았을 때, 그래서 이따금 얼굴이 빨개져서

and she bit her lip / and turned away.
입술을 깨문 채 멀리 돌아가곤 했다.

163

In the evening, / when she passed houses / whose
저녁에,   집들을 지나칠 때면

windows were lighted up, / she used to look into the
창문에 불이 켜진,   따뜻한 방 안을 들여다 보며

warm rooms / and amuse herself / by imagining things
즐거워 하곤 했다   상상하면서

/ about the people / she saw / sitting before the fires /
사람들에 대해   자신이 본   난로 앞에 앉아 있거나

or about the tables. It always interested her / to catch
탁자에 둘러 앉아 있는.   항상 흥미로웠다

glimpses of rooms / before the shutters were closed.
방을 살짝 엿보는 것은   덧문이 닫히기 전에.

There were several families / in the square / in which
여러 가족들이 있었다   광장에는

Miss Minchin lived, / with which / she had become quite
민친 교장이 살고 있는,   그리고 그 가족들에게 새라는 꽤 친숙해졌다

familiar / in a way of her own. The one she liked best
자신만의 방식으로.   가장 좋아했던 가족에 대해

/ she called the Large Family. She called it the Large
그녀는 대가족이라고 불렀다.   새라가 그 가족을 대가족이라고 부른 것은

Family / not because the members of it were big / —
그 가족들이 몸집이 커서가 아니라

for, indeed, / most of them were little — / but because
— 왜냐하면, 실제로, 그들은 (몸집이) 작았으니까 —

there were so many of them. There were eight children
그 수가 아주 많았기 때문이었다.   여덟 명의 아이들이 있었고

/ in the Large Family, / and a stout, rosy mother, / and
그 대가족에는,   그리고 풍채가 좋고, 발그레한 얼굴의 엄마와,

a stout, rosy father, / and a stout, rosy grandmother, /
풍채가 좋고, 발그레한 얼굴의 아빠, 그리고 풍채가 좋고, 발그레한 얼굴의 할머니,

and any number of servants. The eight children were
그리고 많은 하인들이 있었다.   여덟 명의 아이들은

/ always either being taken out to walk / or to ride in
항상 산책을 나가거나   유모차를 타고 나가거나

perambulators / by comfortable nurses, / or they were
편한 유모들과 함께,   마차를 타고 나갔다

going to drive / with their mamma, / or they were flying
엄마와 함께,   또는 문으로 달려나가서

to the door / in the evening / to meet their papa / and kiss
저녁이면   아빠를 마중하며   아빠에게 입

him / and dance around him / and drag off his overcoat
맞추고 주위에서 춤추며   외투를 잡아 끌고

/ and look in the pockets / for packages, / or they were
주머니 안을 들여다 보았다   선물 상자를 찾으려고, 또는 모여서

crowding / about the nursery windows / and looking out
놀이방 창문 주위에   밖을 내다보면서

/ and pushing each other / and laughing / — in fact, /
서로 밀치며   웃었다   — 사실,

they were always doing something enjoyable / and suited
그들은 항상 즐거운 일들을 하고 있었으며

to the tastes of a large family.
대가족의 성향에 어울렸다.

---

amuse oneself 즐기다 | shutter 덧문, 셔터 | stout 통통한 | rosy 장밋빛의, 발그레한 | perambulator 유모차 |
package 포장용 상자

Sara was quite fond of them, / and had given them names
새라는 그들을 아주 좋아해서,   이름을 붙였다

/ out of books / — quite romantic names. She called them
책에서 따온   — 참 낭만적인 이름들을.   그녀는 그들을 불렀다

/ the Montmorencys / when she did not call them / the
몽모랑시 가족이라고   부르지 않을 때에는

Large Family. The fat, fair baby / with the lace cap / was
대가족이라고.   통통하고, 흰 피부의 아기는   레이스 달린 모자를 쓴

Ethelberta Beauchamp Montmorency; / the next baby
에셀베르타 보샹 몽모랑시였고;

was Violet Cholmondeley Montmorency; / the little boy
그 다음으로 어린 아기는 바이올렛 콜몬델리 몽모랑시였으며;   작은 남자 아이는

/ who could just stagger / and who had such round legs /
이제 겨우 뒤뚱뒤뚱 걸을 수 있는,   그리고 포동포동한 다리의

was Sydney Cecil Vivian Montmorency; / and then came
시드니 세실 비비안 몽모랑시였고;   그 다음으로는

/ Lilian Evangeline Maud Marion, / Rosalind Gladys, /
릴리안 에반젤린 모드 매리언,   로잘린드 글래디스,

Guy Clarence, / Veronica Eustacia, / and Claude Harold
가이 클래런스,   베로니카 유스타샤,   클로드 해럴드 헥터였다.

Hector.

Key Expression 🔑

fair의 다양한 의미
흔히 '공정한'이란 의미로 알고 있는 fair는 그 밖에도 다양한 의미를 가지고 있어요. 형용사, 부사, 명사로 쓰이는 fair의 의미를 알아볼까요.

▶ 형용사
① 타당한 공정한, 공평한
② (수·크기·양이) 상당한
③ 꽤 괜찮은, 제법인
④ 옅은색의, 금발의, 흰 피부의
⑤ 날씨가 맑은, 바람이 잔잔한
⑥ 어여쁜
▶ 부사
공정하게, 타당하게
▶ 명사
축제, 박람회

ex) The fat, fair baby with the lace cap was Ethelberta Beauchamp Montmorency.
레이스 달린 모자를 쓴 통통하고 흰 피부의 아기는 에셀베르타 보샹 몽모랑시였다.

166 A Little Princess

One evening / a very funny thing happened / — though, /
어느 날 저녁　　　　아주 웃긴 일이 벌어졌다　　　　　　　— 그러나,

perhaps, / in one sense / it was not a funny thing / at all.
어쩌면,　　　어떤 면에서는　　　그것은 웃긴 일이 아니었지만　　　전혀.

Several of the Montmorencys / were evidently going to a
몽모랑시 가족 중 몇 명이　　　　　분명히 어린이 파티에 가는 모양이었다.

children's party, / and just as Sara was abou to pass the
　　　　　　그리고 막 새라가 문을 지나려고 했을 때

door / they were crossing the pavement / to get into the
문을　　그들이 길을 건너고 있었다　　　　　　마차에 타려고

carriage / which was waiting for them. Veronica Eustacia
마차에　그들을 기다리고 있는.　　　　　　　베로니카 유스타샤와 로잘린드

and Rosalind Gladys, / in white-lace frocks and lovely
글래디스는,　　　　　　하얀 레이스가 달린 드레스를 입고 예쁜 띠를 두른,

sashes, / had just got in, / and Guy Clarence, / aged five, /
　　　막 올라탔고,　　　가이 클래런스는,　　　다섯 살인,

was following them. He was such a pretty fellow / and had
그들을 따라가고 있었다.　　　그 아이는 참 귀여운 아이였고

such rosy cheeks / and blue eyes, / and such a darling little
아주 발그레한 뺨과　　　파란 눈에,　　　그리고 엄청 사랑스럽고 작고 동근 머리를

round head / covered with curls, / that Sara forgot / her
가진 아이라서　　곱슬머리로 덮인,　　새라는 잊어버렸다

basket and shabby cloak / altogether / — in fact, / forgot
자신의 바구니와 허름한 망토를　　　모두　　　　— 사실,　　모든 것을

everything / but that she wanted to look at him / for a
잊어버렸다　　그 아이를 보고 싶다는 마음 외에　　　잠시 동안이라도.

moment. So she paused / and looked.
　　　그래서 가던 길을 멈추고　바라보았다.

It was Christmas time, / and the Large Family had been
크리스마스 시즌이었고,　　　　대가족은 듣고 있었다

hearing / many stories / about children / who were poor /
　　　많은 이야기들을　　아이들에 관한　　가난하고

and had no mammas and papas / to fill their stockings / and
엄마도 아빠도 없는　　　　　그들의 양말에 선물로 채워주거나

take them to the pantomime / — children who were,
그리고 연극에 데려다 줄　　　　　— 그러한 아이들의 이야기를,

round 통통한 | sash (몸에 두르는) 띠 | pantomime 팬터마임(영국에서 보통 크리스마스 때 공연하는, 음악, 무용,
코미디가 혼합된 동화 연극), 무언극

/ in fact, / cold and thinly clad / and hungry. In the stories, / kind people / — sometimes / little boys and girls / with tender hearts / — invariably saw the poor children / and gave them / money or rich gifts, / or took them home / to beautiful dinners. Guy Clarence had been affected / to tears / that very afternoon / by the reading / of such a story, / and he had burned with a desire / to find such a poor child / and give her a certain sixpence / he possessed, / and thus provide / for her / for life. An entire sixpence, / he was sure, / would mean affluence / for evermore. As he crossed the strip of red carpet / laid across the pavement / from the door to the carriage, / he had this very sixpence / in the pocket of his very short man-o-war trousers; / and just as Rosalind Gladys got into the vehicle / and jumped on the seat / in order to feel the cushions / spring under her, / he saw / Sara standing / on the wet pavement / in her shabby frock and hat, / with her old basket / on her arm, / looking at him / hungrily.

He thought / that her eyes looked hungry / because she had
아이는 생각했다   그 아이의 눈이 배고파 보인다고

perhaps had nothing to eat / for a long time. He did not
아마도 먹을 것이 없어서   오랫동안.   아이는 몰랐다

know / that they looked so / because she was hungry / for
        그 눈들이 그렇게 보이는 것은   갈망하기 때문임을

the warm, merry life / his home held / and his rosy face
따뜻하고, 즐거운 삶에 대해   자신의 집이 가진   그리고 그의 발그레한 얼굴이

spoke of, / and that she had a hungry wish / to snatch him
나타내는,   그리고 간절한 바람을 가졌다는 것을   그를 와락 껴안고

in her arms / and kiss him. He only knew / that she had
        입맞추고 싶다는.   아이는 단지 알 뿐이었다 그 아이가 큰 눈을 가졌다

big eyes / and a thin face / and thin legs / and a common
는 것을   마른 얼굴과   마른 다리와   평범한 바구니와

basket / and poor clothes. So he put his hand / in his pocket
불쌍한 옷을.   그래서 아이는 손을 넣어   주머니에

/ and found his sixpence / and walked up to her / benignly.
6펜스짜리 은화를 찾아서   그녀에게 걸어갔다   상냥하게.

Key Expression

착용의 의미를 지닌 전치사 in

'~을 입은'이라는 의미는 전치사 in를 사용하여 간단하게 표현할 수 있어요.
'~한 옷을 입다'라는 뜻의 동사 dress를 사용할 때에는 재귀대명사를 써서
dress oneself in이라고 하거나 또는 수동태로 be dressed in이라고 표
현합니다.

ex) He saw Sara standing on the wet pavement in her shabby frock and hat
그는 새라가 초라한 옷을 입고 모자를 쓴 채 젖은 길 위에 서 있는 것을 보았다.
She was dressed only in such clothes.
그녀는 그런 옷만 입었다.

clad ~을 입은 | invariably 변함없이, 언제나 | for life 평생 | affluence 풍족, 부유 | evermore 항상, 언제나 |
strip 가늘고 긴 조각 | man-o-war 군함, 해군 풍 | benignly 상냥하게

169

"Here, poor little girl," / he said. "Here is a sixpence. I will
"저기, 가엾은 아이야." 그는 말했다. "여기 6펜스짜리 은화가 있어.

give it to you."
네게 줄게."

Sara started, / and all at once / realized / that she looked
새라는 깜짝 놀랐고, 갑자기 깨달았다 자신이 보인다는 것을

/ exactly like poor children / she had seen, / in her better
꼭 불쌍한 아이들처럼 자신이 보아왔던, 더 잘 살았던 시절에,

days, / waiting on the pavement / to watch her / as she got
길에서 기다리던 그녀를 보려고

out of her brougham. And she had given them pennies /
사륜마차에서 내릴 때면. 새라는 그 아이들에게 돈을 준 적이 있었다

many a time.
여러 번.

Her face went red / and then it went pale, / and for a
새라의 얼굴이 빨개지더니 그리고는 창백하게 변했고, 잠시 동안

second / she felt / as if she could not take / the dear little
생각이 들었다 받을 수 없다고 그 소중한 6펜스짜리

sixpence.
은화를.

"Oh, no!" / she said. "Oh, no, thank you; / I mustn't take it,
"아, 아니야!" 그녀가 말했다. "아, 고맙지만 사양할게; 그것을 받을 수 없어,

/ indeed!"
정말로!"

Her voice was / so unlike an ordinary street child's voice
새라의 목소리는 거리의 평범한 아이의 목소리와 매우 달랐고

/ and her manner was / so like the manner of a well-bred
그 태도는 부잣집 아이의 태도 같았으므로

little person / that Veronica Eustacia (whose real name was
베로니카 유스타샤(진짜 이름은 자넷이었다)와

Janet) / and Rosalind Gladys (who was really called Nora) /
로잘린드 글래디스(진짜 이름은 노라였다)는

leaned forward to listen.
몸을 앞으로 내밀고 귀를 기울였다.

---

thwart 좌절시키다 | benevolence 자선, 선행 | heartbrokenly 슬픔에 잠겨, 비탄에 젖어

But Guy Clarence was not to be thwarted / in his
하지만 가이 클래런스는 뜻을 굽히지 않으려 했다

benevolence. He thrust the sixpence / into her hand.
선행에 대한.   아이는 6펜스짜리 은화를 밀어 넣었다   그녀의 손에.

"Yes, / you must take it, / poor little girl!" / he insisted /
"아니야,   넌 받아야 해,   가엾은 아이야!"   아이는 고집을 피웠다

stoutly. "You can buy things to eat / with it. It is a whole
완강하게.   "먹을 것을 살 수 있을 거야   그것으로.

sixpence!"
6펜스짜리 은화라고!"

There was something / so honest and kind / in his face, /
뭔가 있었다   매우 정직하고 친절한   아이의 얼굴에는,

and he looked / so likely to be heartbrokenly disappointed
그래서 보였다   슬픔에 잠겨 실망할 것처럼

/ if she did not take it, / that Sara knew / she must not
그것을 받지 않으면,   그래서 새라는 알았다   거절해서는 안 된다는 것을.

refuse him. To be as proud / as that / would be a cruel
자존심을 세우는 것은   그처럼   잔인한 일일테니.

thing. So she actually put her pride in her pocket, / though
그래서 새라는 실제로 자존심을 주머니에 넣었다,

it must be admitted / her cheeks burned.
비록 인정할 수밖에 없지만   뺨이 빨개진 것은.

Key Expression

so와 such의 어순
비슷한 의미를 지닌 so와 such는 의미는 비슷하지만 품사와 어순이 각각 다르기 때문에 쓰임새에 차이가 있습니다.
so는 부사로 '그렇게나, 매우, 너무'라는 의미이며, such는 '그 정도의, 너무 ~한'이란 뜻의 한정사입니다.

▶ so/too + 형용사 + 관사 + 명사
▶ such/quite + 관사 + 형용사 + 명사

ex) Her voice was so unlike an ordinary street child's voice.
새라의 목소리는 거리의 평범한 아이 목소리와 매우 달랐다.
There is such a yellow gentleman next door.
옆집에 얼굴이 아주 노란 신사가 있어.

171

"Thank you," / she said. "You are a kind, kind little darling
"고마워." 새라가 말했다. "넌 친절하고 착한 아이구나."

thing." And as he scrambled joyfully / into the carriage /
그리고 아이가 신나서 빨리 달려가자 마차 안으로

she went away, / trying to smile, / though she caught her
새라는 멀리 갔다. 애써 미소를 지으며, 숨은 가빠지고

breath quickly / and her eyes were shining through a mist.
눈물이 어려 눈은 반짝거렸지만.

She had known / that she looked odd and shabby, / but until
새라는 알고 있었지만 자신이 이상하고 초라해 보인다는 것을 지금까지

now / she had not known / that she might be taken / for a
몰랐었다 자신이 여겨질 수 있다는 것을

beggar.
거지로.

As the Large Family's carriage drove away, / the children
대가족의 마차가 출발하자, 마차 안의 아이들은

inside it / were talking with interested excitement.
흥분하며 떠들어댔다.

"Oh, Donald," / (this was Guy Clarence's name), / Janet
"오, 도날드." (이건 가이 클래런스의 진짜 이름이었다).

exclaimed / alarmedly, / "why did you offer / that little girl
자넷이 소리쳤다 깜짝 놀라서, "왜 줬니 그 여자 아이에게

/ your sixpence? I'm sure / she is not a beggar!"
6펜스짜리 은화를? 확실히 그 아이는 거지가 아닌데!"

"She didn't speak like a beggar!" / cried Nora. "And her
"그 애는 거지같은 말투가 아니었어!" 노라가 소리쳤다.

face didn't really look / like a beggar's face!"
"그리고 얼굴도 정말로 보이지 않았어 거지의 얼굴처럼!"

"Besides, / she didn't beg," / said Janet. "I was so afraid
"게다가, 구걸하지도 않았잖아," 자넷이 말했다. "조마조마 했다고

/ she might be angry with you. You know, / it makes
그 아이가 네게 화낼까 봐. 있잖아, 사람들을 화내게

people angry / to be taken for beggars / when they are not
만드는 거야 거지로 여겨지는 것은 거지가 아닌데."

beggars."

"She wasn't angry," / said Donald, / a trifle dismayed, /
"그 아이는 화내지 않았어." 도날드가 말했다, 약간 당황했지만,

but still firm. "She laughed a little, / and she said / I was a
여전히 완강하게. "살짝 웃으면서, 말했어

kind, kind little darling thing. And I was!" / — stoutly. "It
내가 친절하고 착한 아이라고. 그리고 난 그렇다고!" — 결연하게.

was my whole sixpence."
"그 6펜스는 내가 가진 전부였다고."

Janet and Nora exchanged glances.
자넷과 노라가 눈빛을 교환했다.

"A beggar girl would never have said that," / decided
"거지 여자 아이는 절대 그렇게 말하지 않아." 자넷이 결론지었다.

Janet. "She would have said, / 'Thank yer / kindly, little
"거지라면 말했을 거야. '고맙습니다 친절한, 어린 신사분

gentleman / — thank yer, sir;' / and perhaps she would
— 고마워요, 나리;' 그리고 아마 고개를 숙여 절을 했을 거야."

have bobbed a curtsy."

Sara knew nothing / about the fact, / but from that time /
새라는 아무것도 몰랐다 그 사실에 대해, 하지만 그때부터

the Large Family was as profoundly interested / in her / as
대가족은 깊은 흥미를 느꼈다 새라에게

she was in it. Faces used to appear / at the nursery windows
새라 만큼이나. 얼굴들이 나타나곤 했다 놀이방 창문에

/ when she passed, / and many discussions / concerning her
그녀가 지나갈 때, 그리고 많은 토론들이 그녀에 관한

/ were held / round the fire.
이루어졌다 난로 주변에서.

---

catch one's breath 숨이 턱 막히다 | mist 엷은 안개 | alarmedly 놀라서, 당황하여 | trifle 약간 | dismayed
당황한, 놀란 | firm 확고한 | bob 까닥거리다 | curtsy 절(여성이 서 있는 자세에서 한 쪽 다리를 뒤로 살짝 빼고
무릎을 약간 구부리며 하는 인사법) | profoundly 깊이

"She is a kind of servant / at the seminary," / Janet said.
"그 애는 일종의 하인이야   신학교에서."   자넷이 말했다.

"I don't believe she belongs to anybody. I believe she is
"가족이 아무도 없는 것 같아.   고아라고 생각해.

an orphan. But she is not a beggar, / however shabby she
하지만 그 아이는 거지가 아니야,   아무리 누추해 보여도."

looks."

And afterward / she was called / by all of them, /
그 후로   새라는 불려졌다   그들 모두에게,

"The-little-girl-who-is-not-a-beggar," / which was, / of
"거지가 – 아닌 – 여자 아이"라고,   그것은,

course, / rather a long name, / and sounded very funny /
물론,   다소 긴 이름이었고,   매우 우스꽝스럽게 들렸다

sometimes / when the youngest ones said it in a hurry.
때때로   가장 어린 아이들이 빨리 말할 때면.

Key Expression

however : 아무리 ~하더라도

관계부사 how와 ever가 결합된 복합관계부사 however는 '아무리 ~하더라도'
라는 의미의 양보 부사절을 이끕니다.
관계부사 however가 이끄는 절의 어순은 'however + 형용사/부사 + 주어 + 동
사'라는 사실도 기억해 두세요.
또한 관계부사에는 however 외에도 whenever와 wherever가 있습니다.

▶ however : 아무리 ~하더라도 (=no matter how)
▶ whenever : ~할 때는 언제든지 (=at any time when),
　　　　　　　 언제 ~하더라도 (=no matter when)
▶ wherever : ~한 곳은 어디든지 (=at any place where),
　　　　　　　 어디에서 ~하더라도 (=no matter where)

ex) But she is not a beggar, however shabby she looks."
　　 하지만 아무리 누추해 보여도 그녀는 거지가 아니야.

---

bore (구멍을) 뚫다 | strive 분투하다, 싸우다 | insinuate (신체 일부를) 밀어 넣다, 암시하다 | nestle 따뜻하게 안다
| alight 내리다 | make much of 소중히 여기다

Sara managed to bore a hole / in the sixpence / and hung
새라는 가까스로 구멍을 뚫어   그 6펜스짜리 은화에   매달았다

it / on an old bit / of narrow ribbon / round her neck.
   낡은 조각에   얇은 리본의   목에 건.

Her affection / for the Large Family / increased / — as,
새라의 애정은   대가족을 향한   점점 커졌다

indeed, / her affection / for everything / she could love
— 실제로,   그녀의 애정은   모든 것에 대한   사랑할 수 있는

/ increased. She grew fonder and fonder / of Becky, /
   커져갔다   새라는 점점 더 좋아했고   베키를,

and she used to look forward / to the two mornings a
고대하곤 했다   일주일에 두 번의 아침을

week / when she went into the schoolroom / to give the
       교실로 가는 때인

little ones their French lesson. Her small pupils loved
어린 아이들에게 프랑스어 수업을 가르치러.   어린 학생들은 새라를 사랑했고,

her, / and strove with each other / for the privilege / of
       서로 다퉜다   특권을 차지하려고

standing close to her / and insinuating their small hands
가까이 설 수 있는   그리고 작은 손을 넌지시 밀어넣었다

/ into hers. It fed her hungry heart / to feel them nestling
   그녀의 손 안에. 굶주린 마음에 양분을 주었다   그 아이들이 자신에게 안겨오는 것

up to her. She made such friends / with the sparrows /
을 느끼는 것은. 새라는 아주 친해져서   참새들과

that when she stood upon the table, / put her head and
탁자 위에 올라서서,   머리와 어깨를 내놓은 채

shoulders / out of the attic window, / and chirped, /
           다락방 창문 밖으로,   짹짹거리면,

she heard almost immediately / a flutter of wings / and
곧 들려왔다   날개가 퍼덕거리고

answering twitters, / and a little flock / of dingy town
짹짹거리며 대답하는 소리를,   그리고 작은 무리가   지저분한 도시의 새들의

birds / appeared and alighted / on the slates / to talk to
나타나서 내려앉았고   슬레이트 지붕 위에   그녀에게 말을

her / and make much of the crumbs / she scattered.
걸고   빵부스러기들을 소중히 여겼다   그녀가 뿌려놓은.

With Melchisedec / she had become so intimate /
멜기세덱과는   매우 친숙해져서

that he actually brought Mrs. Melchisedec with him
실제로 멜기세덱 부인을 데려왔고

/ sometimes, / and now and then / one or two of his
때때로,   가끔씩은   한두 명의 자식들도 데려왔다

children. She used to talk to him, / and, / somehow, / he
새라는 쥐에게 말을 걸곤 했으며,   그리고,   어쩐지,

looked quite as if he understood.
쥐는 이해하는 듯 보였다.

There had grown in her mind / rather a strange feeling
새라의 마음속에 자라났다   다소 이상한 감정이

/ about Emily, / who always sat / and looked on /
에밀리에 대한,   항상 앉아서   보고 있는

at everything. It arose / in one of her moments / of
모든 것을.   그 감정은 일어났다   어느 한 순간에

great desolateness. She would have liked / to believe
매우 쓸쓸했던.   새라는 좋아했다   믿거나

/ or pretend to believe / that Emily understood / and
믿는 척 하는 것을   에밀리가 이해하고

sympathized / with her. She did not like to own to
공감한다고   자신을.   새라는 스스로 인정하고 싶지 않았다

herself / that her only companion / could feel and hear
유일한 친구가   느끼거나 들을 수 없다는 것을.

nothing. She used to put her / in a chair / sometimes /
그녀는 에밀리를 올려놓고   의자에   때때로

and sit opposite to her / on the old red footstool, / and
반대편에 앉곤 했다   낡고 빨간 의자 위에,

stare and pretend / about her / until her own eyes would
그리고 바라보며 상상했다   에밀리에 대해   그러다가 눈이 커지곤 했다

grow large / with something / which was almost like fear
     뭔가 때문에   거의 공포와 같은

/ — particularly at night / when everything was so still,
— 특히 밤에   모든 것이 아주 적막하고,

desolateness 황량함, 황폐 | wrought-up 흥분한, 짜증나는 | fancifulness 비현실적임, 공상

/ when the only sound / in the attic / was the occasional
유일한 소리는   다락방에서   이따금 갑자기 뛰어다니거나

sudden scurry and squeak / of Melchisedec's family / in
찍찍거리는 소리뿐일 때   멜기세덱 가족이

the wall. One of her "pretends" / was that Emily was a
벽 속에서.   그녀의 "척 하는 놀이" 중 하나는   에밀리가 착한 마법사라는 것이었다

kind of good witch / who could protect her. Sometimes,
             자신을 지켜주는.   가끔,

/ after she had stared at her / until she was wrought up
에밀리를 바라보다가   새라는 흥분하여

/ to the highest pitch of fancifulness, / she would ask
상상력의 최고조에 이르게 되어,

her questions / and find herself almost feeling / as if she
질문을 했고   느끼기도 했다

would presently answer. But she never did.
에밀리가 정말 대답한 것처럼.   하지만 에밀리는 절대 그러지 않았다.

"As to answering, / though," / said Sara, / trying to console
"대답하는 것에 대해 말하자면, 비록," 새라가 말했다, 자신을 위로하려 애쓰며,

herself, / "I don't answer very often. I never answer / when
"나도 종종 대답하지 않기도 해. 절대 대답하지 않아

I can help it. When people are insulting you, / there is
할 수 있으면. 사람들이 모욕할 때에는,

nothing so good for them / as not to say a word / — just
가장 이로운 일이니까 한 마디도 하지 않는 것이

to look at them / and think. Miss Minchin turns pale with
— 단지 그들을 쳐다보고 생각하는 거야. 민친 교장은 화가 나서 창백해지지

rage / when I do it, / Miss Amelia looks frightened, / and
내가 그러면, 아멜리아 선생은 공포에 떨고,

so do the girls. When you will not fly into a passion /
여자 아이들도 그래. 벌컥 화를 내지 않으면

people know / you are stronger than they are, / because
사람들은 알아 자신들보다 강하다는 것을,

you are strong enough to hold in your rage, / and they are
왜냐하면 화를 참을 만큼 강하다는 뜻이니까, 그리고 그들은 하지 못

not, / and they say stupid things / they wish they hadn't
하니까, 그러면 사람들은 어리석은 말을 하지 말하지 않았으면 좋았을 거라고

said / afterward. There's nothing so strong as rage, / except
이후로는. 분노만큼 강한 것은 없어,

what makes you hold it in / — that's stronger. It's a good
분노를 참는 것 외에는 — 그것이 더 강하지. 좋은 일이야

thing / not to answer your enemies. I scarcely ever do.
적에 반응하지 않는 것은. 난 좀처럼 하지 않아.

Perhaps / Emily is more like me / than I am like myself.
아마도 에밀리는 나같은 것인지 몰라 나 자신보다 더.

Perhaps / she would rather not / answer her friends, / even.
아마도 그녀는 안 하는 것이 나을지 모르지 친구에게 대답하는 것도, 그조차.

She keeps it all in her heart."
마음속에 모두 담아두고 있는 거야."

---

as to ~에 관해서는 | fly into a passion 벌컥 화를 내다 | harsh 가혹한, 귀에 거슬리는 | slighting 경멸하는 |
vulgar 저속한, 천박한 | insolent 버릇없는, 무례한 | sneer 비웃다, 조롱하다 | shabbiness 초라함 | tempest
폭풍 | sawdust 톱밥 | inexpressive 무표정한, 형언할 수 없는

But though she tried to satisfy herself / with these
하지만 만족하려고 애써도   이런 갈등에 대해,

arguments, / she did not find it easy. When, after a long,
쉽지는 않았다.   길고, 힘든 하루를 보낸 후에,

hard day, / in which she had been sent here and there, /
이리저리 돌아다니며,

sometimes / on long errands / through wind and cold and
때때로   멀리까지 심부름을 가느라   바람과 추위와 비를 뚫고,

rain, / she came / in wet and hungry, / and was sent out /
그녀는 돌아와서 젖고 배고픈 채로,   그리고 보내지기도 했다

again / because nobody chose to remember / that she was
또 다시   아무도 기억하지 않으려 했기 때문에   새라는 그저 아이이라는

only a child, / and that her slim legs might be tired / and
것을,   그리고 가냘픈 다리는 지쳤고

her small body might be chilled; / when she had been given
작은 몸이 떨고 있다는 것을;   또 가혹한 말들만 듣게 되었을 때

only harsh words / and cold, slighting looks / for thanks; /
차갑고, 경멸하는 표정과 함께   고맙다는 말 대신;

when the cook had been vulgar and insolent; / when Miss
또 요리사가 천박하고 거만했을 때;

Minchin had been in her worst mood, / and when she
또 민친 교장이 기분이 가장 안 좋았을 때,   그리고 봤을 때

had seen / the girls sneering among themselves / at her
아이들이 비웃는 것을   자신의 초라한

shabbiness / — then she was not always able to comfort /
모습을 보고   — 그러면 새라도 언제나 달랠 수 있는 것은 아니었다

her sore, proud, desolate heart / with fancies / when Emily
자신의 상한 자존심과 쓸쓸한 마음을   상상력으로

merely sat upright / in her old chair / and stared.
에밀리가 똑바로 앉아서   낡은 의자에서   쳐다보기만 하면.

One of these nights, / when she came up to the attic / cold
이런 밤 중 어느 날,   새라가 다락방에 올라왔을 때

and hungry, / with a tempest raging / in her young breast, /
춥고 배고픈 채,   폭풍우가 불어 닥치면서   어린 가슴에,

Emily's stare seemed so vacant, / her sawdust legs and arms
에밀리의 시선은 아주 공허해 보였고,   톱밥 다리와 팔은

/ so inexpressive, / that Sara lost all control over herself.
매우 무표정하게 보여서,   새라는 자신에 대한 평정심을 잃고 말았다.

There was nobody but Emily / — no one / in the world.
에밀리밖에 없었다   — 아무도   세상에는.

And there / she sat.
그리고 그곳에   에밀리는 앉아 있었다.

"I shall die presently," / she said / at first.
"난 곧 죽을 거야."   새라는 말했다   처음으로.

Emily simply stared.
에밀리는 그저 쳐다볼 뿐이었다.

"I can't bear this," / said the poor child, / trembling. "I
"견딜 수 없어."   가여운 아이가 말했다,   몸을 떨면서.

know I shall die. I'm cold; / I'm wet; / I'm starving to
"죽을 것 같다고.   춥고;   비에 젖었어;   배고파 죽겠어.

death. I've walked a thousand miles / today, / and they
수천 마일을 걸었어   오늘,

have done nothing but scold me / from morning until
그런데 사람들은 꾸중만 했어   아침부터 밤까지.

night. And because I could not find / that last thing / the
그리고 찾을 수 없어서   마지막 물건을

cook sent me for, / they would not give me / any supper.
요리사가 사 오라고 시킨,   내게 주지 않았어   저녁을.

Some men laughed at me / because my old shoes made /
어떤 사람들이 날 보고 비웃었어   낡은 신발 때문에

me slip down / in the mud. I'm covered with mud / now.
미끄러지는 바람에   진흙에서.   진흙으로 뒤범벅이 되었지   지금.

And they laughed. Do you hear?"
그런데 사람들은 웃었다고.   내 말 듣는 거야?"

She looked / at the staring glass eyes / and complacent
새라는 보았다   멍하게 쳐다보는 유리로 된 눈과   자기 만족적인 얼굴을.

face, / and suddenly / a sort of heartbroken rage / seized
그리고 갑자기   가슴이 터질 듯한 분노가   그녀를 사로

her. She lifted her little savage hand / and knocked Emily
잡았다. 새라는 작고 사나운 팔을 들어서   에밀리를 의자에서 내동댕이쳤다.

off the chair, / bursting into a passion of sobbing / —
갑자기 격정적인 울음을 터뜨리며

Sara who never cried.
— 절대 울지 않던 새라가.

"You are nothing but a doll!" / she cried. "Nothing but a doll
"넌 인형일 뿐이야!"   그녀가 소리쳤다. "인형일 뿐이야

/ — doll / — doll! You care for nothing. You are stuffed with
— 인형   — 인형이라고! 넌 아무래도 상관없지.   넌 톱밥으로 채워져 있어.

sawdust. You never had a heart. Nothing could ever make
마음도 없지.   아무것도 느끼지 못하겠지.

you feel. You are a doll!"
넌 인형이라고!"

Emily lay on the floor, / with her legs ignominiously doubled
에밀리는 바닥에 누워 있었다.   창피하게도 두 다리를 포개고

up / over her head, / and a new flat place / on the end of her
머리 위로,   그리고 납작해진 채   코 끝이;

nose; / but she was calm, / even dignified. Sara hid her face
하지만 에밀리는 침착했고,   심지어 품위 있었다.   새라는 얼굴을 가렸다

/ in her arms. The rats in the wall / began to fight / and bite
두 팔로.   벽 속에 있는 쥐들이   싸우기 시작하며

each other / and squeak and scramble. Melchisedec was
서로 물어뜯고   난리법석을 떨었다.   멜기세덱은 꾸짖고 있었다

chastising / some of his family.
가족 중 누군가를.

Sara's sobs gradually quieted themselves. It was so unlike
새라의 울음 소리는 점점 조용해졌다.   매우 자신같지 않아서

her / to break down / that she was surprised / at herself.
무너지는 것은   새라는 놀랐다   자신을 보고.

After a while / she raised her face / and looked at Emily,
잠시 후에   얼굴을 들어   에밀리를 보자,

/ who seemed to be gazing at her / round the side of one
에밀리는 새라를 보고 있는 듯 했다   곁눈질로,

angle, / and, / somehow, / by this time / actually / with a
그리고,   어쩐지,   이번에는   진짜로

kind of glassy-eyed sympathy. Sara bent / and picked her up.
유리알 눈에 동정의 빛이 어렸다.   새라는 몸을 굽혀 에밀리를 집어 들었다.

---

complacent 자기 만족적인 | ignominiously 불명예스럽게, 창피하게, 비열하게 | double up (통증이나 웃음
때문에) 몸을 웅크리다 | dignified 품위 있는 | chastise 꾸짖다 | angle 각도 | sympathy 동정, 공감

181

Remorse overtook her. She even smiled / at herself / a
후회가 밀려왔다.   웃음이 나기까지 했다   자신을 보고

very little smile.
아주 엷은 미소였지만.

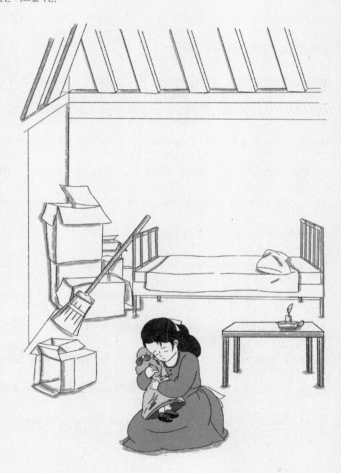

remorse 회한 | overtake (불쾌한 일이) 엄습하다 | resigned 체념한 | sigh 한숨 | prop 받치다 | aperture (작은)
구멍 | under servant 머슴, 허드레 일꾼 | prolonged 오래 계속되는 | van (뒷부분에 지붕이 덮인) 화물차, 밴

"You can't help being a doll," / she said / with a resigned
"너도 어쩔 수 없이 인형이 된 거지," 새라가 말했다 체념한 듯 한숨 쉬며,

sigh, / "any more than Lavinia and Jessie / can help not
"라비니아와 제시가 어쩔 수 없이 분별 없는

having any sense. We are not all made alike. Perhaps / you
아이인 것처럼. 우리는 모두 똑같은 모습으로 태어나지 않았으니. 아마 넌 톱밥

do your sawdust best." And she kissed her / and shook her
인형으로서 최선을 다하고 있는 거야." 새라는 에밀리에게 입맞추고

clothes straight, / and put her back upon her chair.
옷을 털어 가지런히 해 주고, 다시 의자에 앉혔다.

She had wished very much / that someone would take / the
그녀는 간절히 바랐다 누군가 살았으면 하고

empty house next door. She wished it / because of the attic
비어 있는 옆집에. 그것을 바랐다 왜냐하면 다락방 창문이

window / which was so near hers. It seemed / as if it would
사라의 창문과 아주 가까웠기 때문에. 그렇게 보였다

be so nice / to see it propped open / someday / and a head
매우 멋질 것처럼 창문이 벌컥 열리고 언젠가

and shoulders rising / out of the square aperture.
머리와 어깨가 불쑥 나오면 네모난 구멍 밖으로.

"If it looked a nice head," / she thought, / "I might begin
"만약 그 얼굴이 착해 보인다면," 그녀는 생각했다, "난 말을 걸지도 몰라,

by saying, / 'Good morning,' / and all sorts of things might
'안녕하세요'라고, 그리고 모든 일이 벌어질 거야.

happen. But, / of course, / it's not really likely / that anyone
하지만, 물론, 그럴리가 없지 누군가

/ but under servants / would sleep there."
허드레 일꾼 머슴 말고는 거기에서 자는 건.

One morning, / on turning the corner of the square / after
어느 날 아침, 광장의 모퉁이를 돌았을 때

a visit / to the grocer's, / the butcher's, / and the baker's,
방문 후 가게와, 푸줏간과, 빵집을,

/ she saw, / to her great delight, / that during her rather
그녀는 봤다, 무척 기쁘게도, 조금 오래 집을 비운 사이,

prolonged absence, / a van full of furniture / had stopped
가구로 가득 찬 화물차가 멈춰 있는 것을

183

/ before the next house, / the front doors were thrown
바로 옆집 앞에.   대문들이 활짝 열려 있었고,

open, / and men in shirt sleeves / were going in and out /
셔츠 차림의 남자들이   들락날락 하면서

carrying heavy packages and pieces of furniture.
무거운 짐과 가구를 옮기고 있었다.

"It's taken!" / she said. "It really is taken! Oh, I do hope /
"들어왔구나!"   그녀가 말했다. "정말 저기로 이사 왔나 봐!   오, 정말 좋을텐데

a nice head will look / out of the attic window!"
착한 사람의 얼굴이 보이면   다락방 창문 밖으로!"

She would almost have liked to join / the group of
사라는 끼고 싶었다   어슬렁거리는 사람들의 무리에

loiterers / who had stopped / on the pavement / to watch
멈춰서서   길 위에

the things carried in. She had an idea / that if she could
짐 나르는 것을 구경하려고.   사라는 알고 있었다   가구 몇 가지만 볼 수 있으면

see some of the furniture / she could guess something /
짐작할 수 있을 것이라는 사실을

about the people / it belonged to.
사람들에 대해   그것을 소유한.

"Miss Minchin's tables and chairs / are just like her," /
"민친 선생의 탁자와 의자들은   정말 주인과 똑같아."

she thought; / "I remember thinking / that the first minute
그녀는 생각했다.   "생각났던 것이 기억나   처음에

/ I saw her, / even though I was so little. I told papa /
선생님을 봤을 때, 비록 아주 어렸지만.   아빠한테 말씀 드렸더니

afterward, / and he laughed / and said / it was true. I am
나중에,   아빠는 웃으면서   말했어   정말 그렇다고.   난 확신해

sure / the Large Family have fat, comfortable armchairs
대가족의 집에는 푹신하고, 편안한 안락의자와 소파가 있을 거야,

and sofas, / and I can see / that their red-flowery wallpaper
그리고 알 수 있어   그 집의 붉은 꽃무늬 벽지는

/ is exactly like them. It's warm / and cheerful / and kind-
정말 그들과 똑같다는 것을.   그것은 따뜻하고   즐겁고   친절해 보이며

looking / and happy."
행복하지."

She was sent out for parsley / to the greengrocer's / later
새라는 파슬리를 사러 나갔다   채소 가게로

in the day, / and when she came up the area steps / her
그날 오후 늦게,   지하실로 통하는 계단을 올라왔을 때

heart gave quite a quick beat / of recognition. Several
심장은 두근거렸다   뭔가를 보고.

pieces of furniture had been set / out of the van / upon
가구 몇 점이 있었다   화물차 밖에

the pavement. There was a beautiful table / of elaborately
도로 위.   멋진 탁자가 있었다

wrought teakwood, / and some chairs, / and a screen /
공들여 세공한 티크 목재의,   의자 몇 개와,   병풍도

covered with rich Oriental embroidery. The sight of them
호화로운 동양 자수로 뒤덮인.   그것을 보자

/ gave her a weird, homesick feeling. She had seen / things
새라는 묘한 향수에 젖었다.   본 적 있었다   그것들과

so like them / in India. One of the things / Miss Minchin
똑같은 물건들을   인도에서.   그 중 하나는   민친 교장이 가져가 버린

had taken from her / was a carved teakwood desk / her
조각된 티크 목재 책상이었다

father had sent her.
아빠가 그녀에게 보내준.

"They are beautiful things," / she said; / "they look / as
"멋진 물건들이야,"   새라가 말했다;   "보이는데

if they ought to belong / to a nice person. All the things /
그 물건들이 소유인 것처럼   친절한 사람의.   모든 것들이

look rather grand. I suppose it is a rich family."
굉장히 화려해 보이네.   부유한 가족인가 봐."

---

in shirt sleeves 상의를 벗고, 셔츠 차림의 | loiterer 어슬렁거리다 | wallpaper 벽지 | parsley 파슬리 |
greengrocer's 청과물 가게 | recognition 인식 | elaborately 공들여, 정교하게 | wrought worked의 고어 |
teakwood 티크 목재 | screen 칸막이, 가리개 | Oriental 동양의 | embroidery 자수 | weird 기이한, 기묘한 |
homesick 향수병을 앓는 | carved 조각된 | grand 웅장한, 화려한

The vans of furniture / came and were unloaded / and
가구가 실린 화물차들이   도착하여 짐을 내리고

gave place to others / all the day. Several times / it so
다른 차가 뒤를 이었다   하루 종일.   몇 번인가

happened / that Sara had an opportunity of seeing /
아주 우연히   새라도 볼 기회가 있었다

things carried in. It became plain / that she had been
짐들이 안으로 옮겨지는 것을. 분명해졌다   새라가 상상한대로

right in guessing / that the newcomers were / people of
새로 이사오는 사람들은

large means. All the furniture was rich and beautiful, /
대단한 부자일 거라고. 모든 가구는 화려하고 아름다웠으며,

and a great deal of it / was Oriental. Wonderful rugs and
대대수는   동양에서 온 것이었다.

draperies and ornaments / were taken from the vans, /
멋진 양탄자와 휘장과 장식품들이   화물차들에서 내려졌고,

many pictures, and books / enough for a library. Among
많은 그림과, 책들도   서재 하나를 채우기에 충분한.

other things / there was a superb god Buddha / in a
다른 것들 중에는   최상품의 불상도 있었다

splendid shrine.
눈부신 성물함에 들어 있는.

Key Expression ♥

must have+과거분사 : ~였음에 틀림없다

must는 의무(~해야 한다)와 강한 추측(~임에 틀림없다)의 두 가지 뜻을 가진 조동사입니다.
의무의 must의 경우 과거형으로는 비슷한 뜻를 가진 동사 had to를 사용하는 것이 보편적입니다.
반면 과거에 대한 강한 추측을 나타낼 경우에는 must have+과거분사를 사용하여 '~했음에 틀림없다'라고 해석합니다.
추측의 must의 부정형은 cannot(~일리가 없다) 입니다. 따라서 must have+과거분사의 부정형은 cannot have+과거분사 형태가 됩니다.

ex) Someone in the family must have been in India.
     저 가족 중에 누군가 인도에서 살았었나 봐.

---

newcomer 신입자 | means 돈, 재력 | drapery 휘장 | superb 최고의, 최상의, 대단히 훌륭한 | shrine 성지(聖地)

"Someone in the family / must have been in India," / Sara
"저 가족 중에 누군가   인도에서 살았었나 봐."   새라는

thought. "They have got used / to Indian things / and like
생각했다.   "그들은 익숙해졌고   인도 물건들에   좋아하게 된

them. I am glad. I shall feel / as if they were friends, /
거야.   난 기뻐.   느껴질 거야   마치 그들이 친구인 것처럼.

even if a head never looks / out of the attic window."
머리가 전혀 보이지 않는다 해도   다락방 창문 밖으로."

When she was taking in the evening's milk / for the cook
새라가 저녁에 먹을 우유를 가져가고 있을 때   요리사를 위해

/ (there was really no odd job / she was not called upon to
(사실 예외적인 일이 없을 정도였다   새라한테 하라고 시키지 않는),

do), / she saw something occur / which made the situation
그녀는 뭔가 일어난 것을 보았다   아주 흥미진진하게 상황을 만든

more interesting / than ever. The handsome, rosy man /
그 어느 때보다.   잘생기고, 발그레한 피부를 가진 남자가

who was the father of the Large Family / walked across
대가족의 아버지인   광장을 가로질러 걸어가서

the square / in the most matter-of-fact manner, / and ran
매우 사무적인 태도로,   뛰어서 계단을

up the steps / of the next-door house. He ran up them /
올라갔다   옆집 문의.   그는 거기로 뛰어 올라가더니

as if he felt quite at home / and expected to run up and
마치 자기집인 양   계속 오르락내리락 할 것 같았다

down them / many a time / in the future. He stayed inside
여러 번   앞으로.   그는 집 안에 머물렀다

/ quite a long time, / and several times/ came out / and
아주 오랜 시간 동안.   그리고 몇 차례   집 밖으로 나와

gave directions / to the workmen, / as if he had a right to
지시를 내렸다   일꾼들에게.   마치 자신에게 그런 권한이 있다는

do so. It was quite certain / that he was / in some intimate
듯이.   확실했다   그가   친밀한 방식으로

way / connected with the newcomers / and was acting for
새로 이사온 사람들과 관계가 있으며   그들을 대신하여 행동하고 있

them.
다는 것이.

"If the new people have children," / Sara speculated, /
"새로 온 사람들에게 아이들이 있다면,"　　　새라가 추측했다.

"the Large Family children / will be sure to come / and
"대가족의 아이들은　　　분명히 이 집에 와서

play with them, / and they might come up / into the attic
그들과 놀겠지.　　　그리고 올라올지도 몰라　　　다락방으로

/ just for fun."
그저 재미로."

At night, / after her work was done, / Becky came in to
밤에,　　일이 끝난 후,　　베키가 만나러 들어와

see / her fellow prisoner / and bring her news.
동료 죄수를　　새 소식을 전했다.

"It's a' Nindian gentleman / that's comin' to live next
"인도 신사래요　　옆집에 살게 될 사람이.

door, / miss," / she said. "I don't know / whether he's a
아가씨,"　　그녀가 말했다. "모르지만　　흑인인지 아닌지는,

black gentleman or not, / but he's a Nindian one. He's
인도 신사래요.

very rich, / an' he's ill, / an' the gentleman of the Large
아주 부자이고,　　아프대요,　　그리고 대가족의 나리가

Family / is his lawyer. He's had a lot of trouble, / an' it's
그의 변호사래요.　　많은 고난을 겪어서,

made him ill / an' low in his mind. He worships idols,
병이 났고　　마음도 침울해졌대요.　　우상을 숭배한대요,

/ miss. He's an 'eathen / an' bows down / to wood an'
아가씨. 이교도인이고　　절을 한대요　　나무와 돌에게.

stone. I seen a' idol bein' carried in / for him to worship.
우상이 옮겨지는 것을 봤어요　　그 사람이 숭배하는.

Somebody had oughter send him a trac'. You can get a
누군가 그 사람에게 종교책을 보냈을 거예요.　　살 수 있대요

trac' / for a penny."
1페니면.

Sara laughed a little.
새라는 약간 웃었다.

Nindian 인도의(=Indian) | low 기운 없는, 침울한 | worship 숭배하다 | idol 우상 | 'eathen 비종교인, 이교도
(=heathen) | trac' 소책자, 팜플릿(=tract) | inclined ~하는 경향이 있는, ~하고 싶은 | prayer book 기도책

"I don't believe / he worships that idol," / she said; /
"내 생각에는 우상을 숭배하는 것이 아닌 것 같아," 새라가 말했다;

"some people like to keep them / to look at / because
"어떤 사람들은 갖고 있는 것을 좋아해 보기 위해

they are interesting. My papa had a beautiful one, / and
왜냐하면 흥미롭거든. 우리 아빠도 멋진 것을 갖고 계셨는데,

he did not worship it."
숭배하지는 않았어."

But Becky was rather inclined to prefer / to believe /
하지만 베키는 더 좋아하는 경향이 있었다 믿는 것을

that the new neighbor was "an 'eathen." It sounded so
새로 온 이웃이 "이교도인"라고.

much more romantic / than that he should merely be / the
그것이 더 낭만적으로 들렸다 그가 그저

ordinary kind of gentleman / who went to church / with
평범한 신사인 것보다 교회에 다니는

a prayer book. She sat and talked / long / that night / of
기도책을 들고. 그녀는 앉아서 말했다 오랫동안 그날 밤

what he would be like, / of what his wife would be like /
그 사람이 어떤 사람일지, 부인은 어떤 사람일지

if he had one, / and of what his children would be like /
부인이 있다면, 그리고 아이들은 어떤 아이일지에 대해

if they had children. Sara saw / that privately / she could
아이들이 있다면. 새라가 보기에 개인적으로

not help hoping very much / that they would all be black,
베키는 바랄 수밖에 없는 것 같았다 그들이 모두 흑인이며,

/ and would wear turbans, / and, / above all, that / — like
터번을 쓰고, 그리고, 무엇보다도,

their parent — / they would all be "'eathens."
— 부모처럼 — 모두 "이교도"이기를.

"I never lived / next door / to no 'eathens, / miss," / she
"나는 살아본 적이 없어요 옆집에 이교도인의, 아가씨," 베키가

said; / "I should like to see / what sort o' ways they'd
말했다; "난 보고 싶어요 그들이 사는 방식을."

have."

It was several weeks / before her curiosity was satisfied,
몇 주가 지나자 / 베키의 호기심은 풀렸고,

/ and then it was revealed / that the new occupant /
그리고는 밝혀졌다 / 새로 이사온 사람에게는

had neither wife nor children. He was a solitary man /
부인도 아이들도 없다는 것이. / 그는 군인이었고

with no family at all, / and it was evident / that he was
전혀 가족이 없는, / 확실했다

shattered in health / and unhappy in mind.
건강이 완전히 망가졌고 / 마음은 불행하다는 것이.

A carriage drove up / one day / and stopped / before
마차가 도착하여 / 어느 날 / 멈췄다 / 그 집 앞에.

the house. When the footman dismounted from the box
특별석에서 하인이 내려

/ and opened the door / the gentleman / who was the
문을 열었을 때 / 신사가 / 대가족의 아버지인

father of the Large Family / got out first. After him /
먼저 내렸다. / 그의 뒤를 이어

there descended a nurse / in uniform, / then came down
간호사가 내렸고 / 제복을 입은, / 그리고는 계단을 내려왔다

the steps / two men-servants. They came to assist their
두 명의 하인이. / 그들은 주인을 거들어 주러 온 것이었고,

master, / who, / when he was helped / out of the carriage,
그 사람이, 도움을 받아 / 마차에서 나오자,

/ proved to be a man / with a haggard, distressed face, /
사람임이 밝혀졌다 / 초췌하고,고통스러워 하는 얼굴을 하고,

and a skeleton body / wrapped in furs. He was carried
뼈만 남은 몸을 가진 / 모피로 감싼. / 그는 부축 받으며 계단을

up the steps, / and the head of the Large Family / went
올라갔고, / 대가족의 가장이

with him, / looking very anxious. Shortly afterward / a
그와 함께 갔다. 매우 걱정스러운 표정으로. / 곧이어

doctor's carriage arrived, / and the doctor went in / ―
의사의 마차가 도착했고, / 의사가 들어갔다

plainly to take care of him.
― 그를 치료하러 온 것이 분명했다.

"There is such a yellow gentleman / next door, / Sara,"
"얼굴이 아주 노란 신사가 있어   옆집에,   새라."

Lottie whispered / at the French class / afterward. "Do
로티가 속삭였다   프랑스어 수업 시간에   나중에.

you think he is a Chinee? The geography says / the
중국인이라고 생각해?   지리책에 쓰여 있었어

Chinee men are yellow."
중국 사람들은 얼굴이 노란색이라고."

"No, he is not Chinese," / Sara whispered back; / "he
"아니, 그는 중국인이 아니야,"   새라가 속삭이며 대답했다;   "

is very ill. Go on with your exercise, / Lottie. *Non,
"그는 아주 아파. 공부를 계속해,   로티.

monsieur. Je n'ai pas le canif / de mon oncle."'
'농, 므슈.   쥬 내 파 르 카니프   드 몽 언크르.'"

That was the beginning / of the story / of the Indian
그것은 시작이었다   이야기의   영국 신사에 관한.

gentleman.

* No, Mr. I don't have the knife of my uncle. (아니요, 아저씨. 나는 삼촌의 주머니 칼을 가지고 있지 않아요.)

occupant 입주자 | shatter 산산조각 내다, 엄청난 충격을 주다 | footman 하인 | dismount 내리다 | box (극장·법정 등의) 특별석 | haggard 초췌한 | distressed 아파하는, 허약한 | skelton (몹시 여위어서) 뼈만 남은 | shortly 곧 | plainly 분명히 | Chinee 중국인을 가리키는 속어 | geography 지리학 | monsieur ~씨, 님, 귀하 (Mr. 혹은 Sir에 해당하는 프랑스어의 경칭)

 mini test 6

A. 다음 문장을 해석해 보세요.

(1) She had begun to grow very fast, / and, as she was dressed only in / such clothes / as the plainer remnants / of her wardrobe would supply, / she knew / she looked very queer, / indeed.
→

(2) All her valuable garments had been disposed of, / and such as had been left / for her use / she was expected to wear / so long as she could put them on at all.
→

(3) She called it the Large Family / not because the members of it were big / — for, indeed, / most of them were little — / but because there were so many of them.
→

(4) It was several weeks / before her curiosity was satisfied, / and then it was revealed / that the new occupant / had neither wife nor children.
→

B. 다음 주어진 문구가 알맞은 문장이 되도록 순서를 맞춰보세요.

(1) 그녀는 지금까지 자신이 거지로 여겨질 수 있다는 것을 몰랐었다.
(taken / might / beggar / for / she / a / be)
Until now she had not known that ⬚
⬚.

(2) 그녀는 아무리 누추해 보여도, 거지가 아니다.
(shabby / looks / she / however)
She is not a beggar, ⬚.

 Answer

A. (1) 그녀는 매우 빠르게 성장하기 시작했고, 옷장에 남아있는 허름한 천조각같은 그런 옷들만 입었기 때문에, 자신이 아주 이상해 보인다는 것을 알고 있었다. (2) 그녀의 값비싼 옷들은 모두 처분되었고, 사용할 수 있게 남겨진 옷들은 입을 수 있는 한 오랫동안 입어야만 했다. (3) 새라가 그 가족을 대가족이라고 부른

192　A Little Princess

(3) 새라는 점점 더 베키를 좋아했다.
〔grew / and / Becky / She / fonder / of / fonder〕
→

(4) 한 마디도 하지 않는 것이 <u>그들에게 있어 가장 이로운 일이니까.</u>
〔so / nothing / There / for / good / is / as / them〕

_____ not to say a word.

C. 다음 주어진 문장이 본문의 내용과 맞으면 T, 틀리면 F에 동그라미 하세요.

(1) Ermengarde and Lottie visited the attic regularly.
〔T / F〕

(2) Girls from the Large Family became interested in Sara.
〔T / F〕

(3) Teaching French to children was a big burden to Sara.
〔T / F〕

(4) Sara look forward to seeing someone take the empty house next door.
〔T / F〕

D. 의미가 서로 비슷한 것끼리 연결해 보세요.

(1) insolent   ►   ◄ ① scorn

(2) sneer   ►   ◄ ② self-satisfied

(3) complacent   ►   ◄ ③ regret

(4) remorse   ►   ◄ ④ impolite

8

The Magic
마법

When Sara had passed / the house next door / she had
새라가 지나갔을 때   옆집을

seen Ram Dass closing the shutters, / and caught her
람다스가 덧문을 닫는 것을 봤고,   언뜻 보았다

glimpse / of this room also.
        이 방도.

"It is a long time / since I saw a nice place / from the
"오래되었구나   멋진 곳을 본 지도   방 안에서."

inside," / was the thought / which crossed her mind.
        이런 생각이   그녀의 마음을 스쳐 지나갔다.

There was the usual bright fire glowing / in the grate, /
평소처럼 불이 타오르고 있었고   벽난로에서는,

and the Indian gentleman was sitting / before it. His head
인도 신사는 앉아 있었다   그 앞에.

was resting in his hand, / and he looked / as lonely and
손으로 머리를 괴고 있었는데,   그는 보였다   그 어느 때보다도 외롭고

unhappy as ever.
불행하게.

"Poor man!" / said Sara. "I wonder / what you are
"불쌍한 아저씨구나!"   새라는 말했다.   "난 궁금해요   아저씨가 뭘 생각하고 있는지."

supposing."

Key Expression ❗

as ~ as ever (+동사의 과거형) : 지금까지 없었던 만큼, 아주 ~한
as ~ as ever는 최상급의 의미를 가진 표현입니다. ever 뒤에 오는 동사는 과
거형을 사용합니다.

ex) His head was resting in his hand, and he looked as lonely and unhappy as
ever.
그는 손으로 머리를 괴고 있었는데, 그 어느 때보다도 외롭고 불행하게 보였다.

And this was what he was "supposing" / at that very
이것이 바로 그가 "생각하고 있는" 것이었다   바로 그 순간.

moment.

"Suppose," / he was thinking, / "suppose / — even if
"만약,"   그는 생각하고 있었다.   "만약

Carmichael traces the people / to Moscow / — the little
— 카마이클이 그 사람들을 찾아   모스크바로 가더라도 — 그 여자 아이가

girl / they took / from Madame Pascal's school / in
그들이 데려간   마담 파스칼의 학교에서   파리에 있는

Paris / is not the one / we are in search of. Suppose / she
그 아이가 아니라면   우리가 찾고 있는.   만약

proves to be quite a different child. What steps shall I
그 아이가 완전 다른 아이라고 판명되면.   무슨 조치를 취해야 하지

take / next?"
앞으로?

When Sara went into the house / she met Miss Minchin,
새라가 집에 들어섰을 때   민친 교장을 만났다,

/ who had come downstairs / to scold the cook.
아래층으로 내려온   요리사를 꾸짖으러.

"Where have you wasted your time?" / she demanded.
"넌 어디에서 시간을 낭비하는 거냐?"   그녀가 따져 물었다.

"You have been out / for hours."
"넌 밖에 있었구나   몇 시간 동안이나."

"It was so wet and muddy," / Sara answered, / "it was
"질척거리고 진흙투성이라서,"   새라가 대답했다,

hard to walk, / because my shoes were so bad / and
"걷기 힘들었어요,   제 신발이 너무 닳아서

slipped about."
미끄러졌거든요."

"Make no excuses," / said Miss Minchin, / "and tell no
"변명하지 마라,"   민친 교장이 말했다,

falsehoods."
"그리고 거짓말도 하지 마."

---

trace 추적하다 | in search of ~을 찾아서 | falsehoods 거짓말

Sara went in / to the cook. The cook had received a severe
새라는 들어갔다   요리사에게.   요리사는 혹독한 잔소리를 들어서

lecture / and was in a fearful temper / as a result. She was
매우 화가 난 상태였다   그 결과.

only too rejoiced / to have someone / to vent her rage on, /
그녀는 너무 기쁠 뿐이었고   누군가 있다는 것이   분통을 터트릴,

and Sara was a convenience, / as usual.
그리고 새라는 편한 대상이었다.   평소처럼.

"Why didn't you stay / all night?" / she snapped.
"놀다 오지 그랬니   밤새도록?"   요리사가 톡 쏘며 말했다.

Sara laid her purchases / on the table.
새라는 사 온 것을 놓았다   탁자에.

"Here are the things," / she said.
"여기 물건들이 있어요."   그녀가 말했다.

The cook looked them over, / grumbling. She was in a very
요리사가 물건들을 살펴 보았다,   툴툴거리며.   그녀는 심기가 아주 사나웠다

savage humor / indeed.
정말로.

"May I have something / to eat?" / Sara asked rather faintly.
"뭔가 있을까요   먹을 것이?"   새라가 다소 힘없이 물었다.

"Tea's over and done with," / was the answer. "Did you
"티타임은 이미 끝났다,"   라고 대답했다.

expect me / to keep it hot / for you?"
"나한테 기대했냐   차를 뜨겁게 데우리라고   널 위해?

Sara stood silent / for a second.
새라는 조용히 서 있었다   잠시.

"I had no dinner," / she said next, / and her voice was quite
"저녁을 못 먹었어요,"   새라는 이어서 말했는데,   목소리는 매우 낮았다.

low. She made it low / because she was afraid / it would
새라는 목소리를 낮췄다   두려웠기 때문에

tremble.
목소리가 떨릴까 봐.

---

lecture 잔소리, 설교 | convenience 편리 | purchases 구입, 산 물건 | grumble 투덜거리다 | be in ~ humor
심기가 ~하다 | faintly 희미하게, 가냘프게 | pantry 식료품 저장실 | vicious 잔인한, 악랄한 | vent 터뜨리다 |
spite 앙심, 악의 | flight 계단, 층계 | steep 가파른

"There's some bread / in the pantry," / said the cook.
"빵이 있지 식료품 저장실에." 요리사가 말했다.

"That's all you'll get / at this time of day."
"그것이 네가 먹을 전부야 하루 중 이 시간에는."

Sara went / and found the bread. It was old and hard and
새라는 가서 빵을 찾았다. 그것은 오래되고 딱딱하고 말라 있었다.

dry. The cook was in too vicious a humor / to give her
요리사는 너무 포악해서

anything to eat with it. It was always safe / and easy /
그녀에게 먹을 것을 주지 않았다. 항상 안전하고 쉬웠다

to vent her spite / on Sara. Really, / it was hard / for the
분풀이를 하는 것이 새라에게. 실제로, 힘들었다 어린 아이가

child / to climb the three long flights of stairs / leading
세 개의 긴 층계를 오르는 것은

to her attic. She often found them long and steep / when
다락방으로 이어진. 새라는 종종 계단이 길고 가파르게 느껴졌다

she was tired; / but tonight / it seemed / as if she would
피곤할 때면; 하지만 오늘 밤에는 보였다 마치 꼭대기에 도달할 수

never reach the top. Several times / she was obliged to
없는 듯. 여러 번 새라는 멈춰서 쉬어야 했다.

stop to rest. When she reached the top landing / she was
꼭대기에 다다랐을 때 새라는 기뻤다

glad / to see the glimmer of a light / coming from under
희미한 불빛을 보고 자신의 방문 밑에서 새어나오는.

her door. That meant / that Ermengarde had managed
그것은 의미했다 어먼가드가 겨우 올라왔다는 것을

to creep up / to pay her a visit. There was some comfort
자신을 방문하러. 그 방문은 위안이 되었다.

in that. It was better / than to go into the room alone /
훨씬 나았으니까 방에 혼자 들어가

and find it empty and desolate. The mere presence / of
텅 비고 황폐한 것을 보는 것 보다. 그저 그 존재가

plump, comfortable Ermengarde, / wrapped in her red
포동포동하고, 편안한 어먼가드의, 빨간 숄을 두른,

shawl, / would warm it a little.
숄, 방을 조금은 따뜻하게 했다.

Yes; / there Ermengarde was / when she opened the door.
그랬다; 어먼가드가 있었다 새라가 문을 열었을 때.

She was sitting / in the middle of the bed, / with her feet
어먼가드는 앉아 있었다 침대 한가운데,

tucked safely under her. She had never become intimate
다리를 안전하게 접어넣은 채. 어먼가드는 절대 친해지지 못했다

/ with Melchisedec and his family, / though they rather
멜기세덱과 그 가족과는, 그 가족이 다소 흥미를 끌었지만.

fascinated her. When she found herself alone / in the attic
어먼가드는 혼자 있을 때면 다락방에서

/ she always preferred to sit on the bed / until Sara arrived.
항상 침대에 앉아 있는 것을 더 좋아했다 새라가 도착할 때까지.

She had, / in fact, / on this occasion / had time to become
그녀는, 사실, 이런 경우 다소 예민해져 있었다,

rather nervous, / because Melchisedec had appeared / and
왜냐하면 멜기세덱이 나타나서

sniffed about a good deal, / and once / had made her utter
계속 주위를 킁킁거렸기 때문에, 한 번은 억지로 비명을 참기도 했다

a repressed squeal / by sitting up on his hind legs / and, /
멜기세덱이 뒷다리로 번쩍 일어서는 바람에 그리고,

while he looked at her, / sniffing pointedly in her direction.
어먼가드를 쳐다보며, 그녀 쪽으로 예리하게 코를 킁킁거리자.

"Oh, Sara," / she cried out, / "I am glad you have come.
"오, 새라," 그녀가 소리쳤다, "네가 와서 기뻐.

Melchy would sniff about so. I tried to coax him to go back,
멜기가 저렇게 킁킁거리며 다니잖아. 달래서 돌려보내려 했는데,

/ but he wouldn't / for such a long time. I like him, / you
돌아가려 하지 않았어 아주 오랫동안. 난 저 애를 좋아해, 알다시피;

know; / but it does frighten me / when he sniffs / right at
하지만 날 깜짝 놀라게 해 코를 킁킁댈 때 바로 내 앞에서.

me. Do you think / he ever would jump?"
네 생각에는 저 애가 뛰어 오를 것 같니?"

"No," / answered Sara.
"아니," 새라가 대답했다.

Ermengarde crawled forward / on the bed / to look at her.
어먼가드는 앞으로 기어나왔다 침대 위에서 새라를 보러.

"You do look tired, / Sara," / she said; / "you are quite
"넌 피곤해 보이는구나, 새라." 그녀가 말했다; "많이 창백해 보여."

pale."

"I am tired," / said Sara, / dropping on / to the lopsided
"피곤해." 새라가 말했다. 주저 앉으며 한쪽이 기울어진 의자에.

footstool. "Oh, there's Melchisedec, / poor thing. He's
"아, 멜기세덱이 있네. 불쌍한 것.

come to ask for his supper."
저녁거리를 얻으러 왔구나."

Melchisedec had come / out of his hole / as if he had been
멜기세덱이 왔다 구멍 밖으로 마치 듣고 있었다는 듯

listening / for her footstep. Sara was quite sure / he knew
새라의 발소리를. 새라는 아주 확신했다 쥐가 알고 있다고.

it. He came forward / with an affectionate, expectant
앞으로 나왔다 다정하고, 기대하는 표정으로

expression / as Sara put her hand / in her pocket / and
새라가 손을 넣고 주머니에

turned it inside out, / shaking her head. "I'm very
안을 밖으로 뒤집었을 때, 머리를 흔들며. "매우 미안해,"

sorry," / she said. "I haven't one crumb left. Go home, /
새라가 말했다. "남은 빵 부스러기가 하나도 없어. 집에 가,

Melchisedec, / and tell your wife / there was nothing / in
멜기세덱, 그리고 부인한테 말하렴 아무것도 없다고

my pocket. I'm afraid / I forgot / because the cook and
내 주머니에는. 유감이지만 잊어버렸단다

Miss Minchin were so cross."
요리사와 민친 교장이 아주 화가 나는 바람에."

Melchisedec seemed to understand. He shuffled
멜기세덱은 이해하는 듯 보였다. 체념하듯 발을 끌면서 갔다,

resignedly, / if not contentedly, / back to his home.
섭섭하긴 해도, 자신의 집으로.

---

repressed 억압된 | pointedly 날카롭게 | crawl 기다 | lopsided 한쪽으로 처진 | expectant 기대하는 | cross
짜증난, 화난 | resignedly 체념하며 | contentedly 만족해 하며

"I did not expect / to see you / tonight, / Ermie," / Sara
"기대도 못 했어   널 보게 될 줄   오늘 밤에,   어먼가드,"   새라가

said. Ermengarde hugged herself / in the red shawl.
말했다. 어먼가드는 몸을 감쌌다   빨간 숄로.

"Miss Amelia has gone out / to spend the night / with her
"아멜리아 선생이 밖에 나갔어   밤을 보내러   늙은 고모와,"

old aunt," / she explained. "No one else ever comes / and
어먼가드가 설명했다. "아무도 오지 않을 거야

looks into the bedrooms / after we are in bed. I could
침실을 검사하러   우리가 잠든 후에.   여기에 있을 수

stay here / until morning / if I wanted to."
있어   아침까지   내가 원하면."

She pointed toward the table / under the skylight. Sara
어먼가드는 탁자 쪽을 가리켰다   천장의 창문 아래.

had not looked toward it / as she came in. A number of
새라는 그것을 보지 못했었다   들어왔을 때.

books were piled / upon it. Ermengarde's gesture was a
수많은 책들이 쌓여 있었다   그 위에.   어먼가드는 낙담한 모습이었다.

dejected one.

"Papa has sent me / some more books, / Sara," / she said.
"아빠가 보내셨어   책을 몇 권 더,   새라,"   어먼가드가 말했다.

"There they are."
"저기 있어."

Sara looked round / and got up / at once. She ran to the
새라는 주위를 돌아보고   일어났다   즉시.   탁자로 달려가서,

table, / and picking up the top volume, / turned over
맨 위의 책을 집어들고,   책장을 넘겼다

its leaves / quickly. For the moment / she forgot her
재빨리.   그 순간   피곤한 것도 잊어버렸다.

discomforts.

"Ah," / she cried out, / "how beautiful! *Carlyle's
"와,"   새라가 소리쳤다,   "아주 멋지다!

French Revolution. I have so wanted to read that!"
칼라일의 '프랑스 혁명'이네.   정말 읽어보고 싶었어!"

"I haven't," / said Ermengarde. "And papa will be so
"난 그런 적 없어," 어먼가드가 말했다. "우리 아빠는 아주 화가 나실 거야

cross / if I don't. He'll expect me to know / all about it /
내가 안 읽으면, 아빠는 내가 이해하기를 바라실 거야   책 전부

when I go home / for the holidays. What shall I do?"
집에 갈 때   휴일 동안.   어떡하지?"

Sara stopped / turning over the leaves / and looked at her
새라는 멈추고   책장을 넘기는 것을   어먼가드를 보았다

/ with an excited flush / on her cheeks.
흥분해서 홍조를 띤 채   두 뺨에.

"Look here," / she cried, / "if you'll lend me these books,
"나 좀 봐,"   그녀가 외쳤다,   "만약 나한테 이 책들을 빌려 준다면,

/ I'll read them / — and tell you everything / that's in
내가 읽을게   — 그리고 네게 모든 것을 말해 줄게   책 속에 있는

them / afterward / — and I'll tell it / so that you will
나중에   — 내가 말해 줄게   네가 기억할 수 있도록,

remember it, / too."
또한."

Key Expression ♥

so that 주어 may ~ : ~할 수 있도록

so that + 주어 + may + 동사원형은 '~할 수 있도록, ~하기 위하여'라는 의
미의 구문입니다. 이때 may 대신 will이나 can이 와도 같은 의미가 되며 so
that 대신 in order that을 쓸 수도 있습니다

ex) I'll tell it so that you will remember it.
네가 그것을 기억할 수 있도록 내가 말해 줄게.

---

* Carlyle 토머스 칼라일(1795~1881). 영국의 평론가이자 사상가, 역사가. 〈프랑스 혁명〉이란 저서를 통해
혁명을 지지하며 영웅적 지도자의 필요성을 주장했다

skylight 천장에 낸 채광창 | dejected 실의에 빠진, 낙담한 | discomforts 불편

"Oh, goodness!" / exclaimed Ermengarde. "Do you think
"오, 맙소사!" 어먼가드가 외쳤다. "할 수 있을 것 같아?"

you can?"

"I know I can," / Sara answered. "The little ones always
"할 수 있어." 새라가 대답했다. "어린 학생들은 항상 기억해

remember / what I tell them."
내가 말해 준 것을."

"Sara," / said Ermengarde, / hope gleaming / in her
"새라," 어먼가드가 말했다, 희망의 빛이 어리며

round face, / "if you'll do that, / and make me remember,
통통한 얼굴에, "만약 그렇게 해서, 내가 기억하도록 해 준다면,

/ I'll — I'll give you anything."
난 — 난 뭐든 줄게."

"I don't want / you to give me anything," / said Sara. "I
"원하지 않아 내게 뭐든 주는 것을," 새라가 말했다.

want your books / — I want them!" And her eyes grew
"네 책을 원해 — 그것들을 원하지!" 그리고 새라의 눈이 커지며,

big, / and her chest heaved.
가슴이 들썩거렸다.

"Take them, / then," / said Ermengarde. "I wish I wanted
"그것들을 가져가렴 그럼," 어먼가드가 말했다. "나도 책을 원했으면 좋을텐데

them / — but I don't. I'm not clever, / and my father is, /
— 하지만 난 아니야. 난 똑똑하지 않고, 우리 아빠는 똑똑해,

and he thinks / I ought to be."
그리고 아빠는 생각해 나도 그래야 한다고."

Sara was opening / one book after the other. "What are
새라는 펼쳤다 책을 한 권씩 차례로.

you going to tell your father?" / she asked, / a slight
"넌 아빠한테 뭐라고 말할 거니?" 새라가 물었다. 약간의 의심이

doubt / dawning in her mind.
마음속에 일어나면서.

"Oh, he needn't know," / answered Ermengarde. "He'll
"오, 아빠는 아실 필요 없지," 어먼가드가 대답했다. "아빠는 생각

think / I've read them."
할 거야 내가 다 읽었다고."

Sara put down her book / and shook her head / slowly.
새라는 책을 내려놓고　머리를 저었다　천천히.

"That's almost like telling lies," / she said. "And lies
"그것은 거짓말 하는 것과 마찬가지잖아."　그녀가 말했다.　"그리고 거짓말은

— well, you see, / they are not only wicked / — they're
— 음, 있잖아.　나쁜 짓이고　— 천박한 거야.

vulgar. Sometimes" / — reflectively — / "I've thought
때때로"　— 곰곰이 생각하며 —　"생각한 적이 있어

/ perhaps I might do something wicked / — I might
어쩌면 나도 나쁜 짓을 저지를지 모른다고

suddenly fly into a rage / and kill Miss Minchin, / you
— 갑자기 화를 내다가　민친 교장을 죽일지 모른다고.

know, / when she was ill-treating me / — but I couldn't
알다시피,　선생님이 날 학대할 때　— 하지만 난 천박한 짓을

be vulgar. Why can't you tell your father / I read them?"
할 수 없었어.　아빠한테 말씀 드리는 게 어때　내가 책을 읽었다고?"

"He wants / me to read them," / said Ermengarde, / a
"아빠는 원해서　내가 책을 읽기를."　어먼가드가 말했다.

little discouraged / by this unexpected turn of affairs.
약간 낙담하면서　이렇게 예상치 못하게 상황이 뒤바뀌자.

"He wants / you to know / what is in them," / said Sara.
"아빠는 원해서　네가 알기를　책에 있는 내용을."　새라가 말했다.

"And if I can tell it to you / in an easy way / and make
"그리고 내가 그 내용을 네게 이야기 해 주고　쉬운 방법으로

you remember it, / I should think / he would like that."
네가 기억할 수 있도록 하면,　내 생각에　아빠도 좋아하실 거야."

"He'll like it / if I learn anything / in any way," / said
"아빠는 좋아하시겠지　내가 뭐든 배우기만 하면　어떤 식으로든."

rueful Ermengarde. "You would / if you were my father."
유감스러운듯 어먼가드가 말했다.　"너도 그렇겠지　네가 우리 아빠라면."

---

heave 들어 올리다, 들썩거리다 | dawn 밝다, 분명해지다 | discouraged 낙담한 | affair 사건, 일 | rueful
후회하는, 유감스러워 하는

"It's not your fault / that — " / began Sara. She pulled
"네 잘못이 아니야   그것은 — "   새라가 말을 시작했다. 그녀는 멈춰 서서

herself up / and stopped / rather suddenly. She had been
말을 중단했다   갑자기.   새라는 말하려고 했다,

going to say, / "It's not your fault / that you are stupid."
"네 잘못이 아니야   네가 멍청한 것은."

"That what?" / Ermengarde asked.
"그것은 뭐?"   어먼가드가 물었다.

"That you can't learn things / quickly," / amended Sara.
"네가 뭔가를 배울 수 없는 것은   빨리,"   새라가 고쳐 말했다.

"If you can't, / you can't. If I can / — why, I can; / that's
"네가 할 수 없다면,   할 수 없는 거야. 내가 할 수 있으면   — 음, 할 수 있는 것이고;

all."
그 뿐이야."

She always felt / very tender of Ermengarde, / and tried /
새라는 항상 느꼈다   어먼가드의 여린 마음을,   그래서 애썼다

not to let her feel / too strongly / the difference / between
어먼가드가 느끼지 않도록 하려고 너무 강하게   그 차이점을

being able to learn anything at once, / and not being able
즉시 배울 수 있는 것과,   전혀 배울 수 없는 것 사이의.

to learn anything at all. As she looked at her plump face,
새라가 어먼가드의 통통한 얼굴을 쳐다보았을 때,

/ one of her wise, old-fashioned thoughts / came to her.
현명하고, 어른스러운 생각 하나가   그녀에게 떠올랐다.

> ## Key Expression ♪

worth의 사용법

worth는 '~의 가치가 있는'이라는 의미의 형용사이지만 명사를 수식하는 용법으로는 쓰이지 않으며, 다음과 같은 방법으로 '~의 가치가 있다, ~할 가치가 있다'라는 뜻을 나타냅니다.

▶ be + worth + 관사 + 명사 (전치사처럼 쓰여 명사나 동명사 사용)
　　　　　　＋ 동명사
▶ be + worthy of + 관사 + 명사 (전치사 of 뒤에 명사나 동명사)
　　　　　　＋ 동명사
▶ be + worth while to + 부정사 (동명사를 쓰는 경우도 있으나 부정사가 일반적)

ex) To be kind is worth a great deal to other people.
　　친절하다는 것은 다른 사람들에게 매우 큰 가치가 있어.

"Perhaps," / she said, / "to be able to learn things quickly
"아마도," 새라가 말했다, "뭔가를 빨리 배울 수 있다는 것이

/ isn't everything. To be kind / is worth a great deal /
전부는 아닌 것 같아. 친절하다는 것은 매우 큰 가치가 있는 거야

to other people. If Miss Minchin knew / everything on
다른 사람들에게. 민친 교장이 알더라도 세상 모든 것을

earth / and was like what she is now, / she'd still be a
지금의 그녀와 같다면, 여전히 혐오스러운 사람일

detestable thing, / and everybody would hate her. Lots of
것이고, 누구나 싫어할 거야. 똑똑한 사람

clever people / have done harm / and have been wicked.
중 다수가 해로운 짓을 하거나 사악해졌어.

Look at *Robespierre — "
로베스피에르를 봐 —"

She stopped / and examined Ermengarde's countenance,
새라는 말을 멈추고 어먼가드의 표정을 살폈다,

/ which was beginning to look bewildered. "Don't you
당황한 듯 보이기 시작한.

remember?" / she demanded. "I told you / about him /
"기억나지 않니?" 새라가 물었다. "네게 말했는데 그에 대해서

not long ago. I believe you've forgotten."
얼마 전에. 잊어버린 것 같구나."

"Well, I don't remember all of it," / admitted
"음, 전혀 기억 안 나." 어먼가드가 인정했다.

Ermengarde.

"Well, you wait a minute," / said Sara, / "and I'll take off
"그럼, 잠시만 기다려." 새라가 말했다. "젖은 옷을 벗고

my wet things / and wrap myself / in the coverlet / and
몸을 감싸야겠어 이불로 그리고

tell you / over again."
말해 줄게 다시 한 번.

---

* 막시밀리앙 로베스피에르(1758~94). 프랑스 혁명기의 정치가이자 자코뱅당의 지도자로 파리 코뮌의 대표로 추대되어 공포정치를 추진했다

pull up 멈추다, 서다 | amend 수정하다 | tender 예민한, 상처받기 쉬운, 감수성이 강한 | detestable 혐오스러운 |
coverlet 침대보

205

She took off her hat and coat / and hung them / on a nail
새는 모자와 외투를 벗어서 / 걸었다 / 못에

/ against the wall, / and she changed her wet shoes / for
벽에 박힌, / 그리고 젖은 신발을 바꿔 신었다

an old pair of slippers. Then she jumped on the bed, / and
낡은 슬리퍼로. / 그리고는 침대로 뛰어올라가,

drawing the coverlet / about her shoulders, / sat / with her
이불을 끌어당기며 / 어깨까지, / 앉았다

arms round her knees. "Now, listen," / she said.
두 팔로 무릎을 감싸며. / "자, 들어봐," / 새가 말했다.

She plunged / into the gory records / of the French
새는 빠져들었다 / 유혈의 기록들로 / 프랑스 혁명의,

Revolution, / and told such stories of it / that
그것에 관한 이야기들을 아주 많이 해서

Ermengarde's eyes grew round / with alarm / and she
어먼가드의 눈이 동그랗게 커졌고 / 놀라움에

held her breath. But though she was rather terrified, /
숨을 죽였다. / 하지만 다소 무서워도,

there was a delightful thrill / in listening, / and she was
기쁨이 가득 찬 전율이 있어서 / 들으면서, / 어먼가드는 잊어버리지

not likely to forget / Robespierre / again, / or to have any
않을 것 같았다 / 로베스피에르를 / 다시는, / 또는 의문도 갖지 않을 것

doubts / about *the Princesse de Lamballe.
같았다 / 랑발 공비에 대해서도.

"You know / they put her head / on a pike / and danced
"알다시피 / 사람들은 랑발 공비의 머리를 꽂았어 / 창 위에 / 그리고 그 주위에서

round it," / Sara explained. "And she had beautiful
춤을 췄지," / 새가 설명했다. / "그리고 공비는 아름답게 물결치는 금발을

floating blonde hair; / and when I think of her, / I never
가졌었지; / 그래서 랑발 공비를 생각하면, / 몸에 붙어 있는

see her head on her body, / but always on a pike, / with
머리가 보이는 것이 아니라, / 항상 창에 매달린 머리만 보여,

those furious people / dancing and howling."
그 몹시 화가 난 사람들이 / 춤추고 울부짖는 가운데.

It was agreed / that Mr. St. John was to be told / the plan
뜻을 모았다   세인트 존 씨에게 말하기로

they had made, / and for the present / the books were to
그들이 세운 계획을,   그래서 당분간   책들은 남겨두기로 했다

be left / in the attic.
다락방에.

"Now let's tell each other things," / said Sara. "How are
"이제 다른 이야기를 해 보자,"   새라가 말했다.

you getting on / with your French lessons?"
"어떻게 되어가는 중이니   네 프랑스어 공부는?"

"Ever so much better / since the last time / I came up
"아주 좋아졌어   지난번 이래로   내가 여기 올라와서

here / and you explained the conjugations. Miss Minchin
    네가 동사 활용법을 설명해 줬던.

could not understand / why I did my exercises so well /
민친 교장은 알 수 없었지   어떻게 내가 그렇게 잘 공부했는지

that first morning."
그 첫날 아침에."

Sara laughed a little / and hugged her knees.
새라는 약간 웃으며   그녀의 무릎을 감쌌다.

"She doesn't understand / why Lottie is doing her sums
"선생님은 모르셔   어떻게 로티가 계산을 그렇게 잘하는지,"

so well," / she said; / "but it is because / she creeps up
    그녀가 말했다;   "하지만 그 이유는   로티도 여기로 몰래 오기 때

here, / too, / and I help her." She glanced round the
문이지,   역시,   그리고 내가 도와주거든." 새라는 방 주위를 보았다.

room. "The attic would be rather nice / — if it wasn't so
    "다락방도 꽤 멋질 텐데   — 이렇게 끔찍하지만 않다면,"

dreadful," / she said, / laughing again. "It's a good place
    새라가 말했다,   다시 웃으면서.   "좋은 장소야

/ to pretend in."
상상놀이를 하는데."

---

* 랑발 공비 : 루이 16세의 왕비 마리 앙투와네트의 절친한 친구로 프랑스 혁명 때 폭도들에 의해 처형됐다

plunge (갑자기) 뛰어들다, 고꾸라지다 | gory 피투성이의 | thrill 황홀감, 흥분, 전율 | pike 창, 바늘 | floating
유동적인, 흔들리는 | furious 몹시 화가 난 | conjugation 동사 활용형 | sum 합계, 액수

The truth was / that Ermengarde did not know anything /
사실은   어먼가드는 아무것도 몰랐고

of the sometimes / almost unbearable side of life / in the
때때로   참을 수 없는 삶의 단면에 대해   다락방에서의

attic / and she had not a sufficiently vivid imagination /
다락방   충분히 생생한 상상력이 없었다

to depict it / for herself. On the rare occasions / that she
그것을 그려볼   혼자.   아주 드문 경우에는

could reach Sara's room / she only saw the side of it / which
어먼가드가 새라의 방에 올 수 있었던   그 한쪽 면만 보았을 뿐이었다

was made exciting / by things which were "pretended"
흥미진진하게 만들어진   "상상되어진" 것들에 의해

/ and stories which were told. Her visits partook / of the
그리고 듣는 이야기들에 의해.   그녀의 방문은 띠고 있다

character of adventures; / and though sometimes / Sara
모험의 특성을;   그리고 비록 이따금

looked rather pale, / and it was not to be denied / that she
새라가 다소 창백해 보였고,   틀림없었지만

had grown very thin, / her proud little spirit / would not
새라가 매우 야위어 간다는 것은,   새라의 자존심 센 작은 영혼이   인정하지 않으려 했다

admit / of complaints. She had never confessed / that at
불평하는 것을.   절대 털어놓은 적이 없었다   가끔은

times / she was almost ravenous with hunger, / as she
배고파서 거의 죽을 지경이라는 것을,

was tonight. She was growing rapidly, / and her constant
오늘 밤처럼.   새라는 빠르게 성장하는 중이었고,

walking and running about / would have given her a keen
끊임없이 걷고 뛰어다녀서   식욕이 예민해졌다

appetite / even if she had had abundant and regular meals /
푸짐하고 규칙적인 식사를 했어야 했지만

of a much more nourishing nature / than the unappetizing,
훨씬 더 많은 영양분의   식욕을 떨어뜨리는 안 좋은 음식보다

inferior food / snatched at such odd times / as suited the
매우 비정상적인 시간에 빨리 먹어치워야 했던

kitchen convenience. She was growing used / to a certain
부엌 형편에 맞춰서.   새라는 익숙해졌다

gnawing feeling / in her young stomach.
괴로운 통증에   어린 위 속에서.

"I suppose soldiers feel like this / when they are on a long
"군인들이 이처럼 느꼈을 거라고 생각해   길고 피곤한 행군을 할 때,"

and weary march," / she often said to herself. She liked
새라는 자신에게 종종 말했다.

the sound of the phrase, / "long and weary march." It
새라는 그 구절의 소리를 좋아했다   "길고 피곤한 행군"이라는.

made her feel / rather like a soldier. She had also a quaint
그 말은 느끼게 해 주었다 마치 자신이 군인인 듯.   새라는 항상 기묘한 생각을 했다

sense / of being a hostess / in the attic.
여주인이 된 듯   다락방에서.

"If I lived in a castle," / she argued, / "and Ermengarde
"내가 성에 살았다면,"   새라가 말했다,

was the lady of another castle, / and came to see me, /
"그리고 어먼가드가 다른 성의 여주인인데,   나를 보러 오지,

with knights and squires and vassals riding with her, /
기사와 대지주와 봉신들을 거느리고,

and pennons flying, / when I heard the clarions sounding
깃발을 휘날리며,   나팔 소리가 울려 퍼지는 것이 들리면

/ outside the drawbridge / I should go down / to receive
도개교 밖에서   난 내려가서   어먼가드를 영접하고,

her, / and I should spread feasts / in the banquet hall / and
잔치를 벌이겠지   연회 홀에서

call in minstrels / to sing and play / and relate romances.
그리고 음악가들을 불러서 노래하고 놀며   이야기를 들려주겠지.

When she comes / into the attic / I can't spread feasts, /
어먼가드가 올 때   다락방에   잔치를 열 수는 없지만,

but I can tell stories, / and not let her know / disagreeable
이야기를 말해 줄 수 있어,   그래서 그 아이가 모르게 할 수 있어 유쾌하지 못한 일들을.

things. I dare say / poor chatelaines had to do that / in
분명히   가난한 성주 부인은 그렇게 해야 했을 거야

time of famine, / when their lands had been pillaged."
기근의 시기에는,   양들을 약탈당했을 때에는."

---

sufficiently 충분히 | depict 묘사하다 | partake of (특정한 성질을) 띠다, 취하다 | at times 때때로 | ravenous 배가 고파 죽을 지경인 | keen 날카로운, 예민한 | abundant 풍부한 | nourishing 영양이 되는 | gnawing 괴롭히는 | weary 지친, 지루한 | quaint 진기한, 독특한 | squire (과거 잉글랜드의) 대지주 | vassal 봉신(봉건 군주에게서 봉토를 받은 신하), 속국 | pennon 창기(槍旗), 깃 | clarion 클라리온 (명쾌한 음색을 가진 옛 나팔) | drawbridge 도개교(다리를 들어 올려 배가 통과하도록 만들어진 다리) | minstrel (중세의) 음악가, 음유 시인 | chatelaine 여자 성주, 저택의 여주인 | famine 기근 | pillage 약탈하다

She was a proud, brave little chatelaine, / and dispensed
새라는 자랑스럽고, 용감하며, 어린 여자 성주였고,

generously / the one hospitality / she could offer / — the
관대하게 베풀었다   유일한 환대를   자신이 줄 수 있는

dreams she dreamed / — the visions she saw / — the
— 그녀가 꾸었던 꿈들과   — 그녀가 보았던 비전과

imaginings / which were her joy and comfort.
— 상상한 것들을   그녀의 기쁨이고 위안이었던.

So, / as they sat together, / Ermengarde did not know /
그래서, 그들이 함께 앉아 있을 때,   어먼가드는 알지 못했다

that she was faint / as well as ravenous, / and that while
새라가 어지러워 했다는 것을   배고플 뿐 아니라,   그리고 새라가 이야기 하는

she talked / she now and then wondered / if her hunger
동안   이따금 궁금해했다는 사실도   배고픔 때문에 잠이

would let her sleep / when she was left alone. She felt / as
들 수 있을지   혼자 남겨지게 되면.   새라는 느꼈다

if she had never been quite so hungry / before.
마치 그렇게 배고픈 적은 없었던 것처럼   이전에는.

"I wish I was as thin as you, / Sara," / Ermengarde said
"나도 너만큼 날씬하면 좋을 텐데,   새라,"   어먼가드가 말했다

/ suddenly. "I believe / you are thinner / than you used
갑자기.   "내 생각에   넌 더 날씬해진 것 같아   예전보다"

to be. Your eyes look so big, / and look at the sharp little
눈은 정말 커 보이고,   날카로운 작은 뼈가 보여

bones / sticking out of your elbow!"
팔꿈치에서 튀어나와 있는!"

Sara pulled down her sleeve, / which had pushed itself up.
새라는 소맷자락을 끌어 내렸다,   걷어 올렸던.

"I always was a thin child," / she said bravely, / "and I
"난 항상 마른 아이였으니까,"   새라가 씩씩하게 말했다,

always had big green eyes."
"그리고 항상 큰 초록색 눈을 가졌지."

dispense 나누어 주다, 내놓다 | scratchy 긁는 소리가 나는, 거슬리는

"I love your queer eyes," / said Ermengarde, / looking
"난 네 묘한 눈이 좋아," 어먼가드가 말했다. 눈을 보면서

into them / with affectionate admiration. "They always
애정어린 동경을 담아. "네 눈은 항상 보여

look / as if they saw such a long way. I love them / —
마치 아주 멀리 보는 것처럼. 그 눈이 좋아

and I love them to be green / — though they look black
— 네 눈이 초록빛인 것이 좋아 — 평소에는 검은 색으로 보이지만."

generally."

"They are cat's eyes," / laughed Sara; / "but I can't see /
"고양이의 눈이지," 새라가 웃었다; "하지만 난 볼 수 없어

in the dark / with them / — because I have tried, / and I
어둠 속에서는 내 눈으로 — 시도해 봤었는데,

couldn't / — I wish I could."
볼 수 없었어 — 보고 싶기는 해."

It was just at this minute / that something happened /
바로 이때였다 무슨 일이 일어난 것은

at the skylight / which neither of them saw. If either of
채광창에서 두 사람 모두 보지 못한. 만약 둘 중 누군가

them / had chanced to turn and look, / she would have
우연히 돌아보았다면,

been startled / by the sight of a dark face / which peered
깜짝 놀랐을 것이다 어두운 얼굴을 보고 조심스럽게 쳐다보다가

cautiously / into the room / and disappeared / as quickly
방 안을 사라져버린

and almost as silently / as it had appeared. Not quite as
빠르고 조용하게 나타났을 때처럼. 그렇게 조용한 것은

silently, / however. Sara, / who had keen ears, / suddenly
아니었다, 하지만. 새라가, 예민한 귀를 가진, 갑자기 고개를

turned a little / and looked up at the roof.
살짝 돌려 지붕을 올려다봤다.

"That didn't sound like Melchisedec," / she said. "It
"저것은 멜기세덱이 내는 소리가 아닌데," 새라가 말했다.

wasn't scratchy enough."
"긁는 소리가 아니었어."

"What?" / said Ermengarde, / a little startled.
"뭐라고?" 어먼가드가 말했다, 조금 놀라며.

"Didn't you think you heard something?" / asked Sara.
"넌 무슨 소리 들은 것 같지 않아?" 새라가 물었다.

"N-no," / Ermengarde faltered. "Did you?"
"아—아니," 어먼가드가 더듬거렸다. "넌 들었니?"

"Perhaps / I didn't," / said Sara; "but I thought I did.
"어쩌면 못 들었을지도," 새라가 말했다; "들은 것 같아.

It sounded / as if something was on the slates / —
그것은 소리였어 마치 뭔가 슬레이트 지붕 위에 있는 것 같은

something that dragged softly."
— 조용히 끄는 뭔가."

"What could it be?" / said Ermengarde. "Could it be / —
"그건 뭘까?" 어먼가드가 말했다. "혹시

robbers?"
— 강도?"

"No," / Sara began cheerfully. "There is nothing / to
"아니," 새라가 활기차게 말하기 시작했다. "아무것도 없잖아

steal — "
훔칠 것이 —"

She broke off / in the middle of her words. They both
새라는 말을 멈추었다 말하는 중간에. 둘 다 소리를 들었다

heard / the sound that checked her. It was not on the
그녀의 말을 멈추게 했던 소리를. 그것은 지붕 위가 아니라,

slates, / but on the stairs below, / and it was Miss
아래 계단에서 나는 소리였고,

Minchin's angry voice. Sara sprang off the bed, / and put
민친 교장의 화가 난 목소리였다. 새라가 침대에서 벌떡 일어나,

out the candle.
촛불을 껐다.

"She is scolding Becky," / she whispered, / as she stood /
"베키를 혼내고 있어." 새라가 속삭였다, 선 채로

in the darkness. "She is making her cry."
어둠 속에서. "베키를 울리고 있어."

---

falter (자신이 없어 목소리가) 흔들리다, 더듬거리다 | panic-stricken 공황 상태에 빠진 | dishonest 정직하지 못한

"Will she come in here?" Ermengarde whispered back, /
"선생님이 여기로 들어오실까?" 어먼가드가 속삭이며 대꾸했다

panic-stricken.
공황 상태에 빠져.

"No. She will think I am in bed. Don't stir."
"아니야, 내가 자고 있다고 생각할 거야. 움직이지 마."

It was very seldom / that Miss Minchin mounted / the last
매우 드문 일이었다 민친 교장이 올라오는 것은

flight of stairs. Sara could only remember / that she had
마지막 층계를. 새라는 기억할 뿐이었다 교장이 한 번 올라왔던

done it once / before. But now / she was angry enough / to
적을 전에. 하지만 지금 교장은 엄청 화가 나서

be coming / at least part of the way up, / and it sounded /
올라오고 있었다 적어도 계단의 일부를, 그리고 들렸다

as if she was driving Becky / before her.
마치 베키를 몰고 있는 듯 바로 앞에서.

"You impudent, dishonest child!" / they heard her say.
"넌 무례하고, 정직하지 못한 아이구나!" 그들은 교장이 말하는 것을 들었다.

"Cook tells me / she has missed things / repeatedly."
"요리사가 말했어 물건들을 잃어버린다고 자꾸."

"'T warn't me, / mum," / said Becky sobbing. "I was
"그것은 제가 아니에요, 마님," 베키가 울면서 말했다. "전 엄청 배가

'ungry enough, / but 't warn't me / — never!"
고프기는 했지만, 전 아니에요 — 절대로!"

"You deserve to be sent to prison," / said Miss Minchin's
"넌 감옥에 보내져야 마땅해." 민친 교장의 목소리가 말했다.

voice. "Picking and stealing! Half a meat pie, / indeed!"
"좀도둑질을 하다니! 고기 파이 반쪽을, 정말!"

"'T warn't me," / wept Becky. "I could 'ave eat a whole un
"제가 안 그랬어요." 베키가 흐느꼈다. "그것을 전부 먹을 수도 있었지만

/ — but I never laid a finger on it."
— 손가락 하나도 대지 않았어요."

Miss Minchin was out of breath / between temper / and
민친 교장은 숨이 찼다 화를 내면서

mounting the stairs. The meat pie had been intended /
계단을 오르느라고. 그 고기 파이는 준비된 것이었다

for her special late supper. It became apparent / that she
교장의 특별한 밤참으로. 틀림없었다

boxed Becky's ears.
교장이 베키의 따귀를 때린 것이.

"Don't tell falsehoods," / she said. "Go to your room / this
"거짓말 하지 마." 교장이 말했다. "네 방으로 가거라

instant."
지금 당장."

Both Sara and Ermengarde heard the slap, / and then /
새라와 어먼가드 둘 다 찰싹 하는 소리를 들었고, 그리고 나서

heard / Becky run / in her slipshod shoes / up the stairs /
들었다 베키가 뛰어와서 낡은 신발을 신고 계단을 올라와

and into her attic. They heard her door shut, / and knew /
다락방 안으로 들어가는 소리를. 그들은 베키의 방문이 닫히는 소리를 들었고, 알았다

that she threw herself / upon her bed.
베키가 몸을 던졌다는 것을 침대 위로.

"I could 'ave e't two of 'em," / they heard her cry / into
"두 개 다 먹을 수도 있었지만." 그들은 베키가 우는 소리를 들었다

her pillow. "An' I never took a bite. 'T was cook give it /
베개 속에서. "한 입도 먹지 않았어. 요리사가 준 거라고

to her policeman."
경찰관한테."

pick and steal 좀도둑질 | box one's ears 뺨을 때리다 | slap 찰싹 하는 소리 | slipshod 엉성한 | clench 꽉
쥐다, 이를 악물다 | fiercely 사납게, 맹렬하게 | outstretched 죽 뻗은 | burst 갑자기 시작하다 | barrel 통 |
passionate 욕정, 열정을 느끼는, 보이는, 격정적인 | overawed 압도된

Sara stood / in the middle of the room / in the darkness.
새라는 서 있었다   방의 한가운데에   어둠 속에서.

She was clenching her little teeth / and opening and
새라는 작은 이를 악물고   사납게 쥐락펴락 했다

shutting fiercely / her outstretched hands. She could
                쭉 뻗은 손을.

scarcely stand still, / but she dared not move / until Miss
새라는 가만히 있을 수 없었지만,   감히 움직이지 못했다

Minchin had gone down the stairs / and all was still.
민친 교장이 계단을 내려가서   모두 조용해질 때까지.

"The wicked, cruel thing!" / she burst forth. "The cook
"사악하고, 잔인한 인간!"   새라는 갑자기 말을 시작했다. "요리사는 자기가

takes things herself / and then says / Becky steals them.
그것을 가져가고는   말한 거야   베키가 훔쳐갔다고.

She doesn't! She doesn't! She's so hungry / sometimes
베키는 안 그랬어!   안 그랬는데!   베키는 아주 배고파서   이따금씩

/ that she eats crusts / out of the ash barrel!" She
    부스러기를 먹는다고   쓰레기통에서!"

pressed her hands hard against her face / and burst into
새라는 손으로 얼굴을 가리고

passionate little sobs, / and Ermengarde, / hearing this
격정적인 눈물을 터뜨렸다.   그리고 어먼가드는,   이 범상치 않은 소리를

unusual thing, / was overawed by it. Sara was crying!
들으면서,   그 소리에 위압되었다.   새라가 울고 있어!

Key Expression ♥

not A until B : B하고 나서야 (비로소) A하다
not A until B는 직역하면 'B할 때까지는 A하지 않다'라고 해석되지만, 'B하
고 나서야 (비로소) A하다'로 해석하는 것이 자연스러워요.

ex) She dared not move until Miss Minchin had gone down the stairs and all was
   still.
   민친 교장이 계단을 내려가서 모두 조용해진 후에야 그녀는 비로소 움직일 수
   있었다.

215

The unconquerable Sara! It seemed to denote something
그 무적의 새라가!   뭔가 새로운 것을 의미하는 것 같았다

new / — some mood she had never known. Suppose —
— 자신이 알지 못했던 낌새를   만약 — 만약 —

suppose — / a new dread possibility / presented itself / to
새롭고 두려운 가능성이   나타났다

her kind, slow, little mind / all at once. She crept off the
어먼가드의 친절하고, 느리고, 작은 마음에   갑자기.   어먼가드는 침대로 기어가서

bed / in the dark / and found her way to the table / where
어둠 속에서   탁자로 가는 길을 찾았다

the candle stood. She struck a match / and lit the candle.
촛불이 놓여 있던.   성냥을 켜서   촛불에 불을 붙였다.

When she had lighted it, / she bent forward / and looked at
불을 켰을 때,   어먼가드는 앞으로 몸을 숙여   새라를 보았다,

Sara, / with her new thought / growing to definite fear / in
그녀의 새로운 생각이   확실한 두려움으로 변하면서

her eyes.
눈 속에서.

"Sara," / she said / in a timid, / almost awe-stricken voice,
"새라,"   어먼가드가 말했다   겁먹고,   거의 공황에 빠져서,

/ are — are — you never told me / — I don't want to be
넌 — 넌 — 나한테 말한 적 없었고   — 나도 무례해지고 싶지는 않아,

rude, / but — are you ever hungry?"
그렇지만 — 넌 배고픈 적 있니?"

Key Expression ♥

감각동사의 사용법

오감을 나타내는 동사를 감각동사라고 부릅니다. 감각동사에는 look/seem(~처럼 보이다), smell(~같은 냄새가 나다), taste(~같은 맛이 나다), sound(~같이 들린다), feel(~같이 느껴진다)가 있어요.

▶ 감각동사 + 형용사
▶ 감각동사 + like + 명사

ex) You do look tired, Sara.
새라, 넌 피곤해 보이는구나.
I know I look like a street beggar.
나도 내가 거리의 거지처럼 보인다는 것을 알고 있다.

unconquerable 정복할 수 없는, 무적의 | denote 의미하다, 나타내다 | dread 몹시 무서워하다, 두려워하다 |
definite 확실한, 분명한 | woefully 슬픔에 가득 차서, 비참하게

It was too much / just at that moment. The barrier broke
그것은 너무 심한 말이었다   바로 그 순간은.   장벽이 무너져버렸다.

down. Sara lifted her face / from her hands.
          새라는 얼굴을 들었다   손에서.

"Yes," / she said / in a new passionate way. "Yes, I am.
"맞아."   새라가 말했다   새삼 격앙된 말투로.   "그래, 난 배고파.

I'm so hungry now / that I could almost eat you. And it
난 지금 아주 배고파서   널 잡아먹을 수도 있을 것 같아.

makes it worse / to hear poor Becky. She's hungrier than
그래서 더 슬픈 거야   불쌍한 베키 소리를 듣는 것이.   베키는 나보다도 더 배고파."

I am."

Ermengarde gasped.
어먼가드는 숨이 막혔다.

"Oh, oh!" / she cried woefully. "And I never knew!"
"아, 아!"   슬픔에 가득 차서 소리쳤다.   "난 전혀 몰랐어!"

"I didn't want you to know," / Sara said. "It would have
"네가 알게 되는 것을 원하지 않았어."   새라가 말했다.   "그러면 내가 느끼게

made me feel / like a street beggar. I know / I look like a
될 테니까   거리의 거지처럼.   알고 있어   내가 거리의 거지처

street beggar."
럼 보인다는 것을."

"No, you don't / — you don't!" Ermengarde broke in.
"아니야, 넌 그렇지 않아   — 그렇지 않다고!"   어먼가드가 끼어들었다.

"Your clothes are a little queer / — but you couldn't look
"옷은 좀 이상해 보이지만   — 넌 보이지 않아

/ like a street beggar. You haven't a street-beggar face."
거리의 거지처럼.   네 얼굴은 거지의 얼굴이 아니거든."

"A little boy once gave me / a sixpence for charity," /
"어떤 남자 아이가 내게 준 적 있어   자선으로 6펜스짜리 은화를."

said Sara, / with a short little laugh / in spite of herself.
새라가 말했다,   짧게 웃으며   자신도 모르게.

"Here it is." And she pulled out / the thin ribbon / from
"여기 있어."   그리고 새라는 꺼내었다   얇은 리본을

her neck. "He wouldn't have given me / his Christmas
목에서.   "그 애는 주지 않았을 거야   자신의 크리스마스 선물인

sixpence / if I hadn't looked / as if I needed it."
6펜스 은화를   내가 보이지 않았더라면   돈을 원하는 것처럼."

217

Somehow / the sight of the dear little sixpence / was
어쨌든   소중하고 작은 6펜스짜리 은화를 보자

good for both of them. It made them laugh a little, /
둘 다 기분이 좋아졌다.   그 이야기로 두 사람은 살짝 웃었다.

though they both had tears / in their eyes.
둘 다 눈물이 어려 있었지만   눈에는.

"Who was he?" / asked Ermengarde, / looking at it
"그 애가 누군데?"   어먼가드가 물었다,   은화를 보면서

/ quite as if it had not been / a mere ordinary silver
마치 아닌 듯이   그저 평범한 6펜스짜리 은화가.

sixpence.

"He was a darling little thing / going to a party," / said
"사랑스러운 꼬마 아이야   파티에 가고 있었던."   새라가

Sara. "He was one of the Large Family, / the little one
말했다.   "대가족 중 한 명이고,

with the round legs / — the one I call Guy Clarence. I
통통한 다리를 가진 어린 아이야   — 내가 가이 클래런스라고 부르는 아이지.

suppose / his nursery was crammed / with Christmas
내 생각에   그 애의 놀이방은 가득 차 있을 거야   크리스마스 선물과

presents / and hampers / full of cakes and things, / and
          바구니로   케이크같은 것으로 가득 찬,   그래서

he could see / I had nothing."
알 수 있었던 거야   내게 아무것도 없다는 것을."

Ermengarde gave a little jump backward. The last
어먼가드는 뒤로 살짝 뛰어올랐다.

sentences had recalled something / to her troubled mind /
마지막 말이 뭔가를 생각나게 하고   불안한 마음에

and given her / a sudden inspiration.
그리고 준 것이다   갑작스런 영감을.

"Oh, Sara!" / she cried. "What a silly thing I am / not to
"오, 새라!"   그녀가 외쳤다.   "이렇게 바보같을 수가   그것을

have thought of it!"
생각하지 못하다니!"

ordinary 보통의, 평범한 | cram 밀어 넣다, 가득 차게 하다 | hamper 광주리, 바구니 | tumble 굴러 떨어지다 |
tart 타르트(속에 과일같은 것을 넣고 위에 반죽을 씌우지 않고 만든 파이) | red-currant 레드 커런트(색깔이 붉은
까치밥나무 열매) | fig 무화과 | reel 비틀거리다 | ejaculate (갑자기) 외치다

"Of what?"
"뭔데?"

"Something splendid!" / said Ermengarde, / in an excited
"멋진 게 있어!"　　　　　　어먼가드가 말했다,　　　　　흥분되어 서두르며.

hurry. "This very afternoon / my nicest aunt sent me a
"오늘 오후에　　　　　　제일 착한 고모님이 상자를 보내 주셨어.

box. It is full of good things. I never touched it, / I had so
좋은 것들로 가득 찬 거야.　　　　　건드리지도 않았지,

much pudding at dinner, / and I was so bothered / about
저녁 때 푸딩을 아주 많이 먹은데다,　　　아주 신경이 쓰였거든

papa's books." Her words began to tumble over / each
아빠가 보낸 책들에."　　그녀의 말이 튀어나오기 시작했다

other. "It's got cake in it, / and little meat pies, / and jam
하나씩.　　"그 안에는 케이크가 있고,　　작은 고기 파이,

tarts and buns, / and oranges and red-currant wine, / and
잼 타르트와 빵,　　　　오렌지와 레드커런트 주스,

figs and chocolate. I'll creep back / to my room / and get it
무화과와 초콜릿이 있어.　　내가 몰래 돌아가서　　내 방으로　　가져올게

/ this minute, / and we'll eat it now."
　당장,　　　그리고 지금 먹자."

Sara almost reeled. When one is faint with hunger / the
새라는 거의 비틀거렸다.　　사람이 배고픔으로 현기증을 느끼면

mention of food / has sometimes a curious effect. She
음식을 언급하는 것으로　　때때로 알 수 없는 현상이 생기곤 한다.

clutched Ermengarde's arm.
새라는 어먼가드의 팔을 움켜잡았다.

"Do you think / — you could?" / she ejaculated.
"생각하니　　　— 네가 할 수 있다고?"　새라가 갑자기 외쳤다.

"I know I could," / answered Ermengarde, / and she ran to
"할 수 있어."　　　　어먼가드가 대답했다,　　　　그리고 문으로 달려가서

the door / — opened it softly / — put her head out / into
　　　— 살짝 열어보고는　　　— 머리를 밖으로 내밀고

the darkness, / and listened. Then she went back to Sara.
어둠 속으로,　　귀 기울였다.　　그리고는 새라에게 다시 돌아왔다.

"The lights are out. Everybody's in bed. I can creep / —
"불들이 꺼졌어.　　　　　모두 다 자고 있어.　　　　기어갈 수 있어　　—그

and creep / — and no one will hear."
리고 몰래 가면　　— 아무도 못 들을 거야."

It was so delightful / that they caught each other's hands
매우 기뻐서　　　　둘은 서로 손을 잡았고

/ and a sudden light sprang / into Sara's eyes.
갑작스러운 빛이 일어났다　　　새라의 눈에.

"Ermie!" / she said. "Let us pretend! Let us pretend / it's
"어면가드!"　　새라가 말했다. "우리 상상해 보자!　　상상해 보자

a party! And oh, / won't you invite the prisoner / in the
파티라고!　　그리고 아,　　죄수를 초대하지 않을래

next cell?"
옆방에 있는?"

"Yes! Yes! Let us knock / on the wall / now. The jailer
"그래!　좋아!　노크해 보자　　벽에　　　지금.

won't hear."
교도소장은 듣지 못할 거야."

Sara went to the wall. Through it / she could hear / poor
새라가 벽으로 갔다.　　　벽을 통해　　새라는 들을 수 있었다

Becky crying more softly. She knocked four times.
불쌍한 베키가 더 작은 소리로 우는 것을.　네 번 노크했다.

Key Expression

지각동사의 목적보어

지각동사에는 보다(see, look at, watch), 듣다(hear, listen to), 느끼다 (feel) 등이 있으며, 이외에도 비슷한 의미를 지닌 동사들이 지각동사와 같은 용법 으로 사용되기도 해요.

지각동사는 '동사 + 목적어 + 목적보어(동사원형/현재분사)'의 5형식 구문으로 쓰 이며 '~가 …하고 있는 것을 보다/듣다/느끼다'라고 해석합니다.

이때 목적보어 자리에는 동사 원형이나 현재분사(-ing)가 옵니다. 현재분사는 진 행 중인 동작을 강조하는 경우에 쓰입니다.

ex) Through it she could hear poor Becky crying more softly.
그것을 통해 그녀는 불쌍한 베키가 더 작은 소리로 우는 것을 들을 수 있었다.

"That means, / 'Come to me / through the secret passage
"그것은 의미해,   '내게로 와   비밀의 통로를 통해

/ under the wall,' / she explained. 'I have something to
벽 아래 있는.'   그녀가 설명했다.   '할 말이 있어'라는 뜻이야.

communicate.'"

Five quick knocks answered her.
다섯 번의 빠른 노크가 새라에게 대답했다.

"She is coming," / she said.
"베키가 올 거야."   그녀가 말했다.

Almost immediately / the door of the attic opened / and
곧 이어   다락방 문이 열렸고

Becky appeared. Her eyes were red / and her cap was
베키가 나타났다.   눈은 충혈되었고   모자는 미끄러져 내려와 있었다,

sliding off, / and when she caught sight of Ermengarde /
그리고 어먼가드를 보자

she began to rub her face / nervously / with her apron.
얼굴을 문지르기 시작했다   신경질적으로   앞치마로.

"Don't mind me a bit, / Becky!" / cried Ermengarde.
"날 조금도 신경 쓰지 마,   베키!"   어먼가드가 소리쳤다.

"Miss Ermengarde has asked / you to come in," / said
"어먼가드 아가씨가 청한 거야   네게 와 달라고,"   새라가

Sara, / "because she is going / to bring a box of good
말했다,   "가지고 올 거거든   좋은 것들이 들어있는 상자를

things / up here / to us."
여기로   우리에게."

Becky's cap almost fell off entirely, / she broke in / with
베키의 모자가 거의 떨어질 뻔 했고,   베키가 끼어들었다

such excitement.
매우 흥분하여.

"To eat, miss?" / she said. "Things that's good to eat?"
"먹을 거요, 아가씨?"   그녀가 말했다.   "맛있는 건가요?"

"Yes," / answered Sara, / "and we are going / to pretend
"맞아."   새라가 대답했다,   "그리고 우리는 할 거야

a party."
파티인 척."

"And you shall have / as much as you want to eat," / put
"먹게 될 거야   네가 먹고 싶은 만큼,"

in Ermengarde. "I'll go / this minute!"
어먼가드가 끼어들었다.   "갈게   지금!"

She was in such haste / that as she tiptoed / out of the
어먼가드가 매우 서두르는 바람에   발끝으로 걸었을 때   다락방에서 나와

attic / she dropped her red shawl / and did not know / it
빨간 숄을 떨어뜨렸지만   알지 못했다

had fallen. No one saw it / for a minute or so. Becky was
떨어진 사실을.   아무도 보지 못했다   그 순간에는.

too much overpowered / by the good luck / which had
베키는 가슴이 벅차올랐다   행운에

befallen her.
자신에게 닥친.

"Oh, miss! Oh, miss!" she gasped; / "I know / it was you
"아, 아가씨!   아, 아가씨!"   숨이 가빠왔다;   "알고 있어요   아가씨라는 것을

/ that asked her to let me come. It — it makes me cry / to
저를 부르자고 부탁한 사람이.   그것은 — 눈물이 나요

think of it." And she went to Sara's side / and stood / and
그것을 생각하면."   그리고 새라 쪽으로 가더니   서서

looked at her / worshipingly.
새라를 보았다   존경하며.

But in Sara's hungry eyes / the old light had begun to
하지만 새라의 굶주린 눈에는   예전의 그 빛이 빛나기 시작했고

glow / and transform her world for her. Here in the attic
그녀의 세상을 바꾸기 시작했다.   이곳 다락방에서

/ — with the cold night outside / — with the afternoon in
— 밖에서 보냈던 추운 밤과   — 질척한 거리에서 보낸 오후와

the sloppy streets / barely passed / — with the memory
가까스로 걸어갔던   — 심하게 굶주린 표정의 기억들이

of the awful unfed look / in the beggar child's eyes / not
거지 아이의 눈 속에 있던   아직

yet faded / — this simple, cheerful thing had happened /
사라지지 않은 채   — 이 단순하고, 즐거운 일이 일어났다

like a thing of magic.
마법과 같이.

She caught her breath.
새라는 숨을 내쉬었다.

"Somehow, / something always happens," / she cried, /
"어쨌든, 무슨 일인가는 항상 일어나게 마련이지," 새라가 외쳤다.

"just before / things get to the very worst. It is as if the
"바로 직전에 상황이 최악으로 변하기. 그것은 마법이 하는 것

Magic did it. If I could only just remember that / always.
같아. 그것을 기억하기만 하면 되는 거야 항상.

The worst thing never quite comes."
최악의 상황은 절대 오지 않는 거야."

She gave Becky a little cheerful shake.
새라는 베키의 어깨를 살짝 흔들었다.

"No, no! You mustn't cry!" / she said. "We must make
"안 돼, 안 돼! 울면 안 돼!" 새라가 말했다. "서둘러야 해

haste / and set the table."
식탁을 차리자."

"Set the table, miss?" / said Becky, / gazing round the
"식탁을 차려요, 아가씨?" 베키가 말했다, 방을 돌아보며.

room. "What'll we set it with?"
"무엇으로 차리죠?"

Sara looked round the attic, / too.
새라도 다락방을 둘러 보았다, 역시.

"There doesn't seem to be much," / she answered, / half
"별로 없는 것 같구나," 새라가 말했다.

laughing.
반쯤 웃으며.

That moment / she saw something / and pounced upon it.
그 순간 그녀는 뭔가를 보았고 갑자기 그것을 향해 달려갔다.

It was Ermengarde's red shawl / which lay upon the floor.
그것은 어먼가드의 빨간 숄이었다 바닥에 놓여져 있던 .

"Here's the shawl," / she cried. "I know she won't mind it.
"숄이 있네," 그녀가 소리쳤다. "그 애는 신경 쓰지 않을 거라고 생각해.

It will make such a nice red tablecloth."
그것은 아주 멋진 빨간 식탁보가 될 거야."

---

overpowered 매혹되어서 | befall 닥치다 | worshipingly 숭배하여, 존경하여 | sloppy 질척한 | unfed 음식을
먹지 못한 | pounce 갑자기 달려들다, 와락 덤벼들다

They pulled the old table forward, / and threw the shawl
그들은 낡은 탁자를 끌어내서, 숄을 그 위에 덮어 씌웠다.

over it. Red is a wonderfully kind / and comfortable
빨간 색은 굉장히 따뜻하고 편안한 색깔이었다.

color. It began to make the room look furnished /
식탁보로 인해 방이 잘 갖춰진 것처럼 보였다

directly.
직접적으로.

"How nice a red rug would look / on the floor!" /
"빨간 양탄자가 있다면 정말 멋질텐데 바닥에도!"

exclaimed Sara. "We must pretend there is one!"
새라가 외쳤다. "있는 척 해야 해!"

Her eye swept the bare boards / with a swift glance of
새라의 시선이 맨 바닥을 훑었다 감탄이 담긴 재빠른 눈길로.

admiration. The rug was laid down / already.
양탄자는 깔려 있었다 이미.

"How soft and thick it is!" / she said, / with the little
"참 부드럽고 두툼하구나!" 새라가 말했다. 살짝 웃으면서

laugh / which Becky knew / the meaning of; / and she
베키는 알았다 그 의미를;

raised and set her foot down again / delicately, / as if she
그리고 베키는 발을 들었다가 내려 놓았다 살며시,

felt something / under it.
마치 뭔가를 느끼는 듯 발 아래.

"Yes, miss," / answered Becky, / watching her / with
"그래요, 아가씨," 베키가 대답했다, 새라를 바라보며

serious rapture. She was always quite serious.
진지하게 황홀해 하며, 베키는 언제나 진지했다.

"What next, / now?" / said Sara, / and she stood still /
"다음에는 뭘까, 이제?" 새라가 말했다, 그리고 가만히 서서

and put her hands over her eyes. "Something will come /
눈 위에 손을 올려놓았다. "뭔가 올 거야

if I think and wait a little" / — in a soft, expectant voice.
잠시만 생각하며 기다리면" — 부드럽고, 기대하는 목소리로.

---

delicately 우아하게, 섬세하게 | rapture 황홀 | enlightened 깨우친, 개화된

"The Magic will tell me."
"마법이 나한테 말해 줄 거야."

One of her favorite fancies was / that on "the outside,"
새라가 가장 좋아하는 이야기 중 하나는   "바깥 세계"에서,

/ as she called it, / thoughts were waiting / for people to
새라가 그렇게 이름 붙인,   상상이 기다리고 있다는 것이었다   사람들이 그 상상을

call them. Becky had seen / her stand and wait / many
불러낼 때까지. 베키는 보았다   새라가 서서 기다리는 것을

a time before, / and knew / that in a few seconds / she
전에도 여러 번,   그래서 알았다   잠시 후에

would uncover / an enlightened, laughing face.
새라가 드러내리라는 것을   밝고, 웃는 얼굴을.

In a moment / she did.
잠시 후   새라는 정말 그렇게 했다.

"There!" / she cried. "It has come! I know now! I must
"저기!"   새라가 외쳤다.   "왔다!   이제 알겠어!   봐야겠어

look / among the things / in the old trunk / I had / when I
물건들을   낡은 가방에 있는   내가 가졌던

was a princess."
공주였을 때."

She flew to its corner / and kneeled down. It had not been
새라는 방 구석으로 달려가서   무릎을 꿇고 앉았다.   그 가방은 둔 것이 아니라

put / in the attic / for her benefit, / but because there was
다락방에   새라를 위해서,   공간이 없기 때문이었다

no room for it / elsewhere. Nothing had been left in it / but
다른 곳에는.   아무것도 남아 있지 않았다

rubbish. But she knew / she should find something. The
쓰레기 외에는.   하지만 새라는 알았다   뭔가 찾아낼 것이라는 것을.

Magic always arranged / that kind of thing / in one way or
마법이 항상 마련해 주었다   그런 종류의 것을

another.
이런저런 방법으로.

In a corner / lay a package / so insignificant-looking / that
한 구석에는   짐 꾸러미가 있었다   아주 하찮게 보여서

it had been overlooked, / and when she herself had found
내버려 두었던.   새라가 발견하여

it / she had kept it / as a relic. It contained / a dozen small
보관하고 있었다   유물처럼.   거기에는 들어있었다

white handkerchiefs. She seized them joyfully / and ran to
수십여 개의 작고 하얀 손수건들이. 새라는 즐겁게 그것들을 집어서   탁자로 달려왔다.

the table. She began to arrange them / upon the red table-
그것을 가지런히 놓기 시작했고   빨간 식탁보 위에.

cover, / patting and coaxing them / into shape / with the
그것을 두드리고 매만지면서   모양을 내서

narrow lace edge curling outward, / her Magic working its
좁은 레이스 장식을 바깥쪽으로 말아서,   자신의 마법이 주문을 걸도록 했다

spells for her / as she did it.
자신에게 통했던 것처럼.

"These are the plates," / she said. "They are golden plates.
"이것들은 접시야."   새라가 말했다.   "황금 접시들이야.

These are the richly embroidered napkins. Nuns worked
이것들은 화려하게 수놓은 냅킨이야.   수녀들이 만들었어

them / in convents / in Spain."
수녀원에서   스페인에 있는."

insignificant 대수롭지 않은, 사소한 | relic 유물, 유적 | narrow 좁은 | nun 수녀, 여승 | convent 수녀원 |
devote onself to ~에 몰두하다 | accomplish 성취하다, 해내다 | convulsive 경련성의, 발작적인 | contortion
뒤틀림, 일그러짐 | with a start 깜짝 놀라서 | sheepishly 양처럼 순하게 | grin (소리 없이) 활짝 웃음

"Did they, miss?" / breathed Becky, / her very soul uplifted
"정말 그랬어요, 아가씨?"　　베키는 헐떡거리며 물었다.　자신의 영혼이 고양된 듯

/ by the information.
그 말에.

"You must pretend it," / said Sara. "If you pretend it
"그런 척 해야 해."　　새라가 말했다.　"네가 그렇게 상상하면,

enough, / you will see them."
그것들을 볼 수 있을 거야."

"Yes, miss," / said Becky; / and as Sara returned to the
"네, 아가씨."　베키가 말했다;　새라가 가방 쪽으로 돌아가자

trunk / she devoted herself to / the effort of accomplishing
베키는 몰두했다　　이루려는 노력에

an end so much to be desired.
그토록 간절히 바랐던 목적을.

Sara turned suddenly / to find her standing / by the table, /
새라가 갑자기 돌아보자　　베키가 서 있는 것이 보였다　　탁자 옆에.

looking very queer indeed. She had shut her eyes, / and was
정말 매우 이상한 표정을 지으며.　　베키는 두 눈을 감고,

twisting her face / in strange convulsive contortions, / her
얼굴을 찡그렸다　　이상하게 덜덜 떨면서 찡그리고,

hands hanging stiffly clenched / at her sides. She looked /
주먹을 꽉 쥐고는　　양 옆에 붙이면서.　베키는 보였다

as if she was trying / to lift some enormous weight.
마치 애쓰는 것처럼　　무거운 것을 들어올리려고.

"What is the matter, Becky?" / Sara cried. "What are you
"왜 그래, 베키?"　　새라가 외쳤다.　"뭐 하는 거야?"

doing?"

Becky opened her eyes / with a start.
베키가 눈을 떴다　　깜짝 놀라서.

"I was a-'pretendin',' miss," / she answered / a little
"저는 상상하고 있었어요, 아가씨."　베키가 대답했다　약간 소심하게;

sheepishly; / "I was tryin' to see it / like you do. I almost
"그것을 보려고 노력하는 중이었어요 아가씨가 하는 것처럼. 거의 해낼 뻔

did," / with a hopeful grin. "But it takes a lot o' stren'th."
했어요."　희망 가득 찬 활짝 웃음을 지으며.　"하지만 엄청 힘드네요."

227

"Perhaps / it does / if you are not used to it," / said Sara, /
"아마도   그럴 거야   네가 아직 익숙지 않아서."   새라가 말했다,

with friendly sympathy; / "but you don't know / how easy
우정 어린 동정심으로;   "하지만 넌 모를 거야   얼마나 쉬운지

it is / when you've done it often. I wouldn't try so hard /
그것을   자주 해 봤다면.   그렇게 힘들게 애쓰지 마

just at first. It will come to you / after a while. I'll just tell
처음부터.   곧 알게 될 거야   조만간.   네게 말해 줄게

you / what things are. Look at these."
그것이 뭔지.   이것들을 봐."

She held an old summer hat / in her hand / which she
새라는 낡은 여름 모자를 집었다   손에   찾아낸

had fished out / of the bottom of the trunk. There was a
가방 바닥에서.   화관이 있었다

wreath / of flowers on it. She pulled the wreath off.
꽃으로 장식된.   새라는 화관을 떼어냈다.

"These are garlands / for the feast," / she said grandly.
"이것들은 화환이야   연회를 위한."   새라는 우아하게 말했다.

"They fill all the air with perfume. There's a mug / on the
"이 꽃들이 향기로 가득 채울 거야.   머그잔이 있어

wash-stand, / Becky. Oh — and bring the soap dish / for
세면대 위에,   베키.   아 — 비누 받침대도 갖다 줘

a centerpiece."
테이블 중앙 장식에 놓을."

Becky handed them to her / reverently.
베키는 그것들을 새라에게 건네 주었다   공손하게.

"What are they now, / miss?" / she inquired. "You'd think
"이제 저것들은 뭐예요,   아가씨?"   베키가 물었다.   "생각하겠지만

/ they was made of crockery / — but I know / they ain't."
그것들은 그릇으로 만들어졌다고   — 하지만 난 알아요   그렇지 않다는 것을."

"This is a carven flagon," / said Sara, / arranging tendrils
"이것은 조각을 새긴 포도주병이야,"   새라가 말했다.   화환 덩굴을 배열하며

of the wreath / about the mug. "And this" / — bending
머그잔 주변에.   "그리고 이것은"

tenderly over the soap dish / and heaping it with roses /
— 비누 받침대 위로 몸을 숙이고   장미꽃들을 거기에 수북하게 쌓으면서 —

— / "is purest alabaster / encrusted with gems."
"아주 하얀 설화 석고상이야   보석으로 아로새겨진."

fish out 찾아내다 | garland 화환 | mug 머그잔(손잡이는 있고 받침 접시는 안 딸린 큰 잔) | wash-stand 세면대 | centerpiece 테이블 중앙에 놓는 장식 | reverently 경건하게 | crockery 그릇(특히 도자기류) | carven 조각한 | flagon (포도주 등을 담는 손잡이가 달린) 큰 병 | tendrils (식물의) 덩굴손 | alabaster 설화 석고 | encrust 외피로 덮다, 새기다 | gem 보석

She touched the things gently, / a happy smile / hovering
새라는 물건들을 살살 만졌고,   행복한 미소가

about her lips / which made her look / as if she were a
입술 주변에 맴돌면서   사라의 표정을 보이게 했다   마치 꿈 속에 있는 것처럼.

creature in a dream.

"My, ain't it lovely!" / whispered Becky.
"세상에, 정말 아름답잖아요!"   베키가 속삭였다.

"If we just had something / for bonbon dishes," / Sara
"뭔가 있으면 될텐데   봉봉 캔디를 담은 그릇으로 쓸,"

murmured. "There!" / — darting to the trunk / again. "I
새라가 중얼거렸다.   "저기다!"   — 가방으로 돌진했다   다시.

remember / I saw something / this minute."
"기억나   뭔가를 봤어   방금 전에."

It was only a bundle of wool / wrapped in red and white
그것은 털실 뭉치였을 뿐이었다   빨갛고 하얀 포장지로 감싸진,

tissue paper, / but the tissue paper was soon twisted /
하지만 곧 포장지를 꼬아

into the form of little dishes, / and was combined / with
작은 접시 모양으로 만들었고,   함께 놓여졌다

the remaining flowers / to ornament the candlestick /
남은 꽃들과   촛대를 장식하기 위해

which was to light the feast. Only the Magic could have
연회를 밝혀 줄.   오직 마법만이 만들 수 있었다

made / it more than an old table / covered with a red
그 식탁을 낡은 탁자 이상의 것으로   빨간 숄로 덮이고

shawl / and set with rubbish / from a long-unopened
쓰레기로 차려놓은   오랫동안 열어보지도 않던.

trunk. But Sara drew back / and gazed at it, / seeing
하지만 새라는 다시 돌아와   그것을 보았고,   경이로운 모습을

wonders; / and Becky, / after staring in delight, / spoke
바라보며;   그리고 베키는,   기쁨에 차서 쳐다본 후,

with bated breath.
숨을 죽이고 말했다.

"This 'ere," / she suggested, / with a glance round the
"여기는," 베키가 말을 꺼냈다, 다락방을 둘러보며

attic / — "is it the Bastille / now / — or has it turned /
— "바스티유 감옥인가요 지금 — 아니면 바뀐 건가요

into somethin' different?"
다른 곳으로?"

"Oh, yes, yes!" / said Sara. "Quite different. It is a
"아, 맞아, 맞아!" 새라가 말했다. "완전히 다른 곳이야.

banquet hall!"
여기는 연회장이야!"

"My eye, miss!" / ejaculated Becky. "A blanket 'all!" /
"오 세상에, 아가씨!" 베키가 외쳤다. "연회장이라고요!"

and she turned to view the splendors / about her / with
그리고 화려한 방 안으로 시선을 돌렸다 주위의

awed bewilderment.
감탄하고 어리둥절하며.

"A banquet hall," / said Sara. "A vast chamber / where
"연회장은 말이지," 새라가 말했다. "아주 큰 방이야

feasts are given. It has a vaulted roof, / and a minstrels'
연회가 열리는. 아치형의 지붕이 있고 악단들을 위한 자리와,

gallery, / and a huge chimney / filled with blazing oaken
커다란 벽난로가 있어 불타는 오크나무 장작들로 가득 찬,

logs, / and it is brilliant / with waxen tapers twinkling /
그리고 멋지지 왁스로 만든 양초들이 빛나면서

on every side."
곳곳에서.

"My eye, Miss Sara!" / gasped Becky / again.
"오 세상에, 아가씨!" 베키는 숨이 턱 막혔다 다시.

Then the door opened, / and Ermengarde came in, /
그때 문이 열렸고, 어먼가드가 들어왔다,

rather staggering / under the weight of her hamper.
조금 비틀비틀하며 바구니의 무게에 눌려.

---

dart 쏜살같이 달리다 | wool 털실 | tissue paper 박엽지, 티슈 페이퍼 | bate 줄이다 | bewilderment
어리둥절함 | vast 거대한 | vaulted 아치형의, 둥근 천장의 | gallery 좌석, 관람석 | blazing 타는 듯이 더운 |
oaken 오크 나무의 | brilliant 훌륭한, 멋진 | waxen 왁스로 만든 | taper (길고 가느다란) 양초

She started back / with an exclamation of joy. To enter from
어먼가드는 주춤했다   기쁨으로 가득 찬 비명을 지르며.

the chill darkness outside, / and find one's self confronted /
춥고 어두운 밖에서 들어왔는데,   마주하게 된다면

by a totally unanticipated festal board, / draped with red, /
전혀 기대하지 못했던 잔칫상과,   붉은 식탁보로 덮이고,

adorned with white napery, / and wreathed with flowers, /
흰 식탁용 린넨으로 장식됐으며,   꽃으로 둘러싸인,

was to feel / that the preparations were brilliant / indeed.
느낄 것이다   준비가 기막히다고   정말로.

"Oh, Sara!" / she cried out. "You are the cleverest girl / I
"와, 새라!"   그녀가 외쳤다.   "넌 가장 똑똑한 소녀야

ever saw!"
내가 본 중에!"

"Isn't it nice?" / said Sara. "They are things / out of my old
"멋지지 않니?"   새라가 말했다.   "이것들은 물건이야   내 낡은 가방에서

trunk. I asked my Magic, / and it told me / to go and look."
나온.   마법에게 물었더니,   마법이 말해 줬어   가서 보라고."

"But oh, miss," / cried Becky, / "wait / till she's told you
"하지만 아, 아가씨."   베키가 외쳤다.   "기다려요 새라 아가씨가 말해 줄 때까지

/ what they are! They ain't just / — oh, miss, / please tell
저것들이 뭔지!   저것들은 단순하지 않아요   — 아, 아가씨,   제발 말해 주세요,"

her," / appealing to Sara.
새라에게 호소하면서.

So Sara told her, / and because her Magic helped her / she
그래서 새라가 말했다.   그녀의 마법이 베키를 도와서

made her almost see it all: / the golden platters / — the
베키도 거의 볼 수 있게 해 줬다고: 금색 접시들과

vaulted spaces / — the blazing logs / — the twinkling
— 아치형의 지붕과   — 불타는 장작들과   — 반짝반짝 빛나는 밀랍 촛불까지.

waxen tapers. As the things were taken / out of the hamper
물건들은 꺼내놓자   바구니에서

/ — the frosted cakes / — the fruits / — the bonbons and
— 설탕을 입힌 케이크와   — 과일들과   — 봉봉 캔디와 주스까지

the wine / — the feast became a splendid thing.
와인   — 연회는 화려한 것이 되었다.

"It's like a real party!" / cried Ermengarde.
"진짜 파티 같아!"   어먼가드가 외쳤다.

"It's like a queen's table," / sighed Becky.
"여왕님의 식탁 같아요."   베키가 탄성을 질렀다.

Then Ermengarde had / a sudden brilliant thought.
그때 어먼가드에게 떠올랐다   갑작스런 기막힌 생각이.

"I'll tell you what, Sara," / she said. "Pretend you are a
"할 말이 있어, 새라."   그녀가 말했다. "네가 공주인 척 하자

princess / now / and this is a royal feast."
지금   그리고 이것은 왕실의 연회이고."

"But it's your feast," / said Sara; / "you must be the
"하지만 이것은 네 연회잖아."   새라가 말했다: "네가 공주여야 해,

princess, / and we will be your maids of honor."
그리고 우리는 네 시녀가 될게."

"Oh, I can't," / said Ermengarde. "I'm too fat, / and I
"아, 난 할 수 없어."   어먼가드가 말했다.   "난 너무 뚱뚱하고,

don't know how. You be her."
어떻게 하는지도 몰라.   네가 공주여야 해."

"Well, if you want me to," / said Sara.
"음, 내가 하길 원한다면."   새라가 말했다.

But suddenly / she thought of something else / and ran to
하지만 갑자기   뭔가 다른 것이 생각났고

the rusty grate.
녹슨 벽난로로 달려갔다.

"There is a lot of paper and rubbish stuffed / in here!"
"종이와 쓰레기들이 가득 있어   이 안에!"

/ she exclaimed. "If we light it, / there will be a bright
새라가 외쳤다.   "여기에 불을 밝히면,   환하게 타오를 거야

blaze / for a few minutes, / and we shall feel / as if it was
잠시 동안,   그러면 느낄 수 있을 거야   그것이 진짜 난롯불

a real fire." She struck a match / and lighted it up / with a
인 듯."   새라가 성냥을 켜서   거기에 불을 붙였다

great specious glow / which illuminated the room.
아주 그럴 듯한 빛이 나면서   방을 환하게 밝혔다.

festal 축제의, 즐거운 | drape 가리다. 장식하다 | napery 식탁용 리넨 | appeal 호소하다. 간청하다 | platter (큰 서빙용)
접시 | frosted 서리에 뒤덮인 | maid of honor (여왕·왕녀의) 시녀 | stuffed 속을 채운 | specious 허울만 그럴 듯한

"By the time / it stops blazing," / Sara said, / "we shall
"때쯤이면   불타는 것이 멈출,"   새라가 말했다,   "우리는 잊게 될 거야

forget / about its not being real."
그것이 진짜가 아니라는 것도."

She stood / in the dancing glow / and smiled.
새라는 서서   다 춤추듯 타오르는 불빛 속에   그리고 웃었다.

"Doesn't it look real?" / she said. "Now we will begin
"진짜처럼 보이지 않니?"   새라가 말했다.   "이제 우리 파티를 시작하자."

the party."

She led the way / to the table. She waved her hand
새라가 발걸음을 옮겼다   식탁으로.   손을 우아하게 흔들었다

graciously / to Ermengarde and Becky. She was in the
어먼가드와 베키에게.

midst of her dream.
새라는 꿈 속 한가운데에 있었다.

"Advance, fair damsels," / she said / in her happy
"어서 오세요, 아름다운 아가씨들,"   새라가 말했다   행복하게 꿈꾸는 목소리로,

dream-voice, / "and be seated / at the banquet table.
"앉으세요   연회 식탁에.

My noble father, the king, / who is absent on a long
고결한 아버지, 왕께서는,   지금 긴 여정으로 출타 중이신데,

journey, / has commanded me / to feast you." She turned
제게 명령하셨습니다   당신들에게 연회를 베풀라고."

her head slightly / toward the corner / of the room.
새라는 고개를 살짝 돌렸다   한 구석으로   방의.

"What, ho, there, minstrels! Strike up / with your viols
"자, 어이, 거기, 악단이여!   켜거라   비올과 바순을.

and bassoons. Princesses," / she explained rapidly / to
공주님들은"   새라는 재빠르게 설명했다

Ermengarde and Becky, / "always had minstrels to play
어먼가드와 베키에게,   "항상 연주할 음악가들이 있어

/ at their feasts. Pretend there is a minstrel gallery / up
연회에는.   악단의 자리가 있는 척 해 봐

there / in the corner. Now we will begin."
저 위에   구석의.   이제 우리는 시작하는 거야."

They had barely had time / to take their pieces of cake
그들은 거의 시간이 없었다   케이크를 한 조각씩 집을

/ into their hands / — not one of them had time / to do
손으로   — 셋 중 아무도 시간이 없었다   더 이상 할

more, / when / — they all three sprang / to their feet /
수 있는,   그때   — 그들 셋 모두 벌떡 일어나   두 발로

and turned pale faces / toward the door / — listening —
창백해진 얼굴을 돌렸고   문 쪽으로   — 귀를 기울이고 — 또

listening.
기울였다.

Someone was coming up the stairs. There was no
누군가 계단을 올라오고 있었다.   틀림없었다.

mistake about it. Each of them recognized / the angry,
세 사람 모두 알아차렸고   그 성난, 발걸음의

mounting tread / and knew / that the end of all things
주인공을   알았다   모든 것이 끝장이라는 사실을.

had come.

"It's — the missus!" / choked Becky, / and dropped her
"저것은 — 마님이에요!"   베키는 목이 메어,   케이크 조각을 떨어뜨렸다

piece of cake / upon the floor.
바닥 위로.

graciously 우아하게 | damsel 처녀 | noble 고결한, 고귀한, 숭고한 | viol 비올(바이올린과 비슷한 초기 현악기) |
tread 발걸음, 계단의 디딤판 | choke 숨이 막히다, 목이 메다

"Yes," / said Sara, / her eyes growing shocked and large
"맞아." 새라가 말했다, 새라의 눈은 충격으로 커졌다

/ in her small white face. "Miss Minchin has found us
작고 하얗게 질린. "민친 교장이 우리를 알아채신 거야."

out."

Miss Minchin struck the door open / with a blow of her
민친 교장이 문을 열었다 손으로 쾅 치며.

hand. She was pale herself, / but it was with rage. She
교장 자신도 창백해졌지만, 그것은 분노 때문이었다. 교장은 시선

looked / from the frightened faces / to the banquet table,
을 옮겼다 공포에 질린 얼굴들에서 연회 식탁으로,

/ and from the banquet table / to the last flicker / of the
연회 식탁에서 마지막 불꽃으로

burnt paper / in the grate.
타다 남은 종이의 벽난로에 있는.

"I have been suspecting / something of this sort," / she
"의심했었어 이런 종류의 일을."

exclaimed; / "but I did not dream / of such audacity.
그녀가 외쳤다: "하지만 꿈에도 몰랐지 이렇게 뻔뻔한 짓을 벌일 줄은.

Lavinia was telling the truth."
라비니아가 사실을 말한 거였군."

So they knew / that it was Lavinia / who had somehow
그래서 그들은 알았다 라비니아였다는 것을

guessed their secret / and had betrayed them. Miss
어떻게든 자신들의 비밀을 추측하고 자신들을 고자질한 사람이.

Minchin strode over / to Becky / and boxed her ears / for
민친 교장을 성큼성큼 걸어가서 베키에게 따귀를 때렸다

a second time.
두 번째로.

---

flicker (빛의) 깜박거림 | suspect 의심하다 | audacity 뻔뻔함 | betray 배반하다 | stride 성큼성큼 걷다 |
witheringly 어리둥절하게 하여 | decorate 장식하다 | stamp (발로) ~을 짓밟다 | command 명령하다 | attend
to ~을 처리하다, 돌보다

"You impudent creature!" / she said. "You leave the
"이 뻔뻔한 것 같으니!"   교장이 말했다.   "이 집을 떠나거라

house / in the morning!"
아침에!"

Sara stood quite still, / her eyes growing larger, / her face
새라는 아주 가만히 서 있었다,   눈이 점점 커지고,   얼굴은 더 창백

paler. Ermengarde burst into tears.
해지면서. 어먼가드는 눈물을 터뜨렸다.

"Oh, don't send her away," / she sobbed. "My aunt sent
"아, 저 애를 내쫓지 마세요,"   어먼가드가 흐느꼈다. "우리 고모가제게 바구니

me the hamper. We're — only — having a party."
를 보내줬어요.   우리는 — 단지 — 파티를 하는 중이었어요."

"So I see," / said Miss Minchin, / witheringly. "With
"그래 이제 알겠다," 민친 교장이 말했다,   면박을 주면서.

the Princess Sara / at the head of the table." She turned
"새라 공주를 모셨군   식탁 상석에."   교장은 사납게 돌아보

fiercely / on Sara. "It is your doing, / I know," / she
았다   새라를.   "네 짓이구나,   알고 있어."   교장이 외쳤다.

cried. "Ermengarde would never have thought / of such a
"어먼가드는 절대로 생각해내지 못했겠지   그런 것들을.

thing. You decorated the table, / I suppose / — with this
네가 식탁을 꾸몄겠지,   내 생각에는   — 이런 쓰레기로."

rubbish." She stamped her foot / at Becky. "Go to your
교장은 발을 구르며   베키를 보았다.   "네 다락방으로 가!"

attic!" / she commanded, / and Becky stole away, / her
교장이 명령하자,   베키는 뛰어갔다,

face hidden in her apron, / her shoulders shaking.
얼굴을 앞치마로 가린 채,   어깨를 들썩이며.

Then / it was Sara's turn / again.
그러자   이번에는 새라의 차례였다   다시.

"I will attend to you / tomorrow. You shall have neither
"널 손봐주겠어   내일.   넌 아침도, 점심도, 저녁도 없다!"

breakfast, dinner, nor supper!"

"I have not had / either dinner or supper / today, / Miss
"전 먹지 못했어요   점심도 저녁도   오늘,   민친 교장님,"

Minchin," / said Sara, / rather faintly.
새라가 말했다,   어지러움을 느끼며.   237

"Then / all the better. You will have something to
"그렇다면 더 잘됐구나. 넌 명심해야 해.

remember. Don't stand there. Put those things / into the
거기 서 있지 마라. 저것들을 집어넣어 바구니에

hamper / again."
다시."

She began to sweep them / off the table / into the hamper
교장은 물건들을 쓸어 담기 시작했다 식탁에서 바구니로

/ herself, and caught sight / of Ermengarde's new books.
직접, 그리고 보았다 어먼가드의 새 책들을.

"And you" / — to Ermengarde — / "have brought / your
"그리고 넌" — 어먼가드에게 — "갖고 왔구나

beautiful new books / into this dirty attic. Take them
네 좋은 새 책들을 이 더러운 다락방에. 저것들을 집어서

up / and go back / to bed. You will stay there / all day
다시 가져가 네 침대로. 넌 거기에서 꼼짝하지 말고 있어

tomorrow, / and I shall write / to your papa. What would
내일 하루 종일, 그리고 난 편지를 써야겠다 네 아버지께. 뭐라고 하실까

he say / if he knew / where you are tonight?"
아버지가 아신다면 네가 오늘 밤 어디 있었는지?"

Something she saw / in Sara's grave, fixed gaze / at this
교장은 뭔가를 보고 새라의 심각하고, 고정된 시선 속에서 이 순간

moment / made her turn on her / fiercely.
새라 쪽을 돌아보았다 화가 나서.

grave 심각한 | notable 주목할 만한, 중요한, 유명한 | pertness 버릇 없음, 건방짐 | infuriated 극도로 화난,
노발대발 하는 | intemperate 무절제한 | insolent 버릇없는, 무례한 | unmanageable 다루기 힘든

"What are you thinking of?" / she demanded. "Why do
"넌 뭘 생각하는 거냐?"   따지듯 물었다.

you look at me / like that?"
"왜 날 쳐다보는 거냐   그렇게?"

"I was wondering," / answered Sara, / as she had
"전 궁금해하고 있었어요."   새라가 대답했다.   대답했던 것처럼

answered / that notable day / in the schoolroom.
             그 유명했던 날에   교실에서.

"What were you wondering?"
"뭐가 궁금했다는 거지?"

It was very like / the scene in the schoolroom. There was
그것은 거의 흡사했다   교실에서의 상황과.   건방진 기색은

no pertness / in Sara's manner. It was only sad and quiet.
없었다   새라의 태도에는.   그저 슬프고 조용했을 뿐이었다.

"I was wondering," / she said / in a low voice, / "what my
"전 궁금했어요."   새라가 대답했다, 낮은 목소리로,

papa would say / if he knew / where I am tonight."
"아빠는 뭐라 하셨을까요   아신다면   제가 오늘 밤 어디 있는지."

Miss Minchin was infuriated / just as she had been
민친 교장은 노발대발 했고   전에도 그랬듯이

before / and her anger expressed itself, / as before, / in an
이전처럼,   분노가 폭발했다   이전처럼,

intemperate fashion. She flew at her / and shook her.
화를 잠지 못하는 모습으로.   교장은 새라에게 달려가   그녀를 흔들었다.

"You insolent, unmanageable child!" / she cried. "How
"버릇없고, 대책 없는 아이 같으니라고!"   교장이 외쳤다.

dare you! How dare you!"
"네가 어찌 감히! 네가 어찌 감히!"

She picked up the books, / swept the rest of the feast /
교장은 책을 집어 들었고,   식탁에 남아있던 것까지 쓸어 넣더니

back into the hamper / in a jumbled heap, / thrust it / into
바구니로   뒤죽박죽으로,   떠안겼다

Ermengarde's arms, / and pushed her before her / toward
어먼가드의 팔에,   그리고 어먼가드를 밀어붙였다

the door.
문을 향해.

"I will leave you to wonder," / she said. "Go to bed / this
"궁금해하든지 상관없어." 교장이 말했다. "잠이나 자

instant." And she shut the door behind / herself and poor
지금 당장." 그리고 교장은 문을 닫고 나갔고

stumbling Ermengarde, / and left Sara / standing quite alone.
불쌍하게 비틀거리는 어먼가드와 함께. 새라를 남겨뒀다 혼자 서 있는.

The dream was quite at an end. The last spark had died /
꿈은 끝이 났다. 마지막 불꽃은 사라졌고

out of the paper / in the grate / and left only black tinder;
종이가 부족해 벽난로에 있는 검은 불쏘시개만 남았다;

/ the table was left bare, / the golden plates / and richly
식탁은 텅 비어 있었고, 금빛 접시들과

embroidered napkins, / and the garlands / were transformed
화려하게 수놓인 냅킨들과. 화관들은 다시 바뀌어 버렸다

again / into old handkerchiefs, / scraps of red and white
낡은 손수건들과, 빨갛고 하얀 종이 조각들과,

paper, / and discarded artificial flowers / all scattered on the
버려진 조화들로 모두 바닥에 흩어진 채;

floor; / the minstrels / in the minstrel gallery / had stolen
음악가들은 악단석에 있던 사라져 버렸고,

away, / and the viols and bassoons were still. Emily was
비올과 바순들도 조용했다. 에밀리는 앉아 있었다

sitting / with her back against the wall, / staring very hard.
등을 벽에 기댄 채. 강하게 노려보면서.

Sara saw her, / and went and picked her up / with trembling
새라가 에밀리를 보았고, 가서 집어 올렸다 떨리는 손으로.

hands.

"There isn't any banquet left, / Emily," / she said. "And there
"더 이상 연회는 없어. 에밀리." 새라가 말했다.

isn't any princess. There is nothing left / but the prisoners /
"그리고 더 이상 공주도 없어. 아무것도 없어 죄수뿐이야

in the Bastille." And she sat down / and hid her face.
바스티유 감옥에 있는." 그리고 앉아서 얼굴을 감쌌다.

---

stumbling 비틀거리는 | tinder 불쏘시개 | embroidered 수놓은 | discard 버리다 | artificial 인공적인

What would have happened / if she had not hidden it
무슨 일이 벌어졌을까 　　　　　 새라가 얼굴을 감싸지 않았다면

/ just then, / and if she had chanced to look up / at the
바로 그때, 　　 그리고 그녀가 우연히 올려다 보았다면 　　　 채광창을

skylight / at the wrong moment, / I do not know / —
적절치 않은 순간에, 　　　　　　 알 수 없다

perhaps the end of this chapter / might have been quite
— 아마도 이 장의 끝부분이 　　　　 꽤 달라졌을지도 모른다 —

different — / because if she had glanced / at the skylight
　　　　　 왜냐하면 새라가 보았다면 　　　　　 채광창을

/ she would certainly have been startled / by what she
분명히 놀랐을 것이다 　　　　　　　　　　 본 것 때문에.

would have seen. She would have seen / exactly the same
보았을 것이다 　　　　　　　　　　　 똑같은 얼굴이

face / pressed against the glass / and peering in at her /
유리창에 눌린 채 　　　　 자신를 쳐다보고 있는

as it had peered / in earlier in the evening / when she had
보았던 것과 같은 　　 아까 저녁 때 　　　　　　 이야기 하고 있었을 때

been talking / to Ermengarde.
　　　　　 어먼가드에게.

But she did not look up. She sat / with her little black
하지만 새라는 올려다보지 않았다. 　　 앉아 있었다 　 작고 검은 머리를 팔에 파묻은 채

head in her arms / for some time. She always sat / like
　　　　　　　 한동안. 　　　　　　 새라는 언제나 앉아 있었다

that / when she was trying to bear / something / in
그렇게 　　 참아내려고 할 때면 　　　　　 뭔가를

silence. Then she got up / and went slowly / to the bed.
침묵 속에서. 그리고는 일어나서 　　 천천히 갔다 　　　　 침대로.

"I can't pretend anything else / — while I am awake," /
"난 다른 것을 상상할 수 없어 　　　　 — 깨어 있는 동안에는."

she said. "There wouldn't be any use / in trying. If I go to
새라가 말했다. "더 이상 소용없을 거야 　　　 노력해도. 　　 내가 잠들면,

sleep, / perhaps a dream will come / and pretend for me."
　　 어쩌면 꿈이 찾아와 　　　　　　 내 대신 상상해 줄지도 몰라."

She suddenly felt so tired / — perhaps through want of
새라는 갑자기 매우 피곤해져서   — 아마도 음식이 부족해서였을 것이다 —

food — / that she sat down / on the edge of the bed / quite
              앉았다   침대 가장자리에

weakly.
매우 힘없이.

"Suppose / there was a bright fire / in the grate, / with lots
"만약   밝은 불이 있다면   벽난로에,

of little dancing flames," / she murmured. "Suppose / there
수많은 작은 불꽃들이 춤추면서,"   새라가 중얼거렸다.   "만약

was a comfortable chair / before it / — and suppose / there
편안한 의자가 있다면   그 앞에   — 그리고 만약

was a small table near, / with a little hot — / hot supper on
작은 탁자가 그 옆에 있다면,   약간 따뜻한 —   따뜻한 저녁 식사가 그 위

it." And "suppose" / — as she drew the thin coverings /
에 차려진 채." 그리고 "만약"   — 새라는 얇은 이불보를 끌어당기면서 말했다

over her / — "suppose / this was a beautiful soft bed, / with
그녀 위로   — "만약   이것이 아름답고 폭신한 침대였다면,   양털같

fleecy blankets / and large downy pillows. Suppose / —
이 폭신한 담요와   크고 보송보송한 베개가 있는.   만약

suppose — " And / her very weariness was good to her, /
— 만약 —"   그리고   피곤이 도움이 되어,

for her eyes closed / and she fell fast asleep.
눈이 감겼고   새라는 바로 잠이 들었다.

She did not know / how long she slept. But she had been
새라는 알지 못했다   얼마나 오래 잤는지.   하지만 매우 피곤하여

tired enough / to sleep deeply and profoundly / — too
              깊고 깊게 잠들 수 있었다

deeply and soundly / to be disturbed / by anything, / even
— 너무 깊게 푹 자서   깨어날 수 없었다   무엇으로도,

by the squeaks and scamperings / of Melchisedec's entire
찍찍거리는 소리나 날쌔게 움직이는 소리로도   멜기세덱의 가족 전체의,

family, / if all his sons and daughters / had chosen to come /
멜기세덱의 아들 딸 모두가   나오기로 결심하고

out of their hole / to fight and tumble and play.
구멍 밖으로   싸우고 넘어지며 놀더라도.

242   A Little Princess

When she awakened / it was rather suddenly, / and she
새라가 깨어났을 때   다소 갑작스러웠는데,

did not know / that any particular thing / had called her
그녀는 몰랐다   어떤 특별한 일이   자신을 깨웠는지.

out of her sleep. The truth was, / however, / that it was a
사실은,   그러나,   그것은 소리였다

sound / which had called her back / — a real sound — /
새라를 잠에서 불러낸 것은   — 진짜 소리 —

the click of the skylight / as it fell in closing / after a lithe
채광창의 딸깍거리는 소리였다   문을 닫을 때 나는

white figure / which slipped through it / and crouched
유연하고 하얀 형체가 창을 통해 몰래 빠져나가   몸을 쭈그리고 앉은 후에

down / close by upon the slates of the roof / — just near
지붕 슬레이트 위에 바짝 붙어서   — 겨우 볼 수 있을 정

enough to see / what happened / in the attic, / but not near
도로   무슨 일이 일어났는지   다락방에서,   하지만 가깝지는 않게

/ enough to be seen.
눈에 띌 정도로.

At first / she did not open her eyes. She felt too sleepy /
처음에는   새라는 눈을 뜨지 않았다.   너무 졸렸고

and / — curiously enough — / too warm and comfortable.
그리고   — 이상하게도 —   너무 따뜻하고 편안했기 때문이었다.

She was so warm and comfortable, / indeed, / that she did
아주 따뜻하고 편안해서,   실제로,

not believe / she was really awake. She never was as warm
믿지 않았다   자신이 진짜로 깨어났다고.   그렇게 따뜻하고 편한 적이 없었다

and cozy / as this / except in some lovely vision.
이처럼   멋진 상상 속 외에는.

"What a nice dream!" / she murmured. "I feel quite warm.
"참 멋진 꿈이야!"   새라는 중얼거렸다.   "아주 따뜻해.

I — don't — want — to — wake — up."
일어나고 — 싶지 — 않아."

fleecy 양털 같은, 푹신한 | downy 솜털이 뒤덮인, 보송보송한 | scamper 날쌔게 움직이다 | lithe 몸이 유연한,
나긋나긋한 | crouch 쭈그리다, 쭈그리고 앉다

243

Of course / it was a dream. She felt / as if warm,
물론   그것은 꿈이었다.   새라는 느꼈다

delightful bedclothes were heaped upon her. She could
따뜻하고, 기분 좋은 침대보가 덮여 있는 듯.

actually feel blankets, / and when she put out her hand / it
실제 담요가 느껴졌고,   손을 뻗어보니

touched something / exactly like a satin-covered eider-
뭔가 만져졌다   꼭 새틴 천으로 된 솜 오리털로 만든 누비이불같은.

down quilt. She must not awaken / from this delight / ──
       깨어나지 말아야 했다   이 기쁨에서

she must be quite still / and make it last.
── 아주 가만히 있어야 했고   그래서 그것이 계속되도록 해야 했다.

But she could not / ── even though she kept her eyes
하지만 할 수 없었다   ── 눈을 꼭 감고 있었지만,

closed tightly, / she could not. Something was forcing
           할 수 없었다.   뭔가가 그녀를 일어나게 했다

her to awaken / ── something in the room. It was a sense
── 방 안의 뭔가가.   그건 불빛같았다,

of light, / and a sound / ── the sound of a crackling, /
       그리고 소리였다   ── 탁탁하는 소리,

roaring little fire.
── 작은 난롯불이 타는 듯한.

Key Expression

suppose를 사용한 가정법

if를 사용하지 않고 가정법을 표현할 수 있는 동사들이 있습니다.
다음의 동사들이 단독으로 쓰여 절을 이끄는 문장을 만났을 때는 '만약 ~한다면'으로 해석해 보세요.

▶ suppose / supposing (that) S + V ~ ┐
▶ provided / providing (that) S + V~   만약 ~한다면
▶ granted / granting (that) S + V ~   ┘

ex) Suppose there was a bright fire in the grate.
    만약 난로 안에 밝은 불이 타고 있다면.
    Suppose she proves to be quite a different child.
    만약 그녀가 전혀 완전 다른 아이라고 판명된다면.

satin 새틴(광택이 곱고 보드라운 견직물) | eider 솜털 오리 | down (새의) 솜털 | crackling (날카롭게) 탁탁하는 소리
| mournfully 애절하게 | come back to earth 현실로 돌아오다 | hiss 쉬익하는 소리를 내다 | crimson 진홍색

"Oh, I am awakening," / she said mournfully. "I can't help
"아, 깨어나고 있어."　　　　　새라가 슬프게 말했다.　　　　　"어쩔 수 없어

it / — I can't."
　— 어쩔 수 없구나."

Her eyes opened / in spite of herself. And then / she
새라의 눈이 떠졌다　　　자신도 모르게.　　　　그리고 나서

actually smiled / — for what she saw / she had never seen
진짜로 웃었다　　　— 자신이 본 것 때문에　　본 적이 없었고

/ in the attic / before, / and knew / she never should see.
　다락방에서　　이전에,　　알고 있었던　절대 볼 수 없으리라고.

"Oh, I haven't awakened," / she whispered, / daring to
"아, 아직 깨지 않았나 봐."　　　새라가 속삭였다.

rise on her elbow / and look all about her. "I am dreaming
팔꿈치로 받치고 몸을 일으켜　주변을 둘러보면서.　　　　"아직 꿈꾸고 있어."

yet." She knew / it must be a dream, / for if she were
새라는 생각했다　그것이 꿈이 틀림없다고,　　왜냐하면 깨어난 거라면

awake / such things could not / — could not be.
깨어　그런 일들은 불가능했으니까　— 있을 수 없으니까.

Do you wonder / that she felt sure / she had not come back
독자 여러분은 이상한가요　새라가 굳게 믿는 것이　아직 현실로 돌아온 것이 아니라고?

to earth? This is what she saw. In the grate / there was
　　새라가 본 장면은 이렇다.　　　벽난로에는

a glowing, blazing fire; / on the hob / was a little brass
환하게 타오르는 난롯불이 있었고;　선반에는　　작은 구리 주전자가 있었으며

kettle / hissing and boiling; / spread upon the floor / was
주전자　쉬익 소리를 내며 끓고 있는;　바닥에 깔려 있는 것은

a thick, warm crimson rug; / before the fire / a folding-
두껍고, 따뜻한 진홍색 양탄자였고;　불 앞에는　접이식 의자가,

chair, / unfolded, / and with cushions on it; / by the chair
펼쳐져 있었고,　그 위에는 쿠션들이 있었다;　의자 옆에는

/ a small folding-table, / unfolded, / covered with a white
작은 접이식 탁자가,　펼쳐진 채,　흰 식탁보로 씌워져 있었고,

cloth, / and upon it / spread small covered dishes, / a cup,
그 위에는　뚜껑 덮인 작은 그릇들이 펼쳐져 있었다.

a saucer, a teapot; / on the bed / were new warm coverings
컵, 컵 받침, 주전자까지;　침대 위에는　따뜻한 새 이불보와

/ and a satin-covered down quilt; / at the foot / a curious
새틴 천을 씌운 오리털 누비이불이 있었고;　　　　발치에는

*wadded silk robe, / a pair of quilted slippers, / and some
워디드 실크 가운과,　　　　누비 슬리퍼 한 벌,　　　　그리고 책 몇 권이

books. The room of her dream / seemed changed / into
있었다.　　새라의 꿈 속의 방이　　　　바뀐 듯 보였다

fairyland / — and it was flooded / with warm light, / for
동화 속 나라로　　— 그리고 가득 차 있었다　　따뜻한 불빛으로,

a bright lamp stood / on the table / covered with a rosy
밝은 램프가 서 있었으므로　　식탁 위에는　　장밋빛 전등갓이 씌어진.

shade.

She sat up, / resting on her elbow, / and her breathing came
새라는 몸을 일으켜, 팔꿈치를 기댔고,　　　　숨이 가빠졌다.

short and fast.

"It does not — melt away," / she panted. "Oh, I never had
"사라지지 — 않네,"　　숨을 헐떡였다.　　"아, 이런 꿈은 꾼 적이 없어

such a dream / before." She scarcely dared to stir; / but at
전에는."　　그녀는 좀처럼 꼼짝할 수 없었지만;

last / she pushed the bedclothes aside, / and put her feet /
마침내　침대 이불을 한쪽으로 밀고,　　　　발을 디뎠다

on the floor / with a rapturous smile.
바닥에　　황홀해 하는 미소를 지으며.

"I am dreaming / — I am getting out of bed," / she heard
"꿈을 꾸면서　　— 난 침대 밖으로 나오고 있어,"　　자신의 목소리가

her own voice say; / and then, / as she stood up / in the
말하는 것을 들었다;　　그리고는,　　일어서서　　방

midst of it all, / turning slowly / from side to side / — "I
한가운데,　　천천히 돌아보았다　　이쪽에서 저쪽으로

am dreaming / it stays — real! I'm dreaming / it feels real.
— "꿈꾸고 있는 거야　　진짜 — 로!　　꿈꾸고 있어　　진짜처럼 느껴지는.

* 워디드 : 가로골의 속에 메우는 이중직을 말하는데, 여기에서 워드는 '마른 풀·마 부스러기·고무 등 부드러
운 물건을 뭉친 것·메우는 물건·솜뭉치' 등을 말한다. 메우는 것으로 구멍을 막는 것을 의미하기도 한다.

robe 예복, 가운 | fairyland 요정의 나라, 동화의 나라 | pant 헐떡거리다 | rapturous 황홀해 하는

It's bewitched / — or I'm bewitched. I only think / I see it
꿈이 마법에 걸린 거야   — 아니면 내가 마법에 걸렸거나. 생각하고 있는 것 뿐이야 모두 보인

all." Her words began to hurry themselves. "If I can only
다고." 새라의 말이 빨라지기 시작되었다.   "만약 계속 상상할 수만

keep on thinking it," / she cried, / "I don't care! I don't
있다면."   새라가 외쳤다.   "상관없어!

care!"
상관없어!"

She stood panting a moment longer, / and then / cried out
새라는 숨을 헐떡이며 서 있다가,   그리고 나서   다시 외쳤다.

again.

"Oh, it isn't true!" / she said. "It can't be true! But oh, / how
"아, 이것은 진짜가 아니야!"   새라가 말했다. "진짜일 리가 없어!   하지만 아,

true it seems!"
어쩌면 이렇게 진짜같은지!"

The blazing fire drew her to it, / and she knelt down / and
타오르는 난롯불이 새라를 이끌었고,   새라는 무릎을 꿇고

held out her hands / close to it / — so close / that the heat
손을 뻗었다   불 가까이로   — 아주 가까워서

made her start back.
열 때문에 깜짝 놀라 물러섰다.

"A fire I only dreamed / wouldn't be hot," / she cried.
"꿈 속에서의 난롯불이라면   뜨겁지 않을 거야,"   새라가 외쳤다.

She sprang up, / touched the table, the dishes, the rug; / she
새라는 벌떡 일어나,   탁자와, 접시와, 양탄자를 만졌다;

went to the bed / and touched the blankets. She took up the
침대로 가서   담요를 만졌다.

soft wadded dressing-gown, / and suddenly clutched it / to
부드러운 솜이 꽉 찬 누비 가운을 집어 들었고,   갑자기 그것을 움켜쥐어

her breast / and held it to her cheek.
가슴에 안고   뺨에 대 보았다.

"It's warm. It's soft!" / she almost sobbed. "It's real. It must
"따뜻해.   부드러워!"   새라는 거의 울 지경이었다.   "이것은 진짜야.

be!"
틀림없이!"

She threw it over her shoulders, / and put her feet / into the
새라는 그 옷을 어깨에 걸치고,   발을 넣었다

slippers.
슬리퍼 안으로.

"They are real, / too. It's all real!" / she cried. "I am not /
"이것들도 진짜야,   역시.   모두 진짜야!"   그녀가 외쳤다.   "난 아니야

— I am not dreaming!"
— 난 꿈꾸고 있는 게 아니야!"

She almost staggered / to the books / and opened the one
새라는 거의 비틀거리며   책으로 다가가   한 권을 펼쳤다

/ which lay upon the top. Something was written / on the
맨 위에 놓인.   뭔가 쓰여 있었다   책의 맨 앞

flyleaf / — just a few words, / and they were these:
백지에   — 몇 개의 단어로,   그 내용은 이러했다:

"To the little girl / in the attic. From a friend."
"어린 소녀에게   다락방에 있는.   친구로부터."

When she saw that / — wasn't it a strange thing / for her to
새라는 그 글을 보자   — 이상한 일이 아니었다   새라가 그러는

do / — she put her face down / upon the page / and burst
것은   — 얼굴을 숙이고   그 페이지 위에

into tears.
눈물을 터뜨렸다.

"I don't know who it is," / she said; / "but somebody cares
"누구인지 모르지만."   새라가 말했다;   "누군가 나를 좋아해 주는 거야.

for me a little. I have a friend."
난 친구가 있어."

She took her candle / and stole out of her own room / and
새라는 촛불을 들고   방을 살짝 빠져나가

into Becky's, / and stood by her bedside.
베키의 방으로 들어가서, 침대 옆에 섰다.

"Becky, Becky!" / she whispered / as loudly as she dared.
"베키, 베키!"   새라가 속삭였다   조심스럽게 목소리를 높여.

"Wake up!"
"일어나!"

---

flyleaf 책 앞뒤의 백지 | care for 돌보다, 좋아하다 | aghast 경악한, 겁에 질린 | smudge 얼룩을 남기다

When Becky wakened, / and she sat upright / staring
베키가 잠에서 깨어,   일어나 앉았을 때   놀라서 쳐다보며,

aghast, / her face still smudged / with traces of tears, /
베키의 얼굴은 여전히 얼룩져 있었다   눈물 자국으로,

beside her / stood a little figure / in a luxurious wadded
자신의 옆에   작은 사람이 서 있었다   화려한 누비 가운을 입은

robe / of crimson silk. The face she saw / was a shining,
진홍빛 실크로 된.   베키가 본 얼굴은   환하게 빛나고, 아름다웠다.

wonderful thing. The Princess Sara / — as she remembered
새라 공주가   — 베키가 기억하고 있는 대로

her / — stood at her very bedside, / holding a candle / in
— 침대 바로 옆에 서 있었다,   촛불을 들고

her hand.
손에는.

"Come," / she said. "Oh, Becky, come!"
"이리 와,"   새라가 말했다.   "아, 베키, 어서!"

Becky was too frightened to speak. She simply got up / and
베키는 너무 놀라서 말할 수 없었다.   그냥 일어나서

followed her, / with her mouth and eyes open, / and without
새라를 따라왔다.   입을 벌리고 눈을 크게 뜨고,   한 마디 말도 없이.

a word.
한 마디 말도 없이.

And when they crossed the threshold, / Sara shut the door
그들이 문지방을 건넜을 때,   새라가 문을 조용히 닫았고

gently / and drew her / into the warm, glowing midst of
베키를 끌었다   따뜻하고, 빛나는 방 한가운데로

things / which made her brain reel / and her hungry senses
그 광경은 베키의 머리를 어지럽게 만들고   배고픔이 사라지게 했다.

faint. "It's true! It's true!" / she cried. "I've touched them
"이것은 진짜야! 진짜라고!"   새라가 외쳤다.   "내가 모두 만져봤어.

all. They are as real / as we are. The Magic has come and
그것들은 진짜야   우리처럼.   마법이 한 것이야,

done it, / Becky, / while we were asleep / — the Magic /
베키,   우리가 자는 동안   — 마법이

that won't let those worst things / ever quite happen."
최악의 상황을 내버려 두지 않는   정말 일어난 거야."

A. 다음 문장을 해석해 보세요.

(1) It was better / than to go into the room alone / and find it empty and desolate.
→

(2) She always felt / very tender of Ermengarde, / and tried / not to let her feel / too strongly / the difference.
→

(3) As they sat together, / Ermengarde did not know / that she was faint / as well as ravenous, / and that while she talked / she now and then wondered / if her hunger would let her sleep / when she was left alone.
→

(4) The truth was / that Ermengarde did not know anything / of the sometimes / almost unbearable side of life / in the attic / and she had not a sufficiently vivid imagination / to depict it / for herself.
→

B. 다음 주어진 문장이 되도록 빈칸에 써 넣으세요.

(1) 네가 그것을 기억할 수 있도록 말해 줄게.

I'll tell it _____.

(2) 새라는 한 권씩 차례대로 펼쳤다.

Sara was opening _____.

(3) 친절하다는 것은 다른 사람들에게 매우 큰 가치가 있는 거야.

To be kind is _____.

(4) 그녀의 눈은 <u>자신도 모르게</u> 떠졌다.
Her eyes opened _____.

C. 다음 주어진 문구가 알맞은 문장이 되도록 순서를 맞춰 보세요.

(1) 네가 먹고 싶은 만큼 먹게 될 것이다.
(have / You / shall / you / want / much / as / to / as / eat)
→

(2) 시도해 봐야 소용없을 것이다.
(be / There / in / trying / use / wouldn't / any)
→

(3) 그녀는 아주 가만히 있으면서 그것이 계속되도록 해야 했다.
(still / must / She / be / it / quite / and / last / make)
→

(4) 뭔가가 그녀를 일어나게 만들었다.
(was / Something / her / forcing / awaken / to)
→

D. 다음 단어에 대한 맞는 설명과 연결해 보세요.

(1) savage   ▶   ◀ ① represent them in a work of art

(2) depict   ▶   ◀ ② squeeze your teeth together firmly

(3) clench   ▶   ◀ ③ feel very anxious and unhappy

(4) dread   ▶   ◀ ④ extremely cruel and violent

배고픔 때문에 잠이 들 수 있을지 이따금 궁금해했다는 사실을 알지 못했다. (4) 사실은 어딘가든는 다락방에서 사는 삶이 때때로 견딜 수 없다는 것을 몰랐고 그것을 혼자서 그려볼 만한 충분히 생생한 상상력도 없었다. | B. (1) so that you will remember it (2) one book after the other (3) worth a great deal to other people (4) in spite of herself | C. (1) You shall have as much as you want to eat, (2) There wouldn't be any use in trying. (3) She must be quite still and make it last. (4) Something was forcing her to awaken. | D. (1) ④ (2) ① (3) ② (4) ③

# 9

"It Is the Child!"
"바로 그 아이야!"

The next afternoon / three members of the Large Family
다음 날 오후   대가족 중 세 명이 앉아서

sat / in the Indian gentleman's library, / doing their best
인도 신사의 서재에.   최선을 다하고 있었다

/ to cheer him up. They had been allowed to come in /
그를 즐겁게 해 주려고.   그들은 들어오도록 허락 받았다

to perform this office / because he had specially invited
사무실 방문을 위해   인도 신사가 특별히 초대했기 때문에.

them. He had been living / in a state of suspense / for
그는 살아왔다   불안한 상태에서

some time, / and today / he was waiting / for a certain
얼마 동안,   그리고 오늘   그는 기다리고 있었다   어떤 특별한 사건을

event / very anxiously. This event was / the return of
매우 흥분하며.   그 사건이란   카마이클 씨가 돌아오는

Mr. Carmichael / from Moscow. His stay there had been
것이었다   모스크바로부터.   그가 그곳에 머무는 기간은 늘어났다

prolonged / from week to week. On his first arrival there,
한 주 또 한 주.   처음 거기에 도착했을 때에는,

/ he had not been able satisfactorily / to trace the family
그는 제대로 할 수 없었다   그 가족을 찾는 일을

/ he had gone in search of. When he felt at last sure /
찾으러 갔었던.   마침내 확신을 느끼며

that he had found them / and had gone to their house, /
그들을 찾았다고   그들의 집에 갔을 때,

he had been told / that they were absent / on a journey.
그는 들었다   그들이 없다는 것을   여행을 떠나서.

His efforts to reach them / had been unavailing, / so he
그들에게 가려는 노력은   계속 효과가 없었기에,

had decided to remain / in Moscow / until their return.
남기로 결심했었다   모스크바에   그들이 돌아올 때까지.

suspense 서스펜스, 긴장감 | satisfactorily 만족스럽게 | unavailing 소용없는, 효과 없는 | reclining chair
안락의자 | astride 두 다리를 벌리고 | chirrup (새나 벌레가) 소리를 내다 | pat 쓰다듬다, 토닥거리다 | bridle 굴레
| bounce 깡충깡충 뛰다

Mr. Carrisford sat / in his reclining chair, / and Janet sat
캐리스포드 씨는 앉았다   안락의자에,   그리고 자넷도 앉았다

/ on the floor / beside him. He was very fond of Janet.
바닥에   그의 옆에.   그는 자넷을 매우 좋아했다.

Nora had found a footstool, / and Donald was astride /
노라는 의자를 찾아 앉았고,   도날드는 두 다리를 벌린 채

the tiger's head / which ornamented the rug / made of the
호랑이의 머리 위에 앉았다   양탄자를 장식하고 있던

animal's skin. It must be owned / that he was riding it /
동물의 가죽으로 만든. 말해야 할 것이다   호랑이를 타고 있었다고

rather violently.
다소 거칠게.

"Don't chirrup so loud, / Donald," / Janet said. "When
"그렇게 크게 소리내지 마,   도날드,"   자넷이 말했다.

you come to cheer an ill person up / you don't cheer
아픈 사람의 기운을 북돋우러 와서   기운 빠지게 하잖아

him up / at the top of your voice. Perhaps / cheering up
그렇게 목소리가 크면.   아마   기운 차리기에 너무

is too loud, / Mr. Carrisford?" / turning to the Indian
시끄럽죠,   캐리스포드 씨?   인도 신사를 돌아보며 말했다.

gentleman.

But he only patted her shoulder.
하지만 그는 자넷의 어깨를 토닥거릴 뿐이었다.

"No, it isn't," / he answered. "And it keeps me / from
"아니, 그렇지 않아,"   그가 대답했다.   "오히려 막아주는 구나

thinking too much."
너무 생각에 빠지지 않도록."

"I'm going to be quiet," / Donald shouted. "We'll all be
"조용히 하겠어요,"   도날드가 소리쳤다.   "모두 조용히 있을게요

as quiet / as mice."
쥐처럼."

"Mice don't make a noise / like that," / said Janet.
"쥐는 시끄럽게 굴지 않아   그렇게,"   자넷이 말했다.

Donald made a bridle / of his handkerchief / and
도날드는 굴레를 만들고는   손수건으로

bounced up and down / on the tiger's head.
펄쩍펄쩍 뛰었다   호랑이 머리 위에서.

"A whole lot of mice might," / he said cheerfully. "A
"많은 쥐가 한꺼번에 그런다면 시끄러울지도," 그가 신나서 말했다.

thousand mice might."
"천 마리라면 그럴 수도 있지."

"I don't believe fifty thousand mice would," / said Janet, /
"5만 마리가 있어도 그렇지 않을 걸." 자넷은 말했다.

severely; / "and we have to be as quiet / as one mouse."
엄하게; "그리고 우리는 조용히 해야 해 쥐 한 마리만 있는 것처럼."

Mr. Carrisford laughed / and patted her shoulder / again.
캐리스포드 씨가 웃으며 그녀의 어깨를 토닥거렸다 또.

"Papa won't be very long / now," / she said. "May we talk
"아빠는 곧 오실 거예요 이제," 자넷이 말했다. "우리 이야기 할까요

/ about the lost little girl?"
그 잃어버린 어린 소녀에 대해?"

"I don't think I could talk much / about anything else /
"말할 수 있을 것 같지 않구나 그밖의 다른 것에 대해

just now," / the Indian gentleman answered, / knitting his
지금 당장은," 인도 신사가 말했다. 이맛살을 찌푸리며

forehead / with a tired look.
피곤한 표정으로.

"We like her / so much," / said Nora. "We call her / the
"우린 그 아이를 좋아해요 아주 많이." 노라가 말했다. "우리는 불러요

little un-fairy princess."
요정이 아닌 어린 공주라고."

"Why?" / the Indian gentleman inquired, / because the
"왜?" 인도 신사가 물었다.

fancies of the Large Family / always / made him forget
왜냐하면 대가족의 공상 이야기를 들으면 항상 잊을 수 있었기 때문이다

things / a little.
약간은.

It was Janet / who answered.
자넷이었다 대답한 것은.

"It is because, / though she is not exactly a fairy, / she
"그 이유는요, 비록 그 아이는 진짜 요정은 아니지만,

will be so rich / when she is found / that she will be
엄청 부자가 될 테니까요 발견되기만 하면 공주처럼 될 거예요

knit one's forehead 이맛살을 찌푸리다

like a princess / in a fairy tale. We called her / the fairy
동화 속 이야기에 나오는. 우리는 그 애를 불렀어요

princess / at first, / but it didn't quite suit."
요정 공주라고   처음에는,   하지만 그것은 딱 어울리지 않았어요."

"Is it true," / said Nora, / "that her papa gave all his
"사실인가요,"   노라가 말했다,   "그 아이의 아빠는 가진 돈을 모두 줬고

money / to a friend / to put in a mine / that had diamonds
친구에게   광산에 투자하도록   다이아몬드가 있는,

in it, / and then / the friend thought / he had lost it all /
그리고는   그 친구는 생각하며   그 돈을 전부 잃었다고

and ran away / because he felt / as if he was a robber?"
도망갔다는 것이   느꼈기 때문에   사기꾼이 된 것처럼?"

"But he wasn't really, / you know," / put in Janet, / hastily.
"하지만 그는 정말 그런 것이 아니야, 알잖아,"   자넷이 끼어들었다,   서둘러.

The Indian gentleman / took hold of her hand / quickly.
인도 신사가   그녀의 손을 잡았다   재빨리.

"No, he wasn't really," / he said.
"아니야, 그는 정말 그런 것이 아니었어," 그가 말했다.

"I am sorry / for the friend," / Janet said; / "I can't help it.
"안됐어요   그 친구분이,"   자넷이 말했다;   "어쩔 수 없어요.

He didn't mean to do it, / and it would break his heart. I
그는 그러려고 한 것이 아니었는데,   그 일 때문에 마음이 아팠을 거예요.

am sure / it would break his heart."
전 확신해요   그 일로 마음이 아팠을 거라고."

"You are an understanding little woman, / Janet," / the
"넌 이해심이 많은 아이로구나,   자넷,"

Indian gentleman said, / and he held her hand close.
인도 신사가 말했다,   그리고 그녀의 손을 꽉 잡았다.

"Did you tell Mr. Carrisford," / Donald shouted again,
"누나가 캐리스포드 씨한테 말했어,"   도날드가 다시 소리쳤다,

/ "about the little-girl-who-is-n't-a-beggar? Did you tell
"거지가 - 아닌 - 어린 - 여자애에 관해?   얘기했어

him / she has new nice clothes? P'r'aps she's been found
그 애가 멋진 새 옷을 입었다고?   아마도 누군가 그 아이를 찾은 거야

by somebody / when she was lost."
잃어버렸다가."

"There's a cab!" / exclaimed Janet. "It's stopping before
"마차가 와요!"   자넷이 소리쳤다.   "문 앞에 멈췄어요.

the door. It is papa!"
아빠예요!"

They all ran to the windows / to look out.
모두 함께 창문으로 달려나갔다   내다보려고.

"Yes, it's papa," / Donald proclaimed. "But there is no
"맞아, 아빠예요,"   도날드가 소리쳤다.   "하지만 여자 아이는 없어요."

little girl."

All three of them / incontinently fled from the room / and
그들 셋 모두   방에서 경솔하게 뛰쳐 나가

tumbled into the hall. It was in this way / they always
거실로 몰려갔다.   이런 식이었다

welcomed their father. They were to be heard / jumping
아빠를 맞이할 때면 언제나.   그들은 말하려 했다

up and down, / clapping their hands, / and being caught
깡총깡총 뛰면서,   손뼉을 치면서,   안겨서

up / and kissed.
입맞춤을 받으며.

Mr. Carrisford made an effort to rise / and sank back /
캐리스포드 씨는 일어나려고 하다가   주저앉았다

again.
다시.

Key Expression ♪

비교급을 강조하는 부사들

비교급 앞에 붙어 '훨씬, 더욱'의 뜻으로 의미를 강조하는 부사들이 있습니다.
원급이나 최상급를 강조하는 부사와 함께 기억하세요.

▶ so, very, quite + 원급
▶ even, much, far, a lot, still + 비교급
▶ much, by far, the very + 최상급

ex) She is much younger than Captain Crewe's little girl.
그 아이는 크루 대위의 딸보다 훨씬 더 어려요.

"It is no use," / he said. "What a wreck I am!"
"소용없어," 그가 말했다. "완전히 만신창이가 됐군!"

Mr. Carmichael's voice / approached the door.
카마이클 씨의 목소리가 문 가까이로 들려 왔다.

"No, children," / he was saying; / "you may come in /
"안 돼, 애들아," 그는 말하고 있었다; "너희는 들어오렴

after I have talked to Mr. Carrisford. Go and play / with
아빠가 캐리스포드 씨와 이야기를 끝낸 후에. 가서 놀아라

Ram Dass."
람 다스와."

Then / the door opened / and he came in. He looked
그때 문이 열렸고 카마이클 씨가 들어왔다. 그는 전보다 혈색이

rosier than ever, / and brought an atmosphere of freshness
좋아 보였고, 팔팔하고 건강한 기운을 가지고 왔다

and health / with him; / but his eyes were disappointed
그에게; 하지만 두 눈에는 실망과 근심이 어려 있었다

and anxious / as they met the invalid's look / of eager
환자의 눈빛과 마주치자 간절한 질문을

question / even as they grasped each other's hands.
하는 듯한 서로의 손을 잡았을 때에도.

"What news?" / Mr. Carrisford asked. "The child / the
"새 소식은?" 캐리스포드 씨가 물었다. "그 아이는

Russian people adopted?"
러시아인 부부가 입양했던?"

"She is not the child we are looking for," / was Mr.
"그 애는 우리가 찾고 있는 아이가 아니었어요,"

Carmichael's answer. "She is much younger / than
카마이클 씨가 대답했다. "그 아이는 훨씬 더 어려요

Captain Crewe's little girl. Her name is Emily Carew. I
크루 대위의 딸보다. 이름은 에밀리 커루예요.

have seen / and talked to her. The Russians were able to
내가 만나서 그 아이와 이야기 했었어요. 그 러시아인 부부가 해 주었죠

give / me every detail."
내게 세세한 설명을."

---

incontinently 경솔하게 | wreck 만신창이 | approach 다가가다 | invalid 환자, 지체 부자유자

How wearied and miserable / the Indian gentleman
얼마나 지치고 비참하게   인도 신사가 보였는지!

looked! His hand dropped / from Mr. Carmichael's.
그의 손은 떨어졌다   카마이클의 손에서.

"Then / the search has to be begun / over again," / he said.
"그러면   수색을 시작해야겠군   또 다시,"   그가 말했다.

"That is all. Please sit down."
"그 수밖에 없군.   앉게."

Mr. Carmichael took a seat. Somehow, / he had gradually
카마이클 씨가 자리에 앉았다.   어쩐지.   그는 점점 좋아하게 되었다

grown fond / of this unhappy man. He was himself so
              이 불행한 남자를.   그 자신은 아주 건강하고 행복하고,

well and happy, / and so surrounded by cheerfulness and
              활기와 사랑에 둘러 싸여 있어서,

love, / that desolation and broken health / seemed pitifully
        쓸쓸하고 병든 몸이   견딜 수 없을 만큼 측은해

unbearable things. If there had been the sound / of just
보였다.   소리만 있었다면

one gay little high-pitched voice / in the house, / it would
즐겁게 떠드는 높은 톤의 작은 목소리의   그 집에,

have been so much less forlorn. And / that a man should
그렇게 외롭지 않았을 텐데.   그리고   품고 살아가야만 한다는 것은

be compelled to carry about / in his breast / the thought /
                              가슴 속에   생각을

that he had seemed to wrong / and desert a child / was not
자신이 잘못해서   아이를 버렸다는

a thing one could face.
감당하기 힘든 것이었다.

"Come, come," / he said / in his cheery voice; / "we'll find
"자, 자."   그가 말했다   활기찬 목소리로,   "그 아이를 찾게

her yet."
될 겁니다."

---

desolation 황량함, 적막함 | pitifully 측은하게, 가련하게 | be compelled to 할 수 없이 ~하다 | carry 지니고
다니다 | fret 조바심 내다 | restless 초조한 | pace 서성거리다

"We must begin at once. No time must be lost," / Mr.
"당장 시작해야 하네.   지체할 시간이 없어."

Carrisford fretted. "Have you any new suggestion to
캐리스포드 씨가 조바심을 냈다. "새로운 제안이라도 있을까

make / — any whatsoever?"
— 무엇이든지?"

Mr. Carmichael felt rather restless, / and he rose / and
카마이클 씨는 다소 초조해져서,   일어나서

began to pace the room / with a thoughtful, / though
방을 서성거리기 시작했다   생각에 잠겨,

uncertain face.
확신하지 못하는 표정이었지만.

"Well, perhaps," / he said. "I don't know what it may be
"음, 어쩌면,   그가 말했다. "해 볼 만한 일인지도 모르겠어요.

worth. The fact is, / an idea occurred to me / as I was
사실은,   어떤 생각이 떠올랐어요

thinking the thing over / in the train / on the journey /
곰곰이 생각하는 동안   기차 안에서   여정 중

from Dover."
도버에서 출발한."

"What was it? If she is alive, / she is somewhere."
"그것이 뭐였나?   그 아이가 살아있다면,   어딘가에 있을 거야."

"Yes; / she is somewhere. We have searched / the schools
"맞아요;   어딘가에 있어요.   샅샅이 찾아봤죠   학교들을

/ in Paris. Let us give up Paris / and begin in London.
파리에 있는. 파리는 관둡시다   그리고 런던에서 시작해요.

That was my idea / — to search London."
그것이 제 생각이었어요   — 런던에서 찾자는 것이."

"There are schools enough / in London," / said Mr.
"학교는 많이 있지   런던에,"   캐리스포드 씨가 말했다.

Carrisford. Then he slightly started, / roused by a
그때 살짝 놀랐다.   기억이 떠오르면서.

recollection. "By the way, / there is one next door."
"그런데 말이야,   옆집에 한 곳이 있어."

"Then we will begin there. We cannot begin / nearer
"그럼 거기에서 시작해 보죠.   시작할 수는 없을테니

than next door."
옆집보다 가까운 곳에서."

"No," / said Carrisford. "There is a child there / who
"없겠지." 캐리스포드가 말했다. "그곳에 아이가 하나 있는데

interests me; / but she is not a pupil. And she is a little
내 관심을 끄는: 하지만 그 애는 학생이 아니야. 그리고 그 애는 작고 어두운,

dark, forlorn creature, / as unlike poor Crewe as a child
버려진 아이야. 가엾은 크루의 딸처럼 보이지는 않아."

could be."

Perhaps / the Magic was at work again / at that very
아마도 마법이 다시 발휘된 것 같았다 바로 그 순간

moment / — the beautiful Magic. It really seemed /
— 아름다운 마법이. 정말 보였다

as if it might be so. What was it that / brought Ram
그런 것처럼. 도대체 무엇이 람 다스를 데려간 것일까

Dass / into the room / — even as his master spoke / —
그 방으로 — 주인이 대화하는 중이었는데도

salaaming respectfully, / but with a scarcely concealed /
— 공손하게 인사하면서, 하지만 좀처럼 감춰질 수 없는

touch of excitement / in his dark, flashing eyes?
흥분의 감정을 담아 검은 눈을 빛내며?

"Sahib," / he said, / "the child herself has come / — the
"사히브," 그가 말했다. "그 아이가 직접 왔어요 — 사히브

child the sahib felt pity for. She brings back the monkey
께서 가엾게 여기셨던 그 아이요. 원숭이를 데려왔습니다

/ who had again run away / to her attic under the roof.
또 도망쳤던 그 아이의 지붕 밑 다락방으로.

I have asked that she remain. It was my thought / that it
그 아이에게 기다려 달라고 부탁했어요. 제 생각에

would please the sahib / to see and speak with her."
사히브가 기뻐하실 것 같아서요 그 아이를 만나 이야기를 나누시면."

"Who is she?" / inquired Mr. Carmichael.
"그 아이가 누구예요?" 카마이클 씨가 물었다.

"God knows," / Mr. Carrrisford answered. "She is the
"누가 알겠나." 캐리스포드 씨가 답했다. "그 아이가 내가 말한

child I spoke of. A little drudge / at the school." He
아이야. 허드렛일 하는 아이지 학교에서."

waved his hand / to Ram Dass, / and addressed him. "Yes,
그가 손을 흔들어   람 다스에게,   말했다.

I should like to see her. Go and bring her in." Then he
"좋아, 그 아이를 보고 싶군.   가서 그 아이를 들여보내."   그리고 돌아보았다

turned / to Mr. Carmichael. "While you have been away,"
카마이클 씨를.   "자네가 떠나 있던 동안,"

/ he explained, / "I have been desperate. The days were so
그가 설명했다.   "난 절망적이었네.   아주 어둡고 긴 날들이었지.

dark and long. Ram Dass told me / of this child's miseries,
람 다스가 내게 말해 주었고   이 아이의 불행을,

/ and together / we invented a romantic plan / to help her.
그래서 함께   낭만적인 계획을 고안했지   그 아이를 도와줄.

I suppose / it was a childish thing to do; / but it gave me
생각해 보면   유치한 짓이었지만;   내게 뭔가를 주었어

something / to plan and think of. Without the help / of an
계획하고 생각할.   도움이 없었다면

agile, soft-footed Oriental / like Ram Dass, / however, / it
날렵하고, 조용히 걷는 동양인의   람 다스처럼,   그렇지만,

could not have been done."
할 수 없는 일이었겠지."

Key Expression ♪

what is it that ~ : 도대체 무엇이 ~일까

what is it that으로 시작하는 의문문은 It is ~ that 강조구문의 의문문 버전이에요. 'What is it that~'으로 시작하는 의문문은 '도대체 무엇이 ~일까?' 혹은 '~는 도대체 뭐야?'로 해석한다고 외워두시면 편해요.

ex) What brought Ram Dass into the room?
→ It is what that brought Ram Dass into the room?
(강조를 위해 It is ~ that 삽입)
→ What was it that brought Ram Dass into the room?
(의문문 형식에 맞추기 위해 의문사를 앞으로 빼고 주어와 동사의 어순 도치)
도대체 뭐가 람 다스를 그 방으로 데려갔던 것일까?

God knows 누가 알겠나, 아무도 모른다 | address 말하다 | desperate 절망적인 | agile 날렵한, 민첩한 | soft-footed 조용히 걷는

Then Sara came into the room. She carried the monkey
그때 새라가 방으로 들어왔다.   새라는 원숭이를 안고 있었는데

/ in her arms, / and he evidently did not intend to part /
팔에,   분명 원숭이는 떨어지고 싶지 않은 듯 했다

from her, / if it could be helped. He was clinging to her /
새라에게서.   그럴 수 있다면.   원숭이는 새라에게 매달려

and chattering, / and the interesting excitement / of finding
떠들어댔다.   그리고 흥분으로 들떠서

herself in the Indian gentleman's room / had brought a
인도 신사의 방에 있다는 것에

flush to Sara's cheeks.
새라의 뺨이 붉어졌다.

"Your monkey ran away again," / she said, / in her pretty
"원숭이가 또 도망쳤어요."   새라가 말했다.   예쁜 목소리로.

voice. "He came to my garret window / last night, / and I
         "제 다락방 창문으로 들어와서   지난 밤,

took him in / because it was so cold. I would have brought
들어오게 했어요   매우 추웠기 때문에.   다시 데려왔을텐데요

him back / if it had not been so late. I knew / you were ill /
시간이 그렇게 늦지 않았다면.   알고 있어서   편찮으신 것을

and might not like to be disturbed."
방해 받고 싶지 않으실까 싶어서요."

The Indian gentleman's hollow eyes / dwelt on her / with
인도 신사의 움푹 꺼진 두 눈이   새라에게 고정되었다

curious interest.
묘한 관심으로.

"That was very thoughtful of you," / he said.
"매우 사려 깊은 아이로구나."   그가 말했다.

Sara looked toward Ram Dass, / who stood near the door.
새라는 람 다스를 보았다.   문 가까이에 서 있던.

"Shall I give him to the Lascar?" / she asked.
"원숭이를 '라스카르'에게 줄까요?"   그녀는 물었다.

"How do you know / he is a Lascar?" / said the Indian
"어떻게 알았니   그가 '라스카르'라는 것을?"   인도 신사가 말했다,

gentleman, / smiling a little.
              살짝 웃으면서.

"Oh, I know Lascars," / Sara said, / handing over the
"아, 저는 '라스카르'를 알아요." 새라가 말했다, 내키지 않아하는 원숭이를 건네며.

reluctant monkey. "I was born in India."
"전 인도에서 태어났거든요."

The Indian gentleman sat upright / so suddenly, / and with
인도 신사가 벌떡 일어나 앉았다 아주 갑자기.

such a change of expression, / that she was / for a moment
그리고 표정이 갑자기 달라져서, 새라는 순간적으로

/ quite startled.
매우 놀랐다.

"You were born in India," / he exclaimed, / "were you?
"인도에서 태어났단 말이냐," 그가 소리쳤다, "네가?

Come here." And he held out his hand.
이리 오렴." 인도 신사가 손을 내밀었다.

Sara went to him / and laid her hand / in his, / as he
새라는 그에게 가서 손을 내밀었다 그의 손에,

seemed to want to take it. She stood still, / and her green-
손을 잡고 싶어 하는 듯 보여서. 새라는 가만히 서서, 초록빛 회색 눈으로

gray eyes met his / wonderingly. Something seemed to be
신사의 눈을 보았다 의아해 하며. 뭔가 문제가 생긴듯 했다

the matter / with him.
신사에게.

"You live next door?" / he demanded.
"넌 옆집에 살지?" 그가 캐물었다.

"Yes; / I live at Miss Minchin's seminary."
"네; 민친 신학교에 살아요."

"But you are not one of her pupils?"
"하지만 넌 학생이 아니잖니?"

A strange little smile hovered / about Sara's mouth. She
야릇한 미소가 살짝 맴돌았다 새라의 입가에.

hesitated / a moment.
새라는 주저했다 잠시.

hollow 텅 빈, 멍한 | dwell on 머무르다 | Lascar 동인도인 선원을 일컫는 말 | reluctant 마지못해 하는, 주저하는
| hover 맴돌다

263

"I don't think I know exactly / what I am," / she replied.
"저도 정확히 모르겠어요   제가 누군지."   새라가 대답했다.

"Why not?"
"왜 그러지?"

"At first / I was a pupil, / and a parlor boarder; / but now — "
"처음에는   저도 학생이었어요.   그것도 특별 우대 학생;   하지만 지금은 — "

"You were a pupil! What are you now?"
"넌 학생이었구나!   지금은 뭘 하지?"

The queer little sad smile / was on Sara's lips / again.
묘한 슬픈 미소가   새라의 입가에 떠올랐다   다시.

"I sleep in the attic, / next to the scullery maid," / she said. "I
"전 다락방에서 잠을 자요,   부엌데기 하녀 옆방에 있는,"   새라가 말했다. "

run errands for the cook / — I do anything / she tells me; /
"요리사의 심부름을 해요   — 뭐든지 해요   요리사가 시키는 일은;

and I teach the little ones their lessons."
그리고 어린 학생들에게 공부도 가르치고요."

"Question her, Carmichael," / said Mr. Carrisford, / sinking
"그 아이에게 질문해 보게, 카마이클,"   캐리스포드 씨가 말했다,   다시 주저앉으며

back / as if he had lost his strength. "Question her; / I
마치 힘을 잃어버린 듯.   "그 아이에게 질문해 보게;

cannot."
난 못 하겠어."

The big, kind father / of the Large Family / knew / how to
덩치 큰, 친절한 아빠는   대가족의   알고 있었다

question little girls. Sara realized / how much practice he
여자 아이에게 질문하는 방법을. 새라는 깨달았다   그가 얼마나 많은 연습을 했었는지

had had / when he spoke to her / in his nice, encouraging
자신에게 말을 거는 순간   친절하고, 격려하는 목소리로.

voice.

"What do you mean / by 'At first,' / my child?" / he inquired.
"무슨 뜻이니   '처음에'라니,   얘야?"   그가 물었다.

"When I was first taken there / by my papa."
"처음 이곳에 맡겨졌을 때요   우리 아빠에 의해."

boarder 기숙사 거주 학생

"Where is your papa?"
"네 아빠는 어디 계시니?"

"He died," / said Sara, / very quietly. "He lost all his money
"돌아가셨어요." 새라가 말했다, 아주 조용히. "아빠는 돈을 전부 잃었고

/ and there was none left for me. There was no one / to take
제게 남은 것은 아무것도 없었어요. 아무도 없었고요

care of me / or to pay Miss Minchin."
저를 돌봐주거나 민친 교장에게 돈을 지불할."

"Carmichael!" / the Indian gentleman cried out / loudly.
"카마이클!" 인도 신사가 소리쳤다 큰 소리로.

"Carmichael!"
"카마이클!"

"We must not frighten her," / Mr. Carmichael said aside / to
"그 애를 놀라게 하면 안 돼요," 카마이클 씨가 따로 말했다

him / in a quick, low voice. And he added aloud / to Sara, /
그에게 빠르고, 낮은 목소리로. 그리고 큰 소리로 덧붙였다 새라에게.

"So you were sent up into the attic, / and made into a little
"그래서 넌 다락방으로 보내져서, 허드렛 일꾼이 되었던 거로구나.

drudge. That was about it, / wasn't it?"
그런 거군, 그렇지 않니?"

"There was no one / to take care of me," / said Sara. "There
"아무도 없었어요 절 돌봐줄," 새라가 말했다.

was no money; / I belong to nobody."
"돈도 없었고; 아무도 없었어요."

"How did your father lose his money?" / the Indian
"네 아빠는 어쩌다 돈을 다 잃으셨지?" 인도 신사가 끼어들었다

gentleman broke in / breathlessly.
숨을 헐떡이면서.

"He did not lose it himself," / Sara answered, / wondering
"직접 잃으신 것은 아니에요." 새라가 대답했다, 훨씬 더 의아해 하며

still more / each moment. "He had a friend / he was very
매 순간. "아빠에게는 친구가 있었는데 매우 좋아하시던

fond of / — he was very fond of him. It was his friend /
— 정말 좋아하셨죠. 그 친구 분이었어요

who took his money. He trusted his friend / too much."
아빠의 돈을 가져간 사람은. 아빠는 친구를 믿으셨지요 너무 많이."

The Indian gentleman's breath came / more quickly.
인도 신사의 숨소리가 변했다   더 빠르게.

"The friend might have meant / to do no harm," / he said.
"그 친구는 의도했을지 모르지   해를 깨치지 않으려고."   그가 말했다.

"It might have happened / through a mistake."
"그런 일이 벌어졌을지 모르잖아   실수로."

Sara did not know / how unrelenting / her quiet young
새라는 알지 못했다   얼마나 매몰차게   자신의 조용하고 어린 목소리가

voice sounded / as she answered. If she had known, /
들렸는지   대답할 때.   만약 알았다면,

she would surely have tried / to soften it / for the Indian
정말 노력했을 텐데   부드럽게 말하려고

gentleman's sake.
인도 신사를 위해.

"The suffering was just as bad / for my papa," / she said.
"그 고통은 아주 심했어요   아빠에게,"   그녀가 말했다.

"It killed him."
"그 고통이 아빠를 죽였으니까요."

"What was your father's name?" / the Indian gentleman
"아빠의 성함이 뭐지?"   인도 신사가 말했다.

said. "Tell me."
            "말해다오."

Key Expression

do good & do harm
do good to ~는 '~에게 도움이 되다, 이롭다'라는 의미이며 do harm to ~은
'~에게 해를 깨치다'라는 뜻을 가지는 표현입니다.

ex) The friend might have meant to do no harm.
그 친구는 해를 깨치지 않으려 했던 것일지도 몰라.

"His name was Ralph Crewe," / Sara answered, / feeling
"아빠 성함은 랄프 크루예요."   새라가 대답했다.   놀라워 하며.

startled. "Captain Crewe. He died in India."
"크루 대위예요.   인도에서 돌아가셨어요."

The haggard face contracted, / and Ram Dass sprang / to
초췌한 얼굴이 일그러졌고,   람 다스가 뛰어왔다

his master's side.
주인 곁으로.

"Carmichael," / the invalid gasped, / "it is the child / ——
"카마이클,"   환자는 숨이 턱 막히며 말했다.   "바로 그 아이야

the child!"
—— 그 아이!"

For a moment / Sara thought / he was going to die. Ram
잠시 동안   새라는 생각했다   그가 죽을 것 같다고.

Dass poured out drops from a bottle, / and held them to
람 다스는 병에서 몇 방울을 따라,   그의 입술로 가져갔다.

his lips. Sara stood near, / trembling a little. She looked /
새라는 가까이 서 있었다.   약간 떨면서.   그녀는 바라보았다

in a bewildered way / at Mr. Carmichael.
당황하며   카마이클을.

"What child am I?" / she faltered.
"제가 무슨 아이라는 말씀인가요?"   주저하며 말했다.

"He was your father's friend," / Mr. Carmichael
"저 분이 네 아버지의 친구란다,"   카마이클 씨가 대답했다.

answered her. "Don't be frightened. We have been
"놀라지 말아라.

looking for you / for two years."
우리는 찾고 있었단다   2년 동안."

Sara put her hand up to her forehead, / and her mouth
새라는 손을 이마에 올리고,   입술이 떨렸다.

trembled. She spoke / as if she were in a dream.
새라는 말했다   마치 꿈속에 있는 듯.

"And I was at Miss Minchin's / all the while," / she half
"그런데 전 민친 교장의 집에 있었군요   그 동안 내내,"   반쯤 속삭이며

whispered. "Just on the other side of the wall."
말했다.   "바로 벽의 반대편에 말이죠."

A. 다음 문장을 해석해 보세요.

(1) "It is because, / though she is not exactly a fairy, / she will be so rich / when she is found / that she will be like a princess / in a fairy tale."
→

(2) "Is it true," / said Nora, / "that her papa gave all his money / to a friend / to put in a mine / that had diamonds in it, / and then / the friend thought / he had lost it all / and ran away / because he felt / as if he was a robber?"
→

(3) Without the help / of an agile, soft-footed Oriental / like Ram Dass, / however, / it could not have been done.
→

(4) Sara realized / how much practice he had had / when he spoke to her / in his nice, encouraging voice.
→

B. 다음 주어진 문구가 알맞은 문장이 되도록 순서를 맞춰보세요.

(1) 그것이 내가 생각을 너무 많이 하지 않도록 막아준단다.
(it / keeps / me / from / thinking / too / much)
→

(2) 그 아이는 크루 대위의 딸보다 훨씬 더 어려요.
(She / is / much / younger / than / Captain Crewe's / little girl)
→

A. (1) 그 이유는요, 비록 그 애가 진짜 요정은 아니지만, 발견되기만 하면 엄청난 부자가 되어 동화 속에 나오는 공주처럼 될 거예요. (2) 노라가 말했다. "그 아이의 아빠가 가진 돈을 모두 친구에게 줘서 다이아몬드 광산에 투자하도록 했고, 그리고 나서 그 친구는 돈을 다 잃었다고 생각하며 자신이 사기꾼이 된 것처럼 느껴서 도망갔

(3) 인도 신사의 표정이 얼마나 지치고 비참했는지!
(How / wearied / and / miserable / the Indian gentleman / looked)
→

(4) 도대체 무엇이 람 다스를 방으로 데려간 것일까?
(What / was / it / that / brought / Ram Dass / into / the room)
→

C. 다음 주어진 문장이 본문의 내용과 맞으면 T, 틀리면 F에 동그라미 하세요.

(1) The Indian gentleman has been looking for a girl of his friend's.
(T / F)

(2) The father of Large Family came home with a girl from Russia.
(T / F)

(3) Sara was guided to meet The Indian gentleman's room by Ram Dass.
(T / F)

(4) Sara could finally meet her father's friend.
(T / F)

D. 의미가 서로 비슷한 것끼리 연결해 보세요.

(1) unavailing ▶   ◀ ① nimble

(2) fret ▶   ◀ ② unsuccessful

(3) agile ▶   ◀ ③ shorten

(4) contract ▶   ◀ ④ worry

다는 것이 사실인가요?" (3) 하지만, 람 다스처럼 날렵하고 조용히 걷는 동양인의 도움이 없었다면 그 일은 할 수 없었을 것이다. (4) 새라는 그가 친절하고, 격려하는 목소리로 자신에게 말을 걸자 그가 얼마나 많은 연습을 했었는지 깨달았다. | B. (1) it keeps me from thinking too much. (2) She is much younger than Captain Crewe's little girl. (3) How wearied and miserable the Indian gentleman looked! (4) What was it that brought Ram Dass into the room? | C. (1) T (2) F (3) T (4) T | D. (1) ② (2) ④ (3) ① (4) ③

A Little Princess를 다시 읽어 보세요.

 1

Sara

Once on a dark winter's day, when the yellow fog hung so thick and heavy in the streets of London that the lamps were lighted and the shop windows blazed with gas as they do at night, an odd-looking little girl sat in a cab with her father and was driven rather slowly through the big thoroughfares.

She sat with her feet tucked under her, and leaned against her father, who held her in his arm, as she stared out of the window at the passing people with a queer old-fashioned thoughtfulness in her big eyes.

She was such a little girl that one did not expect to see such a look on her small face. It would have been an old look for a child of twelve, and Sara Crewe was only seven.

The fact was, however, that she was always dreaming and thinking odd things and could not herself remember any time when she had not been thinking things about grown-up people and the world they belonged to. She felt as if she had lived a long, long time.

At this moment she was remembering the voyage she had just made from Bombay with her father, Captain Crewe. She was thinking of the big ship, of the Lascars passing silently to and fro on it, of the children playing about on the hot deck, and of some young officers' wives who used to try to make her talk to them and laugh at the things she said.

Principally, she was thinking of what a queer thing it was that at one time one was in India in the blazing sun, and then in the middle of the ocean, and then driving in a strange vehicle through strange streets where the day was as dark as the night. She found this so puzzling that she moved closer to her father.

"Papa," she said in a low, mysterious little voice which was almost a whisper, "papa."

"What is it, darling?" Captain Crewe answered, holding her closer and looking down into her face. "What is Sara thinking of?"

"Is this the place?" Sara whispered, cuddling still closer to him. "Is it, papa?"

"Yes, little Sara, it is. We have reached it at last." And though she was only seven years old, she knew that he felt sad when he said it.

It seemed to her many years since he had begun to prepare her mind for "the place," as she always called it. Her mother had died when she was born, so she had never known or missed her. Her young, handsome, rich, petting father seemed to be the only relation she had in the world. They had always played together and been fond of each other. She only knew he was rich because she had heard people say so when they thought she was not listening, and she had also heard them say that when she grew up she would be rich, too. She did not know all that being rich meant. She had always lived in a beautiful bungalow, and had been used to seeing many servants who made salaams to her and called her "Missee Sahib," and gave her her own way in everything. She had had toys and pets and an ayah who worshipped her, and she had gradually learned that people who were rich had these things. That, however, was all she knew about it. During her short life only one thing had troubled her, and that thing was "the place" she was to be taken to some day. The climate of India was very bad for children, and as soon as possible they were sent away from it — generally to England and to school. She had seen other children go away, and had heard their fathers and mothers talk about the letters they received from them. She had known that she would be obliged to go also, and though sometimes her father's stories of the voyage and the new country had attracted her, she had been troubled by the thought that he could not stay with her.

"Couldn't you go to that place with me, papa?" she had asked when she was five years old. "Couldn't you go to school, too? I would help you with your lessons." "But you will not have to stay for a very long time, little Sara," he had always said. "You will go to a nice house where there will be a lot of little girls, and you will play together, and I will send you plenty of books, and you will grow so fast that it will seem scarcely a year before you are big enough and clever enough to come back and take care of papa."

She had liked to think of that. To keep the house for her father; to ride with him, and sit at the head of his table when he had dinner parties; to talk to him and read his books — that would be what she would like most in the world, and if one must go away to "the place" in England to attain it, she must make up her mind to go. She did not care very much for other little girls, but if she had plenty of books she could console herself. She liked books more than anything else, and was, in fact, always inventing stories of beautiful things and telling them to herself. Sometimes she had told them to her father, and he had liked them as much as she did.

"Well, papa," she said softly, "if we are here I suppose we must be resigned." He laughed at her old-fashioned speech and kissed her. He was really not at all resigned himself, though he knew he must keep that a secret. His quaint little Sara had been a great companion to him, and he felt he should be a lonely fellow when, on his return to India, he went into his bungalow knowing he need not expect to see the small figure in its white frock come forward to meet him. So he held her very closely in his arms as the cab rolled into the big, dull square in which stood the house which was their destination.

It was a big, dull, brick house, exactly like all the others in its row, but that on the front door there shone a brass plate on which was engraved in black letters: MISS MINCHIN, Select Seminary for Young Ladies.

"Here we are, Sara," said Captain Crewe, making his voice sound as cheerful as possible. Then he lifted her out of the cab and they mounted the steps and rang the bell. Sara often thought afterward that the house was somehow exactly like

Miss Minchin. It was respectable and well furnished, but everything in it was ugly; and the very armchairs seemed to have hard bones in them. In the hall everything was hard and polished — even the red cheeks of the moon face on the tall clock in the corner had a severe varnished look. The drawing room into which they were ushered was covered by a carpet with a square pattern upon it, the chairs were square, and a heavy marble timepiece stood upon the heavy marble mantel.

As she sat down in one of the stiff mahogany chairs, Sara cast one of her quick looks about her.

"I don't like it, papa," she said. "But then I dare say soldiers — even brave ones — don't really like going into battle."

Captain Crewe laughed outright at this. He was young and full of fun, and he never tired of hearing Sara's queer speeches.

"Oh, little Sara," he said. "What shall I do when I have no one to say solemn things to me? No one else is as solemn as you are."

"But why do solemn things make you laugh so?" inquired Sara.

"Because you are such fun when you say them," he answered, laughing still more. And then suddenly he swept her into his arms and kissed her very hard, stopping laughing all at once and looking almost as if tears had come into his eyes.

It was just then that Miss Minchin entered the room. She was very like her house, Sara felt: tall and dull, and respectable and ugly. She had large, cold, fishy eyes, and a large, cold, fishy smile. It spread itself into a very large smile when she saw Sara and Captain Crewe. She had heard a great many desirable things of the young soldier from the lady who had recommended her school to him. Among other things, she had heard that he was a rich father who was willing to spend a great deal of money on his little daughter.

"It will be a great privilege to have charge of such a beautiful and promising child, Captain Crewe," she said, taking Sara's hand and stroking it. "Lady Meredith has told me of her unusual cleverness. A clever child is a great treasure in an establishment like mine."

Sara stood quietly, with her eyes fixed upon Miss Minchin's face. She was thinking something odd, as usual.

"Why does she say I am a beautiful child?" she was thinking. "I am not beautiful at all. Colonel Grange's little girl, Isobel, is beautiful. She has dimples and rose-colored cheeks, and long hair the color of gold. I have short black hair and green eyes; besides which, I am a thin child and not fair in the least. I am one of the ugliest children I ever saw. She is beginning by telling a story."

She was mistaken, however, in thinking she was an ugly child. She was not in the least like Isobel Grange, who had been the beauty of the regiment, but she had an odd charm of her own. She was a slim, supple creature, rather tall for her age, and had an intense, attractive little face. Her hair was heavy and quite black and only curled at the tips; her eyes were greenish gray, it is true, but they were big, wonderful eyes with long, black lashes, and though she herself did not like the color of them, many other people did. Still she was very firm in her belief that she was an ugly little girl, and she was not at all elated by Miss Minchin's flattery.

"I should be telling a story if I said she was beautiful," she thought; "and I should know I was telling a story. I believe I am as ugly as she is — in my way. What did she say that for?"

After she had known Miss Minchin longer she learned why she had said it. She discovered that she said the same thing to each papa and mamma who brought a child to her school.

Sara stood near her father and listened while he and Miss Minchin talked. She had been brought to the seminary because Lady Meredith's two little girls had been educated there, and Captain Crewe had a great respect for Lady Meredith's experience. Sara was to be what was known as "a parlor boarder," and she was to enjoy even greater privileges than parlor boarders usually did. She was to have a pretty bedroom and sitting room of her own; she was to have a pony and a carriage, and a maid to take the place of the ayah who had been her nurse in India.

"I am not in the least anxious about her education," Captain Crewe said, with his gay laugh, as he held Sara's hand and patted it. "The difficulty will be to keep her from learning too fast and too much. She is always sitting with her little nose burrowing into books. She doesn't read them, Miss Minchin; she gobbles them up as if she were a little wolf instead of a little girl. She is always starving for new books to gobble, and she wants grown-up books — great, big, fat ones — French and German as well as English — history and biography and poets, and all sorts of things. Drag her away from her books when she reads too much. Make her ride her pony in the Row or go out and buy a new doll. She ought to play more with dolls."

"Papa," said Sara, "you see, if I went out and bought a new doll every few days I should have more than I could be fond of. Dolls ought to be intimate friends. Emily is going to be my intimate friend."

Captain Crewe looked at Miss Minchin and Miss Minchin looked at Captain Crewe.

"Who is Emily?" she inquired.

"Tell her, Sara," Captain Crewe said, smiling.

Sara's green-gray eyes looked very solemn and quite soft as she answered.

"She is a doll I haven't got yet," she said. "She is a doll papa is going to buy for me. We are going out together to find her. I have called her Emily. She is going to be my friend when papa is gone. I want her to talk to about him."

Miss Minchin's large, fishy smile became very flattering indeed.

"What an original child!" she said. "What a darling little creature!"

"Yes," said Captain Crewe, drawing Sara close. "She is a darling little creature. Take great care of her for me, Miss Minchin."

Sara stayed with her father at his hotel for several days; in fact, she remained with him until he sailed away again to India. They went out and visited many big shops together, and bought a great many things. They bought, indeed, a great many more things than Sara needed; but Captain Crewe was a rash, innocent young man and wanted his little girl to have everything she admired and everything he admired himself, so between them they collected a wardrobe much too grand for a child of seven. There were velvet dresses trimmed with costly furs, and lace dresses, and embroidered ones, and hats with great, soft ostrich feathers, and ermine coats and muffs, and boxes of tiny gloves and handkerchiefs and silk stockings in such abundant supplies that the polite young women behind the counters whispered to each other that the odd little girl with the big, solemn eyes must be at least some foreign princess — perhaps the little daughter of an Indian rajah.

And at last they found Emily, but they went to a number of toy shops and looked at a great many dolls before they discovered her.

"I want her to look as if she wasn't a doll really," Sara said. "I want her to look as if she listens when I talk to her. The trouble with dolls, papa" — and she put her head on one side and reflected as she said it — "the trouble with dolls is that they never seem to hear." So they looked at big ones and little ones — at dolls with black eyes and dolls with blue — at dolls with brown curls and dolls with golden braids, dolls dressed and dolls undressed.

"You see," Sara said when they were examining one who had no clothes. "If, when I find her, she has no frocks, we can take her to a dressmaker and have her things made to fit. They will fit better if they are tried on."

After a number of disappointments they decided to walk and look in at the shop windows and let the cab follow them. They had passed two or three places without even going in, when, as they were approaching a shop which was really not a very large one, Sara suddenly started and clutched her father's arm.

"Oh, papa!" she cried. "There is Emily!"

A flush had risen to her face and there was an expression in her green-gray eyes as if she had just recognized someone she was intimate with and fond of.

"She is actually waiting there for us!" she said. "Let us go in to her."

"Dear me," said Captain Crewe, "I feel as if we ought to have someone to introduce us."

"You must introduce me and I will introduce you," said Sara. "But I knew her the minute I saw her — so perhaps she knew me, too."

Perhaps she had known her. She had certainly a very intelligent expression in her eyes when Sara took her in her arms. She was a large doll, but not too large to carry about easily; she had naturally curling golden-brown hair, which hung like a mantle about her, and her eyes were a deep, clear, gray-blue, with soft, thick eyelashes which were real eyelashes and not mere painted lines.

"Of course," said Sara, looking into her face as she held her on her knee, "of course papa, this is Emily."

So Emily was bought and actually taken to a children's outfitter's shop and measured for a wardrobe as grand as Sara's own. She had lace frocks, too, and velvet and muslin ones, and hats and coats and beautiful lace-trimmed underclothes, and gloves and handkerchiefs and furs.

"I should like her always to look as if she was a child with a good mother," said Sara. "I'm her mother, though I am going to make a companion of her."

Captain Crewe would really have enjoyed the shopping tremendously, but that a sad thought kept tugging at his heart. This all meant that he was going to be separated from his beloved, quaint little comrade.

He got out of his bed in the middle of that night and went and stood looking down at Sara, who lay asleep with Emily in her arms. Her black hair was spread out on the pillow and Emily's golden-brown hair mingled with it, both of them had lace-ruffled nightgowns, and both had long eyelashes which lay and curled up on their cheeks. Emily looked so like a real child that Captain Crewe felt glad she was there. He drew a big sigh and pulled his mustache with a boyish expression.

"Heigh-ho, little Sara!" he said to himself "I don't believe you know how much your daddy will miss you."

The next day he took her to Miss Minchin's and left her there. He was to sail away the next morning. He explained to Miss Minchin that his solicitors, Messrs. Barrow & Skipworth, had charge of his affairs in England and would give her any advice she wanted, and that they would pay the bills she sent in for Sara's expenses. He would write to Sara twice a week, and she was to be given every pleasure she asked for.

"She is a sensible little thing, and she never wants anything it isn't safe to give her," he said.

Then he went with Sara into her little sitting room and they bade each other good-by. Sara sat on his knee and held the lapels of his coat in her small hands, and looked long and hard at his face.

"Are you learning me by heart, little Sara?" he said, stroking her hair.

"No," she answered. "I know you by heart. You are inside my heart." And they put their arms round each other and kissed as if they would never let each other go.

When the cab drove away from the door, Sara was sitting on the floor of her sitting room, with her hands under her chin and her eyes following it until it had turned the corner of the square. Emily was sitting by her, and she looked after it, too. When Miss Minchin sent her sister, Miss Amelia, to see what the child was doing, she found she could not open the door.

"I have locked it," said a queer, polite little voice from inside. "I want to be quite by myself, if you please."

Miss Amelia was fat and dumpy, and stood very much in awe of her sister. She was really the better-natured person of the two, but she never disobeyed Miss Minchin. She went downstairs again, looking almost alarmed.

"I never saw such a funny, old-fashioned child, sister," she said. "She has locked herself in, and she is not making the least particle of noise."

"It is much better than if she kicked and screamed, as some of them do," Miss Minchin answered. "I expected that a child as much spoiled as she is would set the whole house in an uproar. If ever a child was given her own way in everything, she is."

"I've been opening her trunks and putting her things away," said Miss Amelia. "I never saw anything like them — sable and ermine on her coats, and real Valenciennes lace on her underclothing. You have seen some of her clothes. What do you think of them?"

"I think they are perfectly ridiculous," replied Miss Minchin, sharply; "but they will look very well at the head of the line when we take the schoolchildren to church on Sunday. She has been provided for as if she were a little princess."

And upstairs in the locked room Sara and Emily sat on the floor and stared at the corner round which the cab had disappeared, while Captain Crewe looked backward, waving and kissing his hand as if he could not bear to stop.

 2

Ermengarde

On that first morning, when Sara sat at Miss Minchin's side, aware that the whole schoolroom was devoting itself to observing her, she had noticed very soon one little girl, about her own age, who looked at her very hard with a pair of light, rather dull, blue eyes. She was a fat child who did not look as if she were in the least clever, but she had a goodnaturedly pouting mouth. Her flaxen hair was braided in a tight pigtail, tied with a ribbon, and she had pulled this pigtail around her neck, and was biting the end of the ribbon, resting her elbows on the desk, as she stared wonderingly at the new pupil. When Monsieur Dufarge began to speak to Sara, she looked a little frightened; and when Sara stepped forward and, looking at him with the innocent, appealing eyes, answered him, without any warning, in French, the fat little girl gave a startled jump, and grew quite red in her awed amazement. Having wept hopeless tears for weeks in her efforts to remember that "la mere" meant "the mother," and "le pere," "the father," — when one spoke sensible English — it was almost too much for her suddenly to find herself listening to a child her own age who seemed not only quite familiar with these words, but apparently knew any number of others, and could mix them up with verbs as if they were mere trifles.

She stared so hard and bit the ribbon on her pigtail so fast that she attracted the attention of Miss Minchin, who, feeling extremely cross at the moment, immediately pounced upon her.

"Miss St. John!" she exclaimed severely. "What do you mean by such conduct? Remove your elbows! Take your ribbon out of your mouth! Sit up at once!"

Upon which Miss St. John gave another jump, and when Lavinia and Jessie tittered she became redder than ever — so red, indeed, that she almost looked as if tears were coming into her poor, dull, childish eyes; and Sara saw her and was so sorry for her that she began rather to like her and want to be her friend. It was a way of hers always to want to spring into any fray in which someone was made uncomfortable or unhappy.

"If Sara had been a boy and lived a few centuries ago," her father used to say, "she would have gone about the country with her sword drawn, rescuing and defending everyone in distress. She always wants to fight when she sees people in trouble."

So she took rather a fancy to fat, slow, little Miss St. John, and kept glancing toward her through the morning. She saw that lessons were no easy matter to her, and that there was no danger of her ever being spoiled by being treated as a show pupil. Her French lesson was a pathetic thing. Her pronunciation made even Monsieur Dufarge smile in spite of himself, and Lavinia and Jessie and the more fortunate girls either giggled or looked at her in wondering disdain. But Sara did not laugh. She tried to look as if she did not hear when Miss St. John called "le bon pain," "lee bong pang." She had a fine, hot little temper of her own, and it made her feel rather savage when she heard the titters and saw the poor, stupid, distressed child's face.

"It isn't funny, really," she said between her teeth, as she bent over her book. "They ought not to laugh."

When lessons were over and the pupils gathered together in groups to talk, Sara looked for Miss St. John, and finding her bundled rather disconsolately in a window-seat, she walked over to her and spoke. She only said the kind of thing little girls always say to each other by way of beginning an acquaintance, but there was something friendly about Sara, and people always felt it.

"What is your name?" she said.

To explain Miss St. John's amazement one must recall that a new pupil is, for a short time, a somewhat uncertain thing; and of this new pupil the entire school had talked the night before until it fell asleep quite exhausted by excitement and contradictory stories. A new pupil with a carriage and a pony and a maid, and a voyage from India to discuss, was not an ordinary acquaintance.

"My name's Ermengarde St. John," she answered.

"Mine is Sara Crewe," said Sara. "Yours is very pretty. It sounds like a story book."

"Do you like it?" fluttered Ermengarde. "I — I like yours."

Miss St. John's chief trouble in life was that she had a clever father. Sometimes this seemed to her a dreadful calamity. If you have a father who knows everything, who speaks seven or eight languages, and has thousands of volumes which he has apparently learned by heart, he frequently expects you to be familiar with the contents of your lesson books at least; and it is not improbable that he will feel you ought to be able to remember a few incidents of history and to write a French exercise. Ermengarde was a severe trial to Mr. St. John. He could not understand how a child of his could be a notably and unmistakably dull creature who never shone in anything.

"Good heavens!" he had said more than once, as he stared at her, "there are times when I think she is as stupid as her Aunt Eliza!"

If her Aunt Eliza had been slow to learn and quick to forget a thing entirely when she had learned it, Ermengarde was strikingly like her. She was the monumental dunce of the school, and it could not be denied.

"She must be made to learn," her father said to Miss Minchin.

Consequently Ermengarde spent the greater part of her life in disgrace or in tears. She learned things and forgot them; or, if she remembered them, she did not understand them. So it was natural that, having made Sara's acquaintance, she should sit and stare at her with profound admiration.

"You can speak French, can't you?" she said respectfully.

Sara got on to the window-seat, which was a big, deep one, and, tucking up her feet, sat with her hands clasped round her knees.

"I can speak it because I have heard it all my life," she answered. "You could speak it if you had always heard it."

"Oh, no, I couldn't," said Ermengarde. "I never could speak it!"

"Why?" inquired Sara, curiously.

Ermengarde shook her head so that the pigtail wobbled.

"You heard me just now," she said. "I'm always like that. I can't say the words. They're so queer."

She paused a moment, and then added with a touch of awe in her voice, "You are clever, aren't you?"

Sara looked out of the window into the dingy square, where the sparrows were hopping and twittering on the wet, iron railings and the sooty branches of the trees. She reflected a few moments. She had heard it said very often that she was "clever," and she wondered if she was — and if she was, how it had happened.

"I don't know," she said. "I can't tell." Then, seeing a mournful look on the round, chubby face, she gave a little laugh and changed the subject.

"Would you like to see Emily?" she inquired.

"Who is Emily?" Ermengarde asked, just as Miss Minchin had done.

"Come up to my room and see," said Sara, holding out her hand.

They jumped down from the window-seat together, and went upstairs.

"Is it true," Ermengarde whispered, as they went through the hall — "is it true that you have a playroom all to yourself?"

"Yes," Sara answered. "Papa asked Miss Minchin to let me have one, because — well, it was because when I play I make up stories and tell them to myself, and I don't like people to hear me. It spoils it if I think people listen."

They had reached the passage leading to Sara's room by this time, and Ermengarde stopped short, staring, and quite losing her breath.

"You make up stories!" she gasped. "Can you do that — as well as speak French? Can you?"

Sara looked at her in simple surprise.

"Why, anyone can make up things," she said. "Have you never tried?"

She put her hand warningly on Ermengarde's.

"Let us go very quietly to the door," she whispered, "and then I will open it quite suddenly; perhaps we may catch her."

She was half laughing, but there was a touch of mysterious hope in her eyes which fascinated Ermengarde, though she had not the remotest idea what it meant, or whom it was she wanted to "catch," or why she wanted to catch her. Whatsoever she meant, Ermengarde was sure it was something delightfully exciting. So, quite thrilled with expectation, she followed her on tiptoe along the passage. They made not the least noise until they reached the door. Then Sara suddenly turned the handle, and threw it wide open. Its opening revealed the room quite neat and quiet, a fire gently burning in the grate, and a wonderful doll sitting in a chair by it, apparently reading a book.

"Oh, she got back to her seat before we could see her!" Sara explained. "Of course they always do. They are as quick as lightning."

Ermengarde looked from her to the doll and back again.

"Can she — walk?" she asked breathlessly.

"Yes," answered Sara. "At least I believe she can. At least I pretend I believe she can. And that makes it seem as if it were true. Have you never pretended things?"

"No," said Ermengarde. "Never. I — tell me about it."

She was so bewitched by this odd, new companion that she actually stared at Sara instead of at Emily — notwithstanding that Emily was the most attractive doll person she had ever seen.

"Let us sit down," said Sara, "and I will tell you. It's so easy that when you begin you can't stop. You just go on and on doing it always. And it's beautiful. Emily, you must listen. This is Ermengarde St. John, Emily. Ermengarde, this is Emily. Would you like to hold her?"

"Oh, may I?" said Ermengarde. "May I, really? She is beautiful!" And Emily was put into her arms.

Never in her dull, short life had Miss St. John dreamed of such an hour as the one she spent with the queer new pupil before they heard the lunch-bell ring and were obliged to go downstairs.

Sara sat upon the hearth-rug and told her strange things. She sat rather huddled up, and her green eyes shone and her cheeks flushed. She told stories of the voyage, and stories of India; but what fascinated Ermengarde the most was her fancy about the dolls who walked and talked, and who could do anything they chose when the human beings were out of the room, but who must keep their powers a secret and so flew back to their places "like lightning" when people returned to the room.

"We couldn't do it," said Sara, seriously. "You see, it's a kind of magic."

Once, when she was relating the story of the search for Emily, Ermengarde saw her face suddenly change. A cloud seemed to pass over it and put out the light in her shining eyes. She drew her breath in so sharply that it made a funny, sad little sound, and then she shut her lips and held them tightly closed, as if she was determined either to do or not to do something. Ermengarde had an idea that if she had been like any other little girl, she might have suddenly burst out sobbing and crying. But she did not.

"Have you a — a pain?" Ermengarde ventured.

"Yes," Sara answered, after a moment's silence. "But it is not in my body." Then she added something in a low voice which she tried to keep quite steady, and it was this: "Do you love your father more than anything else in all the whole world?"

Ermengarde's mouth fell open a little. She knew that it would be far from behaving like a respectable child at a select seminary to say that it had never occurred to you that you could love your father, that you would do anything desperate to avoid being left alone in his society for ten minutes. She was, indeed, greatly embarrassed.

"I — I scarcely ever see him," she stammered. "He is always in the library — reading things."

"I love mine more than all the world ten times over," Sara said. "That is what my pain is. He has gone away."

She put her head quietly down on her little, huddled-up knees, and sat very still for a few minutes.

"She's going to cry out loud," thought Ermengarde, fearfully.

But she did not. Her short, black locks tumbled about her ears, and she sat still. Then she spoke without lifting her head.

"I promised him I would bear it," she said. "And I will. You have to bear things. Think what soldiers bear! Papa is a soldier. If there was a war he would have to bear marching and thirstiness and, perhaps, deep wounds. And he would never say a word — not one word."

Ermengarde could only gaze at her, but she felt that she was beginning to adore her. She was so wonderful and different from anyone else.

Presently, she lifted her face and shook back her black locks, with a queer little smile.

"If I go on talking and talking," she said, "and telling you things about pretending, I shall bear it better. You don't forget, but you bear it better."

Ermengarde did not know why a lump came into her throat and her eyes felt as if tears were in them.

"Lavinia and Jessie are 'best friends,'" she said rather huskily. "I wish we could be 'best friends.' Would you have me for yours? You're clever, and I'm the stupidest child in the school, but I — oh, I do so like you!"

"I'm glad of that," said Sara. "It makes you thankful when you are liked. Yes. We will be friends. And I'll tell you what" — a sudden gleam lighting her face — "I can help you with your French lessons."

3

Lottie

If Sara had been a different kind of child, the life she led at Miss Minchin's Select Seminary for the next few years would not have been at all good for her. She was treated more as if she were a distinguished guest at the establishment than as if she were a mere little girl. If she had been a self-opinionated, domineering child, she might have become disagreeable enough to be unbearable through being so much indulged and flattered. If she had been an indolent child, she would have learned nothing. Privately Miss Minchin disliked her, but she was far too worldly a woman to do or say anything which might make such a desirable pupil wish to leave her school. She knew quite well that if Sara wrote to her papa to tell him she was uncomfortable or unhappy, Captain Crewe would remove her at once. Miss Minchin's opinion was that if a child were continually praised and never forbidden to do what she liked, she would be sure to be fond of the place where she was so treated. Accordingly, Sara was praised for her quickness at her lessons, for her good manners, for her amiability to her fellow pupils, for her generosity if she gave sixpence to a beggar out of her full little purse; the simplest thing she did was treated as if it were a virtue, and if she had not had a disposition and a clever little brain, she might have been a very self-satisfied young person. But the clever little brain told her a great many sensible and true things about herself and her circumstances, and now and then she talked these things over to Ermengarde as time went on.

"Things happen to people by accident," she used to say. "A lot of nice accidents have happened to me. It just happened that I always liked lessons and books, and could remember things when I learned them. It just happened that I was born with a father who was beautiful and nice and clever, and could give me everything I liked. Perhaps I have not really a good temper at all, but if you have everything you want and everyone is kind to you, how can you help but be good-tempered? I don't know" — looking quite serious — "how I shall ever find out whether I am really a nice child or a horrid one. Perhaps I'm a hideous child, and no one will ever know, just because I never have any trials."

"Lavinia has no trials," said Ermengarde, stolidly, "and she is horrid enough."

Sara rubbed the end of her little nose reflectively, as she thought the matter over.

"Well," she said at last, "perhaps — perhaps that is because Lavinia is growing." This was the result of a charitable recollection of having heard Miss Amelia say that Lavinia was growing so fast that she believed it affected her health and temper.

Lavinia, in fact, was spiteful. She was inordinately jealous of Sara. Until the new pupil's arrival, she had felt herself the leader in the school. She had led because she was capable of making herself extremely disagreeable if the others did not follow her. She domineered over the little children, and assumed grand airs with those big enough to be her companions. She was rather pretty, and had been the best-dressed pupil in the procession when the Select Seminary walked out two by two, until Sara's velvet coats and sable muffs appeared, combined with drooping ostrich feathers, and were led by Miss Minchin at the head of the line. This, at the beginning, had been bitter enough; but as time went on it became apparent that Sara was a leader, too, and not because she could make herself disagreeable, but because she never did.

"There's one thing about Sara Crewe," Jessie had enraged her "best friend" by saying honestly, "she's never 'grand' about herself the least bit, and you know she might be, Lavvie. I believe I couldn't help being — just a little — if I had so many fine things and was made such a fuss over. It's disgusting, the way Miss Minchin shows her off when parents come."

"'Dear Sara must come into the drawing room and talk to Mrs. Musgrave about India,'" mimicked Lavinia, in her most highly flavored imitation of Miss Minchin. "'Dear Sara must speak French to Lady Pitkin. Her accent is so perfect.' She didn't learn her French at the Seminary, at any rate. And there's nothing so clever in her knowing it. She says herself she didn't learn it at all. She just picked it up, because she always heard her papa speak it. And, as to her papa, there is nothing so grand in being an Indian officer."

"Well," said Jessie, slowly, "he's killed tigers. He killed the one in the skin Sara has in her room. That's why she likes it so. She lies on it and strokes its head, and talks to it as if it was a cat."

"She's always doing something silly," snapped Lavinia. "My mamma says that way of hers of pretending things is silly. She says she will grow up eccentric."

It was quite true that Sara was never "grand." She was a friendly little soul, and shared her privileges and belongings with a free hand. The little ones, who were accustomed to being disdained and ordered out of the way by mature ladies aged ten and twelve, were never made to cry by this most envied of them all. She was a motherly young person, and when people fell down and scraped their knees, she ran and helped them up and patted them, or found in her pocket a bonbon or some other article of a soothing nature. She never pushed them out of her way or alluded to their years as a humiliation and a blot upon their small characters.

"If you are four you are four," she said severely to Lavinia on an occasion of her having — it must be confessed — slapped Lottie and called her "a brat;" "but you will be five next year, and six the year after that. And," opening large, convicting eyes, "it takes sixteen years to make you twenty."

"Dear me," said Lavinia, "how we can calculate!" In fact, it was not to be denied that sixteen and four made twenty — and twenty was an age the most daring were scarcely bold enough to dream of.

So the younger children adored Sara. More than once she had been known to have a tea party, made up of these despised ones, in her own room. And Emily had been played with, and Emily's own tea service used — the one with cups which held quite a lot of much-sweetened weak tea and had blue flowers on them. No one had seen such a very real doll's tea set before. From that afternoon Sara was regarded as a goddess and a queen by the entire alphabet class.

Lottle Legh worshipped her to such an extent that if Sara had not been a motherly person, she would have found her tiresome. Lottie had been sent to school by a rather flighty young papa who could not imagine what else to do with her. Her young mother had died, and as the child had been treated like a favorite doll or a very spoiled pet monkey or lap dog ever since the first hour of her life, she was a very appalling little creature. When she wanted anything or did not want anything she wept and howled; and, as she always wanted the things she could not have, and did not want the things that were best for her, her shrill little voice was usually to be heard uplifted in wails in one part of the house or another.

Her strongest weapon was that in some mysterious way she had found out that a very small girl who had lost her mother was a person who ought to be pitied and made much of. She had probably heard some grown-up people talking her over in the early days, after her mother's death. So it became her habit to make great use of this knowledge.

The first time Sara took her in charge was one morning when, on passing a sitting room, she heard both Miss Minchin and Miss Amelia trying to suppress the angry wails of some child who, evidently, refused to be silenced. She refused so strenuously indeed that Miss Minchin was obliged to almost shout — in a stately and severe manner — to make herself heard.

"What is she crying for?" she almost yelled.

"Oh — oh — oh!" Sara heard; "I haven't got any mam — ma-a!"

"Oh, Lottie!" screamed Miss Amelia. "Do stop, darling! Don't cry! Please don't!"

"Oh! Oh! Oh! Oh! Oh!" Lottle howled tempestuously. "Haven't — got — any —

mam — ma-a!"

"She ought to be whipped," Miss Minchin proclaimed. "You shall be whipped, you naughty child!"

Lottle wailed more loudly than ever. Miss Amelia began to cry. Miss Minchin's voice rose until it almost thundered, then suddenly she sprang up from her chair in impotent indignation and flounced out of the room, leaving Miss Amelia to arrange the matter.

Sara had paused in the hall, wondering if she ought to go into the room, because she had recently begun a friendly acquaintance with Lottie and might be able to quiet her. When Miss Minchin came out and saw her, she looked rather annoyed. She realized that her voice, as heard from inside the room, could not have sounded either dignified or amiable.

"Oh, Sara!" she exclaimed, endeavoring to produce a suitable smile.

"I stopped," explained Sara, "because I knew it was Lottie — and I thought, perhaps — just perhaps, I could make her be quiet. May I try, Miss Minchin?"

"If you can, you are a clever child," answered Miss Minchin, drawing in her mouth sharply. Then, seeing that Sara looked slightly chilled by her asperity, she changed her manner. "But you are clever in everything," she said in her approving way. "I dare say you can manage her. Go in." And she left her.

When Sara entered the room, Lottie was lying upon the floor, screaming and kicking her small fat legs violently, and Miss Amelia was bending over her in consternation and despair, looking quite red and damp with heat. Lottie had always found, when in her own nursery at home, that kicking and screaming would always be quieted by any means she insisted on. Poor plump Miss Amelia was trying first one method, and then another.

"Poor darling," she said one moment, "I know you haven't any mamma, poor — "
Then in quite another tone, "If you don't stop, Lottie, I will shake you. Poor little angel! There —! You wicked, bad, detestable child, I will smack you! I will!"

Sara went to them quietly. She did not know at all what she was going to do, but she had a vague inward conviction that it would be better not to say such different kinds of things quite so helplessly and excitedly.

"Miss Amelia," she said in a low voice, "Miss Minchin says I may try to make her stop — may I?"

Miss Amelia turned and looked at her hopelessly. "Oh, do you think you can?" she gasped.

"I don't know whether I can," answered Sara, still in her half-whisper; "but I will try."

Miss Amelia stumbled up from her knees with a heavy sigh, and Lottie's fat little legs kicked as hard as ever.

"If you will steal out of the room," said Sara, "I will stay with her."

"Oh, Sara!" almost whimpered Miss Amelia. "We never had such a dreadful child before. I don't believe we can keep her."

But she crept out of the room, and was very much relieved to find an excuse for doing it.

Sara stood by the howling furious child for a few moments, and looked down at her without saying anything. Then she sat down flat on the floor beside her and waited. Except for Lottie's angry screams, the room was quite quiet. This was a new state of affairs for little Miss Legh, who was accustomed, when she screamed, to hear other people protest and implore and command and coax by turns. To lie and kick and shriek, and find the only person near you not seeming to mind in the least, attracted her attention. She opened her tight-shut streaming eyes to see who this person was. And it was only another little girl. But it was the one who owned Emily and all the nice things. And she was looking at her steadily and as if she was merely thinking. Having paused for a few seconds to find this out, Lottie thought she must begin again, but the quiet of the room and of Sara's odd, interested face made her first howl rather half-hearted.

"I — haven't — any — ma — ma — ma-a!" she announced; but her voice was not so strong.

Sara looked at her still more steadily, but with a sort of understanding in her eyes.

"Neither have I," she said.

This was so unexpected that it was astounding. Lottie actually dropped her legs, gave a wriggle, and lay and stared. A new idea will stop a crying child when nothing else will. Also it was true that while Lottie disliked Miss Minchin, who was cross, and Miss Amelia, who was foolishly indulgent, she rather liked Sara, little as she knew her. She did not want to give up her grievance, but her thoughts were distracted from it, so she wriggled again, and, after a sulky sob, said, "Where is she?"

Sara paused a moment. Because she had been told that her mamma was in heaven, she had thought a great deal about the matter, and her thoughts had not been quite like those of other people.

"She went to heaven," she said. "But I am sure she comes out sometimes to see me — though I don't see her. So does yours. Perhaps they can both see us now. Perhaps they are both in this room."

Lottle sat bolt upright, and looked about her. She was a pretty, little, curly-headed creature, and her round eyes were like wet forget-me-nots. If her mamma had seen her during the last half-hour, she might not have thought her the kind of child who ought to be related to an angel.

Sara went on talking. Perhaps some people might think that what she said was rather like a fairy story, but it was all so real to her own imagination that Lottie began to listen in spite of herself. She had been told that her mamma had wings and a crown, and she had been shown pictures of ladies in beautiful white nightgowns, who were said to be angels. But Sara seemed to be telling a real story about a lovely country where real people were.

"There are fields and fields of flowers," she said, forgetting herself, as usual, when she began, and talking rather as if she were in a dream, "fields and fields of lilies — and when the soft wind blows over them it wafts the scent of them into the air — and everybody always breathes it, because the soft wind is always blowing. And little children run about in the lily fields and gather armfuls of them, and laugh and make little wreaths. And the streets are shining. And people are never tired, however far they walk. They can float anywhere they like. And there are walls made of pearl and gold all round the city, but they are low enough for the people to go and lean on them, and look down on to the earth and smile, and send beautiful messages."

Whatsoever story she had begun to tell, Lottie would, no doubt, have stopped crying, and been fascinated into listening; but there was no denying that this story was prettier than most others. She dragged herself close to Sara, and drank in every word until the end came — far too soon. When it did come, she was so sorry that she put up her lip ominously.

"I want to go there," she cried. "I — haven't any mamma in this school."

Sara saw the danger signal, and came out of her dream. She took hold of the chubby hand and pulled her close to her side with a coaxing little laugh.

"I will be your mamma," she said. "We will play that you are my little girl. And Emily shall be your sister."

Lottie's dimples all began to show themselves.

"Shall she?" she said.

"Yes," answered Sara, jumping to her feet. "Let us go and tell her. And then I will wash your face and brush your hair."

To which Lottie agreed quite cheerfully, and trotted out of the room and upstairs with her, without seeming even to remember that the whole of the last hour's tragedy had been caused by the fact that she had refused to be washed and brushed for lunch and Miss Minchin had been called in to use her majestic authority.

And from that time Sara was an adopted mother.

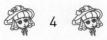 4

Becky

Of course the greatest power Sara possessed and the one which gained her even more followers than her luxuries and the fact that she was "the show pupil," the power that Lavinia and certain other girls were most envious of, and at the same time most fascinated by in spite of themselves, was her power of telling stories and of making everything she talked about seem like a story, whether it was one

287

or not.

Anyone who has been at school with a teller of stories knows what the wonder means — how he or she is followed about and besought in a whisper to relate romances; how groups gather round and hang on the outskirts of the favored party in the hope of being allowed to join in and listen. Sara not only could tell stories, but she adored telling them. When she sat or stood in the midst of a circle and began to invent wonderful things, her green eyes grew big and shining, her cheeks flushed, and, without knowing that she was doing it, she began to act and made what she told lovely or alarming by the raising or dropping of her voice, the bend and sway of her slim body, and the dramatic movement of her hands. She forgot that she was talking to listening children; she saw and lived with the fairy folk, or the kings and queens and beautiful ladies, whose adventures she was narrating. Sometimes when she had finished her story, she was quite out of breath with excitement, and would lay her hand on her thin, little, quick-rising chest, and half laugh as if at herself.

"When I am telling it," she would say, "it doesn't seem as if it was only made up. It seems more real than you are — more real than the schoolroom. I feel as if I were all the people in the story — one after the other. It is queer."

She had been at Miss Minchin's school about two years when, one foggy winter's afternoon, as she was getting out of her carriage, comfortably wrapped up in her warmest velvets and furs and looking very much grander than she knew, she caught sight, as she crossed the pavement, of a dingy little figure standing on the area steps, and stretching its neck so that its wide-open eyes might peer at her through the railings. Something in the eagerness and timidity of the smudgy face made her look at it, and when she looked she smiled because it was her way to smile at people.

But the owner of the smudgy face and the wide-open eyes evidently was afraid that she ought not to have been caught looking at pupils of importance. She dodged out of sight like a jack-in-the-box and scurried back into the kitchen, disappearing so suddenly that if she had not been such a poor little forlorn thing, Sara would have laughed in spite of herself. That very evening, as Sara was sitting in the midst of a group of listeners in a corner of the schoolroom telling one of her stories, the very same figure timidly entered the room, carrying a coal box much too heavy for her, and knelt down upon the hearth rug to replenish the fire and sweep up the ashes.

She was cleaner than she had been when she peeped through the area railings, but she looked just as frightened. She was evidently afraid to look at the children or seem to be listening. She put on pieces of coal cautiously with her fingers so that she might make no disturbing noise, and she swept about the fire irons very softly. But Sara saw in two minutes that she was deeply interested in what was going on, and that she was doing her work slowly in the hope of catching a word here and there. And realizing this, she raised her voice and spoke more clearly. "The Mermaids swam softly about in the crystal-green water, and dragged after them a fishing-net woven of deep-sea pearls," she said. "The Princess sat on the white rock and watched them."

It was a wonderful story about a princess who was loved by a Prince Merman, and went to live with him in shining caves under the sea.

The small drudge before the grate swept the hearth once and then swept it again. Having done it twice, she did it three times; and, as she was doing it the third time, the sound of the story so lured her to listen that she fell under the spell and actually forgot that she had no right to listen at all, and also forgot everything else. She sat down upon her heels as she knelt on the hearth rug, and the brush hung idly in her fingers. The voice of the storyteller went on and drew her with it into winding grottos under the sea, glowing with soft, clear blue light, and paved with pure golden sands. Strange sea flowers and grasses waved about her, and far away faint singing and music echoed.

The hearth brush fell from the work-roughened hand, and Lavinia Herbert looked round.

"That girl has been listening," she said.

The culprit snatched up her brush, and scrambled to her feet. She caught at the coal box and simply scuttled out of the room like a frightened rabbit.

Sara felt rather hot-tempered.

"I knew she was listening," she said. "Why shouldn't she?"

Lavinia tossed her head with great elegance.

"Well," she remarked, "I do not know whether your mamma would like you to tell stories to servant girls, but I know my mamma wouldn't like me to do it."

"My mamma!" said Sara, looking odd. "I don't believe she would mind in the least. She knows that stories belong to everybody."

"I thought," retorted Lavinia, in severe recollection, "that your mamma was dead. How can she know things?"

"Do you think she doesn't know things?" said Sara, in her stern little voice. Sometimes she had a rather stern little voice.

"Sara's mamma knows everything," piped in Lottie. "So does my mamma — 'cept Sara is my mamma at Miss Minchin's — my other one knows everything. The streets are shining, and there are fields and fields of lilies, and everybody gathers them. Sara tells me when she puts me to bed."

"You wicked thing," said Lavinia, turning on Sara; "making fairy stories about heaven."

"There are much more splendid stories in Revelation," returned Sara. "Just look and see! How do you know mine are fairy stories? But I can tell you" — with a fine bit of unheavenly temper — "you will never find out whether they are or not if you're not kinder to people than you are now. Come along, Lottie." And she marched out of the room, rather hoping that she might see the little servant again somewhere, but she found no trace of her when she got into the hall.

"Who is that little girl who makes the fires?" she asked Mariette that night.

Mariette broke forth into a flow of description.

Ah, indeed, Mademoiselle Sara might well ask. She was a forlorn little thing who had just taken the place of scullery maid — though, as to being scullery maid, she was everything else besides. She blacked boots and grates, and carried heavy coal-scuttles up and down stairs, and scrubbed floors and cleaned windows, and was ordered about by everybody. She was fourteen years old, but was so stunted in growth that she looked about twelve. In truth, Mariette was sorry for her. She was so timid that if one chanced to speak to her it appeared as if her poor, frightened eyes would jump out of her head.

"What is her name?" asked Sara, who had sat by the table, with her chin on her hands, as she listened absorbedly to the recital.

Her name was Becky. Mariette heard everyone belowstairs calling, "Becky, do this," and "Becky, do that," every five minutes in the day.

Sara sat and looked into the fire, reflecting on Becky for some time after Mariette left her. She made up a story of which Becky was the ill-used heroine. She thought she looked as if she had never had quite enough to eat. Her very eyes were hungry. She hoped she should see her again, but though she caught sight of her carrying things up or down stairs on several occasions, she always seemed in such a hurry and so afraid of being seen that it was impossible to speak to her.

But a few weeks later, on another foggy afternoon, when she entered her sitting room she found herself confronting a rather pathetic picture. In her own special and pet easy-chair before the bright fire, Becky — with a coal smudge on her nose and several on her apron, with her poor little cap hanging half off her head, and an empty coal box on the floor near her — sat fast asleep, tired out beyond even the endurance of her hard-working young body. She had been sent up to put the bedrooms in order for the evening. There were a great many of them, and she had been running about all day. Sara's rooms she had saved until the last. They were not like the other rooms, which were plain and bare. Ordinary pupils were expected to be satisfied with mere necessaries. Sara's comfortable sitting room seemed a bower of luxury to the scullery maid, though it was, in fact, merely a nice, bright little room. But there were pictures and books in it, and curious things from India; there was a sofa and the low, soft chair; Emily sat in a chair of her own, with the air of a presiding goddess, and there was always a glowing fire and a polished grate. Becky saved it until the end of her afternoon's work, because it rested her to go into it, and she always hoped to snatch a few minutes to sit down in the soft chair and look about her, and think about the wonderful good fortune of the child who owned such surroundings and who went out on the cold days in beautiful hats and coats one tried to catch a glimpse of through the area railing.

On this afternoon, when she had sat down, the sensation of relief to her short, aching legs had been so wonderful and delightful that it had seemed to soothe her whole body, and the glow of warmth and comfort from the fire had crept over her like a spell, until, as she looked at the red coals, a tired, slow smile stole over her smudged face, her head nodded forward without her being aware of it, her eyes drooped, and she fell fast asleep. She had really been only about ten minutes in the room when Sara entered, but she was in as deep a sleep as if she had been, like the Sleeping Beauty, slumbering for a hundred years. But she did not look — poor Becky — like a Sleeping Beauty at all. She looked only like an ugly, stunted, worn-out little scullery drudge.

Sara seemed as much unlike her as if she were a creature from another world. On this particular afternoon she had been taking her dancing lesson, and the afternoon on which the dancing master appeared was rather a grand occasion at the seminary, though it occurred every week. The pupils were attired in their prettiest frocks, and as Sara danced particularly well, she was very much brought forward, and Mariette was requested to make her as diaphanous and fine as possible.

Today a frock the color of a rose had been put on her, and Mariette had bought some real buds and made her a wreath to wear on her black locks. She had been learning a new, delightful dance in which she had been skimming and flying about the room, like a large rose-colored butterfly, and the enjoyment and exercise had brought a brilliant, happy glow into her face.

When she entered the room, she floated in with a few of the butterfly steps — and there sat Becky, nodding her cap sideways off her head.

"Oh!" cried Sara, softly, when she saw her. "That poor thing!"

It did not occur to her to feel cross at finding her pet chair occupied by the small, dingy figure. To tell the truth, she was quite glad to find it there. When the ill-used heroine of her story wakened, she could talk to her. She crept toward her quietly, and stood looking at her. Becky gave a little snore.

"I wish she'd waken herself," Sara said. "I don't like to waken her. But Miss Minchin would be cross if she found out. I'll just wait a few minutes."

She took a seat on the edge of the table, and sat swinging her slim, rose-colored legs, and wondering what it would be best to do. Miss Amelia might come in at any moment, and if she did, Becky would be sure to be scolded.

"But she is so tired," she thought. "She is so tired!"

A piece of flaming coal ended her perplexity for her that very moment. It broke off from a large lump and fell on to the fender. Becky started, and opened her eyes with a frightened gasp. She did not know she had fallen asleep. She had only sat down for one moment and felt the beautiful glow — and here she found herself staring in wild alarm at the wonderful pupil, who sat perched quite near her, like a rose-colored fairy, with interested eyes.

She sprang up and clutched at her cap. She felt it dangling over her ear, and tried wildly to put it straight. Oh, she had got herself into trouble now with a vengeance! To have impudently fallen asleep on such a young lady's chair! She would be turned out of doors without wages.

She made a sound like a big breathless sob.

"Oh, miss! Oh, miss!" she stuttered. "I arst yer pardon, miss! Oh, I do, miss!"

Sara jumped down, and came quite close to her.

"Don't be frightened," she said, quite as if she had been speaking to a little girl like herself. "It doesn't matter the least bit."

"I didn't go to do it, miss," protested Becky. "It was the warm fire — an' me bein' so tired. It — it wasn't imperence!"

Sara broke into a friendly little laugh, and put her hand on her shoulder.

"You were tired," she said; "you could not help it. You are not really awake yet."

How poor Becky stared at her! In fact, she had never heard such a nice, friendly sound in anyone's voice before. She was used to being ordered about and scolded, and having her ears boxed. And this one — in her rose-colored dancing afternoon splendor — was looking at her as if she were not a culprit at all — as if she had a right to be tired — even to fall asleep! The touch of the soft, slim little paw on her shoulder was the most amazing thing she had ever known.

"Ain't — ain't yer angry, miss?" she gasped. "Ain't yer goin' to tell the missus?"

"No," cried out Sara. "Of course I'm not."

The woeful fright in the coal-smutted face made her suddenly so sorry that she could scarcely bear it. One of her queer thoughts rushed into her mind. She put her hand against Becky's cheek.

"Why," she said, "we are just the same — I am only a little girl like you. It's just an accident that I am not you, and you are not me!"

Becky did not understand in the least. Her mind could not grasp such amazing thoughts, and "an accident" meant to her a calamity in which someone was run over or fell off a ladder and was carried to "the 'orspital."

"A' accident, miss," she fluttered respectfully. "Is it?"

"Yes," Sara answered, and she looked at her dreamily for a moment. But the next she spoke in a different tone. She realized that Becky did not know what she meant.

"Have you done your work?" she asked. "Dare you stay here a few minutes?"

Becky lost her breath again.

"Here, miss? Me?"

Sara ran to the door, opened it, and looked out and listened.

"No one is anywhere about," she explained. "If your bedrooms are finished, perhaps you might stay a tiny while. I thought — perhaps — you might like a piece of cake."

The next ten minutes seemed to Becky like a sort of delirium. Sara opened a cupboard, and gave her a thick slice of cake. She seemed to rejoice when it was devoured in hungry bites. She talked and asked questions, and laughed until

Becky's fears actually began to calm themselves, and she once or twice gathered boldness enough to ask a question or so herself, daring as she felt it to be.

"Is that — " she ventured, looking longingly at the rose-colored frock. And she asked it almost in a whisper. "Is that there your best?"

"It is one of my dancing-frocks," answered Sara. "I like it, don't you?"

For a few seconds Becky was almost speechless with admiration. Then she said in an awed voice, "Onct I see a princess. I was standin' in the street with the crowd outside Covin' Garden, watchin' the swells go inter the operer. An' there was one everyone stared at most. They ses to each other, 'That's the princess.' She was a growed-up young lady, but she was pink all over — gownd an' cloak, an' flowers an' all. I called her to mind the minnit I see you, sittin' there on the table, miss. You looked like her."

"I've often thought," said Sara, in her reflecting voice, "that I should like to be a princess; I wonder what it feels like. I believe I will begin pretending I am one."

Becky stared at her admiringly, and, as before, did not understand her in the least. She watched her with a sort of adoration. Very soon Sara left her reflections and turned to her with a new question.

"Becky," she said, "weren't you listening to that story?"

"Yes, miss," confessed Becky, a little alarmed again. "I knowed I hadn't orter, but it was that beautiful I — I couldn't help it."

"I liked you to listen to it," said Sara. "If you tell stories, you like nothing so much as to tell them to people who want to listen. I don't know why it is. Would you like to hear the rest?"

Becky lost her breath again.

"Me hear it?" she cried. "Like as if I was a pupil, miss! All about the Prince — and the little white Mer-babies swimming about laughing — with stars in their hair?"

Sara nodded.

"You haven't time to hear it now, I'm afraid," she said; "but if you will tell me just what time you come to do my rooms, I will try to be here and tell you a bit of it every day until it is finished. It's a lovely long one — and I'm always putting new bits to it."

"Then," breathed Becky, devoutly, "I wouldn't mind how heavy the coal boxes was — or what the cook done to me, if — if I might have that to think of."

"You may," said Sara. "I'll tell it all to you."

When Becky went downstairs, she was not the same Becky who had staggered up, loaded down by the weight of the coal scuttle. She had an extra piece of cake in her pocket, and she had been fed and warmed, but not only by cake and fire. Something else had warmed and fed her, and the something else was Sara.

When she was gone Sara sat on her favorite perch on the end of her table. Her feet were on a chair, her elbows on her knees, and her chin in her hands.

"If I was a princess — a real princess," she murmured, "I could scatter largess to the populace. But even if I am only a pretend princess, I can invent little things to do for people. Things like this. She was just as happy as if it was largess. I'll pretend that to do things people like is scattering largess. I've scattered largess."

 5

In the Attic

The first night she spent in her attic was a thing Sara never forgot. During its passing she lived through a wild, unchildlike woe of which she never spoke to anyone about her. There was no one who would have understood. It was, indeed, well for her that as she lay awake in the darkness her mind was forcibly distracted, now and then, by the strangeness of her surroundings. It was, perhaps, well for her that she was reminded by her small body of material things. If this had not been so, the anguish of her young mind might have been too great for a child to bear. But, really, while the night was passing she scarcely knew that she had a body at all or remembered any other thing than one.

"My papa is dead!" she kept whispering to herself. "My papa is dead!"

It was not until long afterward that she realized that her bed had been so hard that she turned over and over in it to find a place to rest, that the darkness seemed more intense than any she had ever known, and that the wind howled over the roof among the chimneys like something which wailed aloud. Then there was something worse. This was certain scufflings and scratchings and squeakings in the walls and behind the skirting boards. She knew what they meant, because Becky had described them. They meant rats and mice who were either fighting with each other or playing together. Once or twice she even heard sharp-toed feet scurrying across the floor, and she remembered in those after days, when she recalled things, that when first she heard them she started up in bed and sat trembling, and when she lay down again covered her head with the bedclothes.

The change in her life did not come about gradually, but was made all at once. "She must begin as she is to go on," Miss Minchin said to Miss Amelia. "She must be taught at once what she is to expect."

Mariette had left the house the next morning. The glimpse Sara caught of her sitting room, as she passed its open door, showed her that everything had been changed. Her ornaments and luxuries had been removed, and a bed had been placed in a corner to transform it into a new pupil's bedroom.

When she went down to breakfast she saw that her seat at Miss Minchin's side was occupied by Lavinia, and Miss Minchin spoke to her coldly.

"You will begin your new duties, Sara," she said, "by taking your seat with the younger children at a smaller table. You must keep them quiet, and see that they behave well and do not waste their food. You ought to have been down earlier. Lottie has already upset her tea."

That was the beginning, and from day to day the duties given to her were added to. She taught the younger children French and heard their other lessons, and these were the least of her labors. It was found that she could be made use of in numberless directions. She could be sent on errands at any time and in all weathers. She could be told to do things other people neglected. The cook and the housemaids took their tone from Miss Minchin, and rather enjoyed ordering about the "young one" who had been made so much fuss over for so long. They were not servants of the best class, and had neither good manners nor good tempers, and it was frequently convenient to have at hand someone on whom blame could be laid.

During the first month or two, Sara thought that her willingness to do things as well as she could, and her silence under reproof, might soften those who drove her so hard. In her proud little heart she wanted them to see that she was trying to earn her living and not accepting charity. But the time came when she saw that no one was softened at all; and the more willing she was to do as she was told, the more domineering and exacting careless housemaids became, and the more ready a scolding cook was to blame her.

If she had been older, Miss Minchin would have given her the bigger girls to teach and saved money by dismissing an instructress; but while she remained and looked like a child, she could be made more useful as a sort of little superior errand girl and maid of all work. An ordinary errand boy would not have been so clever and reliable. Sara could be trusted with difficult commissions and complicated messages. She could even go and pay bills, and she combined with this the ability to dust a room well and to set things in order.

Her own lessons became things of the past. She was taught nothing, and only after long and busy days spent in running here and there at everybody's orders was she grudgingly allowed to go into the deserted schoolroom, with a pile of old books, and study alone at night.

"If I do not remind myself of the things I have learned, perhaps I may forget them," she said to herself. "I am almost a scullery maid, and if I am a scullery maid who knows nothing, I shall be like poor Becky. I wonder if I could quite forget and begin to drop my h's and not remember that Henry the Eighth had six wives."

One of the most curious things in her new existence was her changed position among the pupils. Instead of being a sort of small royal personage among them, she no longer seemed to be one of their number at all. She was kept so constantly at work that she scarcely ever had an opportunity of speaking to any of them, and she could not avoid seeing that Miss Minchin preferred that she should live a life apart from that of the occupants of the schoolroom.

"I will not have her forming intimacies and talking to the other children," that lady said. "Girls like a grievance, and if she begins to tell romantic stories about herself, she will become an ill-used heroine, and parents will be given a wrong impression. It is better that she should live a separate life — one suited to her circumstances. I am giving her a home, and that is more than she has any right to expect from me."

Sara did not expect much, and was far too proud to try to continue to be intimate with girls who evidently felt rather awkward and uncertain about her. The fact was that Miss Minchin's pupils were a set of dull, matter-of-fact young people. They were accustomed to being rich and comfortable, and as Sara's frocks grew shorter and shabbier and queerer-looking, and it became an established fact that she wore shoes with holes in them and was sent out to buy groceries and carry them through the streets in a basket on her arm when the cook wanted them in a hurry, they felt rather as if, when they spoke to her, they were addressing an under servant.

"To think that she was the girl with the diamond mines," Lavinia commented. "She does look an object. And she's queerer than ever. I never liked her much, but I can't bear that way she has now of looking at people without speaking — just as if she was finding them out."

"I am," said Sara, promptly, when she heard of this. "That's what I look at some people for. I like to know about them. I think them over afterward."

The truth was that she had saved herself annoyance several times by keeping her eye on Lavinia, who was quite ready to make mischief, and would have been rather pleased to have made it for the ex-show pupil.

Sara never made any mischief herself, or interfered with anyone. She worked like a drudge; she tramped through the wet streets, carrying parcels and baskets; she labored with the childish inattention of the little ones' French lessons; as she became shabbier and more forlorn-looking, she was told that she had better take her meals downstairs; she was treated as if she was nobody's concern, and her heart grew proud and sore, but she never told anyone what she felt.

"Soldiers don't complain," she would say between her small, shut teeth, "I am not going to do it; I will pretend this is part of a war."

But there were hours when her child heart might almost have broken with loneliness but for three people.

The first, it must be owned, was Becky — just Becky. Throughout all that first night spent in the garret, she had felt a vague comfort in knowing that on the other side of the wall in which the rats scuffled and squeaked there was another young human creature. And during the nights that followed the sense of comfort grew. They had little chance to speak to each other during the day. Each had her own tasks to perform, and any attempt at conversation would have been regarded as a tendency to loiter and lose time. "Don't mind me, miss," Becky whispered during the first morning, "if I don't say nothin' polite. Some un'd be down on us if I did. I means 'please' an' 'thank you' an' 'beg pardon,' but I dassn't to take time to say it."

But before daybreak she used to slip into Sara's attic and button her dress and give her such help as she required before she went downstairs to light the kitchen fire. And when night came Sara always heard the humble knock at her door which meant that her handmaid was ready to help her again if she was needed. During the first weeks of her grief Sara felt as if she were too stupefied to talk, so it happened that some time passed before they saw each other much or exchanged visits. Becky's heart told her that it was best that people in trouble should be left alone.

The second of the trio of comforters was Ermengarde, but odd things happened before Ermengarde found her place.

When Sara's mind seemed to awaken again to the life about her, she realized that she had forgotten that an Ermengarde lived in the world. The two had always been friends, but Sara had felt as if she were years the older. It could not be contested that Ermengarde was as dull as she was affectionate. She clung to Sara in a simple, helpless way; she brought her lessons to her that she might be helped; she listened to her every word and besieged her with requests for stories. But she had nothing interesting to say herself, and she loathed books of every description. She was, in fact, not a person one would remember when one was caught in the storm of a great trouble, and Sara forgot her.

It had been all the easier to forget her because she had been suddenly called home for a few weeks. When she came back she did not see Sara for a day or two, and when she met her for the first time she encountered her coming down a corridor with her arms full of garments which were to be taken downstairs to be mended. Sara herself had already been taught to mend them. She looked pale and unlike herself, and she was attired in the queer, outgrown frock whose shortness showed so much thin black leg.

Ermengarde was too slow a girl to be equal to such a situation. She could not think of anything to say. She knew what had happened, but, somehow, she had never imagined Sara could look like this — so odd and poor and almost like a servant. It made her quite miserable, and she could do nothing but break into a short hysterical laugh and exclaim — aimlessly and as if without any meaning, "Oh, Sara, is that you?"

"Yes," answered Sara, and suddenly a strange thought passed through her mind and made her face flush. She held the pile of garments in her arms, and her chin rested upon the top of it to keep it steady. Something in the look of her straight-gazing eyes made Ermengarde lose her wits still more. She felt as if Sara had changed into a new kind of girl, and she had never known her before. Perhaps it was because she had suddenly grown poor and had to mend things and work like Becky.

"Oh," she stammered. "How — how are you?"

"I don't know," Sara replied. "How are you?"

"I'm — I'm quite well," said Ermengarde, overwhelmed with shyness. Then spasmodically she thought of something to say which seemed more intimate. "Are you — are you very unhappy?" she said in a rush.

Then Sara was guilty of an injustice. Just at that moment her torn heart swelled within her, and she felt that if anyone was as stupid as that, one had better get away from her.

"What do you think?" she said. "Do you think I am very happy?" And she marched past her without another word.

In course of time she realized that if her wretchedness had not made her forget things, she would have known that poor, dull Ermengarde was not to be blamed for her unready, awkward ways. She was always awkward, and the more she felt, the more stupid she was given to being.

But the sudden thought which had flashed upon her had made her over-sensitive. "She is like the others," she had thought. "She does not really want to talk to me. She knows no one does."

So for several weeks a barrier stood between them. When they met by chance Sara looked the other way, and Ermengarde felt too stiff and embarrassed to speak. Sometimes they nodded to each other in passing, but there were times when they did not even exchange a greeting.

"If she would rather not talk to me," Sara thought, "I will keep out of her way. Miss Minchin makes that easy enough."

Miss Minchin made it so easy that at last they scarcely saw each other at all. At that time it was noticed that Ermengarde was more stupid than ever, and that she looked listless and unhappy. She used to sit in the window-seat, huddled in a heap, and stare out of the window without speaking. Once Jessie, who was passing, stopped to look at her curiously.

"What are you crying for, Ermengarde?" she asked.

"I'm not crying," answered Ermengarde, in a muffled, unsteady voice.

"You are," said Jessie. "A great big tear just rolled down the bridge of your nose and dropped off at the end of it. And there goes another."

"Well," said Ermengarde, "I'm miserable — and no one need interfere." And she turned her plump back and took out her handkerchief and boldly hid her face in it.

That night, when Sara went to her attic, she was later than usual. She had been kept at work until after the hour at which the pupils went to bed, and after that she had gone to her lessons in the lonely schoolroom. When she reached the top of the stairs, she was surprised to see a glimmer of light coming from under the attic door.

"Nobody goes there but myself," she thought quickly, "but someone has lighted a candle."

Someone had, indeed, lighted a candle, and it was not burning in the kitchen candlestick she was expected to use, but in one of those belonging to the pupils' bedrooms. The someone was sitting upon the battered footstool, and was dressed in her nightgown and wrapped up in a red shawl. It was Ermengarde.

"Ermengarde!" cried Sara. She was so startled that she was almost frightened. "You will get into trouble."

Ermengarde stumbled up from her footstool. She shuffled across the attic in her bedroom slippers, which were too large for her. Her eyes and nose were pink with crying.

"I know I shall — if I'm found out." she said. "But I don't care — I don't care a bit. Oh, Sara, please tell me. What is the matter? Why don't you like me any more?"

Something in her voice made the familiar lump rise in Sara's throat. It was so affectionate and simple — so like the old Ermengarde who had asked her to be "best friends." It sounded as if she had not meant what she had seemed to mean during these past weeks.

"I do like you," Sara answered. "I thought — you see, everything is different now. I thought you — were different."

Ermengarde opened her wet eyes wide.

"Why, it was you who were different!" she cried. "You didn't want to talk to me. I didn't know what to do. It was you who were different after I came back."

Sara thought a moment. She saw she had made a mistake.

"I am different," she explained, "though not in the way you think. Miss Minchin does not want me to talk to the girls. Most of them don't want to talk to me. I thought — perhaps — you didn't. So I tried to keep out of your way."

"Oh, Sara," Ermengarde almost wailed in her reproachful dismay. And then after one more look they rushed into each other's arms. It must be confessed that Sara's small black head lay for some minutes on the shoulder covered by the red shawl. When Ermengarde had seemed to desert her, she had felt horribly lonely. Afterward they sat down upon the floor together, Sara clasping her knees with her arms, and Ermengarde rolled up in her shawl. Ermengarde looked at the odd, big-eyed little face adoringly.

"I couldn't bear it any more," she said. "I dare say you could live without me, Sara; but I couldn't live without you. I was nearly dead. So tonight, when I was crying under the bedclothes, I thought all at once of creeping up here and just begging you to let us be friends again."

"You are nicer than I am," said Sara. "I was too proud to try and make friends. You see, now that trials have come, they have shown that I am not a nice child. I was afraid they would. Perhaps" — wrinkling her forehead wisely — "that is what they were sent for."

"I don't see any good in them," said Ermengarde stoutly.

"Neither do I — to speak the truth," admitted Sara, frankly. "But I suppose there might be good in things, even if we don't see it. There might" — doubtfully —

"be good in Miss Minchin."

Ermengarde looked round the attic with a rather fearsome curiosity.

"Sara," she said, "do you think you can bear living here?"

Sara looked round also.

"If I pretend it's quite different, I can," she answered; "or if I pretend it is a place in a story."

She spoke slowly. Her imagination was beginning to work for her. It had not worked for her at all since her troubles had come upon her. She had felt as if it had been stunned.

"Other people have lived in worse places. Think of the Count of Monte Cristo in the dungeons of the Chateau d'If. And think of the people in the Bastille!"

"The Bastille," half whispered Ermengarde, watching her and beginning to be fascinated. She remembered stories of the French Revolution which Sara had been able to fix in her mind by her dramatic relation of them. No one but Sara could have done it.

A well-known glow came into Sara's eyes.

"Yes," she said, hugging her knees, "that will be a good place to pretend about. I am a prisoner in the Bastille. I have been here for years and years — and years; and everybody has forgotten about me. Miss Minchin is the jailer — and Becky" — a sudden light adding itself to the glow in her eyes — "Becky is the prisoner in the next cell."

She turned to Ermengarde, looking quite like the old Sara.

"I shall pretend that," she said; "and it will be a great comfort."

Ermengarde was at once enraptured and awed.

"And will you tell me all about it?" she said. "May I creep up here at night, whenever it is safe, and hear the things you have made up in the day? It will seem as if we were more 'best friends' than ever."

"Yes," answered Sara, nodding. "Adversity tries people, and mine has tried you and proved how nice you are."

 6

Melchisedec

The third person in the trio was Lottie. She was a small thing and did not know what adversity meant, and was much bewildered by the alteration she saw in her young adopted mother. She had heard it rumored that strange things had happened to Sara, but she could not understand why she looked different — why she wore an old black frock and came into the schoolroom only to teach instead of to sit in her place of honor and learn lessons herself. There had been much whispering among the little ones when it had been discovered that Sara no longer lived in the rooms in which Emily had so long sat in state. Lottie's chief difficulty was that Sara said so little when one asked her questions. At seven mysteries must be made very clear if one is to understand them.

"Are you very poor now, Sara?" she had asked confidentially the first morning her friend took charge of the small French class. "Are you as poor as a beggar?" She thrust a fat hand into the slim one and opened round, tearful eyes. "I don't want you to be as poor as a beggar."

She looked as if she was going to cry. And Sara hurriedly consoled her.

"Beggars have nowhere to live," she said courageously. "I have a place to live in."

"Where do you live?" persisted Lottle. "The new girl sleeps in your room, and it isn't pretty any more."

"I live in another room," said Sara.

"Is it a nice one?" inquired Lottie. "I want to go and see it."

"You must not talk," said Sara. "Miss Minchin is looking at us. She will be angry with me for letting you whisper."

She had found out already that she was to be held accountable for everything which was objected to. If the children were not attentive, if they talked, if they were restless, it was she who would be reproved.

But Lottie was a determined little person. If Sara would not tell her where she lived, she would find out in some other way. She talked to her small companions and hung about the elder girls and listened when they were gossiping; and acting upon certain information they had unconsciously let drop, she started late one afternoon on a voyage of discovery, climbing stairs she had never known the existence of, until she reached the attic floor. There she found two doors near each other, and opening one, she saw her beloved Sara standing upon an old table and looking out of a window.

"Sara!" she cried, aghast. "Mamma Sara!" She was aghast because the attic was so bare and ugly and seemed so far away from all the world. Her short legs had seemed to have been mounting hundreds of stairs.

Sara turned round at the sound of her voice. It was her turn to be aghast. What would happen now? If Lottie began to cry and any one chanced to hear, they were both lost. She jumped down from her table and ran to the child.

"Don't cry and make a noise," she implored. "I shall be scolded if you do, and I have been scolded all day. It's — it's not such a bad room, Lottie."

"Isn't it?" gasped Lottie, and as she looked round it she bit her lip. She was a spoiled child yet, but she was fond enough of her adopted parent to make an effort to control herself for her sake. Then, somehow, it was quite possible that any place in which Sara lived might turn out to be nice. "Why isn't it, Sara?" she almost whispered.

Sara hugged her close and tried to laugh. There was a sort of comfort in the warmth of the plump, childish body. She had had a hard day and had been staring out of the windows with hot eyes.

"You can see all sorts of things you can't see downstairs," she said.

"What sort of things?" demanded Lottie, with that curiosity Sara could always awaken even in bigger girls.

"Chimneys — quite close to us — with smoke curling up in wreaths and clouds and going up into the sky — and sparrows hopping about and talking to each other just as if they were people — and other attic windows where heads may pop out any minute and you can wonder who they belong to. And it all feels as high up — as if it was another world."

"Oh, let me see it!" cried Lottie. "Lift me up!"

Sara lifted her up, and they stood on the old table together and leaned on the edge of the flat window in the roof, and looked out.

Anyone who has not done this does not know what a different world they saw. The slates spread out on either side of them and slanted down into the rain gutter-pipes. The sparrows, being at home there, twittered and hopped about quite without fear. Two of them perched on the chimney top nearest and quarrelled with each other fiercely until one pecked the other and drove him away. The garret window next to theirs was shut because the house next door was empty.

"I wish someone lived there," Sara said. "It is so close that if there was a little girl in the attic, we could talk to each other through the windows and climb over to see each other, if we were not afraid of falling."

The sky seemed so much nearer than when one saw it from the street, that Lottie was enchanted. From the attic window, among the chimney pots, the things which were happening in the world below seemed almost unreal. One scarcely believed in the existence of Miss Minchin and Miss Amelia and the schoolroom, and the roll of wheels in the square seemed a sound belonging to another existence.

"Oh, Sara!" cried Lottie, cuddling in her guarding arm. "I like this attic — I like it! It is nicer than downstairs!"

"Look at that sparrow," whispered Sara. "I wish I had some crumbs to throw to him."

"I have some!" came in a little shriek from Lottie. "I have part of a bun in my pocket; I bought it with my penny yesterday, and I saved a bit."

When they threw out a few crumbs the sparrow jumped and flew away to an adjacent chimney top. He was evidently not accustomed to intimates in attics, and unexpected crumbs startled him. But when Lottie remained quite still and Sara chirped very softly — almost as if she were a sparrow herself — he saw that the thing which had alarmed him represented hospitality, after all. He put his head on one side, and from his perch on the chimney looked down at the crumbs with twinkling eyes. Lottie could scarcely keep still.

"Will he come? Will he come?" she whispered.

"His eyes look as if he would," Sara whispered back. "He is thinking and thinking whether he dare. Yes, he will! Yes, he is coming!"

He flew down and hopped toward the crumbs, but stopped a few inches away from them, putting his head on one side again, as if reflecting on the chances that Sara and Lottie might turn out to be big cats and jump on him. At last his heart told him they were really nicer than they looked, and he hopped nearer and nearer, darted at the biggest crumb with a lightning peck, seized it, and carried it away to the other side of his chimney.

"Now he knows," said Sara. "And he will come back for the others."

He did come back, and even brought a friend, and the friend went away and brought a relative, and among them they made a hearty meal over which they twittered and chattered and exclaimed, stopping every now and then to put their heads on one side and examine Lottie and Sara. Lottie was so delighted that she quite forgot her first shocked impression of the attic. In fact, when she was lifted down from the table and returned to earthly things, as it were, Sara was able to point out to her many beauties in the room which she herself would not have suspected the existence of.

"It is so little and so high above everything," she said, "that it is almost like a nest in a tree. The slanting ceiling is so funny. See, you can scarcely stand up at this end of the room; and when the morning begins to come I can lie in bed and look right up into the sky through that flat window in the roof. It is like a square patch of light. If the sun is going to shine, little pink clouds float about, and I feel as if I could touch them. And if it rains, the drops patter and patter as if they were saying something nice. Then if there are stars, you can lie and try to count how many go into the patch. It takes such a lot. And just look at that tiny, rusty grate in the corner. If it was polished and there was a fire in it, just think how nice it would be. You see, it's really a beautiful little room."

She was walking round the small place, holding Lottie's hand and making gestures which described all the beauties she was making herself see. She quite made Lottie see them, too. Lottie could always believe in the things Sara made pictures of.

"You see," she said, "there could be a thick, soft blue Indian rug on the floor; and in that corner there could be a soft little sofa, with cushions to curl up on; and just over it could be a shelf full of books so that one could reach them easily; and there could be a fur rug before the fire, and hangings on the wall to cover up the whitewash, and pictures. They would have to be little ones, but they could be beautiful; and there could be a lamp with a deep rose-colored shade; and a table in the middle, with things to have tea with; and a little fat copper kettle singing on the hob; and the bed could be quite different. It could be made soft and covered with a lovely silk coverlet. It could be beautiful. And perhaps we could coax the sparrows until we made such friends with them that they would come and peck at the window and ask to be let in."

"Oh, Sara!" cried Lottie. "I should like to live here!"

When Sara had persuaded her to go downstairs again, and, after setting her on her way, had come back to her attic, she stood in the middle of it and looked about her. The enchantment of her imaginings for Lottie had died away. The bed was hard and covered with its dingy quilt. The whitewashed wall showed its broken patches, the floor was cold and bare, the grate was broken and rusty, and the battered footstool, tilted sideways on its injured leg, the only seat in the room. She sat down on it for a few minutes and let her head drop in her hands. The mere fact that Lottie had come and gone away again made things seem a little worse — just as perhaps prisoners feel a little more desolate after visitors come and go, leaving them behind.

"It's a lonely place," she said. "Sometimes it's the loneliest place in the world."

She was sitting in this way when her attention was attracted by a slight sound near her. She lifted her head to see where it came from, and if she had been a nervous child she would have left her seat on the battered footstool in a great hurry. A large rat was sitting up on his hind quarters and sniffing the air in an interested manner. Some of Lottie's crumbs had dropped upon the floor and their scent had drawn him out of his hole.

He looked so queer and so like a gray-whiskered dwarf or gnome that Sara was rather fascinated. He looked at her with his bright eyes, as if he were asking a question. He was evidently so doubtful that one of the child's queer thoughts came into her mind.

"I dare say it is rather hard to be a rat," she mused. "Nobody likes you. People jump and run away and scream out, 'Oh, a horrid rat!' I shouldn't like people to scream and jump and say, 'Oh, a horrid Sara!' the moment they saw me. And set traps for me, and pretend they were dinner. It's so different to be a sparrow. But nobody asked this rat if he wanted to be a rat when he was made. Nobody said, 'Wouldn't you rather be a sparrow?'"

She had sat so quietly that the rat had begun to take courage. He was very much afraid of her, but perhaps he had a heart like the sparrow and it told him that she was not a thing which pounced. He was very hungry. He had a wife and a large family in the wall, and they had had frightfully bad luck for several days. He had left the children crying bitterly, and felt he would risk a good deal for a few crumbs, so he cautiously dropped upon his feet.

"Come on," said Sara; "I'm not a trap. You can have them, poor thing! Prisoners in the Bastille used to make friends with rats. Suppose I make friends with you."

How it is that animals understand things I do not know, but it is certain that they do understand. Perhaps there is a language which is not made of words and everything in the world understands it. Perhaps there is a soul hidden in everything and it can always speak, without even making a sound, to another soul. But whatsoever was the reason, the rat knew from that moment that he was safe — even though he was a rat. He knew that this young human being sitting on the red footstool would not jump up and terrify him with wild, sharp noises or throw heavy objects at him which, if they did not fall and crush him, would send him limping in his scurry back to his hole. He was really a very nice rat, and did not mean the least harm. When he had stood on his hind legs and sniffed the air, with his bright eyes fixed on Sara, he had hoped that she would understand this, and would not begin by hating him as an enemy. When the mysterious thing which speaks without saying any words told him that she would not, he went softly toward the crumbs and began to eat them. As he did it he glanced every now and then at Sara, just as the sparrows had done, and his expression was so very apologetic that it touched her heart.

She sat and watched him without making any movement. One crumb was very much larger than the others — in fact, it could scarcely be called a crumb. It was evident that he wanted that piece very much, but it lay quite near the footstool and he was still rather timid.

"I believe he wants it to carry to his family in the wall," Sara thought. "If I do not stir at all, perhaps he will come and get it."

She scarcely allowed herself to breathe, she was so deeply interested. The rat shuffled a little nearer and ate a few more crumbs, then he stopped and sniffed delicately, giving a side glance at the occupant of the footstool; then he darted at the piece of bun with something very like the sudden boldness of the sparrow, and the instant he had possession of it fled back to the wall, slipped down a crack in the skirting board, and was gone.

"I knew he wanted it for his children," said Sara. "I do believe I could make friends with him."

A week or so afterward, on one of the rare nights when Ermengarde found it safe to steal up to the attic, when she tapped on the door with the tips of her fingers Sara did not come to her for two or three minutes. There was, indeed, such a silence in the room at first that Ermengarde wondered if she could have fallen asleep. Then, to her surprise, she heard her utter a little, low laugh and speak coaxingly to someone.

"There!" Ermengarde heard her say. "Take it and go home, Melchisedec! Go home to your wife!"

Almost immediately Sara opened the door, and when she did so she found Ermengarde standing with alarmed eyes upon the threshold.

"Who — who are you talking to, Sara?" she gasped out.

Sara drew her in cautiously, but she looked as if something pleased and amused her.

"You must promise not to be frightened — not to scream the least bit, or I can't tell you," she answered.

Ermengarde felt almost inclined to scream on the spot, but managed to control herself. She looked all round the attic and saw no one. And yet Sara had certainly been speaking to someone. She thought of ghosts.

"Is it — something that will frighten me?" she asked timorously.

"Some people are afraid of them," said Sara. "I was at first — but I am not now."

"Was it — a ghost?" quaked Ermengarde.

"No," said Sara, laughing. "It was my rat."

Ermengarde made one bound, and landed in the middle of the little dingy bed. She tucked her feet under her nightgown and the red shawl. She did not scream, but she gasped with fright.

"Oh! Oh!" she cried under her breath. "A rat! A rat!"

"I was afraid you would be frightened," said Sara. "But you needn't be. I am making him tame. He actually knows me and comes out when I call him. Are you too frightened to want to see him?"

The truth was that, as the days had gone on and, with the aid of scraps brought up from the kitchen, her curious friendship had developed, she had gradually forgotten that the timid creature she was becoming familiar with was a mere rat. At first Ermengarde was too much alarmed to do anything but huddle in a heap upon the bed and tuck up her feet, but the sight of Sara's composed little countenance and the story of Melchisedec's first appearance began at last to rouse her curiosity, and she leaned forward over the edge of the bed and watched Sara go and kneel down by the hole in the skirting board.

"He — he won't run out quickly and jump on the bed, will he?" she said.

"No," answered Sara. "He's as polite as we are. He is just like a person. Now watch!"

She began to make a low, whistling sound — so low and coaxing that it could only have been heard in entire stillness. She did it several times, looking entirely absorbed in it. Ermengarde thought she looked as if she were working a spell. And at last, evidently in response to it, a gray-whiskered, bright-eyed head peeped out of the hole. Sara had some crumbs in her hand. She dropped them, and Melchisedec came quietly forth and ate them. A piece of larger size than the rest he took and carried in the most businesslike manner back to his home.

"You see," said Sara, "that is for his wife and children. He is very nice. He only eats the little bits. After he goes back I can always hear his family squeaking for joy. There are three kinds of squeaks. One kind is the children's, and one is Mrs. Melchisedec's, and one is Melchisedec's own."

Ermengarde began to laugh.

"Oh, Sara!" she said. "You are queer — but you are nice."

"I know I am queer," admitted Sara, cheerfully; "and I try to be nice." She rubbed her forehead with her little brown paw, and a puzzled, tender look came into her face. "Papa always laughed at me," she said; "but I liked it. He thought I was queer, but he liked me to make up things. I — I can't help making up things. If I didn't, I don't believe I could live." She paused and glanced around the attic.

"I'm sure I couldn't live here," she added in a low voice.

Ermengarde was interested, as she always was. "When you talk about things," she said, "they seem as if they grew real. You talk about Melchisedec as if he was a person."

"He is a person," said Sara. "He gets hungry and frightened, just as we do; and he is married and has children. How do we know he doesn't think things, just as we do? His eyes look as if he was a person. That was why I gave him a name." She sat down on the floor in her favorite attitude, holding her knees.

"Besides," she said, "he is a Bastille rat sent to be my friend. I can always get a bit of bread the cook has thrown away, and it is quite enough to support him."

"Is it the Bastille yet?" asked Ermengarde, eagerly. "Do you always pretend it is the Bastille?"

"Nearly always," answered Sara. "Sometimes I try to pretend it is another kind of place; but the Bastille is generally easiest — particularly when it is cold."

Just at that moment Ermengarde almost jumped off the bed, she was so startled by a sound she heard. It was like two distinct knocks on the wall.

"What is that?" she exclaimed.

Sara got up from the floor and answered quite dramatically:

"It is the prisoner in the next cell."

"Becky!" cried Ermengarde, enraptured.

"Yes," said Sara. "Listen; the two knocks meant, 'Prisoner, are you there?'"

She knocked three times on the wall herself, as if in answer.

"That means, 'Yes, I am here, and all is well.'"

Four knocks came from Becky's side of the wall.

"That means," explained Sara, "'Then, fellow-sufferer, we will sleep in peace. Good night.'"

Ermengarde quite beamed with delight.

"Oh, Sara!" she whispered joyfully. "It is like a story!"

"It is a story," said Sara. "Everything's a story. You are a story — I am a story. Miss Minchin is a story."

And she sat down again and talked until Ermengarde forgot that she was a sort of escaped prisoner herself, and had to be reminded by Sara that she could not remain in the Bastille all night, but must steal noiselessly downstairs again and creep back into her deserted bed.

7

The Indian Gentleman

But it was a perilous thing for Ermengarde and Lottie to make pilgrimages to the attic. They could never be quite sure when Sara would be there, and they could scarcely ever be certain that Miss Amelia would not make a tour of inspection through the bedrooms after the pupils were supposed to be asleep. So their visits were rare ones, and Sara lived a strange and lonely life. It was a lonelier life when she was downstairs than when she was in her attic. She had no one to talk to; and when she was sent out on errands and walked through the streets, a forlorn little figure carrying a basket or a parcel, trying to hold her hat on when the wind was blowing, and feeling the water soak through her shoes when it was raining, she felt as if the crowds hurrying past her made her loneliness greater. When she had been the Princess Sara, driving through the streets in her brougham, or walking, attended by Mariette, the sight of her bright, eager little face and picturesque coats and hats had often caused people to look after her. A happy, beautifully cared for little girl naturally attracts attention. Shabby, poorly dressed children are not rare enough and pretty enough to make people turn around to look at them and smile. No one looked at Sara in these days, and no one seemed to see her as she hurried along the crowded pavements. She had begun to grow very fast, and, as she was dressed only in such clothes as the plainer remnants of her wardrobe would supply, she knew she looked very queer, indeed. All her valuable garments had been disposed of, and such as had been left for her use she was expected to wear so long as she could put them on at all. Sometimes, when she passed a shop window with a mirror in it, she almost laughed outright on catching a glimpse of herself, and sometimes her face went red and she bit her lip and turned away.

In the evening, when she passed houses whose windows were lighted up, she used to look into the warm rooms and amuse herself by imagining things about the people she saw sitting before the fires or about the tables. It always interested her to catch glimpses of rooms before the shutters were closed. There were several families in the square in which Miss Minchin lived, with which she had become quite familiar in a way of her own. The one she liked best she called the Large Family. She called it the Large Family not because the members of it were big — for, indeed, most of them were little — but because there were so many of them. There were eight children in the Large Family, and a stout, rosy mother, and a stout, rosy father, and a stout, rosy grandmother, and any number of servants. The eight children were always either being taken out to walk or to ride in perambulators by comfortable nurses, or they were going to drive with their mamma, or they were flying to the door in the evening to meet their papa and kiss him and dance around him and drag off his overcoat and look in the pockets for packages, or they were crowding about the nursery windows and looking out and pushing each other and laughing — in fact, they were always doing something enjoyable and suited to the tastes of a large family. Sara was quite fond of them, and had given them names out of books — quite romantic names. She called them the Montmorencys when she did not call them the Large Family. The fat, fair baby with the lace cap was Ethelberta Beauchamp Montmorency; the next baby was Violet Cholmondeley Montmorency; the little boy who could just stagger and who had such round legs was Sydney Cecil Vivian Montmorency; and then came Lilian Evangeline Maud Marion, Rosalind Gladys, Guy Clarence, Veronica Eustacia, and Claude Harold Hector.

One evening a very funny thing happened — though, perhaps, in one sense it was not a funny thing at all.

Several of the Montmorencys were evidently going to a children's party, and just as Sara was about to pass the door they were crossing the pavement to get into the carriage which was waiting for them. Veronica Eustacia and Rosalind Gladys, in white-lace frocks and lovely sashes, had just got in, and Guy Clarence, aged five, was following them. He was such a pretty fellow and had such rosy cheeks and blue eyes, and such a darling little round head covered with curls, that Sara forgot her basket and shabby cloak altogether — in fact, forgot everything but that she wanted to look at him for a moment. So she paused and looked.

It was Christmas time, and the Large Family had been hearing many stories about children who were poor and had no mammas and papas to fill their stockings and take them to the pantomime — children who were, in fact, cold and thinly clad and hungry. In the stories, kind people — sometimes little boys and girls with tender hearts — invariably saw the poor children and gave them money or rich gifts, or took them home to beautiful dinners. Guy Clarence had been affected to tears that very afternoon by the reading of such a story, and he had burned with a desire to find such a poor child and give her a certain sixpence he possessed, and thus provide for her for life. An entire sixpence, he was sure, would mean affluence for evermore. As he crossed the strip of red carpet laid across the pavement from the door to the carriage, he had this very sixpence in the pocket of his very short man-o-war trousers; And just as Rosalind Gladys got into the vehicle and jumped on the seat in order to feel the cushions spring under her, he saw Sara standing on the wet pavement in her shabby frock and hat, with her old basket on her arm, looking at him hungrily.

He thought that her eyes looked hungry because she had perhaps had nothing to eat for a long time. He did not know that they looked so because she was hungry for the warm, merry life his home held and his rosy face spoke of, and that she had a hungry wish to snatch him in her arms and kiss him. He only knew that she had big eyes and a thin face and thin legs and a common basket and poor clothes. So he put his hand in his pocket and found his sixpence and walked up to her benignly.

"Here, poor little girl," he said. "Here is a sixpence. I will give it to you."

Sara started, and all at once realized that she looked exactly like poor children she had seen, in her better days, waiting on the pavement to watch her as she got out of her brougham. And she had given them pennies many a time.

Her face went red and then it went pale, and for a second she felt as if she could not take the dear little sixpence.

"Oh, no!" she said. "Oh, no, thank you; I mustn't take it, indeed!"

Her voice was so unlike an ordinary street child's voice and her manner was so like the manner of a well-bred little person that Veronica Eustacia (whose real name was Janet) and Rosalind Gladys (who was really called Nora) leaned forward to listen.

But Guy Clarence was not to be thwarted in his benevolence. He thrust the sixpence into her hand.

"Yes, you must take it, poor little girl!" he insisted stoutly. "You can buy things to eat with it. It is a whole sixpence!"

There was something so honest and kind in his face, and he looked so likely to be heartbrokenly disappointed if she did not take it, that Sara knew she must not refuse him. To be as proud as that would be a cruel thing. So she actually put her pride in her pocket, though it must be admitted her cheeks burned.

"Thank you," she said. "You are a kind, kind little darling thing." And as he scrambled joyfully into the carriage she went away, trying to smile, though she caught her breath quickly and her eyes were shining through a mist. She had known that she looked odd and shabby, but until now she had not known that she might be taken for a beggar.

As the Large Family's carriage drove away, the children inside it were talking with interested excitement.

"Oh, Donald," (this was Guy Clarence's name), Janet exclaimed alarmedly, "why did you offer that little girl your sixpence? I'm sure she is not a beggar!"

"She didn't speak like a beggar!" cried Nora. "And her face didn't really look like a beggar's face!"

"Besides, she didn't beg," said Janet. "I was so afraid she might be angry with you. You know, it makes people angry to be taken for beggars when they are not beggars."

"She wasn't angry," said Donald, a trifle dismayed, but still firm. "She laughed a little, and she said I was a kind, kind little darling thing. And I was!" — stoutly. "It was my whole sixpence."

Janet and Nora exchanged glances.

"A beggar girl would never have said that," decided Janet. "She would have said, 'Thank yer kindly, little gentleman — thank yer, sir;' and perhaps she would have bobbed a curtsy."

Sara knew nothing about the fact, but from that time the Large Family was as profoundly interested in her as she was in it. Faces used to appear at the nursery windows when she passed, and many discussions concerning her were held round the fire.

"She is a kind of servant at the seminary," Janet said. "I don't believe she belongs to anybody. I believe she is an orphan. But she is not a beggar, however shabby she looks."

And afterward she was called by all of them, "The-little-girl-who-is-not-a-beggar," which was, of course, rather a long name, and sounded very funny sometimes when the youngest ones said it in a hurry.

Sara managed to bore a hole in the sixpence and hung it on an old bit of narrow ribbon round her neck. Her affection for the Large Family increased — as, indeed, her affection for everything she could love increased. She grew fonder and fonder of Becky, and she used to look forward to the two mornings a week when she went into the schoolroom to give the little ones their French lesson. Her small pupils loved her, and strove with each other for the privilege of standing close to her and insinuating their small hands into hers. It fed her hungry heart to feel them nestling up to her. She made such friends with the sparrows that when she stood upon the table, put her head and shoulders out of the attic window, and chirped, she heard almost immediately a flutter of wings and answering twitters, and a little flock of dingy town birds appeared and alighted on the slates to talk to her and make much of the crumbs she scattered. With Melchisedec she had become so intimate that he actually brought Mrs. Melchisedec with him sometimes, and now and then one or two of his children. She used to talk to him, and, somehow, he looked quite as if he understood. There had grown in her mind rather a strange feeling about Emily, who always sat and looked on at everything. It arose in one of her moments of great desolateness. She would have liked to believe or pretend to believe that Emily understood and sympathized with her. She did not like to own to herself that her only companion could feel and hear nothing. She used to put her in a chair sometimes and sit opposite to her on the old red footstool, and stare and pretend about her until her own eyes would grow large with something which was almost like fear — particularly at night when everything was so still, when the only sound in the attic was the occasional sudden scurry and squeak of Melchisedec's family in the wall. One of her "pretends" was that Emily was a kind of good witch who could protect her. Sometimes, after she had stared at her until she was wrought up to the highest pitch of fancifulness, she would ask her questions and find herself almost feeling as if she would presently answer. But she never did. "As to answering, though," said Sara, trying to console herself, "I don't answer very often. I never answer when I can help it. When people are insulting you, there is nothing so good for them as not to say a word — just to look at them and think. Miss Minchin turns pale with rage when I do it, Miss Amelia looks frightened, and so do the girls. When you will not fly into a passion people know you are stronger than they are, because you are strong enough to hold in your rage, and they are not, and they say stupid things they wish they hadn't said afterward. There's nothing so strong as rage, except what makes you hold it in — that's stronger. It's a good thing not to answer your enemies. I scarcely ever do. Perhaps Emily is more like me than I am like myself. Perhaps she would rather not answer her friends, even. She keeps it all in her heart."

But though she tried to satisfy herself with these arguments, she did not find it easy. When, after a long, hard day, in which she had been sent here and there, sometimes on long errands through wind and cold and rain, she came in wet and hungry, and was sent out again because nobody chose to remember that she was only a child, and that her slim legs might be tired and her small body might be chilled; when she had been given only harsh words and cold, slighting looks for thanks; when the cook had been vulgar and insolent; when Miss Minchin had been in her worst mood, and when she had seen the girls sneering among themselves at her shabbiness — then she was not always able to comfort her sore, proud, desolate heart with fancies when Emily merely sat upright in her old chair and stared.

One of these nights, when she came up to the attic cold and hungry, with a tempest raging in her young breast, Emily's stare seemed so vacant, her sawdust legs and arms so inexpressive, that Sara lost all control over herself. There was nobody but Emily — no one in the world. And there she sat.

"I shall die presently," she said at first.

Emily simply stared.

"I can't bear this," said the poor child, trembling. "I know I shall die. I'm cold; I'm wet; I'm starving to death. I've walked a thousand miles today, and they have done nothing but scold me from morning until night. And because I could not find that last thing the cook sent me for, they would not give me any supper. Some men laughed at me because my old shoes made me slip down in the mud. I'm covered with mud now. And they laughed. Do you hear?"

She looked at the staring glass eyes and complacent face, and suddenly a sort of heartbroken rage seized her. She lifted her little savage hand and knocked Emily off the chair, bursting into a passion of sobbing — Sara who never cried.

"You are nothing but a doll!" she cried. "Nothing but a doll — doll — doll! You care for nothing. You are stuffed with sawdust. You never had a heart. Nothing could ever make you feel. You are a doll!"

Emily lay on the floor, with her legs ignominiously doubled up over her head, and a new flat place on the end of her nose; but she was calm, even dignified. Sara hid her face in her arms. The rats in the wall began to fight and bite each other and squeak and scramble. Melchisedec was chastising some of his family. Sara's sobs gradually quieted themselves. It was so unlike her to break down that she was surprised at herself. After a while she raised her face and looked at Emily, who seemed to be gazing at her round the side of one angle, and, somehow, by this time actually with a kind of glassy-eyed sympathy. Sara bent and picked her up. Remorse overtook her. She even smiled at herself a very little smile.

"You can't help being a doll," she said with a resigned sigh, "any more than Lavinia and Jessie can help not having any sense. We are not all made alike. Perhaps you do your sawdust best." And she kissed her and shook her clothes straight, and put her back upon her chair.

She had wished very much that someone would take the empty house next door. She wished it because of the attic window which was so near hers. It seemed as if it would be so nice to see it propped open someday and a head and shoulders rising out of the square aperture.

"If it looked a nice head," she thought, "I might begin by saying, 'Good morning,' and all sorts of things might happen. But, of course, it's not really likely that anyone but under servants would sleep there."

One morning, on turning the corner of the square after a visit to the grocer's, the butcher's, and the baker's, she saw, to her great delight, that during her rather prolonged absence, a van full of furniture had stopped before the next house, the front doors were thrown open, and men in shirt sleeves were going in and out carrying heavy packages and pieces of furniture.

"It's taken!" she said. "It really is taken! Oh, I do hope a nice head will look out of the attic window!"

She would almost have liked to join the group of loiterers who had stopped on the pavement to watch the things carried in. She had an idea that if she could see some of the furniture she could guess something about the people it belonged to. "Miss Minchin's tables and chairs are just like her," she thought; "I remember thinking that the first minute I saw her, even though I was so little. I told papa afterward, and he laughed and said it was true. I am sure the Large Family have fat, comfortable armchairs and sofas, and I can see that their red-flowery wallpaper is exactly like them. It's warm and cheerful and kind-looking and happy."

She was sent out for parsley to the greengrocer's later in the day, and when she came up the area steps her heart gave quite a quick beat of recognition. Several pieces of furniture had been set out of the van upon the pavement. There was a beautiful table of elaborately wrought teakwood, and some chairs, and a screen covered with rich Oriental embroidery. The sight of them gave her a weird, homesick feeling. She had seen things so like them in India. One of the things Miss Minchin had taken from her was a carved teakwood desk her father had sent her.

"They are beautiful things," she said; "they look as if they ought to belong to a nice person. All the things look rather grand. I suppose it is a rich family."

The vans of furniture came and were unloaded and gave place to others all the day. Several times it so happened that Sara had an opportunity of seeing things carried in. It became plain that she had been right in guessing that the newcomers were people of large means. All the furniture was rich and beautiful, and a great deal of it was Oriental. Wonderful rugs and draperies and ornaments were taken from the vans, many pictures, and books enough for a library. Among other things there was a superb god Buddha in a splendid shrine.

"Someone in the family must have been in India," Sara thought. "They have got used to Indian things and like them. I am glad. I shall feel as if they were friends, even if a head never looks out of the attic window."

When she was taking in the evening's milk for the cook (there was really no odd job she was not called upon to do), she saw something occur which made the situation more interesting than ever. The handsome, rosy man who was the father of the Large Family walked across the square in the most matter-of-fact manner, and ran up the steps of the next-door house. He ran up them as if he felt quite at home and expected to run up and down them many a time in the future. He stayed inside quite a long time, and several times came out and gave directions to the workmen, as if he had a right to do so. It was quite certain that he was in some intimate way connected with the newcomers and was acting for them.

"If the new people have children," Sara speculated, "the Large Family children will be sure to come and play with them, and they might come up into the attic just for fun."

At night, after her work was done, Becky came in to see her fellow prisoner and bring her news.

"It's a' Nindian gentleman that's comin' to live next door, miss," she said. "I don't know whether he's a black gentleman or not, but he's a Nindian one. He's very rich, an' he's ill, an' the gentleman of the Large Family is his lawyer. He's had a lot of trouble, an' it's made him ill an' low in his mind. He worships idols, miss. He's an 'eathen an' bows down to wood an' stone. I seen a' idol bein' carried in for him to worship. Somebody had oughter send him a trac'. You can get a trac' for a penny."

Sara laughed a little.

"I don't believe he worships that idol," she said; "some people like to keep them to look at because they are interesting. My papa had a beautiful one, and he did not worship it."

But Becky was rather inclined to prefer to believe that the new neighbor was "an 'eathen." It sounded so much more romantic than that he should merely be the ordinary kind of gentleman who went to church with a prayer book. She sat and talked long that night of what he would be like, of what his wife would be like if he had one, and of what his children would be like if they had children. Sara saw that privately she could not help hoping very much that they would all be black, and would wear turbans, and, above all, that — like their parent — they would all be "'eathens."

"I never lived next door to no 'eathens, miss," she said; "I should like to see what sort o' ways they'd have."

It was several weeks before her curiosity was satisfied, and then it was revealed that the new occupant had neither wife nor children. He was a solitary man with no family at all, and it was evident that he was shattered in health and unhappy in mind.

A carriage drove up one day and stopped before the house. When the footman dismounted from the box and opened the door the gentleman who was the father of the Large Family got out first. After him there descended a nurse in uniform, then came down the steps two men-servants. They came to assist their master, who, when he was helped out of the carriage, proved to be a man with a haggard, distressed face, and a skeleton body wrapped in furs. He was carried up the steps, and the head of the Large Family went with him, looking very anxious. Shortly afterward a doctor's carriage arrived, and the doctor went in — plainly to take care of him.

"There is such a yellow gentleman next door, Sara," Lottie whispered at the French class afterward. "Do you think he is a Chinee? The geography says the Chinee men are yellow."

"No, he is not Chinese," Sara whispered back; "he is very ill. Go on with your exercise, Lottie. 'Non, monsieur. Je n'ai pas le canif de mon oncle.'"

That was the beginning of the story of the Indian gentleman.

8

The Magic

When Sara had passed the house next door she had seen Ram Dass closing the shutters, and caught her glimpse of this room also.

"It is a long time since I saw a nice place from the inside," was the thought which crossed her mind.

There was the usual bright fire glowing in the grate, and the Indian gentleman was sitting before it. His head was resting in his hand, and he looked as lonely and unhappy as ever.

"Poor man!" said Sara. "I wonder what you are supposing."

And this was what he was "supposing" at that very moment.

"Suppose," he was thinking, "suppose — even if Carmichael traces the people to Moscow — the little girl they took from Madame Pascal's school in Paris is not the one we are in search of. Suppose she proves to be quite a different child. What steps shall I take next?"

When Sara went into the house she met Miss Minchin, who had come downstairs to scold the cook.

"Where have you wasted your time?" she demanded. "You have been out for hours."

"It was so wet and muddy," Sara answered, "it was hard to walk, because my shoes were so bad and slipped about."

"Make no excuses," said Miss Minchin, "and tell no falsehoods."

Sara went in to the cook. The cook had received a severe lecture and was in a fearful temper as a result. She was only too rejoiced to have someone to vent her rage on, and Sara was a convenience, as usual.

"Why didn't you stay all night?" she snapped.

Sara laid her purchases on the table.

"Here are the things," she said.

The cook looked them over, grumbling. She was in a very savage humor indeed.

"May I have something to eat?" Sara asked rather faintly.

"Tea's over and done with," was the answer. "Did you expect me to keep it hot for you?"

Sara stood silent for a second.

"I had no dinner," she said next, and her voice was quite low. She made it low because she was afraid it would tremble.

"There's some bread in the pantry," said the cook. "That's all you'll get at this time of day."

Sara went and found the bread. It was old and hard and dry. The cook was in too vicious a humor to give her anything to eat with it. It was always safe and easy to vent her spite on Sara. Really, it was hard for the child to climb the three long flights of stairs leading to her attic. She often found them long and steep when she was tired; but tonight it seemed as if she would never reach the top. Several times she was obliged to stop to rest. When she reached the top landing she was glad to see the glimmer of a light coming from under her door. That meant that Ermengarde had managed to creep up to pay her a visit. There was some comfort in that. It was better than to go into the room alone and find it empty and desolate. The mere presence of plump, comfortable Ermengarde, wrapped in her red shawl, would warm it a little.

Yes; there Ermengarde was when she opened the door. She was sitting in the middle of the bed, with her feet tucked safely under her. She had never become intimate with Melchisedec and his family, though they rather fascinated her. When she found herself alone in the attic she always preferred to sit on the bed until Sara arrived. She had, in fact, on this occasion had time to become rather nervous, because Melchisedec had appeared and sniffed about a good deal, and once had made her utter a repressed squeal by sitting up on his hind legs and, while he looked at her, sniffing pointedly in her direction.

"Oh, Sara," she cried out, "I am glad you have come. Melchy would sniff about so. I tried to coax him to go back, but he wouldn't for such a long time. I like him, you know; but it does frighten me when he sniffs right at me. Do you think he ever would jump?"

"No," answered Sara.

Ermengarde crawled forward on the bed to look at her.

"You do look tired, Sara," she said; "you are quite pale."

"I am tired," said Sara, dropping on to the lopsided footstool. "Oh, there's Melchisedec, poor thing. He's come to ask for his supper."

Melchisedec had come out of his hole as if he had been listening for her footstep. Sara was quite sure he knew it. He came forward with an affectionate, expectant expression as Sara put her hand in her pocket and turned it inside out, shaking her head. "I'm very sorry," she said. "I haven't one crumb left. Go home, Melchisedec, and tell your wife there was nothing in my pocket. I'm afraid I forgot because the cook and Miss Minchin were so cross."

Melchisedec seemed to understand. He shuffled resignedly, if not contentedly, back to his home.

"I did not expect to see you tonight, Ermie," Sara said. Ermengarde hugged herself in the red shawl.

"Miss Amelia has gone out to spend the night with her old aunt," she explained. "No one else ever comes and looks into the bedrooms after we are in bed. I could stay here until morning if I wanted to."

She pointed toward the table under the skylight. Sara had not looked toward it as she came in. A number of books were piled upon it. Ermengarde's gesture was a dejected one.

"Papa has sent me some more books, Sara," she said. "There they are."

Sara looked round and got up at once. She ran to the table, and picking up the top volume, turned over its leaves quickly. For the moment she forgot her discomforts.

"Ah," she cried out, "how beautiful! Carlyle's French Revolution. I have so wanted to read that!"

"I haven't," said Ermengarde. "And papa will be so cross if I don't. He'll expect me to know all about it when I go home for the holidays. What shall I do?"

Sara stopped turning over the leaves and looked at her with an excited flush on her cheeks.

"Look here," she cried, "if you'll lend me these books, I'll read them — and tell you everything that's in them afterward — and I'll tell it so that you will remember it, too."

"Oh, goodness!" exclaimed Ermengarde. "Do you think you can?"

"I know I can," Sara answered. "The little ones always remember what I tell them."

"Sara," said Ermengarde, hope gleaming in her round face, "if you'll do that, and make me remember, I'll — I'll give you anything."

"I don't want you to give me anything," said Sara. "I want your books — I want them!" And her eyes grew big, and her chest heaved.

"Take them, then," said Ermengarde. "I wish I wanted them — but I don't. I'm not clever, and my father is, and he thinks I ought to be."

Sara was opening one book after the other. "What are you going to tell your father?" she asked, a slight doubt dawning in her mind.

"Oh, he needn't know," answered Ermengarde. "He'll think I've read them."

Sara put down her book and shook her head slowly. "That's almost like telling lies," she said. "And lies — well, you see, they are not only wicked — they're vulgar. Sometimes" — reflectively — "I've thought perhaps I might do something wicked — I might suddenly fly into a rage and kill Miss Minchin, you know, when she was ill-treating me — but I couldn't be vulgar. Why can't you tell your father I read them?"

"He wants me to read them," said Ermengarde, a little discouraged by this unexpected turn of affairs.

"He wants you to know what is in them," said Sara. "And if I can tell it to you in an easy way and make you remember it, I should think he would like that."

"He'll like it if I learn anything in any way," said rueful Ermengarde. "You would if you were my father."

"It's not your fault that — " began Sara. She pulled herself up and stopped rather suddenly. She had been going to say, "It's not your fault that you are stupid."

"That what?" Ermengarde asked.

"That you can't learn things quickly," amended Sara. "If you can't, you can't. If I can — why, I can; that's all."

She always felt very tender of Ermengarde, and tried not to let her feel too strongly the difference between being able to learn anything at once, and not being able to learn anything at all. As she looked at her plump face, one of her wise, old-fashioned thoughts came to her.

"Perhaps," she said, "to be able to learn things quickly isn't everything. To be kind is worth a great deal to other people. If Miss Minchin knew everything on earth and was like what she is now, she'd still be a detestable thing, and everybody would hate her. Lots of clever people have done harm and have been wicked. Look at Robespierre — "

She stopped and examined Ermengarde's countenance, which was beginning to look bewildered. "Don't you remember?" she demanded. "I told you about him not long ago. I believe you've forgotten."

"Well, I don't remember all of it," admitted Ermengarde.

"Well, you wait a minute," said Sara, "and I'll take off my wet things and wrap myself in the coverlet and tell you over again."

She took off her hat and coat and hung them on a nail against the wall, and she changed her wet shoes for an old pair of slippers. Then she jumped on the bed, and drawing the coverlet about her shoulders, sat with her arms round her knees. "Now, listen," she said.

She plunged into the gory records of the French Revolution, and told such stories of it that Ermengarde's eyes grew round with alarm and she held her breath. But though she was rather terrified, there was a delightful thrill in listening, and she was not likely to forget Robespierre again, or to have any doubts about the Princesse de Lamballe.

"You know they put her head on a pike and danced round it," Sara explained. "And she had beautiful floating blonde hair; and when I think of her, I never see her head on her body, but always on a pike, with those furious people dancing and howling."

It was agreed that Mr. St. John was to be told the plan they had made, and for the present the books were to be left in the attic.

"Now let's tell each other things," said Sara. "How are you getting on with your French lessons?"

"Ever so much better since the last time I came up here and you explained the conjugations. Miss Minchin could not understand why I did my exercises so well that first morning."

Sara laughed a little and hugged her knees.

"She doesn't understand why Lottie is doing her sums so well," she said; "but it is because she creeps up here, too, and I help her." She glanced round the room. "The attic would be rather nice — if it wasn't so dreadful," she said, laughing again. "It's a good place to pretend in."

The truth was that Ermengarde did not know anything of the sometimes almost unbearable side of life in the attic and she had not a sufficiently vivid imagination to depict it for herself. On the rare occasions that she could reach Sara's room she only saw the side of it which was made exciting by things which were "pretended" and stories which were told. Her visits partook of the character of adventures; and though sometimes Sara looked rather pale, and it was not to be denied that she had grown very thin, her proud little spirit would not admit of complaints. She had never confessed that at times she was almost ravenous with hunger, as she was tonight. She was growing rapidly, and her constant walking and running about would have given her a keen appetite even if she had had abundant and regular meals of a much more nourishing nature than the unappetizing, inferior food snatched at such odd times as suited the kitchen convenience. She was growing used to a certain gnawing feeling in her young stomach.

"I suppose soldiers feel like this when they are on a long and weary march," she often said to herself. She liked the sound of the phrase, "long and weary march." It made her feel rather like a soldier. She had also a quaint sense of being a hostess in the attic.

"If I lived in a castle," she argued, "and Ermengarde was the lady of another castle, and came to see me, with knights and squires and vassals riding with her, and pennons flying, when I heard the clarions sounding outside the drawbridge I should go down to receive her, and I should spread feasts in the banquet hall and call in minstrels to sing and play and relate romances. When she comes into the attic I can't spread feasts, but I can tell stories, and not let her know disagreeable things. I dare say poor chatelaines had to do that in time of famine, when their lands had been pillaged." She was a proud, brave little chatelaine, and dispensed generously the one hospitality she could offer — the dreams she dreamed — the visions she saw — the imaginings which were her joy and comfort.

So, as they sat together, Ermengarde did not know that she was faint as well as ravenous, and that while she talked she now and then wondered if her hunger would let her sleep when she was left alone. She felt as if she had never been quite so hungry before.

"I wish I was as thin as you, Sara," Ermengarde said suddenly. "I believe you are thinner than you used to be. Your eyes look so big, and look at the sharp little bones sticking out of your elbow!"

Sara pulled down her sleeve, which had pushed itself up.

"I always was a thin child," she said bravely, "and I always had big green eyes."

"I love your queer eyes," said Ermengarde, looking into them with affectionate admiration. "They always look as if they saw such a long way. I love them — and I love them to be green — though they look black generally."

"They are cat's eyes," laughed Sara; "but I can't see in the dark with them — because I have tried, and I couldn't — I wish I could."

It was just at this minute that something happened at the skylight which neither of them saw. If either of them had chanced to turn and look, she would have been startled by the sight of a dark face which peered cautiously into the room and disappeared as quickly and almost as silently as it had appeared. Not quite as silently, however. Sara, who had keen ears, suddenly turned a little and looked up at the roof.

"That didn't sound like Melchisedec," she said. "It wasn't scratchy enough."

"What?" said Ermengarde, a little startled.

"Didn't you think you heard something?" asked Sara.

"N-no," Ermengarde faltered. "Did you?"

"Perhaps I didn't," said Sara; "but I thought I did. It sounded as if something was on the slates — something that dragged softly."

"What could it be?" said Ermengarde. "Could it be — robbers?"

"No," Sara began cheerfully. "There is nothing to steal — "

She broke off in the middle of her words. They both heard the sound that checked her. It was not on the slates, but on the stairs below, and it was Miss Minchin's angry voice. Sara sprang off the bed, and put out the candle.

"She is scolding Becky," she whispered, as she stood in the darkness. "She is making her cry."

"Will she come in here?" Ermengarde whispered back, panic-stricken.

"No. She will think I am in bed. Don't stir."

It was very seldom that Miss Minchin mounted the last flight of stairs. Sara could only remember that she had done it once before. But now she was angry enough to be coming at least part of the way up, and it sounded as if she was driving Becky before her.

"You impudent, dishonest child!" they heard her say. "Cook tells me she has missed things repeatedly."

"'T warn't me, mum," said Becky sobbing. "I was 'ungry enough, but 't warn't me — never!"

"You deserve to be sent to prison," said Miss Minchin's voice. "Picking and stealing! Half a meat pie, indeed!"

"'T warn't me," wept Becky. "I could 'ave eat a whole un — but I never laid a finger on it."

Miss Minchin was out of breath between temper and mounting the stairs. The meat pie had been intended for her special late supper. It became apparent that she boxed Becky's ears.

"Don't tell falsehoods," she said. "Go to your room this instant."

Both Sara and Ermengarde heard the slap, and then heard Becky run in her slipshod shoes up the stairs and into her attic. They heard her door shut, and knew that she threw herself upon her bed.

"I could 'ave e't two of 'em," they heard her cry into her pillow. "An' I never took a bite. 'T was cook give it to her policeman."

Sara stood in the middle of the room in the darkness. She was clenching her little teeth and opening and shutting fiercely her outstretched hands. She could scarcely stand still, but she dared not move until Miss Minchin had gone down the stairs and all was still.

"The wicked, cruel thing!" she burst forth. "The cook takes things herself and then says Becky steals them. She doesn't! She doesn't! She's so hungry sometimes that she eats crusts out of the ash barrel!" She pressed her hands hard against her face and burst into passionate little sobs, and Ermengarde, hearing this unusual thing, was overawed by it. Sara was crying! The unconquerable Sara! It seemed to denote something new — some mood she had never known.

Suppose — suppose — a new dread possibility presented itself to her kind, slow, little mind all at once. She crept off the bed in the dark and found her way to the table where the candle stood. She struck a match and lit the candle. When she had lighted it, she bent forward and looked at Sara, with her new thought growing to definite fear in her eyes.

"Sara," she said in a timid, almost awe-stricken voice, are — are — you never told me — I don't want to be rude, but — are you ever hungry?"

It was too much just at that moment. The barrier broke down. Sara lifted her face from her hands.

"Yes," she said in a new passionate way. "Yes, I am. I'm so hungry now that I could almost eat you. And it makes it worse to hear poor Becky. She's hungrier than I am."

Ermengarde gasped.

"Oh, oh!" she cried woefully. "And I never knew!"

"I didn't want you to know," Sara said. "It would have made me feel like a street beggar. I know I look like a street beggar."

"No, you don't — you don't!" Ermengarde broke in. "Your clothes are a little queer — but you couldn't look like a street beggar. You haven't a street-beggar face."

"A little boy once gave me a sixpence for charity," said Sara, with a short little laugh in spite of herself. "Here it is." And she pulled out the thin ribbon from her neck. "He wouldn't have given me his Christmas sixpence if I hadn't looked as if I needed it."

Somehow the sight of the dear little sixpence was good for both of them. It made them laugh a little, though they both had tears in their eyes.

"Who was he?" asked Ermengarde, looking at it quite as if it had not been a mere ordinary silver sixpence.

"He was a darling little thing going to a party," said Sara. "He was one of the Large Family, the little one with the round legs — the one I call Guy Clarence. I suppose his nursery was crammed with Christmas presents and hampers full of cakes and things, and he could see I had nothing."

Ermengarde gave a little jump backward. The last sentences had recalled something to her troubled mind and given her a sudden inspiration.

"Oh, Sara!" she cried. "What a silly thing I am not to have thought of it!"

"Of what?"

"Something splendid!" said Ermengarde, in an excited hurry. "This very afternoon my nicest aunt sent me a box. It is full of good things. I never touched it, I had so much pudding at dinner, and I was so bothered about papa's books." Her words began to tumble over each other. "It's got cake in it, and little meat pies, and jam tarts and buns, and oranges and red-currant wine, and figs and chocolate. I'll creep back to my room and get it this minute, and we'll eat it now."

Sara almost reeled. When one is faint with hunger the mention of food has sometimes a curious effect. She clutched Ermengarde's arm.

"Do you think — you could?" she ejaculated.

"I know I could," answered Ermengarde, and she ran to the door — opened it softly — put her head out into the darkness, and listened. Then she went back to Sara. "The lights are out. Everybody's in bed. I can creep — and creep — and no one will hear."

It was so delightful that they caught each other's hands and a sudden light sprang into Sara's eyes.

"Ermie!" she said. "Let us pretend! Let us pretend it's a party! And oh, won't you invite the prisoner in the next cell?"

"Yes! Yes! Let us knock on the wall now. The jailer won't hear."

Sara went to the wall. Through it she could hear poor Becky crying more softly. She knocked four times.

"That means, 'Come to me through the secret passage under the wall,' she explained. 'I have something to communicate.'"

Five quick knocks answered her.

"She is coming," she said.

Almost immediately the door of the attic opened and Becky appeared. Her eyes were red and her cap was sliding off, and when she caught sight of Ermengarde she began to rub her face nervously with her apron.

"Don't mind me a bit, Becky!" cried Ermengarde.

"Miss Ermengarde has asked you to come in," said Sara, "because she is going to bring a box of good things up here to us."

Becky's cap almost fell off entirely, she broke in with such excitement.

"To eat, miss?" she said. "Things that's good to eat?"

"Yes," answered Sara, "and we are going to pretend a party."

"And you shall have as much as you want to eat," put in Ermengarde. "I'll go this minute!"

She was in such haste that as she tiptoed out of the attic she dropped her red shawl and did not know it had fallen. No one saw it for a minute or so. Becky was too much overpowered by the good luck which had befallen her.

"Oh, miss! Oh, miss!" she gasped; "I know it was you that asked her to let me come. It — it makes me cry to think of it." And she went to Sara's side and stood and looked at her worshipingly.

But in Sara's hungry eyes the old light had begun to glow and transform her world for her. Here in the attic — with the cold night outside — with the afternoon in the sloppy streets barely passed — with the memory of the awful unfed look in the beggar child's eyes not yet faded — this simple, cheerful thing had happened like a thing of magic.

She caught her breath.

"Somehow, something always happens," she cried, "just before things get to the very worst. It is as if the Magic did it. If I could only just remember that always. The worst thing never quite comes."

She gave Becky a little cheerful shake.

"No, no! You mustn't cry!" she said. "We must make haste and set the table."

"Set the table, miss?" said Becky, gazing round the room. "What'll we set it with?"

Sara looked round the attic, too.

"There doesn't seem to be much," she answered, half laughing.

That moment she saw something and pounced upon it. It was Ermengarde's red shawl which lay upon the floor.

"Here's the shawl," she cried. "I know she won't mind it. It will make such a nice red tablecloth."

They pulled the old table forward, and threw the shawl over it. Red is a wonderfully kind and comfortable color. It began to make the room look furnished directly.

"How nice a red rug would look on the floor!" exclaimed Sara. "We must pretend there is one!"

Her eye swept the bare boards with a swift glance of admiration. The rug was laid down already.

"How soft and thick it is!" she said, with the little laugh which Becky knew the meaning of; and she raised and set her foot down again delicately, as if she felt something under lt.

"Yes, miss," answered Becky, watching her with serious rapture. She was always quite serious.

"What next, now?" said Sara, and she stood still and put her hands over her eyes. "Something will come if I think and wait a little" — in a soft, expectant voice. "The Magic will tell me."

One of her favorite fancies was that on "the outside," as she called it, thoughts were waiting for people to call them. Becky had seen her stand and wait many a time before, and knew that in a few seconds she would uncover an enlightened, laughing face.

In a moment she did.

"There!" she cried. "It has come! I know now! I must look among the things in the old trunk I had when I was a princess."

She flew to its corner and kneeled down. It had not been put in the attic for her benefit, but because there was no room for it elsewhere. Nothing had been left in it but rubbish. But she knew she should find something. The Magic always arranged that kind of thing in one way or another.

In a corner lay a package so insignificant-looking that it had been overlooked, and when she herself had found it she had kept it as a relic. It contained a dozen small white handkerchiefs. She seized them joyfully and ran to the table. She began to arrange them upon the red table-cover, patting and coaxing them into shape with the narrow lace edge curling outward, her Magic working its spells for her as she did it.

"These are the plates," she said. "They are golden plates. These are the richly embroidered napkins. Nuns worked them in convents in Spain."

"Did they, miss?" breathed Becky, her very soul uplifted by the information.

"You must pretend it," said Sara. "If you pretend it enough, you will see them."

"Yes, miss," said Becky; and as Sara returned to the trunk she devoted herself to the effort of accomplishing an end so much to be desired.

Sara turned suddenly to find her standing by the table, looking very queer indeed. She had shut her eyes, and was twisting her face in strange convulsive contortions, her hands hanging stiffly clenched at her sides. She looked as if she was trying to lift some enormous weight.

"What is the matter, Becky?" Sara cried. "What are you doing?"

Becky opened her eyes with a start.

"I was a-'pretendin',' miss," she answered a little sheepishly; "I was tryin' to see it like you do. I almost did," with a hopeful grin. "But it takes a lot o' stren'th."

"Perhaps it does if you are not used to it," said Sara, with friendly sympathy; "but you don't know how easy it is when you've done it often. I wouldn't try so hard just at first. It will come to you after a while. I'll just tell you what things are. Look at these."

She held an old summer hat in her hand which she had fished out of the bottom of the trunk. There was a wreath of flowers on it. She pulled the wreath off.

"These are garlands for the feast," she said grandly. "They fill all the air with perfume. There's a mug on the wash-stand, Becky. Oh — and bring the soap dish for a centerpiece."

Becky handed them to her reverently.

"What are they now, miss?" she inquired. "You'd think they was made of crockery — but I know they ain't."

"This is a carven flagon," said Sara, arranging tendrils of the wreath about the mug. "And this" — bending tenderly over the soap dish and heaping it with roses — "is purest alabaster encrusted with gems."

She touched the things gently, a happy smile hovering about her lips which made her look as if she were a creature in a dream.

"My, ain't it lovely!" whispered Becky.

"If we just had something for bonbon dishes," Sara murmured. "There!" — darting to the trunk again. "I remember I saw something this minute."

It was only a bundle of wool wrapped in red and white tissue paper, but the tissue paper was soon twisted into the form of little dishes, and was combined with the remaining flowers to ornament the candlestick which was to light the feast. Only the Magic could have made it more than an old table covered with a red shawl and set with rubbish from a long-unopened trunk. But Sara drew back and gazed at it, seeing wonders; and Becky, after staring in delight, spoke with bated breath.

"This 'ere," she suggested, with a glance round the attic — "is it the Bastille now — or has it turned into somethin' different?"

"Oh, yes, yes!" said Sara. "Quite different. It is a banquet hall!"

"My eye, miss!" ejaculated Becky. "A blanket 'all!" and she turned to view the splendors about her with awed bewilderment.

"A banquet hall," said Sara. "A vast chamber where feasts are given. It has a vaulted roof, and a minstrels' gallery, and a huge chimney filled with blazing oaken logs, and it is brilliant with waxen tapers twinkling on every side."

"My eye, Miss Sara!" gasped Becky again.

Then the door opened, and Ermengarde came in, rather staggering under the weight of her hamper. She started back with an exclamation of joy. To enter from the chill darkness outside, and find one's self confronted by a totally unanticipated festal board, draped with red, adorned with white napery, and wreathed with flowers, was to feel that the preparations were brilliant indeed.

"Oh, Sara!" she cried out. "You are the cleverest girl I ever saw!"

"Isn't it nice?" said Sara. "They are things out of my old trunk. I asked my Magic, and it told me to go and look."

"But oh, miss," cried Becky, "wait till she's told you what they are! They ain't just — oh, miss, please tell her," appealing to Sara.

So Sara told her, and because her Magic helped her she made her almost see it all: the golden platters — the vaulted spaces — the blazing logs — the twinkling waxen tapers. As the things were taken out of the hamper — the frosted cakes — the fruits — the bonbons and the wine — the feast became a splendid thing.

"It's like a real party!" cried Ermengarde.

"It's like a queen's table," sighed Becky.

Then Ermengarde had a sudden brilliant thought.

"I'll tell you what, Sara," she said. "Pretend you are a princess now and this is a royal feast."

"But it's your feast," said Sara; "you must be the princess, and we will be your maids of honor."

"Oh, I can't," said Ermengarde. "I'm too fat, and I don't know how. You be her."

"Well, if you want me to," said Sara.

But suddenly she thought of something else and ran to the rusty grate.

"There is a lot of paper and rubbish stuffed in here!" she exclaimed. "If we light it, there will be a bright blaze for a few minutes, and we shall feel as if it was a real fire." She struck a match and lighted it up with a great specious glow which illuminated the room.

"By the time it stops blazing," Sara said, "we shall forget about its not being real."

She stood in the dancing glow and smiled.

"Doesn't it look real?" she said. "Now we will begin the party."

She led the way to the table. She waved her hand graciously to Ermengarde and Becky. She was in the midst of her dream.

"Advance, fair damsels," she said in her happy dream-voice, "and be seated at the banquet table. My noble father, the king, who is absent on a long journey, has commanded me to feast you." She turned her head slightly toward the corner of the room. "What, ho, there, minstrels! Strike up with your viols and bassoons. Princesses," she explained rapidly to Ermengarde and Becky, "always had minstrels to play at their feasts. Pretend there is a minstrel gallery up there in the corner. Now we will begin."

They had barely had time to take their pieces of cake into their hands — not one of them had time to do more, when — they all three sprang to their feet and turned pale faces toward the door — listening — listening.

Someone was coming up the stairs. There was no mistake about it. Each of them recognized the angry, mounting tread and knew that the end of all things had come.

"It's — the missus!" choked Becky, and dropped her piece of cake upon the floor.

"Yes," said Sara, her eyes growing shocked and large in her small white face. "Miss Minchin has found us out."

Miss Minchin struck the door open with a blow of her hand. She was pale herself, but it was with rage. She looked from the frightened faces to the banquet table, and from the banquet table to the last flicker of the burnt paper in the grate.

"I have been suspecting something of this sort," she exclaimed; "but I did not dream of such audacity. Lavinia was telling the truth."

So they knew that it was Lavinia who had somehow guessed their secret and had betrayed them. Miss Minchin strode over to Becky and boxed her ears for a second time.

"You impudent creature!" she said. "You leave the house in the morning!"

Sara stood quite still, her eyes growing larger, her face paler. Ermengarde burst into tears.

"Oh, don't send her away," she sobbed. "My aunt sent me the hamper. We're — only — having a party."

"So I see," said Miss Minchin, witheringly. "With the Princess Sara at the head of the table." She turned fiercely on Sara. "It is your doing, I know," she cried. "Ermengarde would never have thought of such a thing. You decorated the table, I suppose — with this rubbish." She stamped her foot at Becky. "Go to your attic!" she commanded, and Becky stole away, her face hidden in her apron, her shoulders shaking.

327

Then it was Sara's turn again.

"I will attend to you tomorrow. You shall have neither breakfast, dinner, nor supper!"

"I have not had either dinner or supper today, Miss Minchin," said Sara, rather faintly.

"Then all the better. You will have something to remember. Don't stand there. Put those things into the hamper again."

She began to sweep them off the table into the hamper herself, and caught sight of Ermengarde's new books.

"And you" — to Ermengarde — "have brought your beautiful new books into this dirty attic. Take them up and go back to bed. You will stay there all day tomorrow, and I shall write to your papa. What would he say if he knew where you are tonight?"

Something she saw in Sara's grave, fixed gaze at this moment made her turn on her fiercely.

"What are you thinking of?" she demanded. "Why do you look at me like that?"

"I was wondering," answered Sara, as she had answered that notable day in the schoolroom.

"What were you wondering?"

It was very like the scene in the schoolroom. There was no pertness in Sara's manner. It was only sad and quiet.

"I was wondering," she said in a low voice, "what my papa would say if he knew where I am tonight."

Miss Minchin was infuriated just as she had been before and her anger expressed itself, as before, in an intemperate fashion. She flew at her and shook her.

"You insolent, unmanageable child!" she cried. "How dare you! How dare you!"

She picked up the books, swept the rest of the feast back into the hamper in a jumbled heap, thrust it into Ermengarde's arms, and pushed her before her toward the door.

"I will leave you to wonder," she said. "Go to bed this instant." And she shut the door behind herself and poor stumbling Ermengarde, and left Sara standing quite alone.

The dream was quite at an end. The last spark had died out of the paper in the grate and left only black tinder; the table was left bare, the golden plates and richly embroidered napkins, and the garlands were transformed again into old handkerchiefs, scraps of red and white paper, and discarded artificial flowers all scattered on the floor; the minstrels in the minstrel gallery had stolen away, and the viols and bassoons were still. Emily was sitting with her back against the wall, staring very hard. Sara saw her, and went and picked her up with trembling hands.

"There isn't any banquet left, Emily," she said. "And there isn't any princess.

There is nothing left but the prisoners in the Bastille." And she sat down and hid her face.

What would have happened if she had not hidden it just then, and if she had chanced to look up at the skylight at the wrong moment, I do not know — perhaps the end of this chapter might have been quite different — because if she had glanced at the skylight she would certainly have been startled by what she would have seen. She would have seen exactly the same face pressed against the glass and peering in at her as it had peered in earlier in the evening when she had been talking to Ermengarde.

But she did not look up. She sat with her little black head in her arms for some time. She always sat like that when she was trying to bear something in silence. Then she got up and went slowly to the bed.

"I can't pretend anything else — while I am awake," she said. "There wouldn't be any use in trying. If I go to sleep, perhaps a dream will come and pretend for me."

She suddenly felt so tired — perhaps through want of food — that she sat down on the edge of the bed quite weakly.

"Suppose there was a bright fire in the grate, with lots of little dancing flames," she murmured. "Suppose there was a comfortable chair before it — and suppose there was a small table near, with a little hot — hot supper on it. And suppose" — as she drew the thin coverings over her — "suppose this was a beautiful soft bed, with fleecy blankets and large downy pillows. Suppose — suppose — " And her very weariness was good to her, for her eyes closed and she fell fast asleep.

She did not know how long she slept. But she had been tired enough to sleep deeply and profoundly — too deeply and soundly to be disturbed by anything, even by the squeaks and scamperings of Melchisedec's entire family, if all his sons and daughters had chosen to come out of their hole to fight and tumble and play.

When she awakened it was rather suddenly, and she did not know that any particular thing had called her out of her sleep. The truth was, however, that it was a sound which had called her back — a real sound — the click of the skylight as it fell in closing after a lithe white figure which slipped through it and crouched down close by upon the slates of the roof — just near enough to see what happened in the attic, but not near enough to be seen.

At first she did not open her eyes. She felt too sleepy and — curiously enough — too warm and comfortable. She was so warm and comfortable, indeed, that she did not believe she was really awake. She never was as warm and cozy as this except in some lovely vision.

"What a nice dream!" she murmured. "I feel quite warm. I — don't — want — to — wake — up."

Of course it was a dream. She felt as if warm, delightful bedclothes were heaped upon her. She could actually feel blankets, and when she put out her hand it touched something exactly like a satin-covered eider-down quilt. She must not awaken from this delight — she must be quite still and make it last.

But she could not — even though she kept her eyes closed tightly, she could not. Something was forcing her to awaken — something in the room. It was a sense of light, and a sound — the sound of a crackling, roaring little fire.

"Oh, I am awakening," she said mournfully. "I can't help it — I can't."

Her eyes opened in spite of herself. And then she actually smiled — for what she saw she had never seen in the attic before, and knew she never should see.

"Oh, I haven't awakened," she whispered, daring to rise on her elbow and look all about her. "I am dreaming yet." She knew it must be a dream, for if she were awake such things could not — could not be.

Do you wonder that she felt sure she had not come back to earth? This is what she saw. In the grate there was a glowing, blazing fire; on the hob was a little brass kettle hissing and boiling; spread upon the floor was a thick, warm crimson rug; before the fire a folding-chair, unfolded, and with cushions on it; by the chair a small folding-table, unfolded, covered with a white cloth, and upon it spread small covered dishes, a cup, a saucer, a teapot; on the bed were new warm coverings and a satin-covered down quilt; at the foot a curious wadded silk robe, a pair of quilted slippers, and some books. The room of her dream seemed changed into fairyland — and it was flooded with warm light, for a bright lamp stood on the table covered with a rosy shade.

She sat up, resting on her elbow, and her breathing came short and fast.

"It does not — melt away," she panted. "Oh, I never had such a dream before."

She scarcely dared to stir; but at last she pushed the bedclothes aside, and put her feet on the floor with a rapturous smile.

"I am dreaming — I am getting out of bed," she heard her own voice say; and then, as she stood up in the midst of it all, turning slowly from side to side — "I am dreaming it stays — real! I'm dreaming it feels real. It's bewitched — or I'm bewitched. I only think I see it all." Her words began to hurry themselves. "If I can only keep on thinking it," she cried, "I don't care! I don't care!"

She stood panting a moment longer, and then cried out again.

"Oh, it isn't true!" she said. "It can't be true! But oh, how true it seems!"

The blazing fire drew her to it, and she knelt down and held out her hands close to it — so close that the heat made her start back.

"A fire I only dreamed wouldn't be hot," she cried.

She sprang up, touched the table, the dishes, the rug; she went to the bed and touched the blankets. She took up the soft wadded dressing-gown, and suddenly clutched it to her breast and held it to her cheek.

"It's warm. It's soft!" she almost sobbed. "It's real. It must be!"

She threw it over her shoulders, and put her feet into the slippers.

"They are real, too. It's all real!" she cried. "I am not — I am not dreaming!"

She almost staggered to the books and opened the one which lay upon the top. Something was written on the flyleaf — just a few words, and they were these: "To the little girl in the attic. From a friend."

When she saw that — wasn't it a strange thing for her to do — she put her face down upon the page and burst into tears.

"I don't know who it is," she said; "but somebody cares for me a little. I have a friend."

She took her candle and stole out of her own room and into Becky's, and stood by her bedside.

"Becky, Becky!" she whispered as loudly as she dared. "Wake up!"

When Becky wakened, and she sat upright staring aghast, her face still smudged with traces of tears, beside her stood a little figure in a luxurious wadded robe of crimson silk. The face she saw was a shining, wonderful thing. The Princess Sara — as she remembered her — stood at her very bedside, holding a candle in her hand.

"Come," she said. "Oh, Becky, come!"

Becky was too frightened to speak. She simply got up and followed her, with her mouth and eyes open, and without a word.

And when they crossed the threshold, Sara shut the door gently and drew her into the warm, glowing midst of things which made her brain reel and her hungry senses faint. "It's true! It's true!" she cried. "I've touched them all. They are as real as we are. The Magic has come and done it, Becky, while we were asleep — the Magic that won't let those worst things ever quite happen."

 9

"It Is the Child!"

The next afternoon three members of the Large Family sat in the Indian gentleman's library, doing their best to cheer him up. They had been allowed to come in to perform this office because he had specially invited them. He had been living in a state of suspense for some time, and today he was waiting for a certain event very anxiously. This event was the return of Mr. Carmichael from Moscow. His stay there had been prolonged from week to week. On his first arrival there, he had not been able satisfactorily to trace the family he had gone in search of. When he felt at last sure that he had found them and had gone to their house, he had been told that they were absent on a journey. His efforts to reach them had been unavailing, so he had decided to remain in Moscow until their return. Mr. Carrisford sat in his reclining chair, and Janet sat on the floor beside him. He was very fond of Janet. Nora had found a footstool, and Donald was astride the tiger's head which ornamented the rug made of the animal's skin. It must be owned that he was riding it rather violently.

"Don't chirrup so loud, Donald," Janet said. "When you come to cheer an ill person up you don't cheer him up at the top of your voice. Perhaps cheering up is too loud, Mr. Carrisford?" turning to the Indian gentleman.

But he only patted her shoulder.

"No, it isn't," he answered. "And it keeps me from thinking too much."

"I'm going to be quiet," Donald shouted. "We'll all be as quiet as mice."

"Mice don't make a noise like that," said Janet.

Donald made a bridle of his handkerchief and bounced up and down on the tiger's head.

"A whole lot of mice might," he said cheerfully. "A thousand mice might."

"I don't believe fifty thousand mice would," said Janet, severely; "and we have to be as quiet as one mouse."

Mr. Carrisford laughed and patted her shoulder again.

"Papa won't be very long now," she said. "May we talk about the lost little girl?"

"I don't think I could talk much about anything else just now," the Indian gentleman answered, knitting his forehead with a tired look.

"We like her so much," said Nora. "We call her the little un-fairy princess."

"Why?" the Indian gentleman inquired, because the fancies of the Large Family always made him forget things a little.

It was Janet who answered.

"It is because, though she is not exactly a fairy, she will be so rich when she is found that she will be like a princess in a fairy tale. We called her the fairy princess at first, but it didn't quite suit."

"Is it true," said Nora, "that her papa gave all his money to a friend to put in a mine that had diamonds in it, and then the friend thought he had lost it all and ran away because he felt as if he was a robber?"

"But he wasn't really, you know," put in Janet, hastily.

The Indian gentleman took hold of her hand quickly.

"No, he wasn't really," he said.

"I am sorry for the friend," Janet said; "I can't help it. He didn't mean to do it, and it would break his heart. I am sure it would break his heart."

"You are an understanding little woman, Janet," the Indian gentleman said, and he held her hand close.

"Did you tell Mr. Carrisford," Donald shouted again, "about the little-girl-who-is-n't-a-beggar? Did you tell him she has new nice clothes? P'r'aps she's been found by somebody when she was lost."

"There's a cab!" exclaimed Janet. "It's stopping before the door. It is papa!"

They all ran to the windows to look out.

"Yes, it's papa," Donald proclaimed. "But there is no little girl."

All three of them incontinently fled from the room and tumbled into the hall. It was in this way they always welcomed their father. They were to be heard jumping up and down, clapping their hands, and being caught up and kissed. Mr. Carrisford made an effort to rise and sank back again.

"It is no use," he said. "What a wreck I am!"

Mr. Carmichael's voice approached the door.

"No, children," he was saying; "you may come in after I have talked to Mr. Carrisford. Go and play with Ram Dass."

Then the door opened and he came in. He looked rosier than ever, and brought an atmosphere of freshness and health with him; but his eyes were disappointed and anxious as they met the invalid's look of eager question even as they grasped each other's hands.

"What news?" Mr. Carrisford asked. "The child the Russian people adopted?"

"She is not the child we are looking for," was Mr. Carmichael's answer. "She is much younger than Captain Crewe's little girl. Her name is Emily Carew. I have seen and talked to her. The Russians were able to give me every detail."

How wearied and miserable the Indian gentleman looked! His hand dropped from Mr. Carmichael's.

"Then the search has to be begun over again," he said. "That is all. Please sit down."

Mr. Carmichael took a seat. Somehow, he had gradually grown fond of this unhappy man. He was himself so well and happy, and so surrounded by cheerfulness and love, that desolation and broken health seemed pitifully unbearable things. If there had been the sound of just one gay little high-pitched voice in the house, it would have been so much less forlorn. And that a man should be compelled to carry about in his breast the thought that he had seemed to wrong and desert a child was not a thing one could face.

"Come, come," he said in his cheery voice; "we'll find her yet."

"We must begin at once. No time must be lost," Mr. Carrisford fretted. "Have you any new suggestion to make — any whatsoever?"

Mr. Carmichael felt rather restless, and he rose and began to pace the room with a thoughtful, though uncertain face.

"Well, perhaps," he said. "I don't know what it may be worth. The fact is, an idea occurred to me as I was thinking the thing over in the train on the journey from Dover."

"What was it? If she is alive, she is somewhere."

"Yes; she is somewhere. We have searched the schools in Paris. Let us give up Paris and begin in London. That was my idea — to search London."

"There are schools enough in London," said Mr. Carrisford. Then he slightly started, roused by a recollection. "By the way, there is one next door."

"Then we will begin there. We cannot begin nearer than next door."

"No," said Carrisford. "There is a child there who interests me; but she is not a pupil. And she is a little dark, forlorn creature, as unlike poor Crewe as a child could be."

Perhaps the Magic was at work again at that very moment — the beautiful Magic. It really seemed as if it might be so. What was it that brought Ram Dass into the room — even as his master spoke — salaaming respectfully, but with a scarcely concealed touch of excitement in his dark, flashing eyes?

"Sahib," he said, "the child herself has come — the child the sahib felt pity for. She brings back the monkey who had again run away to her attic under the roof. I have asked that she remain. It was my thought that it would please the sahib to see and speak with her."

"Who is she?" inquired Mr. Carmichael.

"God knows," Mr. Carrrisford answered. "She is the child I spoke of. A little drudge at the school." He waved his hand to Ram Dass, and addressed him.

"Yes, I should like to see her. Go and bring her in." Then he turned to Mr. Carmichael. "While you have been away," he explained, "I have been desperate. The days were so dark and long. Ram Dass told me of this child's miseries, and together we invented a romantic plan to help her. I suppose it was a childish thing to do; but it gave me something to plan and think of. Without the help of an agile, soft-footed Oriental like Ram Dass, however, it could not have been done."

Then Sara came into the room. She carried the monkey in her arms, and he evidently did not intend to part from her, if it could be helped. He was clinging to her and chattering, and the interesting excitement of finding herself in the Indian gentleman's room had brought a flush to Sara's cheeks.

"Your monkey ran away again," she said, in her pretty voice. "He came to my garret window last night, and I took him in because it was so cold. I would have brought him back if it had not been so late. I knew you were ill and might not like to be disturbed."

The Indian gentleman's hollow eyes dwelt on her with curious interest.

"That was very thoughtful of you," he said.

Sara looked toward Ram Dass, who stood near the door.

"Shall I give him to the Lascar?" she asked.

"How do you know he is a Lascar?" said the Indian gentleman, smiling a little.

"Oh, I know Lascars," Sara said, handing over the reluctant monkey. "I was born in India."

The Indian gentleman sat upright so suddenly, and with such a change of expression, that she was for a moment quite startled.

"You were born in India," he exclaimed, "were you? Come here." And he held out his hand.

Sara went to him and laid her hand in his, as he seemed to want to take it. She stood still, and her green-gray eyes met his wonderingly. Something seemed to be the matter with him.

"You live next door?" he demanded.

"Yes; I live at Miss Minchin's seminary."

"But you are not one of her pupils?"

A strange little smile hovered about Sara's mouth. She hesitated a moment.

"I don't think I know exactly what I am," she replied.

"Why not?"

"At first I was a pupil, and a parlor boarder; but now — "

"You were a pupil! What are you now?"

The queer little sad smile was on Sara's lips again.

"I sleep in the attic, next to the scullery maid," she said. "I run errands for the cook — I do anything she tells me; and I teach the little ones their lessons."

"Question her, Carmichael," said Mr. Carrisford, sinking back as if he had lost his strength. "Question her; I cannot."

The big, kind father of the Large Family knew how to question little girls. Sara realized how much practice he had had when he spoke to her in his nice, encouraging voice.

"What do you mean by 'At first,' my child?" he inquired.

"When I was first taken there by my papa."

"Where is your papa?"

"He died," said Sara, very quietly. "He lost all his money and there was none left for me. There was no one to take care of me or to pay Miss Minchin."

"Carmichael!" the Indian gentleman cried out loudly. "Carmichael!"

"We must not frighten her," Mr. Carmichael said aside to him in a quick, low voice. And he added aloud to Sara, "So you were sent up into the attic, and made into a little drudge. That was about it, wasn't it?"

"There was no one to take care of me," said Sara. "There was no money; I belong to nobody."

"How did your father lose his money?" the Indian gentleman broke in breathlessly.

"He did not lose it himself," Sara answered, wondering still more each moment. "He had a friend he was very fond of — he was very fond of him. It was his friend who took his money. He trusted his friend too much."

The Indian gentleman's breath came more quickly.

"The friend might have meant to do no harm," he said. "It might have happened through a mistake."

Sara did not know how unrelenting her quiet young voice sounded as she answered. If she had known, she would surely have tried to soften it for the Indian gentleman's sake.

"The suffering was just as bad for my papa," she said. It killed him."

"What was your father's name?" the Indian gentleman said. "Tell me."

"His name was Ralph Crewe," Sara answered, feeling startled. "Captain Crewe. He died in India."

335

The haggard face contracted, and Ram Dass sprang to his master's side.

"Carmichael," the invalid gasped, "it is the child — the child!"

For a moment Sara thought he was going to die. Ram Dass poured out drops from a bottle, and held them to his lips. Sara stood near, trembling a little. She looked in a bewildered way at Mr. Carmichael.

"What child am I?" she faltered.

"He was your father's friend," Mr. Carmichael answered her. "Don't be frightened. We have been looking for you for two years."

Sara put her hand up to her forehead, and her mouth trembled. She spoke as if she were in a dream.

"And I was at Miss Minchin's all the while," she half whispered. "Just on the other side of the wall."